BUST OF THE PRINCESS NEFERET
(Museum, Cairo)

ARS UNA: SPECIES MILLE
GENERAL HISTORY OF ART

ART IN EGYPT

BY

G. MASPERO

MEMBER OF THE INSTITUTE
DIRECTOR GENERAL OF THE SERVICE OF ANTIQUITIES OF EGYPT

ISBN: 978-1-63923-974-0

All Rights reserved. No part of this book maybe reproduced without written permission from the publishers, except by a reviewer who may quote brief passages in a review to be printed in a newspaper or magazine.

Printed: March 2023

Published and Distributed By:
Lushena Books
607 Country Club Drive, Unit E
Bensenville, IL 60106
www.lushenabks.com

ISBN: 978-1-63923-974-0

PREFACE

THE art of Egypt, like all the rest of its civilisation, is the product of the African soil. If it occasionally took ideas or methods of expression from the peoples with which it was brought into contact by the Pharaohs, its levies were not important enough in the first instance to exercise a durable influence upon its constitution. In a few years, it had so completely assimilated the substance of these as to leave us hardly sensible that any alien influences had interfered, even momentarily, with its homogeneity. It was only towards the end, when the race whose mind it had so admirably materialised and translated began to bow beneath the weight of over fifty centuries of existence, that it too declined, lacking strength to defend its superannuated traditions successfully against the new conceptions of beauty set before it by younger races.

I have dealt briefly with the period of its infancy, thinking the reader would forgive me, if I devoted as little as possible of the limited space at my disposal to dubious origins. Besides, unlike some of my *confrères*, I cannot accept as *art* the rude images by which every new-born people seeks to reproduce the objects or the beings it sees around it, and the ideas they evoke. I have therefore dealt with it as almost adult, when it had left

PREFACE

its awkward age behind it. I have indicated the religious and social principles by which it was governed at the time of the Thinite dynasties, and I have then tried to determine the successive stages of its development during the following periods. It has been very erroneously supposed that it presented a perfect uniformity from beginning to end, and that its character was identical in all the different regions of the land, save for certain differences of handling which were the results of degrees of skill in its artists. I have shown how, while drawing everywhere upon a common fund of general ideas, it had so far varied their manifestations in different districts, as to give birth to independent schools, the activity of which augmented or relaxed according to the varying fortunes of the cities which were their homes: the Thinite School, the Memphite School, the Hermopolitan School, the Tanite School, the secondary schools of the Saïd or the Delta. The list is as yet imperfectly established, and I have not been able to make it complete in architecture, for lack of a sufficient number of provincial documents, but it is fairly satisfactory as regards painting and sculpture. Not only is it possible to determine their principal characteristics, but there are some among them, the Theban School, for instance, whose fortunes may be easily followed from the rise of the Eleventh Dynasty to the rule of the Cæsars. Its relics are to be counted by thousands, and each day is marked by discoveries which enable us to fill in the lacunæ of our science in this connection, and to give additional precision to what we already know.

I have put a good deal of my own into this little volume, and much that I owe to others. We may set aside those who wrote when Egypt was a sealed book to the modern world. Although Champollion had from the outset very sound ideas on the nature of Egyptian art, and thoroughly appreciated its fine qualities, the admirable Emmanuel de Rougé was the first to define its characteristics scientifically and to sketch its history, in his *Notice* of 1854 on the monuments of the Louvre *(Oeuvres diverses,* vol. III, p. 36—40) and in his report of 1854

PREFACE

(Ibid. vol. II, p. 213—246). Mariette, when in 1864 he compiled his Catalogue of the Boulak Museum, pointed out many traits which his master had not noted, but the rest of the school, absorbed in deciphering texts, did not follow on the path thus opened, and for many years only amateurs and classical archæologists made their way along it: Charles Blanc *(Voyage dans la Haute Egypte, 8vo,* Paris, 1870, and *Grammaire des Arts du Dessin,* 6th ed., Paris, 1886), Comte du Barry de Mervel *(Etudes sur l'Architecture Egyptienne,* 8vo, Paris, 1873), Soldi *(La Sculpture Egyptienne,* 8vo, Paris, 1876), Marchandon de la Faye *(Histoire de l'Art Egyptien d'apres les Monuments,* 4to, Paris, 1878), Perrot-Chipiez *(Histoire de l'Art dans l'Antiquite, l'Egypte,* 8vo, Paris, 1880), Goodyear *(Grammar of the Lotus,* 4to, New York, 1891), Lübke-Semrau *(Die Kunst des Altertums,* 14th ed., 8vo, Esslingen, 1908), Springer-Michaelis *(Handbuch der Kunstgeschichte,* 9th. ed., 8vo, vol. I, Leipzig, 1911), Sybel *(Weltgeschichte der Kunst im Altertum,* 2nd ed., 8vo, Marburg, 1903), Woermann *(Geschichte der Kunst aller Zeiten und Völker,* 8vo, vol. I, Leipzig, 1904). Finally, however, the Egyptologists took the field, Maspero in Rayet's *Monuments de l'Art antique,* fol. vol. I, 1879—1883, and *Archéologie Egyptienne,* 8vo, Paris, 1887, Flinders Petrie in *Egyptian Decorative Art,* 8vo, London, 1895, Georges Foucart in *Histoire de l'ordre lotiforme,* 8vo, Paris, 1897. Naville insisted on the part played by utilitarian considerations in the formation of sculptural and architectural types *(L'Art Egyptien,* 8vo, Paris, 1907), while Bissing condensed the results of his prolonged studies in a manual *(Einführung in die Geschichte der Ägyptischen Kunst von den ältesten Zeiten bis auf die Römer,* 8vo, Berlin, 1908). In the interval Steindorff had prepared for the curious who visit the Nile each year a substantial *resumé* of our knowledge on the subject (Baedeker's Handbook, *Egypt and the Sudan,* Leipzig, 1908) and Spiegelberg, reviving a theory propounded by Rougé and Mariette, sought to demonstrate the existence of a popular art less rigid than the official art *(Geschichte der Ägyptischen Kunst,* 8vo, Leipzig, 1903). As a fact, there was never

PREFACE

any distinction between the two, but the same artists were allowed more or less liberty according to the nature of the subjects they treated and the social condition of those they portrayed. I have tried as far as possible to reproduce and to appreciate only things I have myself seen and handled, and the good fortune which made me twice the director of the Service of Antiquities has greatly facilitated my task. I should, however, be guilty of ingratitude no less than of injustice if I did not acknowledge my debt to those collections of engravings and photographs in black and white and in colours, in which so many of us, and I myself among them, have been able to study monuments to which personal access was denied us. The architectural drawings of the French Commission have lost little of their value, and it would be difficult to over-estimate the works of Cailliaud, Gau, Champollion, and Rosellini. Lepsius' *Denkmäler* has been of greater service to archæologists and philologists than to art-historians. Weidenbach, who executed the plates for this with the help of his pupils, conceived the unhappy idea of rendering bas-reliefs and paintings by a series of stereotyped designs which he copied and recopied with slight modifications throughout the work. We can hardly be surprised therefore if critics, finding the same persons treated in the same manner from the Memphite period to that of the Roman domination, accused Egyptian art of monotony. Prisse d'Avennes, though his drawing has more warmth and flexibility, was also guilty of conventionalising his models excessively in his *Histoire de l'Art Egyptien*. We may turn from these approximations to the more trustworthy facsimiles of Champollion and Rosellini when we wish to form an opinion of monuments now mutilated or destroyed; for the others, we may consult Maxime Ducamp's *Voyages en Egypte* (fol., Paris, 1852), the photographs Banville tock in concert with Emmanuel de Rougé (fol., Paris, 1868), Béchard's *L'Egypte et la Nubie* (fol., Paris, 1887). the albums of Mariette *(Album du Musée de Boulaq*, fol., Cairo, 1872), Borchardt *(Kunstwerke aus dem Ägyptischen Museum zu Cairo*, fol., Cairo, 1908), Capart

PREFACE

(L'Art Egyptien, 4to, Brussels, 1909) and above all the incomparable atlas which Bissing is completing for the firm of Bruckmann *(Denkmäler ägyptischer Skulptur*, fol., Munich, 1906—1911). The Cairo Museum, in the volumes of its *Catalogue Général* (4to, Cairo, 1900—1911) has reproduced all the objects of its collections which are of interest to artist or historian, and that of Berlin has given us a valuable selection of its treasures *(Ägyptische und Vorderasiatische Altertümer aus den Königlichen Museen zu Berlin*, fol., Berlin, 1897), but the riches of the British Museum, the Louvre, Turin, and Leyden have hardly been exploited as yet, and how many marvels Egypt herself displays to tourists and even to scholars who pass them by indifferently!

Nevertheless, Egyptian Art is no longer the exclusive domain of a privileged few. Artists — painters, sculptors, architects — blind at first to its merits, have come of late years to perceive and feel them keenly; the admiration it inspires increases with closer study. Men of letters and the general public are still disconcerted by the strangeness of some of its conventions, and a certain time will no doubt have to pass before they appreciate it at its true value. May this little book, in which I have followed its fortunes as clearly and completely as lay in my power, help those who misjudge it, to understand, if not to love it!

CONTENTS

PART I
THE BEGINNINGS OF ART IN EGYPT

PAGE

CHAPTER I
THINITE ART 1

CHAPTER II
MEMPHITE ART 26

PART II
THEBAN ART

CHAPTER I
THE FIRST THEBAN AGE FROM THE ELEVENTH TO THE SEVENTEENTH DYNASTY 95

CHAPTER II
THE SECOND THEBAN AGE FROM THE EIGHTEENTH TO THE TWENTY-FIRST DYNASTY 124

PART III
THE SAÏTE AGE AND THE END OF EGYPTIAN ART

INDEX 305

FIG. I.—SHÛNET-EZ-ZEBÎB, ABYDOS. TYPE OF THINITE FORTRESS.

PART I
THE BEGINNINGS OF ART IN EGYPT

CHAPTER I
THINITE ART

Primitive Art in Egypt before Menes — Thinite Art and its Remains: Architecture, Fortresses, Palaces, Temples, Tombs — In it we may trace the Principles and Forms which, developing in the course of centuries, gave to Egyptian Art its characteristic aspect — Memphite Art was developed by contact with it.

THE most ancient tombs, those of the prehistoric period, have so far yielded nothing which indicates any extraordinary development of the artistic sense among the early Egyptians. The objects found in them bear witness to a taste for personal adornment, and for decorated arms and utensils, equal, but by no means superior to that of most semi-civilised nations. They consist of coloured pottery, either glazed or unglazed, plain, or covered with incised or painted ornament, furniture of wood or stone, jewelry of variegated pebbles, of shells, rough or carved, of bone, ivory, glassy pastes, and precious metals; finally, figures of men and animals, some designed for personal use, such as receptacles for cosmetics, others reserved for funerary rites. The persons and things represented on vases are not grouped methodically in superposed rows, but are scattered irregularly over the surface at the will of the designer, here a house, there an animal,

ART IN EGYPT

a palm-tree, a boat, a few fish. They reveal facility in seizing living forms, and a natural skill in translating attitudes and movement by drawing and modelling. But there is nothing to compare with the sculptures and paintings that contemporaries of the Reindeer Period were executing in the regions now known as France and Spain.

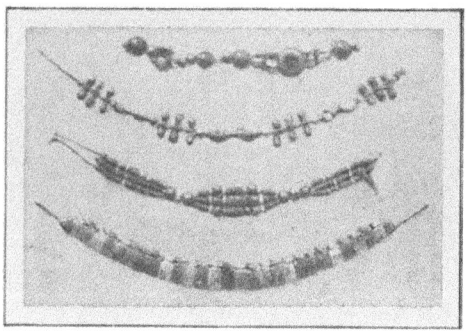

FIG. 2.—THE ABYDOS BRACELETS. (Museum, Cairo.) *(Phot. E. Brugsch.)*

Nevertheless, when we pass from these productions to which no exact date can be assigned, to those of the historic dynasties, we are confronted by thousands of objects and buildings, the execution of which secures a high place for the Egyptians among the nations of the East in the realm of art. Where we had found only the rude essays of laborious apprentices, and the rudiments of a craftsmanship as yet uncertain of itself, we come suddenly, and almost without transition, to the works of masters, and to a highly accomplished technique. Must we conclude that between the two stages, alien races from without had dominated the natives, bringing them a conception of beauty and a power of realising it which they had lacked heretofore? It seems improbable that a sudden efflorescence of art should have followed on a foreign invasion; but if there are no extant monuments by which we may gauge the natural evolution of the Egyptian genius, we are compelled to recognise among the artisans of the Thinite age, the inspiration and even the processes of preceding generations. Their jewelry had preserved the earlier

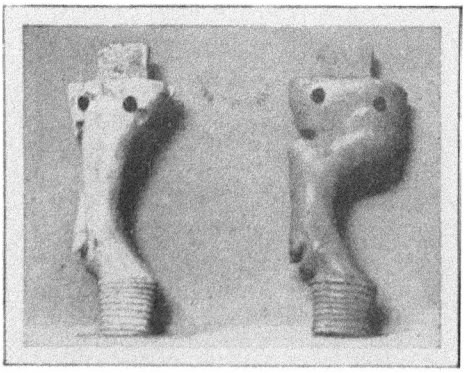

FIG. 3.—IVORY FEET OF A BED AND A STOOL. (Museum, Cairo.) *(Phot. E. Brugsch.)*

THINITE ART

tradition, and their happiest effects were inspired by it. I may cite the four bracelets discovered by Petrie in the necropolis of Abydos (Fig. 2), with their alternating plates of graven gold and

FIG. 4.—FIGURINES OF ANIMALS, MONKEY, LION, DOGS.
(Museum, Cairo.) *(Phot E Brugsch.)*

of turquoise or light blue glass, their beads or pendants of carved amethyst, and the chased floral ornament, the delicacy of which might be envied by our modern goldsmiths. The same might be said of furniture and domestic utensils, feet of bedsteads or stools in wood and in ivory (Fig. 3), figurines of lions, monkeys, and dogs (Fig. 4), stone or crystal fish, statuettes of prisoners or slaves, bone tablets on which the principal episodes of royal sepulture were traced with the style (Fig. 5), cylinders bearing hieroglyphic legends or divine emblems, club-heads, etc. In all these we recognise the early ideas and conventions, with this difference, that what was the result of pure instinct in the beginning has become that of deliberate intention. Craftsmen or artists, the experience of an unknown number of generations had taught

FIG. 5.—THE TABLET OF AHA.
(Museum, Cairo.) *(Phot. E Brugsch)*

them gradually to bring out the principal lines of their models, to fix their contours, to simplify their reliefs, to co-ordinate their

ART IN EGYPT

movements and their postures. They took pleasure in slow and tranquil gestures; if the nature of their subjects, religious processions, hunting and battle-scenes, assaults on cities, the pursuit of enemies, forced them to express violent or rapid action, they did their utmost to minimise its hard abruptness. It will be readily supposed without much insistence on the point, that an art so well regulated implies a long period of preliminary effort and experiment. In spite of external divergences, the elements are those chosen and employed by the ancestors of its practitioners from the beginning; but the workman had handled them so often and for so long that by dint of practice he had at last reduced them to a system, and had replaced the direct observation of nature by the constant use of decorative schemes or of formulæ accepted in the workshop.

FIG. 6.—GROOVED FAÇADE OF THINITE TOMBS AND FORTRESSES.
(After Garstang.)

The impression made by the industrial arts is confirmed by the rarer survivals of the higher arts, architecture, sculpture, and painting. Very little has come down to us of the military and civil or indeed of the religious architecture; we have the ruins of a fortress at Hieraconpolis, in Abydos (cf. Fig. 1) and in one or two small townships of the Saïd, while in some of the ritual tablets and the hieroglyphic writings we find incidental renderings of several very ancient temples (cf. Fig. 8). The fortresses, or rather castles in which the kings and nobles lived, are vast parallelograms of sun-dried brick, the walls of which are sometimes perfectly

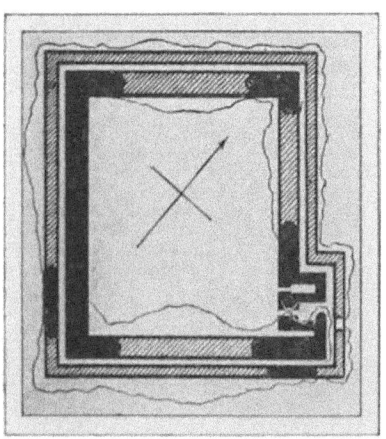

FIG. 7.—PLAN OF THE FORTRESS OF KOM-EL-AHMAR (After Quibell)

THINITE ART

smooth and unadorned from one angle to the other, sometimes divided into panels, the beds of which are alternately horizontal

FIG. 8.—VARIOUS TYPES OF ARCHAIC CHAPELS AND TEMPLES.

and concave, and sometimes finally present a series of vertical prismatic grooves (Fig. 6). The principal doorway is generally relegated to the end of one of the lateral , and is set in a block of masonry solid enought to defy sapll and ram (Fig. 7). Private persons inhabited buildings of beatenpearth or dried brick similar to those of the modern fellahin, and like these, generally of a single storey. The temple was an isolated cell, of variable dimensions, but always of small extent, raised upon an artificial mound at the end of a rectangular enclosure bounded by a low wall or rows of piles; two posts were set up in front of the entrance, and the emblem of the god crowned the roof, or was raised on a pole in the middle of the enclosure (Fig. 8). The cella consisted at first of four wooden uprights, connected by wicker-work plastered with mud; the doorway was closed by a wooden panel or a hanging mat. In some cases, the roof was flat, with or without a cornice; but in general, it described a peculiar curve from front to back, the form of which persisted after the little build-

FIG. 9.—WOODEN NAOS.
(Museum Turin) *(Phot. Lanzone.)*

ing of slight materials had become a naos of wood (Fig. 9) or of stone covered with inscriptions and hieroglyphic scenes (Fig. 10). To this cell other cabins were soon added for the accommodation of auxiliary gods, priests, and offerings, and the whole, symmetrically arranged in an enclosure, constituted a *divine palace,* analogous to the royal dwelling. At a later stage the gods, dissatisfied with so poor a dwelling, demanded thicker walls made of bricks, and stone for thresholds, lintels, architraves, and the bases of columns; then limestone or sandstone was substituted for brick, with granite to surround the bays, and the perishable huts of an earlier age became *houses of eternity,* without, however, changing the main lines of the primitive plan. The fragments which we possess of the temple dedicated to the gods of Hieraconpolis prove that the transformation was already far advanced under the Third Dynasty. They formed part of a doorway of pink granite, the exterior faces of which were decorated with royal legends (Fig. 11), and with bas-reliefs which were effaced during one of the reconstructions of the building; the patterns made by the hammer-strokes enable us to divine that these reliefs represented the sovereign adoring the divinity with the ritual familiar to us on the monuments of the Theban era.

FIG. 10.—SIDE OF NAOS OF SAFT-EL-HENNEH.
(Museum, Cairo.)   *(Phot. L. Brugsch.)*

Like the temples, the tombs of the Thinite age retained the principal features of those of the earlier period at Abydos, at Nakâdah, at Hieraconpolis, and in all places where they have been discovered hitherto. The most famous, that of Nakâdah (Fig. 12), did not belong, as might have been supposed, to the Menes who founded the Egyptian Empire, nor to some other Menes almost contemporary with him; it guarded the mummy of

THINITE ART

some nameless lord, who ruled a portion of the Theban plain. Imagine a rectangle some 176 feet long by 88 wide, running diagonally from north to south. It is composed entirely of unfired bricks cemented and plastered with clay, without either limewash or painting. The exterior surfaces were originally decorated with the usual vertical grooves, and the plan of the interior included a large hall, separated from the enclosing wall by a narrow passage, and divided into five compartments ranged in a line on the main axis. The corpse was laid in the central compartment, and his household goods were arranged partly on the ground around him, partly in the four other chambers. When these were full, they were walled up, and the adjoining passage was parcelled into cells for the reception of surplus provisions, after which the entrance was blocked, and the external decorations were masked by a facing of bricks, whitewashed over. The tombs of the Thinite Pharaohs excavated by Amélineau to the west of Abydos, and by

FIG. 11.—DOOR-JAMB OF THE TEMPLE OF KOM-EL-AHMAR. (Museum, Cairo.) *(Phot. L. Brugsch.*

Garstang at Rekaknah and at Bêt-Khallaf (Figs. 13, 14) were not all exactly similar in arrangement; one was shaped somewhat like a shuttle, wider in the middle than at the two extremities; another was floored and panelled with wood, and their outer surfaces showed neither projections nor recesses. None the less are they of the same type as that of Nakâdah, and if we consider them as a whole, we are struck by their general resemblance to the

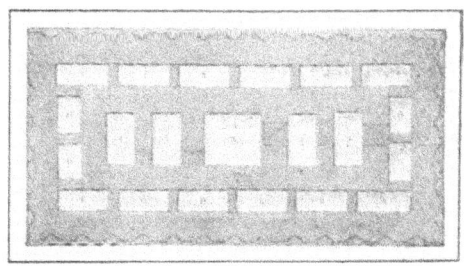

FIG. 12.—PLAN OF THE TOMB AT NAKÂDAH. (After De Morgan.)

fortresses of Abydos and Hieraconpolis. Like these, they have in some cases walls with prismatic niches; they have their store-

ART IN EGYPT

rooms and their lodging reserved for the chief; their doors are hidden away at the least accessible point, and they were blocked up after the deposition of the corpse, just as those of the

FIG. 13.—ROYAL TOMB AT BÊT-KHALLAF. *(Phot Garstang.)*

fortresses were barricaded in the hour of danger (Fig. 14). Thus the same intention governed the construction of each. Just as the fortress was the residence of the living lord or sovereign, the castle in which he held his court in peace, and in which he awaited behind barricaded doors the attacks of his enemies in war, so the tomb was looked upon as the castle of the dead lord or sovereign, in which he intrenched himself for all eternity, safe from the outrages of men and of years. If we remember that the temple was also a palace, the palace of the god, we shall be driven to admit that identity of terms here denotes identity of conception, and that the manner of life of the lord or the Pharaoh before and after interment, was identical with that of the gods. Originally, the monumental tomb had been the privilege of those powerful enough to procure it, chiefs of clans, princes of Nomes, great officers of the crown, and kings; later, with the growth of wealth in the nation, the privilege was extended, and was conferred, under the conditions we shall presently note, on those of the people whose fortunes or the

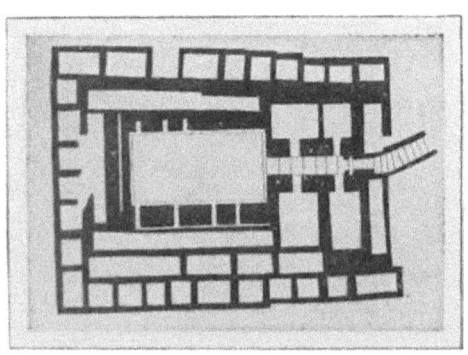

FIG. 14.—PLAN OF THE TOMB *(After Garstang.)*

THINITE ART

favour of the master encouraged to aspire to the luxury of an independent future life.

The internal walls are generally speaking bare, but the priests or the relatives of the defunct stored up in the vault or in the chambers adjoining it the funereal trappings, furniture, provisions, and simulacra more or less rude of the dead man and of the servants who were despatched with him to the next world; they were there in numbers, each in the attitude proper to his rank or function; the master seated, or standing to receive offerings, the servants engaged in preparing or serving these, grinding corn (Fig. 15), kneading dough, brewing beer, plastering a jar (Fig. 16) before putting wine in it, busied with all the duties of the household, apparently inanimate, but impregnated with the latent life breathed into them by virtue of the rites. Gradually, however, the instinct which had moved the primeval Egyptians to decorate their pottery, led those of the archaic age to cover their walls with scenes introducing the persons whose figures had heretofore lain scattered on the ground. These were mute at first; later, they were accompanied by short inscriptions setting forth their deeds, their speeches, their names, the titles which constituted their civil status, and authenticated their rights to posthumous life. The earliest example is that discovered by Quibell at Kom-el-Ahmar. The motives were not as yet arranged in rows with methodical precision, but like those on the vases, they are scattered almost at random over the surface. The first essays are rude figures careless of form and proportion, awkwardly drawn with red ochre, like those with which our children adorn the margins of their books. With these we find the camp or the village on the edge of the desert, gazelles and oryx browsing, running on the plain, or keeping watch on some rocky peak, men armed with darts or clubs, following a trail or fighting

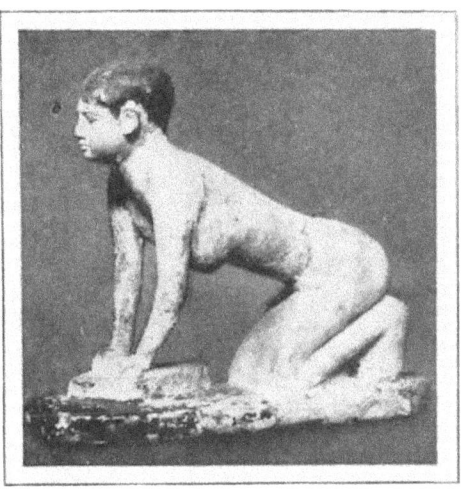

FIG. 15 —WOMAN GRINDING CORN.
(Museum, Cairo.) *(Phot. L. Brugsch.)*

ART IN EGYPT

with hyænas, all the details, in short, which make up the hunter's ideal of a happy life and a desirable Elysium. The noble who ordered the paintings and the artisan who daubed them had no conception of a life of the manes differing in any respect from that of the living, and they believed that the surest way of facilitating access to it was to introduce paintings of it in the tomb near the corpse. This belief was the logical conclusion of a dogma familiar to all semi-barbarians: he who invents or reproduces a figure, no matter what, immediately creates a being, and if he afterwards gives it the name of a man, an animal, or an object, he endows it with a portion of soul stolen from that of the original. The life of the simulacrum ceases with that of its prototype, but the latter can prolong it and himself by means of incantations; and by virtue of these it may even be transmitted to all portraits of an individual executed after his death. Stone or wooden images took the place of the fleshly bodies of master and servants if these were missing, and thus assuming the function of a *double*, they guaranteed its perpetuity as long as they were preserved. The decoration of the tomb produced an identical effect; it prevented the annihilation of the servants and the objects represented, and obliged them to minister to the comfort of the master, as long as substantial traces of what it had reproduced remained upon the walls.

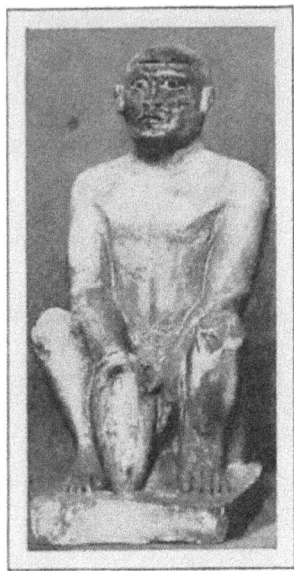

FIG. 16.
SERVANT TARRING A JAR.
(Museum, Cairo.) *(Phot. L. Brugsch.)*

Briefly, all forms of art, architecture, sculpture, and painting, tended not to the disinterested search after beauty, but to the realisation of the useful. The three categories into which reasonable beings were divided, the living, the dead, and the gods, shared an intense desire for duration; they had bent all the most powerful springs of their minds in this direction, and the effort they had made to achieve it had given a special character to the arts. In the first place, it had determined the choice of materials. Men, whose years, however numerous, are but as a moment compared with the innumerable centuries of the dead and the

THINITE ART

gods, were content with slight materials: earth, wood, and freestone. If they made use of metals, it was less for their indestructibility than for the charm of their colour, the fineness of their texture, their ductility and their value. The richest of the Pharaohs did not disdain to dwell in houses of sun-dried bricks, under roofs of beaten mud supported by wooden columns, between ceilings and pavements bedaubed with fragile paintings; if their palaces lasted as long as they lived, they cared little that they should fall into ruin as soon as they themselves had disappeared. The case was very different when the dwelling was destined for the dead or for the gods; then its longevity had to rival theirs, and this result was only to be achieved by the help of the most solid materials. Tombs and temples were accordingly built of limestone or sandstone of the best quality, and even of granite or the breccia of the Arabian mountains, which, however, was generally reserved for the doors, the thresholds, and such portions of the structure as the frequent passage of the faithful and the performance of religious rites tended to wear away rapidly; panegyrics upon the Pharaohs extolled them for having erected houses of eternal stones for their divine fathers. But as the density and durability of the blocks themselves was not sufficient to ensure the longevity of the

FIG. 17.—PAINTINGS AT KOM-EL-AHMAR. (After Quibell.)

FIG. 18.—TEMPLE OF KHONSU AT KARNAK
(Phot. Beato.)

building, care was taken to choose those architectural forms which promised the greatest stability, such as the pyramid, the mastaba, the rectangular temple, set firmly upon the soil under such conditions of equilibrium that only the hand of man or the attacks of the river could overthrow them; time has proved powerless against them. The reliefs with which they were adorned were kept very low, or "left" on sunk surfaces, which diminished the risk of damage from concussion, and protected them from accidental mutilations. It was permissible for persons of modest means to employ wood for statues, and for divine or funerary groups; but if economy was not essential, limestone or sandstone, alabaster, schist, granite, serpentine, and diorite were preferred, and he who had none of these to hand sent into the desert to fetch them. Even then, statues were given one of the three or four attitudes which seemed least fragile; figures were seated upon a complete cube or on a seat with a straight back, or they stood with legs pressed together, arms adhering to the body, back and head engaged in a vertical slab. The care for solidity prevailed over every other consideration both with sculptor and architect.

FIG. 19.—THE SERVANTS OF TI BRINGING OFFERINGS.

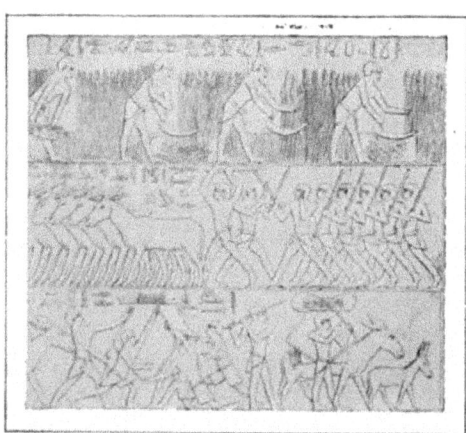

FIG. 20.—HARVEST SCENES IN THE TOMB OF TI.

This gave their works a unity, and also, we must frankly admit, a constant uniformity of invention and execution; the very

THINITE ART

derogations from the determining principle which we seem to note in them prove to be a result and a confirmation of it, when we study them attentively. If indeed the tomb and the temple, supplying the same demands, consist on the whole of the same elements as the palace, it was nevertheless essential that they should be arranged to suit the individual conditions of posthumous existence and of divine life. Each contained a personal dwelling, rooms for guests or slaves, store-rooms, and audience-chambers; but whereas the god consented to receive his priests and to show himself sometimes to the people, the dead person was wholly inaccessible, and never again appeared in public, when the hour of his entry into his private apartments was past. The sanctuary was accordingly so placed that it communicated with the outside world, and that the living could enter it easily on prescribed occasions; the vault, on the other hand, was never opened again after the corpse had been placed in it, and soon, to render the dead more completely inaccessible, the body was placed underground, at the end of a passage or at the bottom of a well which was subsequently filled up to the level of the soil. Thenceforth, whereas the temple, inhabited by a being whose nature did not

FIG. 21.—BRINGING CORN TO THE GRINDER, TREADING AND WINNOWING, IN THE TOMB OF TI.

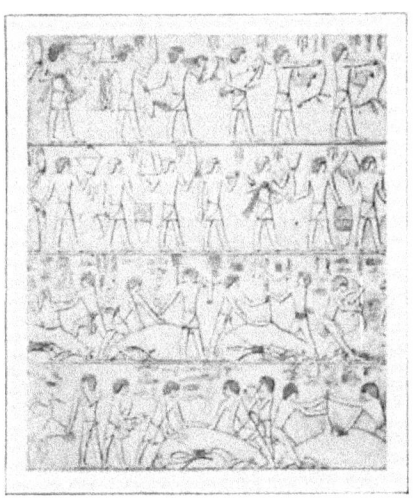

FIG. 22.—SLAUGHTER OF CATTLE, IN THE TOMB OF TI

13

ART IN EGYPT

debar him from official intercourse with the world, tended to increase in size and to expand in the sunlight, the tomb, shunning the light of day, gradually diminished its points of external contact, and ended by displaying only a narrow façade, a roughly hewn panel, the bay of a door, or a rectangular orifice in the rock. During the process of this change, the common plan was modified. As the princely dwelling was converted, on the one hand into a sanctuary, on the other into a vault, the guest-chambers, store-houses, and reception-rooms were modified and adjusted to circumstances. Some of the store-rooms were relegated to the sides, and assimilating to some extent with the guest-chambers, they became, jointly with these, depôts for daily offerings, or chapels for the paredri. The reception rooms were then transformed into hypostyle halls or courts echeloned in a line on the longitudinal axis of the building, and increasing in size in proportion to their distance from the Holy of Holies. Thus the worshippers of the god no more enjoyed equal facilities of approach than the courtiers of Pharaoh; a few were admitted to the presence, many entered halls more or less close to him, as determined by

FIG. 23.—THE NOMES BRINGING OFFERINGS, AT EDFÛ. (Phot. Beato.)

FIG. 24.—A WALL IN THE TEMPLE OF ISIS, AT PHILÆ. (Phot. Beato.)

THINITE ART

the hierarchy, and the rest advanced no farther than the outer courts or the platform before the temple. A dead person of non-royal race, who had not a nation to adore him, but whose family and dependents were necessarily restricted, would have had no use for such vast spaces; a simple chapel sufficed for him, and three or four little rooms, rarely more, and often less, served him for storehouse, reception-rooms, and guest-chambers, without endangering his chances of immortality.

When this point had been reached, the diversity between tomb and temple was so great, that all traces of a common origin seem to have been effaced, what likeness is there at a first glance between a monument such as that of Khonsu (Fig. 18) or of Edfû, and the Theban hypogea of the Saïte period? To perceive the analogy clearly, a long series of deductions and analyses would be requisite.

FIG. 25.—FULL FACE STATUE, THE FEET JOINED.
(Museum, Cairo.)
(Phot. E. Brugsch.)

The difficulty is hardly less when we attempt to refer the decorations of these buildings to a single type; but here again the most extravagant divergencies may be explained by the nature of the personages concerned. Whether gods or mummies, they were incapable of subsisting by their individual energy, and they would have died of starvation but for the daily intervention of the living. The latter accordingly endowed them with appanages, or, if we prefer the term used in Mussulman jurisprudence, *dukaf*, which kept them in good case, as long as the revenues were applied to them. It was not very often, however, that they profited long by their endowments. Their descendants took them away after a certain number of years, or the family became extinct, and its heritage fell to strangers who repudiated the charges on the property; the founder, despoiled of his dues, suffered the slow tortures of starvation, before finally succumbing to that second death which definitively annihilated that remnant of vitality his first death had respected. The statuettes scattered in the rooms, and the scenes represented upon the walls of the tomb averted the danger, and the greater their number, the more certain he was to lack nothing, even if his actual possessions had been taken from him. Interminable processions of men and women simulated his houses, his ponds,

ART IN EGYPT

FIG. 26.—FULL FACE STATUE, WALKING. (Museum, Cairo.) (Phot. E Brugsch.)

his woods, his meadows, and brought the rents of their farms to him (Fig. 19), while the serfs and servants of his household, each occupied with his special work, manufactured its products for him eternally. Did he want bread? The field was ploughed before his eyes in simulacrum; the ripe grain fell under the sickle (Fig. 20); the corn was trodden out, winnowed, measured, and poured into the granary (Fig. 21); then the bakers ground it, baked the loaf, and presented it to him. Did he desire to eat meat? In other pictures, the bull was coupled with the cow, the calf was born, grew up, became an ox, fell into the hands of the butchers who cut its throat, caught the blood, skinned and divided the carcase, choosing the best pieces for him (Fig. 22). The gods were less in danger of that complete ruin which resulted in annihilation; when once their appanage had been apportioned, if some impious person appropriated it in the course of time, a benefactor duly appeared to repair the injury. Nevertheless, it was considered prudent to assign to them as to the dead, a fictitious domain to supplement the real one if needful; the Nomes were accordingly represented bringing their tribute (Fig. 23), and sometimes even barbarous peoples subject to Egypt. And as the gods could only be served by the Pharaoh or one of his family, on every occasion when the help of an inferior was not indispensable, we see around them on the walls only kings and queens, princes and princesses; these noble personages, however, were not obliged to perform the vulgar tasks imposed on the kinsfolk of dead persons. It appears that no effort was necessary to obtain all that was required in the sphere in which they moved; objects presented themselves all ready for use,

FIG. 27.—SEATED STATUE OF THE PHARAOH MYCERINUS. (Museum, Cairo.) (Phot. E. Brugsch.)

THINITE ART

the ox decked for the holocaust, water, wine, milk, and oil poured for libation, the incense lighted for sacramental fumigation. Nothing could be less like the varied episodes of human life which abound in the hypogea than these monotonous functions of divine life; and yet the god who might have been suddenly on the verge of starvation by reason of some accident would only have had to cast his eyes around, and the imagery of the walls would have nourished him with delectable realities; in the temple as in the tomb the decoration had an important utilitarian function, and if the elements which composed the two differed materially, the intention which co-ordinated them and the conception from which they were deduced were one and the same.

This insistence on a utilitarian purpose weighed heavily upon the independence both of art and artist. The artist, obliged to think above all of the welfare of those for whom he was working, was not free to abandon himself to his inspiration, nor to diverge from the rules in which religion imprisoned him. Seeing that the statue was the body of a *double*, it was necessary, in order to attach this *double* to it, to reproduce not only the physiognomy and features of the model, but the bearing and the costume of his profession, to the end that in his state of death he should remain what fortune had made him here below; it had to be at once the portrait of an individual, and a type of the class to which he belonged. Scribes, artisans, nobles, priests, Pharaohs, and gods had each their prescribed

FIG. 28.—STANDING STATUE BEARING ENSIGN. (Museum, Cairo.) *(Phot. E. Brugsch.)*

FIG. 29.—GROUP OF PERSONS, STANDING AND SITTING. (Museum, Cairo.) *(Phot. E. Brugsch.)*

ART IN EGYPT

FIG. 30.—STATUE WITH BODY IN A SHEATH. (Museum, Cairo.) *(Phot. E. Brugsch.)*

formula, to which sculptors and painters were required to adhere faithfully, without, however, modifying the characteristic lines of the individual; some thirty positions were permitted: standing still (Fig. 25) or walking (Fig. 26), sitting (Fig. 27), kneeling, crouching, crawling, lying, with a hundred variations of costume, head-dress and insignia. Persons were represented facing the spectator squarely, so that a line drawn perpendicularly through the body always divided it into two equal portions, and this *law of frontality* was rigorously observed down to the last days of pagan Egypt. Mural decoration, by the nature of the episodes proper to it, admitted greater diversity; but here it is necessary to distinguish between that of tombs and that of temples. It both cases the moment chosen is that of the performance of the act which was to produce the result enjoined by dogma; but whereas in the temple the scene, enacted by gods and Pharaohs, rarely required more than three or four persons, always of the same kind, in the tomb all Egypt played its part, men, beasts and things, and the number of the participants had no other limits than those of the surface to be covered. The result in the bas-reliefs of the temple was a uniformity of composition and attitude almost equal to that of the statues. Nothing was modified in the course of ages but the distribution of the pictures and the degree of skill of the execution. In the tombs, neither the moments of rustic or industrial toil, nor those of funereal offerings are so inflexibly treated. Up to a certain point, the artist was free to introduce additional motives, to intermingle and disconnect his episodes, to alternate and break

FIG. 31.—THE DOG NIBÛ. (Museum, Cairo.) *(Phot. E. Brugsch.)*

THINITE ART

them up; but this freedom only stood him in good stead in the somewhat rare cases when the extent of the walls allowed him to give the decoration the necessary breadth. Nine times out of ten, lack of space compelled him to confine himself to those themes which contributed most to the happiness of the dead person, and to condense his material as much as possible. By a progressive series of eliminations, the work became at last an abbreviated panorama of Egyptian life, the motives of which, blurred or decomposed slowly by the lapse of centuries, impress us in each epoch with a sense of monotony hardly less than that which we experience in the temples. It has not yet been very definitely ascertained where this

FIG. 32.—THE LADY NUTIR. (Museum, Cairo.) *(Phot.E.Brugsch.)*

system arose and was developed. It is probable that its materials were evolved spontaneously at first in every quarter, but that they were revised, subjected to a process of selection, and co-ordinated at Heliopolis, in the regions where the popular religions were welded into a body of theology which the whole nation accepted. The Heliopolitan doctrine unquestionably governed the installation of the temples, with its Enneas, its insistence on the predominance of the solar divinities, its ritual of prayers and offerings. And if we pass in review the illustration of the tombs, we shall see that the great number of fishing and hunting scenes in the marshes included in it are more in keeping with the ancient conditions of the upper parts of the Delta and of the marshy districts adjoining the Fayûm than with those of the Saïd.

FIG. 33.—THE DWARF HAPU. (Museum, Cairo.) *(Phot. E. Brugsch.)*

It would seem then that it was in the Heliopolitan plain and in the region about Memphis that the convention of the tombs was instituted, and its northern origin will explain why it has not so far been met with in the Thinite cemeteries of Abydos;

FIG. 34.—THE SOLDIER ABUNI. (Museum, Cairo.) *(Phot. E. Brugsch.)*

it had not had time to impose itself upon the reigning dynasties and their subjects, even if it had penetrated into the region. The most richly ornamented sepulchres here admitted no elements of plastic art other than stelæ, or perhaps statues of the dead and their servants. None of the latter have survived, but there is no lack of stelæ, both royal and private. The private ones, which are by far the most numerous, generally consist of a simple limestone slab, roughly shaped, sometimes rounded at the top, sometimes rectangular, sometimes irregular in shape, on which the figure of a man or animal with an inscription has been hastily carved. It may be the dog Nibû with his straight ears and pointed muzzle (Fig. 31); the dwarf Hapu standing and presenting his misshapen profile to the spectator (Fig. 33); the lady Nutir crouching on the ground (Fig. 32); the soldier Abuni, also crouching, but grasping a bow (Fig. 34). Their luminous *doubles* were as surely attracted by these rudimentary bas-reliefs as by statues, and as they were much less costly, they were a great saving to the family; thanks to them, the *doubles* followed the sovereigns on whose mastabas they were placed, and by serving them, secured a share in their happy destinies. These stelæ were executed by workmen, with small pretensions to art, yet the technique is already so refined that it almost compels us to assume the existence of a more skilful class of craftsmen for aristocratic patrons. An examination of the royal stelæ justifies this hypothesis. They are regular in form, rounded at the top either in a semi-circle, or a slightly curved outline, in imitation, I believe, of the vaulted chambers or corridors found in the hypogea of the Saïd. As they were set up on the summit of

FIG. 35.—STELE OF QA-AU. (Museum, Cairo.) *(Phot. E. Brugsch.)*

THINITE ART

the tombs, they both simulated the entrance door of the sepulchral vault, and served as indications to posterity of the identity of the Pharaohs buried behind them. Thus on all of them we find the same symbol, the falcon of Horus, perched upon the conventional plan of the eternal abode, a rectangle, the lower division of which simulated the façade or doorway of a house, while the upper space bore the name of the inhabitant. The Qâ-âu stele (Fig. 35) suggests the sculptor's struggle with a dark gray schist over which his triumph was not altogether complete; the outline of the falcon is carved with amazing precision; and its specific characteristics, the roundness of the head, and its attachment to the body, the curve of the back, the vigour of the wing, the grip of the claws, are rendered with all the accuracy of a naturalist, but he handling is still somewhat heavy. This is no longer the case in the stele of King Serpent (Fig. 36). Here the artist has mastered his material, rendering it so supple that we are tempted to believe we have before us not the archaic original, but a replica of the time of Seti I. If the work is really of the First Dynasty, as is possible, we may conclude from this solitary instance that in the treatment of animals at any rate, the Thinite masters had attained a degree of perfection occasionally equalled by their successors, but never surpassed.

FIG. 36.—STELE OF KING SERPENT.
(The Louvre, Paris.)

The same cannot be said of the rare bas-reliefs of Sinaï, nor of those figured schist tablets the purpose of which is still uncertain, though it has been alternatively suggested that they were more elegant variants of the toilet palettes of the archaic age, bases for statuettes or divine emblems, or conventionalised imitations of the rams' heads which ornamented the tombs of great personages. The Sinaï bas-reliefs prove that the triumphant attitudes of the Pharaohs familiar to us from later works of art were already stereotyped at this period, but they have suffered so much from exposure to the weather that it would be hazardous to pronounce

ART IN EGYPT

on their style or artistic merit (Fig. 37). Some fifteen of these tablets, perfect or mutilated, are in the museums of Cairo, Paris, Oxford and London. One of the best preserved of these, that of Pharaoh Neter-baiu (Betchau), bears on its summit on either face the royal name enclosed in its triangular cage and flanked by two human heads of Hathor, with the ears and horns of a cow, the latter very much twisted. The principal face is divided into three tiers (Fig. 38). In the first, Pharaoh (on the left), crowned with the red diadem, clad in the short skirt from which hangs the fox-tail, his feet bare, the scourge and club in his hands, advances, followed by his groom bearing vase and sandals, and preceded by four little figures to whom the standards of the four quarters of the world have been confided, towards two rows of the corpses of his enemies, on the right; they are laid flat on the ground, in fives, their wrists loosely bound with a cord, their heads neatly arranged between their legs after the Oriental fashion. The central compartment is occupied by two leopards, confronting each other; their necks, which are extravagantly elongated, curve and interlace round the central hollow, and are crowned by grimacing heads opposed one to the other; their two keepers, in short skirts, round wigs, and pointed beards, strain on their leashes to prevent them from biting each other. At the bottom, a sturdy bull, the symbol of the Pharaohs, demolishes with his horns a brick fortress, and tramples on a naked barbarian who tries in vain to escape. The reverse (Fig. 39) has only two compartments, instead of the three of the principal face. In the centre Baiu, this time mitred with the high white cap and escorted only by his groom, strikes down with his club a chief crouching on the ground before him, and surmounted by a strange group: the hieroglyph of a papyrus marsh from which the head of a man emerges, and a falcon poised with one foot on three of the stems; with the other, which terminates in the arm and hand of a man, the bird holds a cord passed through the nose of the

FIG. 37.—BAS-RELIEF AT SINAÏ.
(Phot. Petrie.)

THINITE ART

head; the meaning of the whole is that the god Horus delivers six thousand Northern prisoners into the hands of the king. Two naked figures, running at their utmost speed, represent the rest of the defeated tribes and their flight. On the other tablets episodes of war and of the chase are represented, lists of towns taken by sap, troops of domestic animals, oxen, asses, sheep, goats, birds, advancing in superposed rows towards a wood (Fig. 40). Though there are differences in these works due to the individuals who executed them, they are all marked by a real sense of composition and design, and by thorough familiarity with the tool used, but also by a stiffness and awkwardness of which there is no trace in the stele of King Serpent; they belong rather to industrial art than to Art pure and simple. Yet they are interesting, for in them we may discern the chief characteristics of the great sculpture of later ages, the systematic deformation of the human figure, the bust and eyes confronting the spectator while the head and legs are in profile, the dry and angular rendering of the shoulder and the arm, the stiff, almost benumbed bearing of many of the persons, and at the same time, their gravity and their purity of line, the truth and spirit of some of their movements, the firmness of the modelling and its learned

FIG. 38.—TABLET OF NETER-BAIU (OBVERSE).
(Museum, Cairo.) *(Phot. E. Brugsch.)*

simplicity, the systematic practice of keeping the relief low, and of indicating the planes by light touches. All this is purely Egyptian, without any foreign admixture.

It would seem then that the art of Egypt, having arisen and developed in the centuries which preceded Menes, reached its consummation under his descendants; when the Memphite dynasties arose, it was already in full possession of its ruling ideas, its conventions, its formulæ, its technique, all the features which give it originality and character. Perhaps the progress of discovery will encourage us some day to enquire under what influences it flourished, and what were the vicissitudes of its childhood and youth; the scarcity of examples forbids any such enquiry at present. The study of later periods, however, justifies the belief

ART IN EGYPT

that from the first, there was no absolute uniformity throughout the land; each of the sovereign cities had its schools, where architecture, sculpture, and painting developed with a vigour proportioned to the intensity of its political or religious life, and the characteristics of its art, once determined, persisted with no serious modifications, to the last years of Egyptian civilisation. The history of these schools has been barely indicated, and their number is uncertain; but their existence has been notified at Memphis, Abydos, Thebes, Hermopolis, Tanis, Saïs, several minor towns of the Saïd or the Delta, in Nubia and in Ethiopia, and it is probable that future excavations will reveal others. The supremacy which their rank as capitals finally secured for Memphis and Thebes, gave their schools a prestige and importance to which the others never attained; their works account for over three-quarters of what has been saved of the artistic patrimony of Egypt, and at present, the history of Egyptian art is mainly the history of their art.

FIG. 30.—TABLET OF NETER-BAIU
(REVERSE).
(Museum, Cairo.) *(Phot. E. Brugsch.)*

THINITE ART

BIBLIOGRAPHY TO CHAPTER I — PART I

Prehistoric ages and archaic period in Egypt: All that is necessary to be known of these will be found in J. Capart, *Les débuts de l'Art en Égypte*, 8vo. Brussels 1904, 316 p.
Thinite Age. — The existence of a Thinite art was first clearly demonstrated by G. Steindorff, *Eine neue Art Ägyptischer Kunst* in *Aegyptiaca, Festschrift für Georg Ebers*, 8vo. Leipzig 1897, p. 123-146. But the monuments of this art only began to be well known after the excavations of Amélineau, Morgan, Flinders Petrie and Quibell: Amélineau, *Les Nouvelles Fouilles d'Abydos*, 8vo. Paris 1896, 47 p., 1897, 47 p. 1898, 65 p., and 4to I 1899, XXXII-307 p. and XLIII pl., II 1902, XI-326 p. and XXIV pl., II 1904, 742 p. and LII pl., and IV 1905, to be read in conjunction with *Le Tombeau d'Osiris*, 4to. Paris 1899, 155 p. and 6 pl. — J. de Morgan, *Recherches sur les origines de l'Égypte*, II. *Ethnographie préhistorique et tombeau royal de Négadah*, 8vo. Paris 1897, IX-396 p. — Flinders Petrie, *The Royal Tombs of the first Dynasty* (Egypt Exploration Fund, vol. XVIII), 4to. London 1900, 51 p. and LXVII pl.; *The Royal Tombs of the earliest Dynasties* (Egypt Exploration Fund, vol. XX), 4to. London 1901, VIII, 60 p. and LXIII pl.; *Abydos* (Egypt Exploration Fund, vol. XXII-XXIV), 4to. London, I 1902, 60 p. and XXX pl., II 1903, 66 p. and LXVI pl., III 1904, 60 p. and LX pl. — J. E. Quibell, *Hierakonpolis* (Egyptian Research Account, vol. IV-V), 4to. London, I 1900, 12 p. and 43 pl., II 1902, 55 p. and LXXIX pl. For military, religious and funerary architecture, see in addition to the works already quoted: J. Garstang, *Mahasna and Bêt Khallaf* (Egyptian Research Account, vol. VII), 4to. London 1902, 42 p. and XLIIL pl.; *Tombs of the Third Egyptian Dynasty*, 4to. London 1904, 70 p. and XXXIII pl. — G. A. Reisner and Mace, *The Early dynastic Cemeteries of Naga-ed-Deir*, 4to. Leipzig, I 1908, 160 p. and 75 pl., II 1910, 88 p. and 60 pl. — Flinders Petrie, *The Development of the Tomb in Egypt*, in the *Journal of the Royal Institute* of Great Britain 1898, session of June 3, and on the form of the temples, A. Jéquier, *Les Temples primitifs et la persistance des types archaïques dans l'architecture religieuse*, in the *Bulletin de l'Institut français d Archéologie orientale*, 1908, vol. VI, p. 25-45. For stelæ and palettes, see the articles of J. E. Quibell, *Slate Palette from Hierakonpolis*, in the *Zeitschrift für Ägyptische Sprache* 1898, vol. XXXVI, p. 81-84. — G. Bénédite, *La Stèle dite du Roi Serpent*, in the *Mémoires de la Fondation Piot*, 1906, vol. XII, p. 1-15, and *Une nouvelle Palette en schiste*, in the same *Mémoires* 1904, vol. X, p. 105-122. Very good résumés of what we know of the art of this period in general are to be found in W. Spiegelberg, *Geschichte der Ägyptischen Kunst*, p. 7-11, and in R. Weill, *Les Origines de l'Égypte pharaonique*, 8vo. Paris 1908, p. 443-500.

FIG. 40.—THINITE TABLET.
(The Louvre, Paris.) *(Phot. E. Brugsch.)*

FIG. 41.—FIELD OF THE PYRAMIDS OF GIZEH.

CHAPTER II

MEMPHITE ART

It reaches its apogee under the Fourth, Fifth and Sixth Dynasties — Architecture: Houses, Palaces, Mastabas and Pyramids, funerary Chapels and Temples — Painting and Sculpture: the decoration of Tombs and Temples considered as a whole. Bas-reliefs and Statues — The minor Arts.

TOWARDS the beginning of the Third Dynasty there were, in the district where the Pyramids afterwards rose, craftsmen capable of executing tombs like those of Nakâdah, or carving a seated or a standing figure of a man more or less passably, but nothing that has survived of their works indicates that their school would ever have risen above mediocrity, if the revolution which brought about the transfer of the royal residence had not suddenly brought it into contact with experienced masters. The architects, masons, painters and sculptors who had worked for the Thinite Court accompanied it in its migration towards the North; Memphite art developed from their teaching or examples as a natural prolongation of Thinite art. The first buildings we owe to it are grouped, some in the mining region of Sinaï, but the greater part in the neighbourhood of Mêdum, Dahshur, and Zawyét-el-Aryân, round the tombs which the last king of the Third Dynasty, Neferka-Ra-Huni, and the first king of the Fourth, Seneferu, had erected for themselves. At this period of history they were few and far between, but the number increased from the time of Cheops onwards; towards the close of the Memphite age, under the Sixth Dynasty, they not only covered all Egypt, but were to be met with beyond the cata-

MEMPHITE ART

racts of Assuân, in the northern districts of Nubia over which the Pharaohs had established their domination. Rude and clumsy at first, they gradually improved under the Third Dynasty, and reached their highest perfection under the Fourth; they became more and more refined, but lost something of their characteristic simplicity and grandeur under the Fifth Dynasty. Under the Sixth Dynasty, the decadence had begun; the little that has come down to us from the following dynasties betrays the hand of the unskilful and unintelligent artisan.

FIG. 42.—SARCOPHAGUS OF KHUFU-ENEKH. (Museum, Cairo.) *(Phot. E. Brugsch.)*

The architecture is known to us mainly by the tombs. The private houses, built of dried bricks, and perpetually modified or replaced for the convenience of their inhabitants, survive only in shapeless pieces of wall in the deeper strata of the existing towns. The palaces, also of brick, though they had certain stone elements in their doorways and internal colonnades, have proved hardly more durable. To judge by the external arrangement of the sarcophagi of Khufu-cnckh (Fig. 42) and Mycerinus (Fig. 43), they were rectangular masses with vertical walls sometimes encircled by a beaded torus, and crowned by a deep cavetto. The fronts were divided into grooved panels like those of the fortresses, and of the tomb of Nakâdah (cf. Fig. 6), but more elaborate in profile, and they were decorated towards the top by an ornament of two lotus-leaves with crossed stems; doors were pierced

FIG. 43.—SARCOPHAGUS OF MYCERINUS. (After Chipiez, Hist. de l'Art. vol. i. fig. 289.)

ART IN EGYPT

FIG. 44.—FAÇADE AND DOOR OF A MEMPHITE HOUSE, FROM THE STELE OF SETI. (Museum, Cairo.) *(Phot. E. Brugsch.)*

between the panels, and above them openwork bays, or rows of little slits through which the light and air entered (Fig. 44). The whole was whitewashed, and the architectural details were enlivened with crude colours: sphinxes with lions' bodies and human heads often watched on either side of the door, or obelisks, stones rising from a square base into a pyramidal point, took their place, proclaiming the names and titles of the master. The façades of private houses were probably similar, or at least those which belonged to persons of distinction, and had any pretensions to elegance. The appearance of the streets in certain African towns (Fig. 45), where the decoration is in mud or clay like the houses, may give an idea of the rich quarters of Memphis at the time of the Pyramids. As to the temples of the city, which were enlarged or remodelled from reign to reign, then pulled down because of their age, and set up again on new plans, all that is left of them consists of fragments, carved or inscribed, which have been utilised in buildings of recent date. We should still be ignorant of their origin, had it not been for the fortunate discovery of certain funerary temples which were attached to the royal pyramids of the Fifth Dynasty; once again the fictitious life beyond the tomb has provided the document necessary for the reconstitution of real life.

FIG. 45.—AFRICAN MUD ARCHITECTURE. A Street in Dienné.

The burial grounds of the Memphite mountains contain

MEMPHITE ART

several hypogea, both vaults and chapels, which are entirely hollowed out in the rock; other sepulchres approximate to the Thinite type, but the proportion between the elements demanded by the earlier conception was no longer observed, and the internal arrangements were accordingly modified. Indeed, as the doctrine gained ground, according to which the images traced upon the wall were of equal, or even of greater importance to the dead than real objects, the tomb-chamber was circumscribed, and the rooms composing the accessible chapel were increased. At Memphis accordingly the tomb-

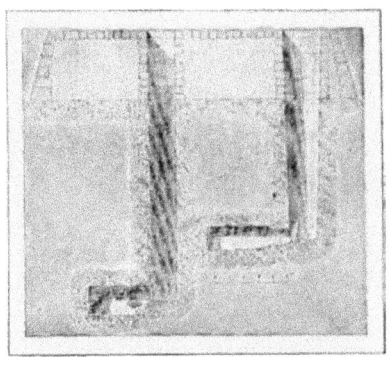

FIG. 46.—VERTICAL SHAFT IN THE MASTABAS OF GIZEH (AFTER LEPSIUS).

chamber is merely a narrow cell, more or less deep beneath the ground, accessible until the day of interment by means of a vertical well (Fig. 46), or an oblique passage (Fig. 47), without any decoration in the way of figures or inscriptions save such as were bestowed on the sarcophagus. On the other hand, the chapel, which had become both a reception-room and a storehouse, forms a building of some importance, a *mastaba*, the visible bulk of which was in direct ratio to the means possessed by the master for ensuring a happy after-life to his *double*. Thus it was not open to everyone to rest under a mastaba. It was a privilege reserved for those whom birth, talents, services rendered to the state, or even some momentary caprice had raised to the summit of the hierarchy. As they had been permitted to approach the master here below, they desired not to be separated from him in the other

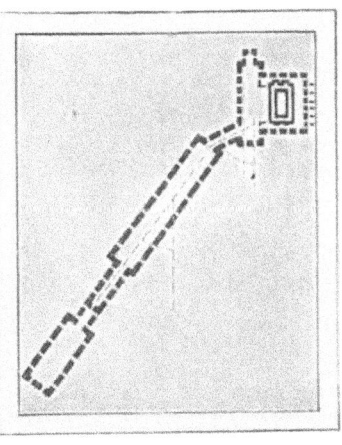

FIG. 47.—THE SLOPING PASSAGE IN THE TOMB OF TI, DRAWN BY A. BAUDRY.

world, that so they might continue to enjoy his favour. However, as they were numerous, and space was limited, Pharaoh was

ART IN EGYPT

obliged to allot it with discretion, if he wished to satisfy his courtiers. Concessions of ground were made methodically, on a predetermined plan, and the mastabas were ranged in regular lines (Fig. 48), the larger ones divided one from another by lanes, the smaller combined into islets of two, three, or more; when his hour had come, Pharaoh had distributed several hundreds of these, which formed a city of the dead around him. Its appearance was monotonous. These houses, or, if we prefer to call them so, these palaces of the necropolis would have been much like those of living cities, if their façades, instead of being straight, had not inclined symmetrically backwards, which gave them a certain vague likeness to an unfinished pyramid (Fig. 49). Some few of these were of sun-dried brick; the majority were of freestone, or small dressed stones, with bare plain facings, the door on the east or the north, and in some cases, a row of apertures just below the line of the summit. Some were from thirty to forty feet high, one hundred and fifty feet in width, and about seventy-five in depth; but this was not usual, and examples occur no more than about nine feet high by fifteen wide. Some are crowned by a cavetto and an entablature; but the majority terminate, without any transition in the last course, in an earthen platform, the soil mixed with fragments of limestone, and dotted with terracotta jars, buried up to the neck. To tell the truth, I see in them the regularisation and consolidation of those heaps of sand and pebbles which the primitive Egyptians piled over their graves; the architect had little to do with their actual form;

FIG. 48.—A CORNER OF THE NECROPOLIS AT GIZEH, RESTORED BY CHIPIEZ.
(Hist. de l'Art, vol. i. fig. 108.)

FIG. 49.—A MASTABA AT GIZEH (After Lepsius).

MEMPHITE ART

tradition had imposed it upon him, and he was obliged to repeat it servilely on the outside.

But there was compensation in the amount of liberty permitted him in the interior. In the beginning, the Memphite mastaba had been solid like the tumulus, whether it was built up over the vault, or constructed beforehand, and pierced with a tunnel which was filled up on the evening or the morrow of interment; in either case the architect was careful to indicate on the eastern front, by means of a panel simulating a door, the place where the *double* was supposed to go out and return (Fig. 50). This feigned entrance was often of natural size, and it would have resembled a practicable door in every way, but for the fact that the back was always closed. It was sometimes doubled, at first only for the king, but later, when private persons ventured to imitate the king, for those noble or wealthy individuals who were concerned that their souls should not lose any of the offering; one of the two was dedicated to the north and its tribute, the other to the south, and its productions.

FIG. 50.—STELE IN THE FORM OF A FALSE DOOR. (Museum, Cairo.) *(Phot. E. Brugsch.)*

The decoration was sober at first: the name of the master on the tympanum over the opening, his titles and image on the jambs sufficed as long as clients were content with a plain door. But very soon, pursuing the imitation of what had at first been the privilege of the sovereign, they required that the slab should represent not merely the door of a dwelling, but the entire building, and the model

ART IN EGYPT

adopted was what is known as the royal banner, in other words, the rectangular structure in which the Pharaohs enclosed their name, Horus. It consisted of two parts; in the lower of these was the façade of a house with a closed door, in the upper one an empty space, a chamber in which the signs which constituted the name were written (Fig. 51). In imitation of this, the slab was divided into two registers, one above the other, enclosed in a flat band which formed a frame common to both (Fig. 52). The lower compartment answered to the false door of the earlier period, often so modified as to be almost unrecognisable. The panels of the rebates were brought forward, the jambs were flattened, and the reliefs as a whole were only a few millimetres above the surface. In the upper compartment, which corresponds to the tomb-chamber, the dead man was seated at a round table, laden with the foods and ornaments he might require in the other world. These were conveyed to him invisibly by means of a special apparatus, a stone table originally fixed between the uprights of the door, and afterwards placed on the ground, against the stele. The celebrant heaped on this all the objects of offering, and the *doubles* of these, detached by virtue of his prayers, were projected upon the round table destined to receive them. This ritual of the dead was carried out in the open air (Fig. 53), in the sight of all, and though in theory this unrestricted publicity did not affect its efficacy, in practice the result was, that when the congregation had dispersed, the offerings were at the mercy of marauders, human and animal; the person for whom they were intended ran the risk of losing the best part of them before he had secured his ration. Two devices were accordingly adopted for their protection: an enclosure of bricks was built, projecting from the east wall, square in the mastaba of Kaâpiru (Fig. 54), irregular in that of Neferhetep (Fig. 55), at Sakkarah; but the more important measure was the imbedding of the false door in the masonry in such a manner as to bring it to the back, sometimes of a niche, sometimes of an actual room. This was very often unique, and so small that it looks to us drowned in the general mass. It is a minute cell, the longer axis of which is parallel to the façade; if the false door

FIG. 51.
THE NAME HORUS
OF CHEPHREN.

MEMPHITE ART

be placed at one of the extremities, the ground-plan forms a figure like a double-headed hammer (Fig. 56); if it be hollowed out opposite the entrance, it suggests a cross the head of which is cut out more or less. Such simple arrangements are found principally in the more archaic quarters, such as Dahshur, Mêdûm, Gizeh and Sakkarah, side by side with more complex types. In the latter, the single chapel was first enlarged, then doubled, and redoubled (Fig. 57), until the mastaba became a series or a labyrinth of rooms large and small: that of Mereruka, under the Sixth Dynasty, contained over thirty compartments (Fig. 58); some of these were passages concealed in the thickness of the structure, sometimes blind, sometimes communicating with the world by conduits so narrow that it is difficult to thrust the hand into them; these were the *serdabs*, in which the statues of the deceased and of his servants were imprisoned, to preserve them from possible destruction. Several were used as warehouses or store-rooms, and for ceremonies, there were rooms upheld by square piers, or by columns with lotus-bud capitals; the entrance is sometimes preceded by a portico (Fig. 59). In the course of time, the false door lost its original character; its hollows were attenuated, its projections flattened, and it was finally resolved into an upright slab, on which the design of a door was indicated on the surface by almost impalpable reliefs; in a word, it

FIG. 52.—STELE-DOOR OF USIRU. (Museum, Cairo.)
(Phot. E. Brugsch.)

became a stele, towards which all the several parts of the tomb converged, just as if it had remained the actual door which had formerly led to the vault. Occasionally, however, its ancient character was revived, at least in appearance. Thus in the tomb of Mereruka (Fig. 60), the life-size statue of the master was introduced into the bay, a flight of three steps was at his feet, by which he was supposed to come down into the chamber, to take the offerings left by the celebrants. In the mastaba of

Atôti (Fig. 61), the statue is set against the stone which fills up the doorway, rather than enframed in the bay. In that of Neferseshemptah (Fig. 62), the conception is more complex; the bust of the dead man rises above the closed door and its lintel, to see what is happening in the chamber, while right and left two statues of him stand erect against the façade, as if keeping guard over him. Later again, the head alone appears over the panel (Fig. 63). The stele thus loses its independent character to become a mere element of the decoration (Fig. 64). The table of offering rests on the ground before it, and sometimes, as among the living, it was flanked by two miniature obelisks, on which the name and titles of the master were proclaimed in large letters (Fig. 65).

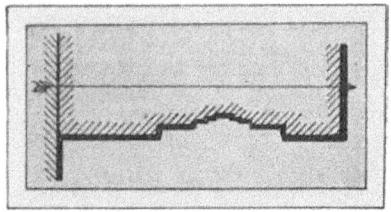

FIG. 53.—FAÇADE OF THE MASTABA OF MENEFER. (After Mariette.)

There is no evidence that this evolution was based on a preconceived idea, nor that it culminated in the creation of a typical mastaba, all the internal parts of which were deduced one from another in logical order. In the mastaba of Ti, at Sakkarah (Fig. 66) there is, indeed, a veritable progression in the successive apartments, from the entrance portico to the point where the stele rises towards the south-western angle: first there is a hall with pillars, where the passage leading up from the vault reached the level, then a corridor divided by a door into two unequal lengths, a little room on the right for the dead man's wife, at the end the chapel with its two stelæ, and, parallel with its south wall, a *serdab* in which the statues were concealed. But this was an exception. In nearly every other instance, the architect did not trouble to arrange the rooms methodically, provided he placed his chapel as far west as possible; he was only concerned to increase their number, and consequently,

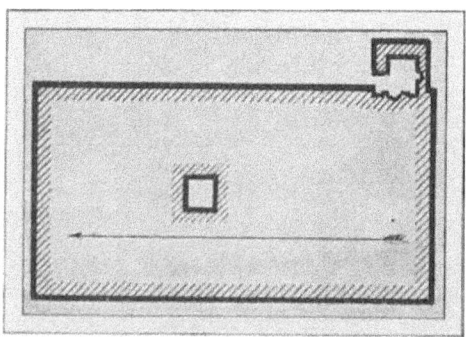

FIG. 54.—CELL AND FORE-COURT OF THE MASTABA OF KAAPIRU (After Mariette.)

MEMPHITE ART

to develope to the utmost surfaces capable of receiving decoration. In this he was influenced by those utilitarian principles which had regulated the arrangement of the tomb from the first; for as the decorator was thus free to repeat the principal scenes in several rooms, if one was defaced, and lost its efficacy, the replica took its place and continued to supply the deceased with his revenues. Towards the end of the Memphite age, he further realised that the tomb-chamber, buried beneath the mastaba and separated from it by a conglomerate cement, offered a greater chance of inviolability

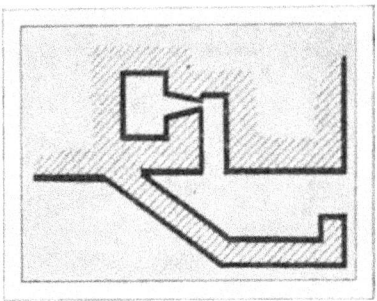

FIG. 55.—FORE-COURT OF THE MASTABA OF NEFER-HETEP. (After Mariette.)

than the super-structure, and he conceived the idea of laying up a reserve of pictures here, in case those above should fail. He accordingly devised a new model (Fig. 67), good examples of which are to be found among the brick tombs discovered from 1881 onwards about the Pyramid of Pepi II. Built of dried bricks, upon the sand itself, this mastaba, like those of the earliest period, at first presents to the spectator either a stele on the west face, or a niche in front of which the family assembled to offer sacrifice. In the interior, the well was replaced by a sort of court, in the western part of which a place was reserved for the tomb-chamber. This consisted of a long, low cell, formed of five limestone slabs; a brick vault, with a radius of from 20

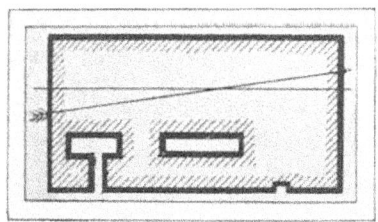

FIG. 56.—THE MASTABA OF ZAZAMENEKH.
(After Mariette.)

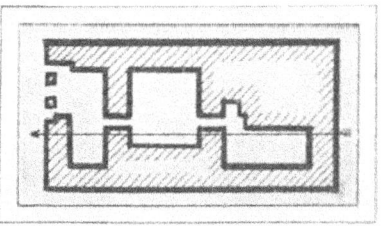

FIG. 57.—THE MASTABA
OF KHABEUPTAH. (After Mariette.)

to 24 inches, relieved the upper slab of the weight of the successive strata rising above it to the level of the terminal platform. The lateral walls, carved and painted, were receptacles for articles of food and clothing; the coffin was pushed along between them, then the opening in front was walled up, and the little court was filled in. When the dead man had a stone sarcophagus, instead of a wooden coffin, the whole building was placed upon this, as offering a more solid foundation; the lid formed the floor of the chamber above, and on this statues and offerings were heaped pell-mell before the mummy was consigned to his eternal rest.

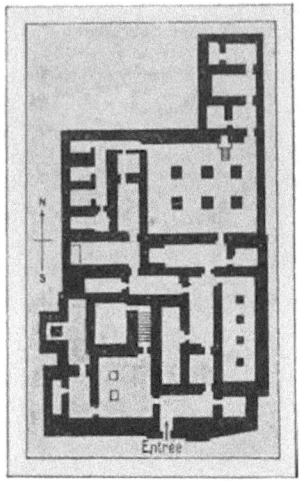

FIG. 58.—THE MASTABA OF MERERUKA. (After Morgan.)

We find then that the Memphite mastaba, in its final development, allowed of two decorated elements, the chapel and the vault, which were connected by a well, or an unornamented passage. It was almost universally adopted among the wealthier classes, from the Fayûm to the centre of the Delta, but it never became general in districts where the court did not habitually reside. The prevalent form in Upper Egypt, in the places where vast sandy spaces at the foot of the mountain-boundaries invited the great nobles to construct mastabas, was derived both from the Thinite and Memphite type, but was more akin to the first than to the second. It is partly buried in the ground, as at El-Kab or Denderah (Fig. 68), and access to it is obtained by an inclined plane, or by a staircase; the corpse is buried not very deep below the soil in a cavity more like a pit than a chamber. Preference was given to the hypogeum hewn in the mountain side, in a vein of lime or sand stone, solid and fine, running horizontally at a good height above the plain. When such a spot had been selected, the members of a family and their servants were laid

FIG. 59.—PORTICO OF THE MASTABA OF TI.

MEMPHITE ART

there from generation to generation, the mighty side by side in a row on the same level, the plebeians haphazard on the slope, in front of, and so to speak, below them, as if to maintain the hierarchical distance even in death. The plan necessitated the three divisions of the mastaba, the vault, the well or sloping passage, and the chapel; but the material in which the architect had to cut them obliged him to modify the detail, at least as far as the chapel was concerned. As the expense would have been very great if he had carried one of those series of chambers such as we find in the mastaba of Mereruka at Memphis right through the living rock, he was nearly always content with a single room for receptions and worship; when more were demanded, they were rarely more than two or three in number. In the mastaba of Zauti, at Kasr-es-sayâd, we find surbased vaults; elsewhere, and indeed generally, the ceiling was flat, like that of the stone mastabas. Where the orientation allowed it, the stele was placed opposite the entrance, in a niche cut towards the centre of the back wall; if this was impracticable it was carved on the west wall, or set against it, and the niche served as *serdab* for the statues of the *double*, these being either separate, or cut in the mass of the rock. The hypogeum thus carried out became a systematised fragment of a quarry, as at Kom-el-Ahmar, Koseir-el-Amarna, Meir, near Akhmim, Dêr-el-Melak, and at Kasr-es-sayâd. Sometimes, however, an artistic intention is revealed. That of Afai, at Kau-el-Kebir, has ceilings the reliefs of which imitate the palm-trunks

FIG. 60.—FALSE DOOR OF MERERUKA. *(Phot. E. Brugsch.)*

FIG. 61.—FALSE DOOR OF ATÔTI. (Museum Cairo). *(Phot. E. Brugsch.)*

which supported the roofs of houses. The chapels of the princes of Elephantine are veritable temple halls; that of Mekhu (Fig. 69), with its triple row of six columns, its niche, and its stele to which a little staircase gives access, its stone three-legged table of offerings, standing between two of the columns of the central aisle; that of Sabni with its fourteen square pillars in two rows, and its narrow door, interrupted at about one third of its height by a triangular lintel which crowns a smaller orifice in the monumental door. All this is rude, ill-proportioned and barbarous compared with what we see at Memphis; but the excellence of the site shows in those who selected it a delicate feeling for nature, and makes amends to some extent for their artistic shortcomings. From the terrace which runs along the storey reserved for the patricians, the eye travels freely to the horizon; the *double*, escaping from the darkness of the vault, was able to take in at a glance the whole expanse of the domain he had ruled, the great river with its hurrying waters, its changing islands, the open country invaded by the sands of the desert, the villages among the palm-trees, and in the distance, the mountains to which he had so often been lured by the pleasures of the chase.

FIG. 62.—FALSE DOOR OF NEFERSESHEM-PTAH.
(Phot. Abbé Thédenat.)

The tombs of the Memphite Pharaohs were also so placed as to command the valley from afar. They stretch out in a line on the edge of the Libyan desert, and succeeding one another from Abu-Roash to Gizeh, from Gizeh to Sakkarah, from Sakkara to Dahshur and thence to Mêdûm, they pursue the traveller who is going up the Nile for days together. Zoser of the Third Dynasty, in his character of King of Upper Egypt, possessed a huge brick *mastaba* of the Thinite type at Bêt-Khallaf (cf. Fig. 12); as King of northern Egypt, he built himself a second tomb of a novel type, at least to us (Fig. 70). The apartments of the *double* are here cut in the rock on a system similar to those of Bêt-Khallaf, but much more com-

MEMPHITE ART

plicated (Fig. 71); it is entered by no less than four doors, the principal one being on the north. After traversing a labyrinth of passages, low chambers, and hypostyle galleries, we find ourselves on the brink of a central well, at the bottom of which is a pit, sealed with a kind of stone stopper; this was doubtless the receptacle for the funerary treasure. The superstructures are not of brick, but of the coarse lime-stone of the surrounding mountains, and it was perhaps this fact which gave rise to the legend that Zoser was the first Egyptian who built with stone. The base on which these upper buildings rest is a parallelogram of about 390 by 350 feet, and their appearance would lead us to suppose that they were composed of five blocks of masonry with sloping surfaces, each receding some 6½ feet from the lower stage, and so diminishing gradually as they rise to terminate in a platform about 190 feet above the level of the ground. But this appearance is deceptive. They are not *mastabas* of decreasing dimensions piled one

FIG. 63.—STELE-DOOR OF NIBERA
(Museum, Cairo.) (Phot. E. Brugsch.)

above the other; the core was raised uninterruptedly, and then dressed on its four sides with parallel courses of masonry, which, ceasing four times at different levels, formed the four successive storeys. The monument is known at present as the *Step Pyramid*, but it is not a true Pyramid. When he ordered his architects to undertake it, Zoser wanted a tomb superior to those of his predecessors, and even to the one he was preparing at Bêt-Khallaf, on the ancient plan. Now the slopes of the *mastaba* approached too closely to the perpendicular to allow of bringing them up to the required height without risking the downfall of the whole, when the small blocks of dressed stone which were in general use at this period were used. It was to obviate this danger that they were compressed between the four graduated facings; these, buttressing them and each other, ensured the stability of the whole. This elevated and reinforced variant of the *mastaba* continued in favour for several generations. Nearly a century and a half after Zoser, Seneferu, the first sovereign of the Fourth Dynasty, still retained it. The false Pyramid at Mêdûm (Fig. 72), where he had taken up his residence as King of Upper Egypt, is, in fact, composed like the so-called Step Pyramid, of vast cubes of masonry with sloping faces, each slightly smaller than the one below; they are, however, square instead of rectangular, and are only four in number. Their progressive diminution is a pure caprice of the architect's, no longer justified by a technical necessity. The core of the fabric is not artificially built up; it is a natural hill, the solidity of which was beyond question, and the masonry which masks it consists of magnificent limestone. The four diminishing cubes are independent one of the other, and it is probable that the last was never finished. .

FIG. 64.—STELE OF NIKHAFITKA.
(Museum, Cairo.) *(Phot. E. Brugsch.)*

After Mêdûm, the Pharaohs built nothing but Pyramids throughout the Memphite age. In my opinion, the pyramid was not derived from the oblong mound with an almost perpendicular incline and a flat top which was the origin of the mastaba, but from a stone tumulus, pointed at the top and sloping gently upwards, which was peculiar to the northern districts. There was a tradition that the fourth king of the First Dynasty, Uennephes, was the author of the one which existed at Kôkômé in

MEMPHITE ART

the Greek period, and this is possible; but the earliest known to us is at Dahshur, where Seneferu built it for himself as king of Lower Egypt. Even then, it did not constitute the entire sepulchre; it was accompanied by a chapel with subterranean store-houses, and a paved *temenos* surrounded it, protected by a square or rectangular enclosure (Fig. 73). A causeway connected the whole with a temple situated in the royal town, towards the fringe of cultivated land. The apartments of the *double* were concealed in or under the pyramid; Seneferu received his revenues in the adjoining chapel, and, as a living god, he was associated with the

FIG. 65.—OBELISKS OF PTAH-HETEP AND ḎAITI.
(Museum, Cairo.) *(Phot. E. Brugsch.)*

other gods in the temple of the city (cf. Fig. 41). We know what the Pyramids are. The heap of stones composing them rests on a square base; the faces confront the four cardinal points as in the *mastabaṣ*, but no more precisely than in the majority of these. Their height varies from 482 feet, as in that of Cheops (Fig. 74) to 62 feet in that of Unas; but whatever the individual dimensions, the general plan was marked out once for all before the work was begun, and the architect proposed to carry it cn without modification to the end. It did sometimes happen, however, that it was altered in the course of building, and that the proportions of the whole were increased, which neccessitated changes in the arrangement of the interior; this was probably the case with the Pyramids of Chephren and Mycerinus, whereas that of

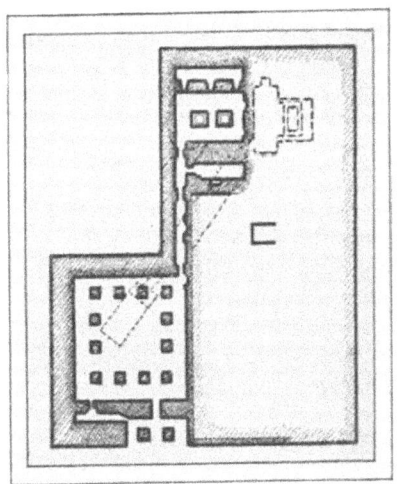

FIG. 66.—PLAN OF THE TOMB OF TI.
(After Mariette.)

ART IN EGYPT

Cheops seems to have been built uninterruptedly on the site of an earlier tomb, the materials of which it absorbed in its rough masonry. This was afterwards covered with a facing of massive blocks (Fig. 75). These modifications in the course of execution were most frequent under the Fourth Dynasty, when the constructive formula had not yet been fixed by prolonged experience, and when architects perhaps allowed themselves to be carried away by daring experiments which imperilled the solidity of their work. Those of Cheops, fearing that, the tomb-chamber might succumb under the weight of over 300 feet of stone, built five chambers, superposed along the central axis, to relieve it; this device, which carried the greater part of the central pressure out to the lateral surfaces, did, in fact, save the building; but it was not repeated. From the middle of the Fifth Dynasty onward, the majority of the Pyramids are almost identical in their plan, in which, though the dimensions were reduced, the inviolability of the mummy was none the less assured (Fig. 76). A sloping passage, rising to the level of the soil under the centre of the north side, just at the height of the first course, led to a low anteroom; this gave access to a horizontal passage, barred almost in the centre by granite portcullises, and a vestibule (Fig. 77), communicating on the right with the tomb-chamber, on the left with a *serdab* or a store-room. The vestibule and the tomb-chamber were crowned by a pointed roof, consisting of three courses

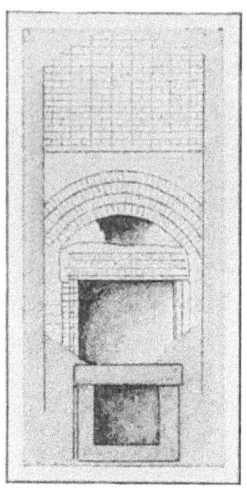

FIG. 67.— MASTABA WITH HOLLOW CHAMBER AND DISCHARGING ARCH.
(Drawing by Bourgoin, communicated by Messis. A. Picard.)

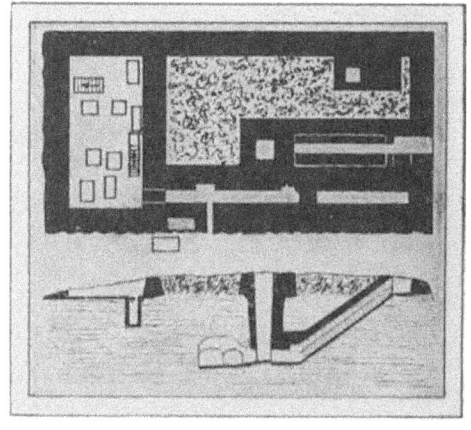

FIG. 68.—TOMB OF ADU, AT DENDERAH.
(After Petrie.)

MEMPHITE ART

of limestone beams, leaning one against the other at the top. Sometimes the superstructures were composed entirely of large blocks of fine limestone, as in the Pyramid of Unas; but more commonly they have a core of coarse limestone from the neighbouring mountains, with a facing of fine limestone.

Little as geometrical figures are calculated, in general, to evoke a sentiment or give artistic enjoyment, the pyramid as realised by the Egyptians on their native soil never fails to move those who see it for the first time profoundly. And when, instead of the finished work, we have as it were the sketch only before our eyes, we are hardly less deeply impressed. The Pharaoh Nefer-ka-Ra, of the Third Dynasty, has left such a sketch at Zawyet-el-Aryân, in the trenches destined for the super-structures of his tomb, and the inclined plane with its slides over which the blocks passed while awaiting the construction of the passage leading to the mortuary chambers (Fig. 78). The works ceased at the moment when the lower courses of granite had been set, and there is nothing above the surface of the ground but an admirable oval basin destined for libations (Fig. 79). The whole is merely a T-shaped ditch, some 100 feet deep; and yet the impression it makes when one goes down into it is unforgettable. The richness and the cutting of the materials, the perfection of the joints and sections, the incomparable finish of the basin, the boldness of the lines and the height of the walls all combine to make up a unique creation. The chapels of the completed pyramids are not marked by this almost brutal strength. They were buildings of medium height, which, projecting from the eastern façade, extended to

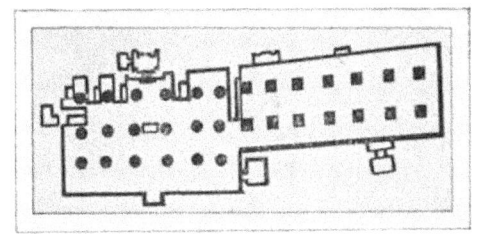

FIG. 69.—TOMB OF MEKHU AND SAHNI AT ASSUÂN. (After Morgan.)

FIG. 70.—THE STEP PYRAMID *(Phot Dumichen.)*

ART IN EGYPT

the enclosing wall. The only one which has come down to us complete, that of Seneferu, consists of two dark little rooms, without ornaments or inscriptions, a courtyard behind them, and in the courtyard, two bare stelæ rising boldly against the pyramid. Only the pavement of the chapel of Cheops remains, and the chapel of Chephren is in ruins (Fig. 80); but recently, several of those which belonged to the sovereigns of the Sixth Dynasty have been excavated, notably those of

FIG. 71.—SECTION OF THE STEP-PYRAMID.
(After Howard-Vyse.)

Sahu-Rā and Rā-en-user. They were approached by propylæa built at the foot of the plateau (Fig. 81), beyond which a long incline rose to the body of the building, the arrangements of which varied. In the chapel of Sahu-Rā (Fig. 82), for instance, there was a dark passage, then a colonnaded court, then a complicated series of cells and storehouses, and in the obscurity of the background, the stele, in the form of a closed door, where the office of the dead king was celebrated. It was a temple, lacking the Holy of Holies, or rather the tomb-chamber was to it what the Holy of Holies was to the real temple, the dwelling where the master of the house was lodged, safe from attacks from without; the stele represented the mysterious door which could no longer be opened, but on the threshold of which offerings were heaped.

Among the inscriptions of Sakkarah, the student occasionally comes upon a certain curious hieroglyph, a truncated pyramid surmounted by an obelisk, and accompanied by a solar disc, which seems sometimes to be poised upon the point of the obelisk. It indicated a temple which Pharaoh had dedicated to Ra, the Sun of Heliopolis, in his royal city, near his tomb; but it seemed uncertain whether it was an exact figure of this, or only a graphic combination of

FIG. 72.—THE FALSE PYRAMID AT MÉDÛM.

44

MEMPHITE ART

elements really separate. The German excavations near Abusir have brought to light fragments which prove that the obelisk rose upon the pyramid itself, and not beside it. An inclined plane between two parapets led from the palace of Rá-en-user to the temple, which consisted of a rectangular court, about 325 feet long by 280 wide, the main axis of which ran from east to west; it was surrounded by a brick wall, which had a sort of pylon in the middle of the east face.

FIG. 73.—THE PYRAMID OF RA-EN-USER, AS RESTORED BY L. BORCHARDT.

The pyramid covered nearly all the western half of the enclosed area; it was not a classic pyramid like those of Gizeh, but a square *mastaba*, analogous to those of which the monument of Mêdûm is composed (Fig. 83). It measured probably from 60 to 100 feet in height, with a base of about 130 feet, and three of its faces were bare; by a door pierced in a chapel attached to the fourth, that of the south, access was obtained to a staircase which led to the platform. Here the obelisk rose, or rather, the facsimile in brick of an immense stone in the shape of a squat obelisk, the point of which rose to about 120 feet. The platform in front of this strange monument was bordered on the east, the south, and the north by long vaulted corridors; that on the south led to the chapel, where the staircase debouched, that on the north to cells where provisions were stored, and where the officiating priests were lodged, together with the materials for worship. In the court itself, a deeply grooved pavement forms

FIG 74.—THE GREAT PYRAMID AND THE SPHINX. *(Phot. Beato.)*

a parallelogram upon the ground, terminating on the east with a row of nine alabaster basins, while on the west, almost at

ART IN EGYPT

the foot of the pyramid, an immense table for offerings, also of alabaster, stood in a little court surrounded by low walls. Many

FIG. 75.—THE FACING SLABS STILL INTACT OF THE GREAT PYRAMID. *(Phot. Covington.)*

details in the arrangement of the various parts are inexplicable or obscure; but one point is now firmly established, namely, that the obelisk stood both for the sanctuary and for the god who was worshipped there. We are so much accustomed to consider the Egyptian divinities as beings of flesh and blood, men or animals, that we are surprised when one of them is revealed as an inanimate object. Here, however, the obelisk was the god himself, and what is more, the Sun-god, and as if to leave no room for doubt on this score, the Egyptians fashioned near the south front a brick model of one of the solar boats, with its special design, and its cargo of sacred insignia (Fig. 84). At the first blush, there seems something paradoxical in the idea of imitating in a heavy substance a thing as light and rapid as a boat, and setting it motionless upon the sand of the desert. And yet this was but the inevitable outcome of that longing for a future life which is

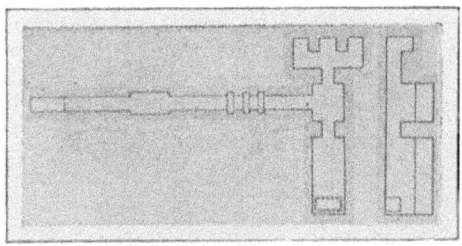

FIG. 76.—PLAN OF THE PYRAMID OF UNAS. (From a drawing by Maspero, communicated by Messrs. A. Picard.)

manifested in all their works. However carefully preserved, the wooden vessel of the god was destined some day to crumble into dust, and perhaps the circumstances of the moment would be such that it would be impossible to make a new one; then the brick vessel would take its place, with more chance of being useful, in that it would be more difficult to damage or destroy; and would continue its function for Rā as long as a fragment of it subsisted.

MEMPHITE ART

The monument of the Sphinx (Fig. 85) was no more a real temple than that of Abusir. It was a kind of waiting hall, built on the edge of the plain in front of the second pyramid, and connected with it by a causeway the line of which is still perceptible; it was the starting-point of the processions which, on fixed days, went to the chapel of Chephren, to perform the worship of the sovereign. The plan is very simple, yet it is not easy to determine the uses of the various parts. The centre is occupied by a hall 79 feet long by 23 wide, with a row of six monolith pillars in the middle. A second hall, 57½ feet by 29, adjoins this, forming a T on plan; it was ornamented with a double row of five pillars, and lighted by oblique vent-holes at the top of the walls. The hall with the six columns is, as it were, the pivot round which the rest of the building was set; it communicates on the east with a gallery, which, running parallel with the façade (Fig. 86), terminates at the two extremities in a rectangular cabinet; at the south-west angle, the hall has a cell containing six niches in superposed pairs, at the north-west angle it communicates with the sloping passage which leads by a gentle incline to the plateau. The core of the masonry is of Turah limestone; the facings, the pillars, the ceilings, the façade (Fig. 87) are of gigantic granite or alabaster blocks, polished and adjusted to perfection, but not decorated. Here, as in the unfin-

FIG. 77.—DOOR BETWEEN ANTE-ROOM AND TOMB-CHAMBER IN THE PYRAMID OF UNAS.

FIG. 78.—INCLINED WAY AT ZAWYET-EL-ARYÂN. (Phot. Oropesa.)

ished tomb of Nefer-ka-Rā, the architecture produces its effect without any adventitious aid, by purity of line and rightness of proportion. The building is almost complete, and it might be supposed that by the help of the data gleaned at Abusir and in the chapels of the Pyramids, we should be able to re- establish the general plan of the ordinary temples from this example; such, however, is not the case, and the problem is still obscured by too many unknown issues to be solved. I think I may venture so far as to say that they lacked certain features proper to those of the later periods, such as pylons, with their high bay flanked by two massive towers. The doors opened directly in the enclosing wall as did later those of Thebes, in the Saïte period. They were accompanied by a portico, and followed by a court, round and in the midst of which the offering-tables and the materials of worship were disposed. The main body of the building rose at the end, but we are unable to say how the different apartments were arranged.

FIG. 79.—FLOOR AND LIBATION-TROUGH OF THE UNFINISHED PYRAMID AT ZAWYET-EL-ARYÂN. (*Phot. Oropesa.*)

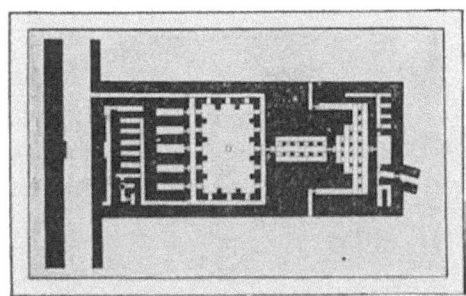

FIG. 80.—PLAN OF THE CHAPEL OF CHEPHREN. (After Steindorff.)

The sanctuary was assuredly quite at the back, but it is a question whether the rooms which flanked it right and left were already assigned to the mother-goddess and the child. The point most clearly established by the ruins is that a good many elements very frequent at a later period were already in use, among them the cornice with its curved gorge, the gargoyles of projecting demi-lions on the stone facings, the images of guardian victims (Fig. 88), the square pillars,

MEMPHITE ART

the palm or lotus column. The former was in favour under the Fifth Dynasty, rather heavy in the temple of Sahu-Rā, light and slender in that of Unas (Fig. 89). Its capital is formed of a bunch of palm-leaves, attached to the shaft by four ribbons, and bending gracefully under the weight of the abacus. The lotus-like columns of Sahu-Rā and Shepsesptah (Fig. 90) are circular, whereas those of Rā-en-user are rectangular at the base, but are gradually rounded as they rise till they become almost circular at the summit (Fig. 91). Save for some slight variations, they consist of four or six lotus-stems in fasces, bulbous at the foot, and adorned with triangular leaves; the buds, bound to the neck of the shaft by four or five bands, are grouped into a bouquet to form the capital, and sometimes young buds, inserted between the half-open ones, fill the spaces above the ligatures. Examination of the ruins leads to the conclusion that Memphite architecture, though it inclined to the gigantic for the tombs of its kings, did not desire it for the temples of the gods; it aimed here at strength and elegance rather than at immensity.

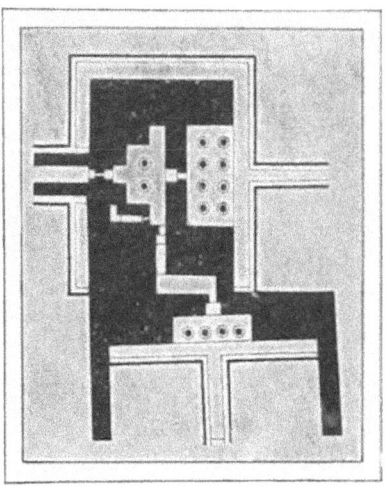

FIG. 81.—PLAN OF THE PROPYLÆA.
(After Borchardt.)

The surfaces it offered nevertheless afforded an almost boundless field for the activity of sculptor and painter. Generally speaking, the Egyptians would not allow even the most beautiful stone to remain bare, while on the other hand, painting alone without sculpture beneath it, did not approve

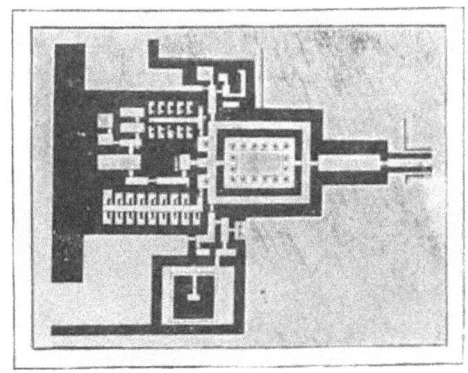

FIG. 82.
SEPULCHRAL CHAPEL OF RĀ-EN-USER.
(After Borchardt.)

ART IN EGYPT

itself to them as possessing the enduring qualities required for the adornment of temples and tombs; with few exceptions, it was tolerated only in houses and palaces. The Pharaohs, indeed, had an instinctive repugnance to taking up their abode in dwellings where others had lived before them; they generally abandoned these to their progeny, and improvised new dwellings for themselves, which always seemed to them good enough if they were of a nature to last as long as themselves. For such ephemeral buildings they were content with a perishable ornamentation of simple painting on the ceilings, pavements, and walls, and the same latitude obtained perforce in hypogea carved in a rock unfit for sculpture, as well as in the chapels of sun-dried bricks which villagers too poor to use stone raised for their gods; everywhere else, colour is only, so to speak, the complement of relief, but a complement so indispensable that it is difficult to imagine a building without it. We understand now why painting in Egypt never acquired the personal development and complexity which characterises it in our own countries. It laid flat tints on the work of the sculptor, and indicated the details of costume and the accessories which he had not noted. The artist's work was therefore rather that of an illuminator than a painter, and the necessity of reliefs to cover was so imperative in his eyes that he did his utmost to suggest them, even

FIG. 83.—SOLAR TEMPLE OF RĀ-EN-USER, AS RESTORED BY BORCHARDT.

FIG. 84.—BRICK BOAT OF RĀ-EN-USER. (After Borchardt.)

MEMPHITE ART

where they did not exist; he surrounded his figures with a red or black outline which defines the contours as sharply as if he had cut them with a style. The deliberate neglect of halftones and of their infinite variety, led him to choose for each object or person a tone which, without deviating too widely from nature sometimes made no attempt to approach it very closely. Thus men are represented with skin of a more or less dark brown, while women are light yellow; a blue, either pure or streaked with black, was reserved for the sea, a bright green for grass and foliage, and a dirty yellow dotted with red stood either for corn piled in heaps or for the sand of the desert.

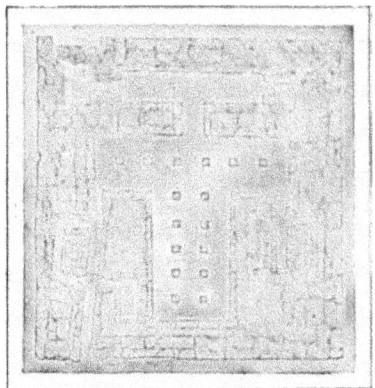

FIG. 85.—TEMPLE OF THE SPHINX. (After Mariette.)

With conventions so harassing, and means so restricted, artists nevertheless man ged to produce works of striking truth and sentiment. Such was the tomb of the time of Seneferu at Mêdûm, where Vassalli saved the famous geese which are now in the Museum of Cairo (Fig. 92). The movement is excellent, and the characteristics which distinguish the male and female in each couple are noted with an accuracy which surprises naturalists; a Chinese or Japanese artist could have done no better. Unfortunately, this is an exceptional example; the painting of the Memphite age rarely rose to the dignity of an autonomous art; it was a servile dependent of sculpture.

FIG. 86.—INTERIOR OF THE TEMPLE OF THE SPHINX (Phot. E. Brugseh).

Such being the case, decoration, whether of tomb or temple, was considered an immense composition, every part of which converged to the same point: in the temple, to the wall at the back of the sanctuary, in the tomb to the stele which had replaced the door of the vault. It is true that every room, and in every room each wall, and on every wall each picture constitutes a whole where the various persons mingle and confront each other in such a manner, that if some are advancing to this *kiblah*[1], others seem either to be going away from it, or at least, not to be making their way towards it; but this contrariety of movement, which might seem to stultify the principle just laid down, is explained when we examine the conditions under which it is produced. In the temple, it is always the god, the supreme deity of the place, and the divinities of his family or of his suite who move in the opposite direction to the rest: the oblationist, priest or king, always advances in the normal direction. Occasionally, but infrequently, a single scene occupies the entire wall; more often, it is divided into panels. Thus the ritual of divine worship was resolved into a definite number of ceremonies, which were at will isolated from their neighbours, or grouped in processions more or less long. When at the beginning of the sacrifice Pharaoh washed the altar, lighted the fire, burnt the incense, poured the libations of water, wine, milk and essences, he provided the material for so many

FIG. 87.—FAÇADE OF THE TEMPLE OF THE SPHINX
(*Phot. Steindorff*).

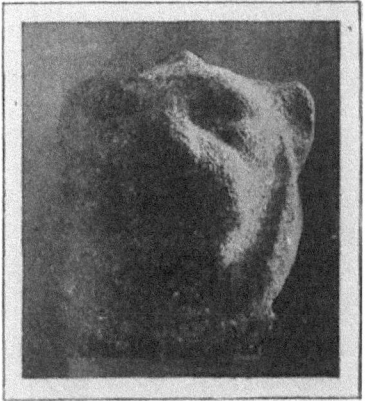

FIG. 88.—HEAD OF A LION FROM SAKKARAH (Museum, Cairo).
(*Phot. E. Brugsch.*)

---
[1] The Arab prayer-niche, facing towards Mecca.

MEMPHITE ART

distinct scenes. And as, to ensure the complete efficacy of these operations, he had to perform them once as the king of the South, and again as the king of the North, the artist was also obliged to depict them twice, but at the same time to distribute them symmetrically from room to room, so that at last the temple came to be, as it were, cut into two parallel sections with corresponding decorations; in the right hand section the sovereign officiated in the name of Upper Egypt, in the left in that of Lower Egypt. He thus proceeded from without to within until he reached the Holy of Holies, and at each stage,

FIG. 89.—TWO COLUMNS WITH PALM-LEAF CAPITALS FROM THE FUNERARY CHAPEL OF UNAS (Museum, Cairo). *(Phot. E. Brugsch.)*

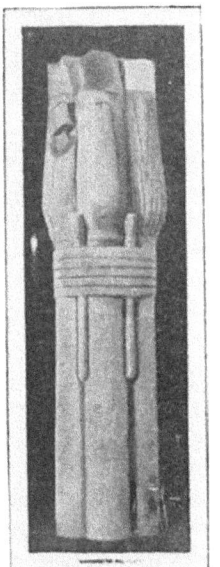

FIG. 90.
LOTUS COLUMN OF SHEPSES-PTAH (Museum, Cairo). *(Phot. E. Brugsch.)*

the god rose before him, like some great lord coming out to meet his subjects, confronting them and receiving their homage from station to station. The concatenation is far less strict in the tombs, for here the deceased plays a double part, and whereas in some places he passively awaits the results of the labours his posterity performs for his benefit, in others he behaves as if he were still reckoned among the living; he passes through his fields or workshops to see what is being done, and superintend. The contradiction in the two parts is accordingly translated by a similar contradiction in the orientation of his images; some of these move or stop facing the *kiblah*, like the faithful who have come from the outer world to do honour to their ancestor, but the majority turn their backs on it and seem to be advancing from it, as becomes the master of the house. If, disregarding these exceptions, which are the result of the ideas held by they Egptians as

ART IN EGYPT

to the material conditions of the after-life, we take the pictures of the hypogeum as a whole, we must admit that they tend uniformly towards the stele, and that they illustrate by their succession the mystic drama, the episodes of which are evolved from the threshold of the chapel to the supposed door of the tomb-chamber.

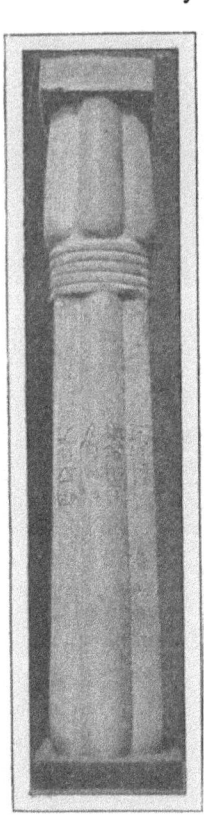

FIG. 91.—LOTUS-COL-
UMN OF RÂ-EN-USER
(Museum, Cairo).
(Phot. E. Brugsch.)

Artists registered them, and as they were used in the same manner in the temples, they finally became a series of designs containing all the elements necessary to decorate the house of the dead or that of the god. It is probable that in the beginning each town had its cartoons, in which the characteristic features of its religion and its burial rites were reproduced, but at the moment when history begins for us, local diversities persisted only in a slight degree, and two general types prevailed, one for the tomb, the other for the temple; the numerous examples of each which we possess were distinguished only by the details of the names and figures. As I have already said, several evidences lead one to conclude that they were definitively fixed in the schools of the Delta, and this I consider a proved fact in the case of the tombs; it is, indeed, in the Delta, and in the Delta alone, that the papyrus reed grows to an immense height, and forms those vast thickets into which the holy dead penetrate at will, to harpoon fish, or hunt water-fowl and hippopotamus (Fig. 93). After the priests of Heliopolis had codified the principles of the worship of the gods and of the dead, they came almost inevitably to lay down rules for the composition and execution of the pictures in which they represented it. They permitted no variation in aught relating to the gods, for when man was invoking these, his most insignificant acts and attitudes had their importance. To carry out his work to perfection, the artist should have decomposed the slightest gestures of the celebrant into as many distinct images, but the theologian did not insist on this. He merely required the artist when rendering each of the episodes, the sequence of which constituted the ritual, to express the

MEMPHITE ART

critical moment when the act was accomplished which produced the maximum effect. In earlier ages, the chief or king himself lassoed the almost wild bull in the fields for sacrifice (Fig. 94).

FIG. 92.—THE GEESE OF MÊDUM (Museum, Cairo). *(Phot. E. Brugsch.)*

He felled it, tied its hoofs together, and then killed it with a wooden pole-axe, partially sharpened, with which he dealt it a blow on the skull between the eyes. At a later period, they cut the beast's throat instead of dealing it a death-blow, but the antique weapon and the gesture it demanded were preserved and inscribed on the walls as the characteristic emblem of the rite. Where we see the king standing before the god and presenting the pole-axe to him, we are contemplating the sacrifice, although the victim is absent; when once the scene had been thus symbolised, it was transmitted from generation to generation in the same form, varying only in the accessories, and it was to be found at Kom-Ombo under the Antonines just as it was under the earliest Pharaohs. If we now return to the mastabas and examine the same motive there, we shall suddenly perceive that it is not treated in accordance with an immutable formula. The draughtsman expands or condenses it regardless of the theologian; he multiplies or suppresses supernumeraries, relaxes or stiffens their gestures, combines their efforts; if so disposed, he devotes entire panels to the ultimate fate of the bull, the cutting-up, and the presentation of the pieces to the master. And what is true of

FIG. 93.—HIPPOPOTAMUS HUNT IN THE TOMB OF TI.

ART IN EGYPT

the sacrifice applies equally to all the rest; composition and rendering are no less varied in the book of the tombs than they are uniform in that of the temples. Dogma, which prescribed to the artist the choice and treatment of the scenes in which the gods were visibly present, allowed him much more liberty in dealing with the dead.

Incoherent as they are, the fragments of the chapels of Unas, Rā-en-user and Sahu-Rā which have come down to us, suffice to prove that the book of the temples comprised even at this period the same kind of pictures, connected almost in the same manner, as those we find under the Second Theban Empire. The decorative scheme changed its nature as it progressed from without to within. In the places accessible to the public, in the columned hall which served as vestibule, and under the porticoes bordering the entrance court, the warlike deeds of the sovereign were set forth, or at least those for which he gave glory to the god, and the spoils of which had helped to build or restore the temple. Thus Sahu-Rā was shown on the south side of his hypostyle hall striking down a king of Libya who is prone at his feet (Fig. 95); further on, three daughters of a Libyan chief implored his mercy, captive herds of oxen, asses, goats and sheep advanced in four rows, while at the base of the wall, beneath the animals, the

FIG. 94.—THE SACRIFICIAL BULL LASSOED BY THE KING, AT ABYDOS (Drawing by Boudier).

FIG. 95.—A LIBYAN CHIEF STRUCK DOWN BY SAHU-RĀ (Museum, Berlin). (Phot. L. Borchardt.)

MEMPHITE ART

family of the vanquished wept over the fate of its chief in the presence of Amentit, Regent of the West, and Ashu, Lord of the Desert. Elsewhere, Pharaoh is engaged in a naval expedition against Asiatics; his fleet advances towards him in two lines, amidst the clamour of the crews. Or he is hunting in the desert, where he pursues birds through the papyrus. All these recollections of his princely life cease when he crosses the threshold of the inner chambers. An escort of offering-bearers accompanies him thither for a few moments, but these soon leave him in their turn, and he remains alone with

FIG. 96.—KING SAHU-RĀ ADOPTED BY THE GODDESS IN THE PRESENCE OF KHNEMU (Museum, Cairo). *(Phot. L. Brugsch.)*

FIG. 97.—MENKHAU-HERU (The Louvre, Paris).

his divine fathers; the goddesses adopt him as their son, suckling him from their breasts (Fig. 96), and the gods receive wine and water from him, and perfumed oil, tribute by which he hopes to gain their goodwill. Several of these motives we have already seen in the mastabas; but until we have studied them on the royal monuments, we can form no idea of the perfection with which the Memphite artists have treated them. The Menkhau-Heru of the Louvre (Fig. 97) had already shown us with what charm they were able to invest the images of their Pharaohs, but this was but an isolated fragment; on the great bas-reliefs of Abusir, each figure, from head to foot, and when several figures in conjunction are in question, each group of figures, is drawn with a continuous line, traced upon the stone with an assurance and freedom that never falter for an instant. The background is hollowed imperceptibly along this

FIG. 98.—TRIUMPHAL BAS-RELIEF OF SENEFERU AT SINAÏ. *(Phot. Petrie.)*

line, to accentuate the relief, but so subtly is it done that we can only perceive it by an effort; the subject is by this means placed in an atmosphere which softens its contours more than might have been thought possible with a relief kept so low. The inner details show a mingling of definite lines and almost imperceptible modellings; the individual elements of the face, the eyes, the nose, the mouth, and the chin are indicated with a vigorous point, and with sharp edges which accentuate the form;

FIG. 99.—PORTION OF A FEMALE FIGURE (Tomb of Gemnikaî).

but the elasticity of muscles and flesh is expressed by mellow strokes and touches which counteract the hardness of the rest (Fig. 99). Beings of supernatural proportions, kings or gods, had eyes of enamel, and this device gave them an appearance of life which was enhanced by the painting. The colour has fallen off nearly everywhere, but where it has been preserved, it is admirably fresh and harmonious. It completes the work of the sculptor, and adds to this a precision which the chisel could hardly have achieved without heaviness; thus it clothes Uzuêri, the god of the sea, with a tunic of undulating blue stripes, symbolising the ocean or covers the god of cereals, Napriti, with a sprinkling of brownish yellow oblong grains, typifying corn (Fig. 100).

MEMPHITE ART

All these were produced in the royal workshops, like the triumphal bas-reliefs of Sinaï (Fig. 98), and also, probably as a result of royal favour, certain funerary bas-reliefs of tombs in which friends of the sovereign were buried. In my opinion, we should include in this category the admirable wood-carvings of Hesi (Fig. 102), one panel at least of which (Fig. 101), ranks among the most astonishing manifestations of Memphite art. It is not surprising that these workshops, installed as they were in the royal residence, in the richest and most highly civilised centre of the age, staffed by families attached for generations to the service of the sovereign, and constantly recruited from all the best elements of the popular workshops, should have produced these fine things; but the level of artistic excellence sinks as soon as we turn away from them, and in certain provinces it falls so low that it is hardly superior to that of the most barbarous people. The local

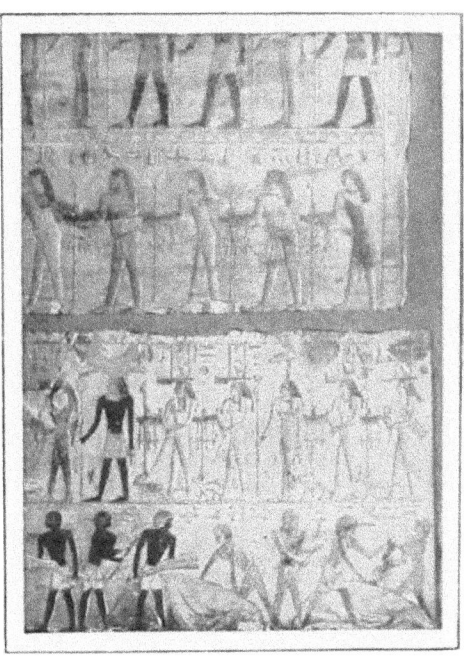

FIG. 100.—BAS-RELIEF OF THE CHAPEL OF SAHU-RĀ (Museum, Cairo)   *(Phot. E. Brugsch.)*

schools, though they had adopted the decorative system of Heliopolis, had not cast aside their individual characteristics, and these are clearly manifested in private tombs. Those of the Saïd have left us but a few specimens of their respective art, and it would perhaps be imprudent to judge them from the examples we have at present. Two or three full length portraits of the barons of Elephantine, incised on the façades of their hypogea, are fairly correct in treatment (Fig. 103), as are also their bas-reliefs (Fig. 104), but the rest are merely rude disjointed figures with ill-matched arms and legs, rugged, twisted, and loaded with crude colour. A stonemason turned sculptor would give a better account of himself after a fortnight's study,

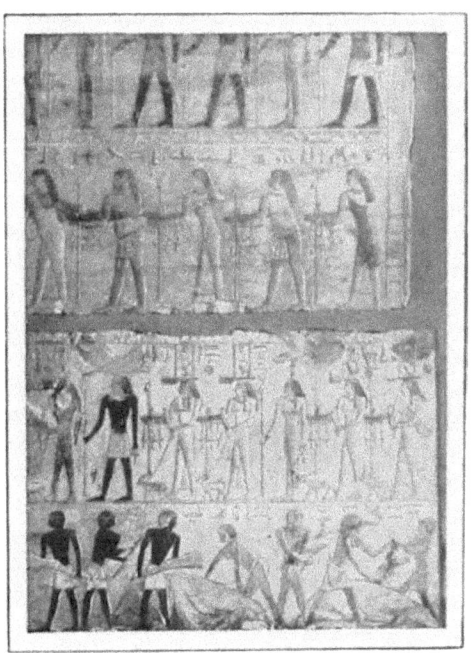

ART IN EGYPT

and we should readily attribute them to a very primitive period, if we did not know from their inscriptions that they were executed under the Sixth Dynasty. The persons who worked in the mastabas of Denderah hardly show a more highly developed artistic sense than those of Elephantine, although they prove themselves more skilful craftsmen. They encircled the human face with two stiff lines, uniting at an almost insensible angle towards the tip of the nose; they furnished the mouth with lips of equal thickness from end to end; they set the almond-shaped eye between two pads which are comic as indications of human eyelids. The slope of the shoulder is over-round in their figures, the elbow too pointed, the knee too knotty; the leg is swollen with muscles which defy the laws of anatomy. We divine a strong ambition to excel, but feeling and technique are not on a level with aspiration. Some few miles west of Denderah, we enter suddenly into a world with higher aptitudes for the plastic arts.

FIG. 101.—ONE OF THE FIGURES OF HESI-RĀ (Museum, Cairo). *(Phot. E. Brugsch.)*

Here the unity of style reveals unity of tradition; and in fact, one single school, the Thinite, reigned supreme from Kasr-es-Sayâd to the burial-grounds of Heracleopolis in Abydos, to Akhmim, to Kau-el-Kebir, to Siût, to Beni-Mohammed-el-Kufur, to Kom-el-Ahmar, everywhere save at Hermopolis. Hermopolis, the city of Thoth, had been from the most remote antiquity, a centre of religious speculation, where theories as to the creation of beings and the essence of things were ela-

FIG. 102.—WOODEN PANELS FROM THE TOMB OF HESI-RĀ (Museum, Cairo). *(Phot. E. Brugsch.)*

MEMPHITE ART

borated; nevertheless, having arrived at reflection and a system after Heliopolis, it had, in the main accepted the doctrines and funerary decorations of the latter, and its originality is revealed to us less by the concept it may have formed of the tomb, than by the details of its scenes and their material execution. Its draughtsmen were remarkable for their sense of life, the intensity and diversity of their movement, and a good humour, the expression of which sometimes verges on caricature. Thus, in one of the tombs of Meir, there are persons evidently suffering from famine; reduced to positive physiological distress, their bones are coming through the skin; this is the procession of the lean (Fig. 105). Another artist near by has reserved his wall for the fat and well-liking, both of man and beast; it shows a kind of carnival of the obese (Fig. 106) Anatomical accuracy is scrupulously observed in both cases, but the lean are perhaps superior to the fat; they come and go with an angular vivacity which would befit the skeletons of our dances of death.

FIG. 103.—A PRINCE OF ELEPHANTINE. *(Phot. J. de Morgan.)*

The Thinite School is only to be distinguished by its air of provincial stiffness, or rather, the Memphite School is in sculpture as in architecture the continuation of the Thinite. The royal workshops of This, transferred to the North at the beginning of the Third Dynasty, taught their methods to the natives, and soon these, gaining in refinement by practice, became capable of executing the commissions of princes and

FIG. 104.—BAS-RELIEF IN THE TOMB OF MEKHU AT ELEPHANTINE. *(Phot. Couyat.)*

ART IN EGYPT

private persons. They were at their full maturity as early as the time of Cheops, and their prosperity endured until the end of the Memphite empire. True, there is not a general level of excellence throughout their burial-places; but if there is a good deal of poor work to be found, there is still more that is good, and examples of a very high quality are not uncommon, even setting aside those mastabas, alloted to their masters by the king's favour, which, are the actual work of the royal artists. The groups of sculptured tombs follow each other regularly enough in chronological order; the earliest, at Mêdûm and Dahshur, rose under the protection of Seneferu, the next towards Gizeh, in the shadow of the great Pyramids, the rest on the sandy plateaux of Abusir and Sakkarah, together with the Pharaohs of the Fifth and Sixth Dynasties; and, as we descend from one group to another, the scheme of decoration expands and becomes more complex. In the first, at Mêdûm and Dahshur, the mastabas, colossal as they sometimes are in the mass, contain but a restricted surface of ornamented wall (Fig. 107). The draughtsman has been content to make a choice among the operations most favourable to the future life; generally speaking, these elements are, in addition to the stele which has the dimensions of a palace door, the procession of domains bringing tribute, the voyage in a ship on the waters of the West, the sacrifice of the bull, the dead man seated before the table awaiting offerings, the principal scenes of the obsequies, and nothing more. They are spaced out widely, with but few figures in each, and the air circulates freely in them. The

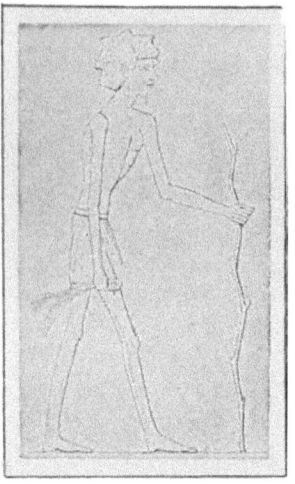

FIG. 105.—ONE OF THE LEAN MEN OF MEIR (Drawing by Clédat).

FIG. 106.—ONE OF THE FAT MEN OF MEIR (Drawing by Clédat).

MEMPHITE ART

relief is fairly high, the modelling precise and supple, the writing careful; each of the hieroglyphs is worked with as much delicacy as if it were an intaglio on a precious stone, and to make the colour more durable, they are sometimes enlivened with incrustations of stones or of paste made of tinted glass. At Gizeh, a few years later, the tendency to enrich the composition is already perceptible; it becomes more and more marked under the Fifth Dynasty, and under the Sixth, at Abusir and Sakkarah, the entire book of the tombs is in use. Here the artist no longer contents himself with an abridged representation of the actual rite of sacrifice (Fig. 108) and of homage (Fig. 109); he traces at great length and with infinite

FIG. 107.—A WALL IN THE TOMB OF RĀ-HETEP AT MÉDŪM (After Petrie).

prolixity the cycle of operations leading up to the consummation; thus, dealing with stuffs and ornaments, he shows on the one hand the reaping of the flax, the stripping of the stalks, the spinning and glazing of the thread, and the weaving of linen; on the other, the weighing of precious metals, their fusion in the crucible, the making of necklaces and bracelets, and finally, the delivery at the shop of chests containing pieces of stuff and jewels, introducing here and there comical episodes which relieve the austerity of the place, such as that of the tame monkey who has fallen out with a bearer of offerings, and seizes him by the leg (Fig. 110); there is, in fact, no longer any limit to the number of the pictures, save that of the

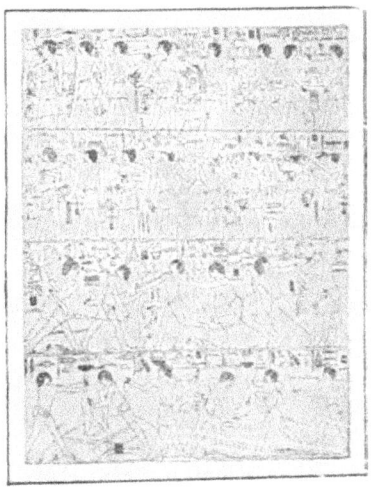

FIG. 108.—SACRIFICE IN THE TOMB OF PTAH-HETEP, AT SAKKARAH.

ART IN EGYPT

time or money allowed to the artist; and in order to multiply them without unduly increasing the surfaces, the number of the registers was augmented, and the inscriptions and figures crowded together and piled one above the other. The tombs look as if they were hung in the interiors with immense tapestries, not an inch of which has been left bare, and if there are unornamented panels and chambers, it is because death snatched away the master before he had finished his "eternal dwelling". The effect upon the modern spectator who enters these sepulchres for the first time is that of stupefaction rather than admiration. His eye, dazzled by the flash of colours and the exuberance of episode, fails to grasp the whole; the general theme escapes him, and he perceives only the amusing detail.

FIG. 109.—A WALL IN THE TOMB OF SABU (Museum, Cairo).

The whole is, however, less homogeneous than he might suppose, if he trusted to his own impression. The small and medium sized tombs were, no doubt, decorated at a breath, so to speak, and we recognise in them the hand of a single craftsman, or at least, the impress of a single enterprise; but this is by no means true of the larger ones; in every period, but more especially under the Fifth and Sixth Dynasties, we find in these from room to room, or even in the same room from wall to wall and from register to register, enough characteristic

MEMPHITE ART

peculiarities to show that one or more companies of craftsmen co-operated. In the Tomb of Ti there is identity of workmanship in the two chapels, and diversity in the corridor, the

FIG. 110.—HUMOROUS EPISODE (Museum, Cairo). *(Phot. E. Brugsch.)*

hypostyle hall, and the exterior portico; but the divergence is of the kind we notice in persons formed in the same school, and does not force us to the conclusion that there was a collaboration of two independent schools; we may rather suppose that while the principal chambers occupied the most dexterous chisels of the company, the less important rooms were left to less skilful workmen. Such inequalities of treatment are more strongly marked in the Tomb of Mereruka, and this is hardly surprising, when we remember that this contained over thirty chambers; three companies at least shared the work of decoration, and if these comprised some good craftsmen, they had also a proportion of very indifferent ones. The examination of some thirty mastabas scattered among the sands of Sakkarah enables me to affirm

FIG. 111.—THE SCULPTOR PTAH-ENEKH. *(Phot. E. Brugsch.)*

the existence of five, and perhaps even six workshops, which flourished under Unas and the two Pepis, each possessing its own version of the Book of the Dead, its own fashion of posing figures and distributing accessories, its own manner of preparing the drawing and then of attacking the stone, even its special colour. Obviously, these were not the only ones, and others existed which will be revealed to us, when the hypogea which are not yet destroyed have all become accessible, and we are able to study their technique in the originals, and not only in pencil sketches and photographs which fail to express its subtleties. Meanwhile, we claim the right to assert that the differences exist solely in slight degrees and that all were inspired by the same traditions; they formed a powerful school, the seat of which was in the Memphite plain, near the royal residences. A few of the masters it produced are known to us, such as that Ptah-enekh, who represented himself as the guest of Ptah-hetep, served by the servants of his patron (Fig. 111), and that other who, taking advantage of an unoccupied panel in the tomb where he was working, used it for his own portrait; seated before his easel, his brush and his pot of colour in his hands, he paints industriously, but he has omitted to tell us his name. These, however, are exceptions, and the finest works of the Memphite age have no responsible authors, as far as we are concerned.

FIG. 112.—COW TURNING ROUND TO HER CALF.

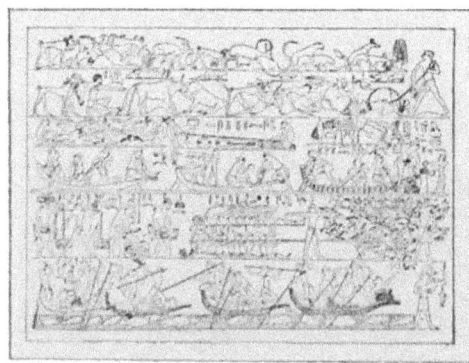

FIG. 113.—PERSPECTIVE OF REGISTERS IN THE TOMB OF PTAH-HETEP (After Dümichen).

The examples known to us are, however, so numerous now that there is no longer any difficulty in defining the characteristics'

MEMPHITE ART

of the school. In the first place, their technique is extraordinarily perfect, even in hastily executed hypogea, and we are inclined to wonder in our surprise, what kind of discipline the heads of workshops can have accepted for themselves and imposed upon their pupils, to produce such confidence and precision in the handling of brush and chisel. The line with which they envelope bodies and objects is not stiff and inflexible as we might think at a first glance; it swells, diminishes, and contracts according to the nature of the forms it indicates and the movements which animate them. Not only do the flat surfaces contain the summary indication of the bony structure and the large planes of the flesh, but the muscles are suggested, each in its place, by projections so slight and depressions so delicate that we fail to understand how the craftsman can have produced them with the

FIG. 114.—THE MEMPHITE FORMULA. PTAH-HETEP AND HIS WIFE (After *Prisse* d'Avesnes).

poor tools at his command; the fine white limestone of Turah could alone have enabled him to preserve them in a relief which in parts is no more than two millimetres high. The science of the composition is, unfortunately, greatly inferior to that of the material execution.

In most cases the participants in a common action, who would be intermingled by an artist of our own times, are arranged separately one after another, as in a procession. Men or beasts, they present themselves in profile against

FIG. 115.—HERDSMEN DRIVING BULLS. TOMB OF PTAH-HETEP. (*Phot. E. Brugsch.*)

the background, their faces turned to the point of common interest or attraction, save in cases where an accidental necessity forces them to inflect some portion of the body in the opposite direction, as when the reaper talks with his neighbour in the interval between two strokes of his sickle, or the cow turns her head to look at the calf she is suckling (Fig. 112), or the herdsman who is milking her; here the head and neck are thrown back upon the shoulder with such force that they would be dislocated permanently if the animal were thus posed in reality. When it was impossible to bring all the figures to the front without destroying the unity, and consequently the ritual efficacy of the scene, the artist made no attempt to fix their relative positions by any artifice of drawing or perspective, but planted them one against the other, as if they had all been standing upon the same vertical plane. The deceased recognised the propriety of this device in dealing with all the episodes of the posthumous life and the details of sacrifice; but he would not tolerate it in the vast panoramas which professed to display to him the sum of pleasures or occupations necessary to his eternal happiness. The artist decomposed these into groups which he staged one above the other; those which with us would occupy the foreground were placed at the bottom of the wall, and the

FIG. 116.—NEFER-SESHEMPTAH WALKING (After Capart).

FIG. 117.—BRAWL ON THE WATER (Museum, Cairo). (Phot. E. Brugsch.)

more distant episodes at the top: boatmen quarrel on a pond or a canal, fowlers snare birds in the thickets of the shore, and

MEMPHITE ART

carpenters build boats above the fowlers, while hunters press the animals of the desert up against the ceiling (Fig. 113). These

FIG. 118.—BRAWL BETWEN BOATMEN. TOMB OF PTAH-HETEP. *(Phot. E. Brugsch.)*

are awkwardnesses which we should wonder to find persisting among the Memphites, if we did not know that at the other extremity of the Oriental world such consummate draughtsmen as the Chinese and Japanese were long the slaves of conventions no less puerile. It would seem as if when once certain habits of seeing and transcribing the object have been contracted, the eye of the races most susceptible of progress is for ever sealed to other impressions, and that it becomes incapable of conceiving representations more consonant with reality than those which sufficed it in the beginning. The Memphite School, perhaps the most gifted of those which flourished on Egyptian soil, accepted the abnormal structure of the human person imposed upon it by its Thinite or pre-historic precursors, in default of knowing how to present the truth correctly on a flat surface; it continued obediently to plant a head in profile with an eye full to the front, upon a bust facing the spectator, and surmounting an abdomen threequarters to the front supported by legs in profile, and this formula, legitimised, as it were, by

FIG. 119.—DANCERS IN THE TOMB OF ANKHMARA (After Capart).

ART IN EGYPT

the talent of those who employed it, was perpetuated without any modifications to the end (Fig. 114). Nevertheless, a certain

FIG. 120.—CRAMMING GEESE, IN THE TOMB OF TI.

liberty of action is allowed in the case of secondary personages, workmen, peasants, scribes, fishermen and hunters, servants and slaves, whose mode of life necessitated attitudes that varied from moment to moment, attitudes which the craftsman was not, indeed, always capable of expressing correctly, as in the case of a man walking (Fig. 115), which he has only succeeded in rendering by dislocating the legs, or by violently twisting the shoulder nearest to the spectator and pressing it flat upon the torso (Fig. 116).

FIG. 121.—THE AGED CHEPHREN (Museum, Cairo). (Phot. E. Brugsch.)

These are faults very well calculated to repel the modern. But if we make an effort, and force ourselves to overcome this initial repugnance, it is impossible not to be fascinated by the merits we discover when we analyse these awkward compositions. As the decoration of the tombs did not, like that of the temples, depict grave and sedate personages, who could not unbend without disrespect to the majesty of the gods, the artists who worked on the former have allowed their figures full liberty of action, and have drawn them with a fidelity which astounds the student, who, knowing how closely the Egypt of the past resembles that of the present, is able to appreciate the truth

MEMPHITE ART

of their observation. These ancient people of the hypogea, intent on their tasks for centuries, scribes or servants, shoemakers, goldsmiths, joiners, potters, are with us still in their offices or their sheds; we recognise their manner of walking or crouching, of preparing their work and handling their tools. And if, passing from the towns where gesture is apt to become constrained and the body to become heavy, we note the outdoor pursuits which necessitate incessant vigour and flexibility, could there be a more rhythmic march or a more lively impulse than among those reapers who advance in a line, cutting down the corn (cf. Fig. 20), or those mountain hunters with arrow strung to pierce the prey, or lasso coiled to entangle it (Fig. 113). Take any one of the brawls between boatmen, that in the Museum of Cairo (Fig. 117), or that which we admire in the Tomb of Ptahhetep (Fig. 118). Three boats are engaged, that in the middle against the two others, and while several of the crew exchange blows, others continue to work the craft. One is planted firmly upon his left leg, his chest expanded, his neck stiffened, his hand thrown back vigorously behind his head, and we await the blow with which he intends to strike down his antagonist; the latter, however, is ready for him, and with his knee against the prow, he thrusts his weapon straight at his assailant's side. In the Tomb of Ankhmara there are dancing girls who, balanced steadily on the right leg, bend back their bodies and kick with the left foot above their heads (Fig. 119). All the bodies are strained, all the muscles work; the figures straddle, lean back, thrust themselves forward, shove with the boathook, stretching wide their arms or throwing back their legs, and among all these violent attitudes, there is not one which

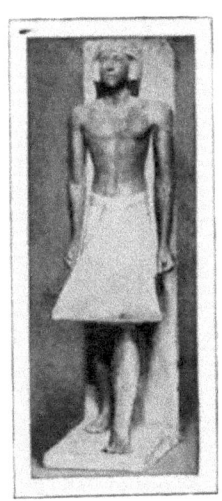

FIG. 122.—RA-NEFER
(Museum, Cairo).
(Phot. E. Brugsch.)

FIG. 123.—THE BREWER
(Museum, Cairo). *(Phot. E. Brugsch.)*

ART IN EGYPT

does not correspond accurately with the effort made. Our modern sculptors might treat the subject differently; they could not treat it better, and how many among them could render the aspect of animals with so much sincerity? Here, in the Tomb of Ti, are ducks and geese which their keepers are fattening by cramming them with large pellets of some apparently unsavoury compound; the ordeal ever, they are walking about to get over their agitation (Fig. 120). The artist has noted the sex characteristics so well that we are able to distinguish his males from his females by the carriage of the head or the outline of the body, and in addition, he has marked the wagging of tails, the arching of necks, the preening of feathers, the stretching out of beaks in which they betray their feelings, and their delight at having got over the evil moment. The geese of Mêdûm are famous (Fig. 92), and they show us what painting might have done if its fragility had not discredited it in the eyes of a nation where nothing impermanent was esteemed. The sculptor has recount-

FIG. 124.—WOMAN GRINDING CORN (Museum, Cairo). *(Phot. E. Brugsch.)*

FIG. 125.—HUSBAND AND WIFE STANDING. (Museum, Cairo). *(Phot. E. Brugsch.)*

FIG. 126.—HUSBAND AND WIFE SEATED (Museum, Cairo). *(Phot. E. Brugsch.)*

MEMPHITE ART

ed the life of the desert beasts with the utmost freshness of design, showing the hare crouching behind a tuft of grass, the hedgehog emerging from his hole to catch a grasshopper, the gazelle suckling her fawn, the oryx in full flight and the greyhound pulling him down; as to the domestic animals, he who has seen the Egyptian flocks of to-day returning from pasture, the sheep and goats in dusty disarray, the donkeys trotting and shaking their ears, the slow, ruminating oxen, outlined in a dry silhouette against the slope, has also seen at a glance the finest bas-reliefs of Ti or Mereruka.

Statuary developed in a domain less vast and consequently with less freedom of inspiration than bas-relief. The attitudes between which the utilitarian tendencies of religion permitted a choice were of two kinds, and these were determined by the condition of the model: either he was noble, and his statue represents him seated or standing, in the costume of his class, or he was of plebeian origin, and in this case it showed him in the most significant of his professional attitudes. There were, however, exceptions to this rule: it happened, perhaps, that some noble attached to the King's household agreed to be represented in a posture characteristic of his office, and not in that proper to his rank, while a low-born scribe or even an artisan might claim the semblance of a person of rank for his stone *double*. But in no case, not even when workers were represented, was it legitimate to give to statues those contorted and ill-balanced attitudes which abound in the bas-reliefs. They continue almost invariably to observe the law of frontality, a convention due, not to the incompetence of the craftsman, but to ritual obligation. They confront the spectator, and the top of the skull, the junction of the neck, the navel and the fork of the legs are in a line on the same vertical plane, without the slightest deviation to right or left. The Egyptians, in fact, were a leisurely race, upon whom the fevers of our age would have had little hold, and to them gravity carried to the verge of hieratic immobility was the supreme mark of birth and authority. The effigy of the prince was expected to be what the

FIG. 127.—HUSBAND AND WIFE OF UNEQUAL HEIGHTS (Museum, Cairo). *(Phot. E. Brugsch.)*

FIG. 128.—THE MOST FREQUENT TYPE OF THE SEATED STATUE (Museum, Cairo). (Phot. E. Brugsch.)

prince himself had been, at least on days of ceremonious reception, serious, impassible, the chin held high, the bust upright, the thighs parallel, and the feet firmly planted on the same line, if seated (Fig. 121), or the left leg advanced and all the weight concentrated on the right leg, if standing (Fig. 122). The plebeian and the slave imitated the bearing of courtiers and nobles, and their images perform their tasks with a calm and sobriety scarcely inferior to the composure of their masters, whether they toil at the kneading trough (Fig. 123) or kneel over the stone to grind corn (Fig. 124). Women were treated according to the class to which they belonged, and the king's daughter or the great lady invested with rights equal to those of her husband possessed like him, her independent image, or, if they were associated in a group, she stood (Fig. 125) or sat on the bench beside him, laying her arm across his shoulders in token of affection (Fig. 126). Nevertheless, as he was the head of the family, round whom all the other members gathered for worship, she allowed herself to be represented either of the same dimensions as he, but standing, while he was seated on the chair of state, or on a much smaller scale, her back against the front of the seat, with her children, or nestling affectionately against his leg (Fig. 127). She is always clothed, but the boys and even the men, both free and slaves, are

FIG. 129. CHEOPS IN IVORY (Museum, Cairo) (Phot. E. Brugsch.)

FIG. 130. IVORY BAS-RELIEF. (Phot. Bouriant.)

MEMPHITE ART

sometimes naked; this may have been in obedience to some religious prescription, or perhaps upon certain occasions these nude figures were dressed in real garments, like the Madonnas of the present day in Italy. Broadly speaking, it may be said that there are only some fifteen attitudes, some of which are very rare, among this nation of statues derived from Memphite tombs, and it is hardly surprising that the visitors to our museums should end by feeling a certain weariness as he confronts them (Fig. 128). This is not altogether the fault of the Egyptians; we ourselves are to blame for having crowded together in two or three gloomy rooms works originally dispersed in a hundred different places.

FIG. 131.—BUST OF A WOODEN STATUE (Museum, Cairo). *(Phot. E. Brugsch.)*

Those who visit the galleries in the Louvre devoted to Greek and Roman sculpture are sometimes oppressed by a kindred sense of monotony and disgust, in spite of the greater variety of types and movements.

Stone was the favourite material, pink or black granite, diorite, green breccia, schist, red sandstone, alabaster, the white limestone of Turah, and the Memphites cut the hardest of these with a dexterity which amazes us, when we remember that they had no knowledge of steel, and that their tools were of flint, bronze, and untempered iron. It was therefore no lack of manual dexterity which caused them not to disengage certain statues and groups entirely, but to keep them nearly always with their backs against a rectangular slab, which protrudes sometimes on either side like a wall against which they are leaning, and sometimes is reduced to the semblance of a pillar terminating squarely at the level of the shoulders or the neck, or in a point

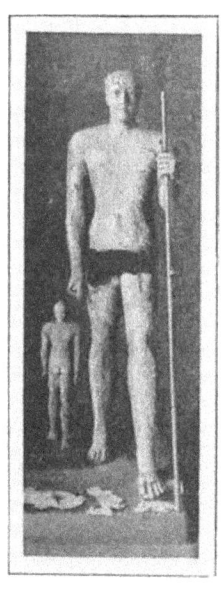

FIG. 132.—THE TWO BRONZE STATUES (Museum, Cairo). *(Phot. E. Brugsch.)*

which is lost in the hair. They had no difficulty in suppressing this buttress when they pleased, and if they generally retained

FIG. 133.—BUST OF THE STATUE OF PEPI I.
(Museum, Cairo). *(Phot. E. Brugsch.)*

FIG. 134.—HEAD OF THE STATUETTE
(Museum, Cairo). *(Phot. E. Brugsch.)*

it, it was out of respect for a tradition established at a time when the artist would have feared to weaken his work and diminish its chances of duration by omitting it. They accordingly continued to the end not to separate the arms from the trunk, and to retain a solid partition between the leg on which the body rested and that which was in advance. I am inclined to believe that the types in which these imperfections occur are the most ancient of those which were invented for the *double*, but that, on the other hand, those in which we do not find them were created later, when the school, after long practice, had so far gained confidence in its strength as to discard them. The ritual, though it regulated artistic themes very strictly in the beginning, did not define those of more ecent invention with the same rigour;

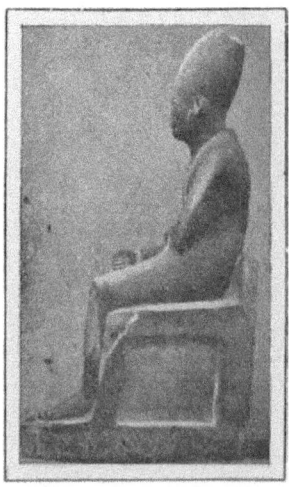

FIG. 135.—THE KHASAKHMUI AT CAIRO. *(Phot. E. Brugsch.)*

MEMPHITE ART

great personages accordingly continued to be represented by statues partially engaged in the stone, while the others, notably the servants of the *double*, millers, bakers, brewers, mourners, and domestic dwarfs had free statues. Very soon, too, the supporting slabs were used for the benefit of individuals; their names, titles, parentage, the formulæ of incantation were inscribed upon them, and the advantages they derived from this practice in their life beyond the tomb was no doubt a factor in the retention of these surfaces. Wood, ivory, and metal had never been regarded with the same distrust as stone, and their firm yet flexible texture enabled the artists who used them to disengage their works entirely; yet they, too, submitted to technical exigencies which must be noted. Ivory was only used for small basreliefs and statuettes, such as the Cheops at Cairo, discovered by Petrie at Abydos (Fig. 129), and the bas-reliefs of the Fifth Dynasty, fragments of which were found at Sakkarah (Fig. 130). Both are very carefully worked, but they have no great artistic merit. Egypt produces little wood fit for carving, and that which was bought in Syria or Caramania, pine, cedar, and cypress, arrived in beams and blocks too small to serve for the carving of a life-size figure. A trunk, a head, and sometimes legs were obtainable, but the arms, unless these were incorporated with the body, and generally speaking the legs, were joined to the rest (Fig. 131); the pieces were

FIG. 136.—THE KNEELING MAN AT CAIRO *(Phot. E. Brugsch.)*

FIG. 137.-STATUE NO. I AT CAIRO. *(Phot. E. Brugsch.)*

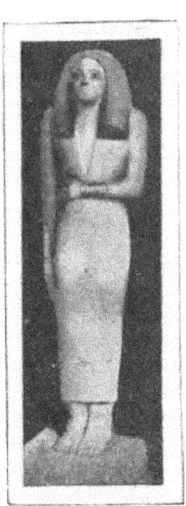

FIG. 138.—THE LADY NASI (The Louvre, Paris). *(Phot. Bouriant).*

ART IN EGYPT

FIG. 139.
ARCHAIC STATUETTE OF A
WOMAN (After Pleyte)
(Museum, Turin).

fitted together by means of rectangular tenons, and as the whole was lightly overlaid with stucco and then painted, the joints disappeared. Metal, gold or silver, bronze or copper would have easily furnished large pieces all in one if the art of the founders had been more advanced; but it seems evident to me that they only dared to operate on modest quantities, and that they did not known how to prepare large moulds. Figurines and amulets were accordingly cast whole, but statues were partially hammered out. The face,

FIG. 140.—ARCHAIC STATUETTE OF A WOMAN (AfterCapart) (Museum, Brussels).

FIG. 141.—THE SPHINX OF GIZEH.
(Phot. E. Brugsch.)

hands and feet, all the parts which demanded delicacy, were made in moulds. The bust, the arms and the legs were merely *repoussé* plates, mounted upon a common core, and put together with rivets. It was thus that the statue of Pepi I., and the statuette found with it at Hierakonpolis (Fig. 132) were ompossed. The framework of these was of wood, the petticoat of gold, and the headdress of lapis-lazuli. As was to be expected, the apron and the wig have disappeared; their material value tempted thieves in ancient times. In spite of the rudeness of the technique and the mutilations they have suffered, they

MEMPHITE ART

are two very remarkable examples (Figs. 133 to 134), which hold their own even beside works like the diorite Chephren.

The earliest statues belong to two schools; those of Pharaoh-Khasakhmui and the crouching man of Kom-el-Ahmar to the Thinite, the No. 1 Cairo statue to the Memphite. The Khasakhmui at Cairo (Fig. 135), the finer of the two, is of schist, half the size of life, and though its author had not thrown off a certain stiffness and awkwardness, it bears witness to a dexterity of no mean order in the use of the chisel. The king is dressed as Osiris for his deification in the festival of *habi sadu*, the high white cap on his head, his short cloak drawn closely about him, and while his left arm and hand are defined under the drapery, the right hand and arm are laid along the knee. The head has lost the right half, but

FIG. 142.—THE GREAT CHEPHREN AT CAIRO.
(Phot. E. Brugsch.)

if we reconstruct it with the limestone fragment at Oxford, we divine the true portrait, modelled with a somewhat rude touch, but with a perfect comprehension of anatomy, and of the processes required for its faithful expression. It is a good example, which I ascribe to the royal workshop, and its merits are the more striking when we compare it with the crouching man (Fig. 136). This is the product of a private workshop, and the style is so rough and heavy that we might naturally suppose it to be earlier than the Pharaoh. But close examination shows that its shortcomings are due less to archaism than to provincial clumsiness, and I hold the same opinion of the granite statue No. 1 at Cairo (Fig. 137); here the head is too large, the neck too short, the torso too thickset, the leg badly formed, the foot perfunctory. These faults are repeated in varying degrees in the similar statues or groups from

FIG. 143.—THE ALABASTER CHEPHREN AT CAIRO
(Phot. E. Brugsch.)

ART IN EGYPT

Sakkarah and Gizeh scattered in European museums. The most famous are the Sapui and the Nasi in the Louvre (Fig. 138), but there are others at Turin (Fig. 139), at Naples, at Munich, at Brussels (Fig. 140) and at Leyden. They have certain stylistic features in common, the short, thick neck, the head pressed down between the shoulders, the round, massive body, the ill-drawn leg and foot. We shall realise the contrast between this provincial art and the art of the Court, if we compare these works with the Ra-hetep and the Neferet of Mêdûm, their contemporaries within a few years (See Frontispiece). These date from the time of Seneferu, the century in which political vicissitudes transported the royal workshop from This to the Memphite plain. The bearing of the man, with his intelligent face, his broad shoulders, his slender torso, and slim legs is full of spirit and vivacity, but the woman is a masterpiece, perhaps *the* masterpiece of this archaic sculpture. Not only do the head and face stand out in the most vigorous manner from the enframing wig, but the bust and hip are revealed with discreet elegance beneath the white mantle. The colour and the enamelled eyes contribute to the effect of reality, and almost produce the illusion of life. Should the Sphinx of Gizeh be assigned to the same period and the same school? It has been the fashion for the last twenty years to rejuvenate the monuments to which the Egyptologists of the first two generations assigned great antiquity. The Sphinx (Fig. 141) has not been spared, and several scholars have brought it down to the Eighteenth Dynasty. It is true that it has undergone countless restorations in the course of its

FIG. 144.—REISNER'S MYCERINUS (Museum, Cairo).*(Phot.E.Brugsch)*.

FIG. 145.—MYCERINUS AND HIS WIFE (Museum, New York). *(Phot. Reisner.)*

MEMPHITE ART

existence, but patched though it be, it retains enough of its primitive appearance to entitle it to be classed as contemporary with the Pyramids, if not anterior to them. In spite of the mutilations which have disfigured it, I believe I can recognise in it the characteristics of the two statues of Mêdûm, works of the Thinite School at its apogee.

There is always, even in the most accomplished works of the Thinites, a something stiff and angular; the Memphite artists whom the Pharaohs summoned to the royal workshops soon lost their awkwardness, but preserving that tendency to roundness shown in their early productions, they evolved a fat and supple touch which distinguishes them from their masters. They had that respect for material truth which was, indeed, enjoined by their religion, but at the same time they permitted themselves to idealise the features of their models as far as this was compatible with the exigencies of likeness. They delicately attenuated certain curves of nose and chin which seemed to them

FIG. 146.—ONE OF THE TRIADS OF MYCERINUS (Museum, Cairo). (Phot. E. Brugsch.)

ungraceful, they filled out hollow cheeks, refrained from sinking the eye too deeply in the orbit, sloped the shoulders slightly, and modified the prominence of the muscles on the arms, legs, and bust. The best among them thus succeeded in creating statues or groups of much harmony and nobility, in which energy was not wanting upon occasion. Their qualities proclaim themselves as early as the middle of the Fourth Dynasty, in the admirable series of royal effigies preserved in the Cairo Museum. The great Chephren (Fig. 142) discovered by Mariette in 1859 in the temple of the Sphinx is in diorite, the most obdurate

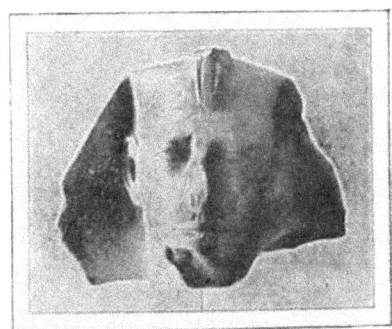

FIG. 147.—HEAD OF DIDUFRIYA (Museum, Cairo). (Phot. E. Brugsch.)

ART IN EGYPT

FIG. 148.—RĀ-NEFER (Museum, Cairo). *(Phot. E. Brugsch.)*

FIG. 149.—THE DWARF OF GIZEH (Museum, Cairo). *(Phot. E. Brugsch.)*

FIG. 150. THE DWARF KHNEMU-HETEP (Museum, Cairo). *(Phot. E. Brugsch.)*

material imaginable; it is attacked here with so much boldness that it seems to have lost its hardness. Like the majority of statues in dark stone, such as black or red granite, or green breccia, it was only painted in parts; parts of the face, the eyes, the nostrils, the lips, and certain details of the costume were heightened with red and white. The polish, and the multiplicity of glazes it entailed, masks the modelling a little: it is necessary to study it for a long time and in a variety of lights to perceive its perfection and its masterly simplicity. What again can be said of the manner in which the king is set on his low-backed seat, while the hawk behind him spreads its wings to shield his head and neck? Rarely has royal majesty been rendered with so much breadth. The sculptor, while faithfully reproducing the features of the reigning Pharaoh, has further succeeded in rendering the idea of sovereignty itself; it is not only Chephren whom he calls up before our eyes, but Pharaoh in general. The same expression of serene grandeur reappears, though in a lesser degree, in the alabaster statuette (Fig. 143), the statue in green breccia which shows Chephren when a little older (cf. Fig. 121) and the alabaster and granite statuettes of Mycerinus, Rā-en-user, and Menkhau-Heru. The

MEMPHITE ART

FIG. 151.—THE SHEIKH-EL-BELED (Museum, Cairo). *(Phot.E.Brugsch.)*

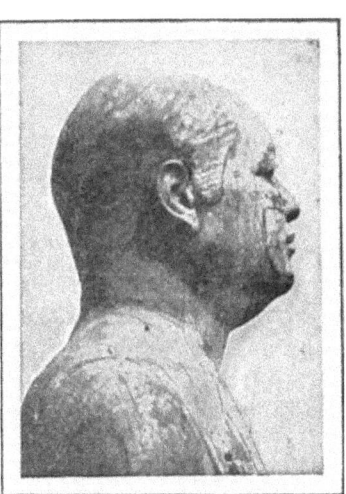

FIG. 152.—THE SHEIKH-EL-BELED IN PROFILE. *(Phot. E. Brugsch.)*

alabaster statue of the seated Mycerinus, which Reisner collected piece by piece in 1908 near the third Pyramid is remarkable above all for the beauty of the stone (Fig. 144); the figure is not well balanced upon the seat, and the head is too small for the body. It may be, however, that here the sculptor faithfully reproduced a peculiarity of the sitter, for the other statues of Mycerinus show the same disproportion. Apart from this, it must be admitted that the group in schist which represents him side by side with his wife (Fig. 145) and the four geographical triads in which he stands between the Goddess Hathor and one of the Nomes of the Saïd deserve nothing but praise (Fig. 146). The statues of Didufriya, the fruits of excavations made by Chassinat at the Pyramid of Abu-roâsh, were almost equal to the Chephren, and may have been by the same sculptor;

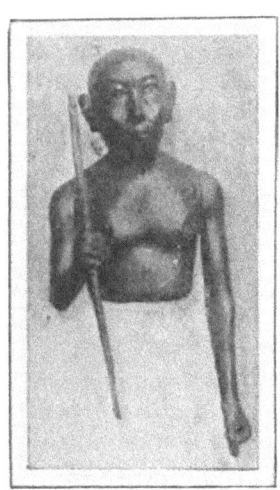

FIG. 153. MYERS' STATUETTE (After Capart).

FIG. 154.—SUPPOSED WIFE OF THE SHEIKH-EL-BELED (Museum, Cairo). *(Phot. E. Brugsch.)*

ART IN EGYPT

FIG. 155.—WOODEN STATUE AT CAIRO.
(Phot. E. Brugsch.)

the heads, which are all that has survived, have been so outrageously mutilated that it would be imprudent to make any assertions in this sense. So far, we know of no stone statues of the last kings of the Fifth Dynasty, or of those of the Sixth; they were not inferior to those of their predecessors, if we may judge by the contemporary statues of private persons which have come down to us.

It is probable that several of these were executed in the royal workshops, notably the Cairo Ra-nefer, whose lofty majesty is almost comparable to that of the Chephren (Fig. 148); but the majority must be attributed to the private ateliers of the Memphite plain, and as the sitters belonged to all classes of society, they present a greater variety of types than the royal iconography. Firstly, we have the courtier and the baron, standing to receive offerings, with arms hanging down, and the left foot advanced; the Ti of the Cairo Museum is a good example, almost equal to the Ra-nefer, but others are interesting chiefly as curiosities; such are the circumcised priest Anisakha, who is completely naked,

FIG. 156.—BUST OF FIG. 155
(Communicated by Messrs. A. Picard.)

and the two dwarfs whose deformities are rendered with medical exactness, without any touch of caricature (Figs. 149—150). These are in white Turah limestone, heightened with vivid colours. Kaâpiru, the famous Sheikh-el-beled (Fig. 151) is in wood, which enabled the sculptor to project the left arm with the ceremonial wand, and to give lightness to the gait by detaching the legs one from another. The Sheikh-el-beled marks the apogee of Memphite art, and if some exhibition of the world's masterpieces were to be inaugurated, I should choose this work to uphold the honour of Egyptian art. It is not only the

MEMPHITE ART

head which is so perfect here (Fig. 152); the modelling of the body has been elaborated *con amore*, and the execution has been carried as far as that of the most realistic of our contemporary sculptors. The man was a rustic, smooth shaven, thickset, short in the leg, of a vigorous but plebeian aspect; he lived in offices more than in the open air, and having passed his fiftieth year, he suffered from the superabundant flesh usual among persons of his class and temperament. Illustrations give but little idea of him: he must be seen in his place in our Museum to be properly appreciated. Both back and front, the artist has noted the tokens of approaching age with a curious insistence, but he has stopped short at the point where truth threatened to trench on brutality.

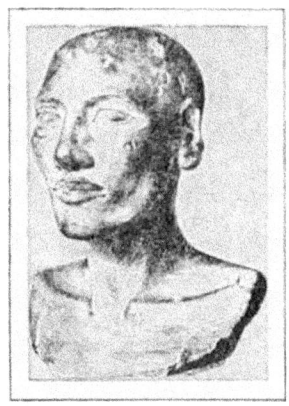

FIG. 157.
HEAD IN THE LOUVRE
(Drawing by Faucher-Gudin).

The bust formerly in the Myers collection (Fig. 153), the two Cairo torsoes, one of a man (cf. Fig. 131), the other of a woman erroneously called the wife of the Sheikh-el-beled (Fig. 154), and the statue of an unknown young man (Figs. 155, 156) are certainly less distinguished; the wood is carved more drily, and the whole makes an impression of hardness which was not perhaps apparent in antiquity, when the form was veiled by painting. For the rest, it may be said that the majority of the stone statues or groups in our museums do not rise above mediocrity: portions of these are often excellent, the heads in particular (Fig. 157), but very often the bodies are imperfect, with the feet and legs barely indicated, the arrangement of the persons is ungraceful, and the gestures by which the women and children manifest their affection for the head of the family are too stiff to be elegant. This is because we have in these objects of current commerce, manufactured in the shops of funeral undertakers by sound and well-trained workmen quite devoid of inspiration. Sometimes, indeed, when they are

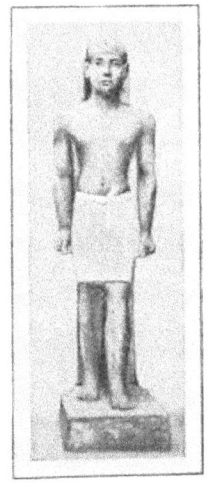

FIG. 158.—NEFERU
(Museum, Cairo).
(Phot. E. Brugsch.)

of small size, the finish of the touch corrects the trivial and impersonal quality of the conception. Our Neferu at Cairo (Fig. 158), Neferu the cooper, who would not be admired at all if he were life-size, appears charming, thanks to his small dimensions. Many visitors would like to take him away and set him up as an ornament on their shelves.

FIG. 159.—THE CROUCHING SCRIBE AT CAIRO. *(Phot. E. Brugsch.)*

The crouching scribe and the reading scribe are sometimes not easily distinguishable on from another; they are differentiated by the head, which is more inclined, and the crossing of the legs, which is flatter in the reader, but very often the sculptor has not insisted on these differences, and the types are interchangeable, or nearly so. They serve, however, to establish the ylink between the aristocracy and the commonalty, citizens, merchants and workpeople. It even happened that a person of high rank, who held the post of secretary to the Sovereign, chose the attitude of a professional scribe for his *double*. It was in itself ungraceful enough, reducing the individual to about half his height, and replacing the slender curves of the leg by a sort of flat angular sole over wich the bust was planted. The Egyptians nevertheless succeeded in evolving a very presentable type from these mediocre premises. They chose the moment when the man, having taken up his position on the ground, his legs bent under him, his skirt drawn tightly over his thighs and his arms stretched across his lap to counterbalance the bust, pre-

FIG. 160.—THE CROUCHING SCRIBE (The Louvre, Paris).

MEMPHITE ART

pares to read or write. Sometimes he holds an unfolded papyrus or a tablet before him, and, his right hand resting on the margin waits for the dictation to begin; sometimes again he has laid aside the scroll, and is meditating. The crossing of the legs is usually execrable. The sculptor has treated it as a kind of reinforcement of the base, and has neglected it. On the other hand, the torso is generally most carefully treated; it is either slightly hunched, as in the Cairo scribe, or drawn up firmly above the haunches, like that in the Louvre. The Cairo Scribe (Fig. 159) is admirable, with his pitiful mien, his peevish mouth, his large eyes which seem to meet those of the visitor with a kind of malevolence, but the

FIG. 161.—SADUNIMÂT
(Museum, Cairo). *(Phot. E. Brugsch.)*

Louvre example (Fig. 160) surpasses it in every way, and if we were called upon to classify masterpieces it might fairly claim a place not much below the Sheikh-el-beled. He is the typical scribe, vigorous, healthy, and sufficiently provided with the stock of intelligence necessary for his craft; he smiles slightly, and his features, as far as they express anything, suggest but little interest in his task, and a good deal of boredom. The seated scribes and readers in pink or black granite at Berlin or Cairo, Sadunimat (Fig. 161), or Rā-hetep have the same peculiar-

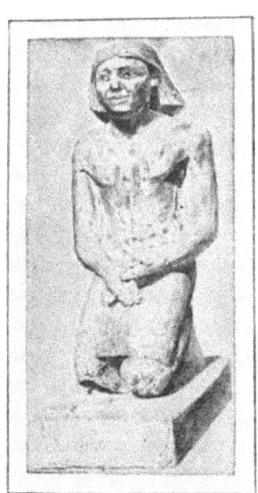

FIG. 162.—KNEELING SCRIBE AT CAIRO (Drawing by Faucher-Gudin).

FIG. 163.
THE COOK AT CAIRO.
(Phot. E. Brugsch.)

ART IN EGYPT

ities more or less accentuated; their faces are stolid, their bodies inert, and in spite of the excellence of the technique, they suggest the hand of the craftsman rather than that of the artist. The kneeling scribe (Fig. 162) is on a different plane altogether; the sculptor to whom we owe this must certainly have studied his model very closely, for he has brought out all the professional traits of the physiognomy. Here is the true scrivener of the *mudirieh*, with his resigned air and timid mien, his hands folded on his lap in sign of submission, his back bent as if anticipating blows. On the last rung of the social ladder, the slaves of the dead man, or sometimes the dead man himself assuming the function of a slave to serve a god, carry on their various occupations, and they would have given opportunities for endless variations, had they been confided to the head of a workshop; but whether in wood or stone, they were generally entrusted to the inferior craftsmen. This explains why the majority of them, grinders of corn, male or female (cf. Fig. 15 and 124) brewers (cf. Fig. 123), glazers of pottery (cf. Fig. 16), crouching mourners, cooks trussing or roasting a goose (Fig. 163) are merely plebeians by the dozen, correct in structure, but devoid of any individual accent; the only one with any originality of appearance, as far as I know, is that wooden servant in our Museum, who walked along following his master, a bag over his shoulder, and his sandals in his hand. (Fig. 164).

FIG. 164.—SERVANT CARRYING HIS MASTER'S BAGGAGE (Museum, Cairo). *(Phot. E. Brugsch.)*

FIG. 165.—BAKERS (Museum, Cairo). *(Phot. E. Brugsch.)*

Towards the close of the Memphite age, these figures of vassals and slaves multiplied, and formed episodical groups; here again

FUNERARY LANDSCAPE
Painted on the Stele of Zadamonefonukhu
(Museum, Cairo)

MEMPHITE ART

the arrangement was a utilitarian one. It was expensive to prepare a tomb with carved or painted walls, so the after-life remained the privilege of rich men and nobles; to extend it to the greatest possible number, the pictures which covered the walls were reproduced in the round by means of small wooden dolls. As the objcet was to procure a cheap immortality

FIG. 166.—THE KITCHEN (Museum, Cairo). *(Phot. E. Brugsch.)*

for the poor, they are nearly always rudely executed, and must rank rather as funerary industry than as art. Thus we have gardens and arbours where the *double* sits to take the air when he pleases, houses and granaries where coopers and scribes gauge the corn, breweries, bakeries (Fig. 165), and kitchens (Fig. 166). A narrow wall separates the building from the street; its rustic door is placed near the corner; butchers kill cattle, and cooks roast geese before a shed arranged as a storehouse, in which we see isolated vessels in the background, and in the front, groups of jars for corn, barley, wine, and oil. A little further, we are present at a concert (Fig. 168). The dead man is enthroned in a kind of stall, and at his right, a little to the front, a young woman, dressed in the apron with braces, is seated on a chair; two harpists, posted on either side, sing, clapping their hands. These festive episodes are rare, but there are innumerable industrial scenes, where the little figures are working busily for the benefit of the deceased. Joiners saw beams for his furniture. Potters turn the wheel and put his crockery into the furnace. A procession of yellow women, each

FIG. 167.—BAND OF OFFERING-BEARERS (Museum, Cairo). *(Phot. P. Brugsch.)*

89

ART IN EGYPT

flanked by a small brown boy, defiles with the produce of his eternal domains (Fig. 167), and boats await him, should he feel inclined to go upon the river. On some of these the sails are set, to go up the Nile favoured by the "soft wind of the North." Others have taken down the mast, for the downward passage; the sailors paddle, and the pilots are at their posts. All these were sold wholesale, and kept in the workshops in sections; the customer ordered at will, according to the sum at his disposal, a full granary, cooks, one or two butchers, brewers, a company of archers or of heavily armed soldiers, vessels with a more or less numerous crew, and the salesman arranged the scenes according to the instructions

FIG. 168.—A CONCERT (Museum, Cairo). *(Phot. E. Brugsch.)*

received. It happened sometimes that the sailors were too large for the boat that had been chosen, or that the coopers were not in proportion with the house, but no one was disturbed by these inequalities; when once they had been blessed and shut up in the tomb, badly composed scenes were just as efficacious as the others. They are amusing to us in spite of their shortcomings, and they are the great delight of visitors to museums; the room in our Museum at Cairo where the archers and pikemen of Meir are exhibited (Fig. 169) is always crowded. They have, indeed, traces of the qualities we find in the bas-reliefs of which they are copies. They live, they act, they move, they adapt themselves to one another, and even when their modelling is summary, we feel that the workmen who carved them had been trained in a good school; by nature and education, they tended to produce works of art, even when they were working at modest prices for the poor and humble.

MEMPHITE ART

Examples of the minor arts are not numerous, or at least of such as have some claim to beauty as well as to utility. Domestic pottery is for the most part coarse; certain forms in use throughout centuries in an earlier age persisted, notably the red variety with a black border, but others had disappeared, and had not been replaced by more refined types. We can scarcely venture to include among works of art the ædiculæ of red terra-cotta which are found in the tombs, and are supposed to furnish the soul with a dwelling duly provided with all the necessaries of life. They are, in fact, simulacra of houses with a court, a portico, lofty chambers, store-rooms, and on the ground of the

FIG. 169.—INFANTRY, FROM MEIR (Museum, Cairo). *(Phot. E. Brugsch.)*

court, opposite to the entrance, a complete meal of bread, vegetables, meats, cakes, and various liquors, the whole of the rudest and most naive description, and quite lacking in artistic value. The potters, however, had already learnt to cover the clay with a vitreous, semi-transparent glaze, tinted with various colours. The polychrome tiles facing the walls of King Zoser's mortuary chamber in the Step Pyramid at Sakkarah (Fig. 170), and the fragments of green plaques found by Petrie among the ruins of Abydos, show that enamelled earthenware was used for the decoration of buildings under the Thinite dynasties, while enamelled beads for necklaces, fragments of vases, yellow, green, and blue bricks have come down to us from the Memphite dynasties; but it is nevertheless evident that the more luxurious table utensils were of stone or metal. The Egyptians had brought the art of piercing stone, and of cutting and polishing it to the highest degree of perfection; not only the softer kinds such as limestone and alabaster, but granite, breccia, diorite, cornelian, onyx and lapis lazuli became flexible under their fingers, and assumed the most varied and graceful forms. We have bronze bowls and ewers which have been discovered in mastabas, but none of those golden and silver vessels mentioned in contemporary texts, or in those of the period immediately following: these all passed into the melting-pot, and we can only wonder by what happy chance the admirable golden hawk's head which Quibell found at Kom-el-Ahmar escaped the common lot (Fig. 171). Its design is no less remarkable than its technique; the physiognomy of the bird is astoundingly vigorous and exact, and the use of red jasper for the eyes gives it an extraordinary vitality. The body was of bronze, but the pieces were too much oxydised to allow of its reconstruction; only the statuette of Pharaoh which was resting against its breast has been preserved.

FIG. 170.—ENAMELLED CHAMBER OF KING ZOSER
(From the Drawing by Segato).

The jewels no doubt equalled those we have discovered in the tombs of the first two Dynasties, but the specimens we possess are of the most trivial kind, strings of enamelled or stone beads, imitations of sea-shells in gold, gold or silver-gilt amulets, plain or ribbed gold beads; there are, however, at Cairo some little figures of gazelles, goats and oxen, *repoussé* in gold leaves, and then retouched with the point to serve as clasps or pendants which are above the general level of mediocrity. We know even less of the furniture than of the jewelry, for we are reduced to seeking information from bas-reliefs as to the appearance of linen-chests, jewel-boxes, seats, beds and tables; the representations of these objects give us a good idea of the inventive taste and skill of the Egyptian joiners. To sum up, the more we study the relics of this age of the Pyramids, the more convinced we become that its industrial art was not unworthy of its higher art; the joiners,

MEMPHITE ART

founders, goldsmiths and potters who catered for the masses had the same instinctive sense of grace and harmony to which I have called attention in the creations of the painters and sculptors who worked for Pharaoh.

BIBLIOGRAPHY TO CHAPTER II — PART I

Architecture: A. The Memphite Mastabas. The classical work for the architectonic study of the Mastabas is still Mariette's, *Les Mastabas de l'ancien Empire*, vol. I, in quarto. Paris, 1882-1886, 592 p.; this must be supplemented by Marie.te, *Voyage de la Haute-Egypte*, vol. I, p. 31-44 and pl. 3-14, and Flinders Petrie, *Dendereh* (Egypt Exploration Fund, vol. XVII) in quarto. London 1900, 78 p. and 78 pl. for the Mastabas of the Saïd, and J. de Morgan, *De la frontière de l'Egypt à Kom-Ombo*, in quarto. Cairo, 1894, XI, 212 p. and N. de G. Davies, *The Rock Tombs of Sheikh Said* (Archæological Survey of Egypt, vol. X) in quarto. London, 1901, XII, 46 p. and 34 pl. for hypogea in the rock. — B. The Pyramids· Lepsius' theory of the construction of the Pyramids, combated by Maspero, *Archéologie Egyptienne*, 1st ed., p. 127-128, has been revived by L. Borchardt, *Lepsius's Theorie des Pyramidenbaues*, in the *Zeitschrift für Ägyptische Sprache*, 1891, vol. XXIX, p. 102-106, and his conclusions have been adopted by W. Spiegelberg, *Geschichte der Ägyptischen Kunst*, p. 17-19. The questions of the construction and alterations of the pyramids of Gizeh and Sakkarah towards the Saïte period are discussed by L. Borchardt, *Zur Baugeschichte der Stufenpyramide bei Sakkarah*, also *Zur Baugeschichte der dritten Pyramide bei Gizeh*, and *Zur Baugeschichte der zweiten Nebenpyramide neben der dritten Pyramide*, in the *Zeitschrift für Ägyptische Sprache*, 1891, vol. XXIX, p. 87, 94, 98, 100; for the general mass of building constituting a royal tomb at Sakkarah, see Barsanti-Maspero, *Fouilles autour de la Pyramide d'Ounas*, in octavo, Cairo, 1902-1906 (Extract from the *Annales du Service des Antiquités*), 175 p.; for the group of Zawyèt-el-Aryân, Barsanti, *Fouilles de Zaouîyèt-el-Aryân*, in the *Annales du Service des Antiquités*, 1906, vol. VII, p. 257-286 with three plates; 1907, vol. VIII, p. 201-210; for the group of Abusir, Fr. W. v. Bissing, *Re-Heiligtum des Königs Ne-woser-Ré Rathourès*: I. L. Borchardt, *Der Bau*, in quarto, Berlin, 1905, 87 p. and 7 pl.; — L. Borchardt, *Das Grabdenkmal des Königs Ne-user-ré (Abusir I)*, in quarto, Leipzig, 1907, 184 p. and 20 pl., *Das Grabdenkmal des Königs Nefer-ir-ké-ré (Abusir V)*, in quarto, Leipzig, 1909, VI, 91 p. and 10 pl., *Das Grabdenkmal des Königs S'ahu-ré (Abusir VI)*, in quarto, Leipzig, 1910, 162 p. and 16 pl., and more especially for the solar or funerary temples: G. Foucart, *Un temple solaire de l'Ancien Empire*, in the *Journal des Savants*, 1906, p. 360-370; — Hölscher-Steindorff, *Die Ausgrabungen des Totentempels der Chephrén-Pyramide durch die Sieglin-Expedition 1908*, in the *Zeitschrift für Ägyptische Sprache* vol. XLVI, p. 1-12; — L. Borchardt, *Der Totentempel der Pyramiden*, in the *Zeitschrift für Geschichte der Architektur*, vol. III, p. 65-88.

Painting and Sculpture. — Several of the Mastabas of the Ancient Empire have been reproduced entirely in works by: Flinders Petrie, *Medum*, in quarto, London, 1892, 52 p. and XXXVI pl.: — Paget-Pirie-Quibell, *The Tomb of Ptah-hetep* (Egyptian Research Account, vol. II), in quarto, London, 1898, p. 25-34 and pl. XXXI-XLI: — N. de G. Davies, *The Mas'aba of Ptahhetep and Akhhetep at Saqqareh* (Archæological Survey of Egypt, vol. VII-X), in quarto, London, I, 1900, 42 p. and XXXI pl., II, 1901, 19 p. and XXV pl.; — M. A. Murray and Hilda Petrie, *Saqqara Mastabas* (Egyptian Research Account, vol. XX-XXI), in quarto, London, 1905, I, 50 p. and XLV pl.; — Fr. W. v. Bissing, *Die Mastaba des Gemnikai*, in quarto, Berlin, I, 1905, VIII, 42 p. and XXXIII pl., II, 1911, 30 p. and XXXV pl.; — J. Capart, *Une rue de tombeaux à Sakkurah*, in quarto, Brussels 1907, I, 79 p., vol. II, 2 p. and CVII pl., *Chambre funéraire de la VIe Dynastie aux Musées royaux du Cinquantenaire*, in quarto, Brussels 1907, 26 p. and 5 pl. For the few names of sculptors given on the monuments, see A. Erman, *Ein Künstler des Alten Reiches*, in the *Zeitschrift für Ägyptische Sprache*, 1894, vol. XXXII, p. 97-99, and for the bas-reliefs of the Hermopolitan School: J. Clédat, *Notes sur quelques figures égyptiennes*, in the *Bulletin de l'Institut français d'Archéologie orientale*, 1901, vol. I, p. 21—24. — The archaic statuary of the Memphite age has been studied by W. Pleyte, *L'Art antique égyptien dans le Musée de Leide*, in the *Verhandlungen des VII. Orientalisten-Kongresses, ägyptisch-afrikanische Sektion* (1888), p. 47-54, — G. Steindorff, *Archaische ägyptische Statuen*, in

ART IN EGYPT

the *Archäologischer Anzeiger*, 1898, p. 64-66; — Grébaut-Maspero, *Le Musée Égyptien*, 1890-1900, p. 12-13 and pl. XIII; — Wiedemann, *Zwei ägyptische Statuen des Museums zu Leiden*, in the *Orientalische Literaturzeitung*, 1898, vol. I, p. 269-273 and pl. I, II, and *Die ägyptische Statue A 39 des Louvre*, in the same journal, 1901, vol. IV, p. 41-43, — Bissing, *Denkmäler ägyptischer Skulptur*, 1906-1911, in folio, Munich, pl. 1-6; — J. Capart, *Recueil de Monuments égyptiens*, in quarto, Brussels, 1902, pl. II-III, VI, LI, and the corresponding portions of text; — R. Weill, *Les Origines de l'Egypte pharaonique*, 1908, p. 143-146, 181-188, 255-260 and pl. I-II, V-VI. For the statues of the fine period, consult in addition to the works already quoted Fr. W. v. Bissing, *Denkmäler ägyptischer Skulptur*, pl. 7-18 and text; — E. de Rougé, *Album photographique*, No. 89-108; — Mariette, *Voyage de la Haute-Egypte*, vol. I, p. 47 and pl. ¡6 and *Album du Musée de Boulak*, pl. 18-21, 25-27; — Borchardt, *Kunstwerke aus dem Ägyptischen Museum zu Kairo*, pl. 1-5, 20-22, 32 and 3-5, 10-11, 14; J. Capart, *Recueil de Monuments égyptiens*, 1908, in quarto, Brussels, pl. IV-XIII, LII-LV, and the corresponding text, and *L'Art Égyptien*, pl. 11-20, 26, the separate articles L. Borchardt, *Über das Alter des Sphinxes bei Gizeh*, in the *Sitzungsberichte der K. Pr. Akademie der Wissenschaften*, 1897, p. 752-760. *Die Dienerstatuen aus den Gräbern des Alten Reiches* and *Über das Alter der Khephrenstatue* in the *Zeitschrift für Ägyptische Sprache*, 1897, vol. XXXV, p. 119-134 and 1898, vol. XXXVI, p. 1-18; — Chassinat, *Les Fouilles d'Abu-Roâsh*, in the *Comptes rendus de l'Académie des Inscriptions et Belles-Lettres*, 1901, p. 616-617; — Daressy, *Sur l'âge du Sphinx*, and *L'Age du Sphinx*, in the *Bulletin de l'Institut Égyptien*, 1906, vol. VII, p. 93-97, and 1909, vol. III, p. 35-38; — Maspero, in O. Rayet, *L'Art Antique*, vol. I, 5 pl. and corresponding text, *Le Nouveau Scribe du Musée de Gizéh*, in the *Gazette des Beaux-Arts*, 3nd. series, 1893, vol. IX, p. 265-270. *Le Scribe accroupi de Gizéh*, in the *Monuments et Mémoires Piot*, 1894, vol. I, p. 1-16 and pl. II, *Le Musée Égyptien*, in quarto, 1890-1900, vol. I, pl. VIII-XII, XIV, XXVI and p. 9-12, 13-14-15, and vol. II, 1901-1907, pl. XI and XVII, and p. 30-33, 47-48. For the Schools of Egyptian Statuary, see Maspero, *La Statuaire égyptienne*, in the *Journal des Savants*, 1908, p. 5-17, and for groups of wooden figurines representing funereal or domestic scenes, Maspero, *Sur les figures et sur les scènes en ronde-bosse qu'on trouve dans les tombeaux égyptiens*, in the *Bulletin de l'Institut Egyptien*, 1904, vol. IV, p. 367-384, *Le Musée Egyptien*, vol. I, pl. XXXIII-XLIII, and p. 30-40, and *Causeries d'Égypte*, in octavo, Paris, 1907, p. 351-357. For polychromy in statues, cf. Fr. W. v. Bissing, *Zur Polychromie der altägyptischen Skulptur*, in the *Recueil de Travaux*, 1898, vol. XX, p. 120-124.

FIG. 171.—GOLDEN
HAWK'S HEAD, AT CAIRO.
(Phot. E. Brugsch.)

FIG. 172.—KARNAK. THE GREAT TEMPLE OF AMON SEEN FROM THE SOUTH IN 1804. (Phot. de Banville.)

PART II

THEBAN ART

CHAPTER I

THE FIRST THEBAN AGE FROM THE ELEVENTH TO THE SEVENTEENTH DYNASTY

The Art of the first Theban Age — Civil, religious and funerary Architecture — Painting begins to detach itself from Sculpture, at least in the Tombs — The provincial Schools of Sculpture: Theban School, Hermopolitan School, Tanite School — The minor Arts: Goldsmith's Work.

THE weakness of the Pharaohs who followed Pepi II., was such that many of the great lords between whom Upper Egypt was divided made themselves almost independent; one Kheti dethroned the Memphites, and reigned over the whole valley; after four or five generations, the Theban barons revolted against his descendants, and fought for the crown. They were at last victorious, and their hegemony lasted from fifteen to twenty centuries, almost without interruption. The first period was a term of feudality, during which the local tyrants exercised in their own domains and the fiefs attached to them an authority almost as complete as that of the suzerain dynasty. Memphis, fallen from her rank as capital, witnessed the gradual decline and, at intervals, the almost complete extinction of her artistic activities; but, on the other hand, the remaining cities of Middle and Upper Egypt, Heracleopolis, Minyeh, Hermopolis, Cusae, Siût, Abydos, Coptos, Thebes, and Elephantine, mingled more and more happily with the artistic life of the nation. They became for the most part the seats of special schools, some of which derived from the Thinite or Memphite, while others were the result and the culmination of provincial schools hitherto embryonic for lack of resources. Relics of these are by no means so numerous, as yet, as those of the earlier periods. There are, however, enough to enable us to determine the general tendencies of each. That of Thebes predominated in the circle of the Pharaohs, as was natural, but its influence over its rivals was restricted, and their originality did not suffer from its preponderance.

FIG. 173.—INTERIOR OF THE TEMPLE OF KOM-ES-SAGHA.
(Phot. Schweinfurt.)

There is little to say of the temples. The Pharaohs of the Eighteenth and Nineteenth Dynasties demolished them for the most part, or preserved only insignificant portions of them. It may be, however, that the chapel at Kom-es-Sagha, on the ancient northern slope of Birket-el-Kurun (Figs. 173—174) is a specimen, so far unique. This seems probable when we consider the elegant shaping of the limestone blocks, and the care with which they are laid together, but as they bear neither sculptures nor inscriptions, we are not justified in pronouncing finally on this point. The remains brought to light by Petrie at Abydos and Sinaï, and by our own Service at Hermopolis, seem to prove that the plan generally adopted was similar to that used by the architects of the following age. The walls

FIG. 174.—TEMPLE OF KOM-ES-SAGHA.
(Phot. Schweinfurt.)

THE FIRST THEBAN AGE

and their facings were of limestone or sandstone, the doors, sphinxes, and obelisks of black or pink granite. The palm-leaf and the lotus capital continued to be generally used, as well as the Hathor capital, but this consisted sometimes of two (Fig. 175), sometimes of four heads of the goddess soldered together at the back, and surmounted by a somewhat low abacus. The excavations at Karnak have restored to us some simple pillars admirable in style, which Sesostris I. erected in the temple of Amon (Fig. 176), and those of his pyramid at Lisht, some Osirian pillars, while throughout the valley, from Assuân to the marshes of the Delta, fragments of various shapes bear witness to the constructive zeal of the first Thebans; but even when brought together and combined, they fail to furnish any data as to the appearance of the temple as a whole. Did the pylon already exist in its classic form, a doorway between two towers? It is doubtful at least, and so far no trace of it has been found. We know, however, that one element, formerly optional, had become a regular feature of the external decoration, a large obelisk modelled upon the minute obelisk of the Memphite tombs. Sesostris I., when he restored the Temple of the Sun at Heliopolis, erected two, and one of these is still standing in the midst of the plains of Matariyeh (Fig. 177). It is of red granite from Syene; it measures 66 feet in height, and the point was crowned by a pyramidium in copper which was still in existence in the fourteenth century of our era. The type of the obelisk as guardian of the temple, and emblem of the founder, was immutably fixed from the beginning of this first Theban age, just as we shall find it down to the Roman period.

FIG. 175.—HATHOR CAPITAL (Museum, Cairo). *(Phot. E. Brugsch.)*

FIG. 176.—A PILLAR AT KARNAK. *(Phot. E. Brugsch.)*

Monumental tombs abound, though they are less numerous

FIG. 177.—THE OBELISK OF HELIOPOLIS. (Phot. Beato.)

than in the Memphite age, and many of them are amazingly well preserved. The rulers had not renounced the pyramid for this purpose, but they modified its structure in various ways. In the beginning, whereas the Heracleopolitans of the Ninth and Tenth Dynasties clung to the traditions of the Sixth, the Thebans of the Eleventh, anxious to appropriate a form originally reserved for royalty, and not daring to usurp it just as it stood, conceived the idea of placing it upon the mastaba. It was, we remember, by a combination of this kind that the Heliopolitans of the Memphite age had created the form of the solar temple in use under the Fifth Dynasty, grafting the obelisk of the Sun upon the mastaba. The semi-independent nobles, or the courtiers who were buried near Abydos or at Drah-abu'l-Nekkah (Fig. 178) seem to have furnished the first examples. These are buildings of coarse, unbaked bricks, consisting of a mastaba, square or rectangular on plan, the longest side of which was rarely more than fifty feet in extent; the pyramid was implanted in this as upon a plinth about 30 or 40 feet high at the most. Sometimes a single

FIG. 178.—PYRAMID-MASTABA OF DRAH-ABU'L-NEKKAH (After Prisse d'Avennes).

FIG. 179.—SECTION OF ONE OF THE PYRAMID-MASTABAS OF ABYDOS (After Mariette).

THE FIRST THEBAN AGE

chamber vaulted on corbels occupies the interior alike of mastaba and pyramid, and the sarcophagus or the coffin was deposited here; very often again, the vault was constructed in the mastaba, and the pyramid contained only a vaulted space designed to bear the weight (Fig. 179). When the Theban barons usurped the royal power, they substituted stone for brick, and increased the proportions of their monuments. That Menthu-hetep who united all Egypt under his sway installed his sepulchre in the southern hollow of the circus of Dêr-el-Bahari (Fig. 180).

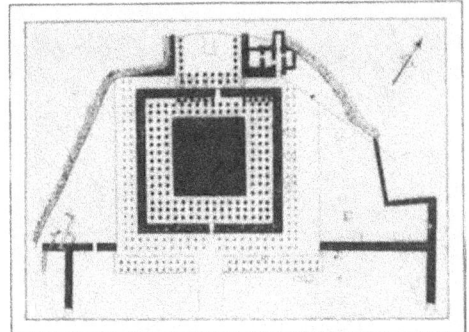

FIG. 180.—PLAN OF THE TOMB OF MENTHU-HETEP (After Naville and Hall).

It was approached on the level, through a court bounded on the west by two porticoes of square pillars; between the two was an inclined causeway leading to a terrace partly made of stones fitted together, partly hewn out of the solid rock. The mastaba rose in the centre, a rectangle some 130 feet long, faced with slabs of carved limestone and furnished at the sides with porticoes corresponding to those of the lower floor. The pyramid crowned the mastaba, so to speak, but it was solid; the royal vault was concealed underground, and was approached by a secret gallery, the door of which opened some way off on the plain, in front of the building. Behind the pyramid, in the temple itself, the sepulchral chapels of the women of the harem were ranged in rows, and behind them a second court with porticoes extending westward, was supported against the cliff (Fig. 181).

FIG. 181.—TOMB OF MENTHU-HETEP, RESTORATION BY SOMERS CLARKE.

Was it a chamber attached to the sepulchre? or a mysterious

ART IN EGYPT

sanctuary, this cell of granite and alabaster, marvellously proportioned, which we reach after traversing a corridor over 550 feet long, whose door stands open at the end of the court. In any case, it dates from the same period as the rest. The Pharaohs of the Thirteenth Dynasty and of the succeeding Dynasties who rest at Thebes, were buried in mastabas with pyramids down to the inauguration of the New Empire; those of the Twelfth and Thirteenth Dynasties, who lived in Middle Egypt, preferred simple pyramids in the Memphite style, with the paved temenos and chapels turned to the east. The external constituents have suffered a good deal, but the bulk of the tombs proper still subsist at Dahshur, Lisht, and Ellâhûn, near Hawara. Those of Amenemhat I. and of Sesostris I. at Lisht are of limestone or granite. Those of their successors at Dahshur and in the Fayûm are of unbaked brick with a peak of black granite (Fig. 182), but they were perhaps originally faced with limestone. They differ from their Memphite models by details of internal arrangement, designed to render access to the sarcophagus even more difficult than in the past, and they are for the most part so decayed that they make no artistic impression upon the spectator. Only one among them, the northern stone pyramid at Dahshur, called the Blunted Pyramid, manifests some attempt at originality. Half way up, the façades are interrupted, and the angle passes suddenly from 54" 41' on the horizon to 42⁰ 59'; we have here a mastaba with a gigantic mansard-roof.

FIG. 182.—PYRAMIDIUM OF DAHSHUR (Museum Cairo). *(Phot. E. Brugsch.)*

FIG. 183.—REMAINS OF THE PORTICO OF SA-RENPUT I. *(Phot. Morgan.)*

Private persons remained no less faithful than the Pharaohs to the local fashions, and retained the mastaba of the old type

THE FIRST THEBAN AGE

in the Memphite necropolis, the pyramid-mastaba at Thebes and Abydos, and hypogea in the mountains elsewhere. These vary in arrangement according to the district. At Assuân, the sepulchre of Sa-Renput I. (Fig. 183) was preceded by a portico; six pillars, cut out in the rock, upheld the architraves and the ceiling of dressed stone. The door gives access to a first chamber, whence a vaulted passage leads to the chamber of statues substituted for the *serdab* of the Memphites. The portico is absent in the hypogeum of Sa-Renput II. (Fig. 184), and we pass directly into a hall with pillars continued by a passage with three niches on either side, containing the mummy-statues of the master. Another pillared room follows, with a niche for the funerary stele. The vault is without any decoration, and the wells which go down to it are flush with the ground, sometimes in one of the rooms, sometimes in the open air on the esplanade outside.

FIG. 184.—PLAN OF THE TOMB OF SA-RENPUT II. (After Morgan).

In Middle Egypt, at Siût, Bersheh, and Beni-Hasan, the plan differs only in detail from one place to another. Hapsefaï's entrance is sheltered by a veritable porch with a rounded arch, about 22 feet high; the first and second hall are connected by a vaulted passage, but they themselves have flat ceilings. At Beni-Hasan the two hypogea of Khnemuhetep and Ameni confront the valley, their porticoes upheld by two polygonal columns (Fig. 185). The chapel consists of a hypostyle hall divided into three vaulted aisles by two double rows of columns; the central aisle terminates in the niche where statues are seated awaiting offerings (Fig. 186). The hypogeum No. 7, which was originally a vaulted hall very much surbased, supported by six columns in three rows, was enlarged to the right subsequently, and the new excavation,

FIG. 185.—THE HYPOGEUM OF KHNEMU-HETEP (After Lepsius).

returning in a square towards the west, there forms a wing with a flat ceiling resting on four columns. All these monuments show a tendency to replace the ceilings of the hypogea and the Memphite mastabas by a curved roof, and the same tendency makes itself felt in the stelæ. This is a natural consequence of progress in religious ideas; as the stele no longer represented only the door of the dead man's apartment, but his whole house, the tomb, it was logical to suggest this by giving it the same aspect. While in Memphis sculptors remained faithful to the square form deduced from the mastaba, in Upper Egypt, and even in Abydos, they preferred the rounded summit which recalled the vaults of the hypogea. Other points on which architects were agreed were the number and the variety of the supports. In the Memphite burial grounds there are scarcely more than two or three examples of columns; at Beni-Hasan and at Bersheh, there is no tomb of any importance without several. By cutting off the angles of a square pillar architects transformed it into an octagonal

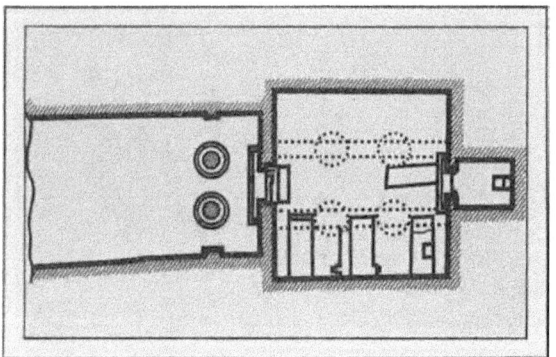

FIG. 186.—PLAN OF THE HYPOGEUM OF AMENI AT BENI-HASAN (After Newberry).

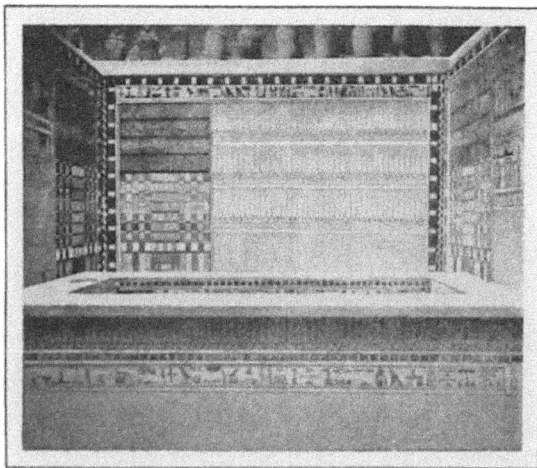

FIG. 187.—PAINTED INTERIOR OF THE TOMB OF HERU-HETEP (Museum, Cairo). *(Phot. E. Brugsch.)*

THE FIRST THEBAN AGE

prism, and by repeating the process on this, they obtained a prism of sixteen facets; these polygonal shafts, imbedded in a low base rounded to a disc, and completed by a square abacus uniting them to the architrave, constitute what Champollion calls by a rough analogy primitive Doric. They appear first at Beni-Hasan, side by side with lotiform capitals of a particular type; in two or three tombs, the base has been left unhewn, or roughly shaped in such a manner as to suggest the junction of a palm-trunk and its roots. Was this an accident, or did the sculptor wish to make his shaft look like a tree? This form has only been found at Beni-Hasan.

We are better informed as to the painting and sculpture,

FIG. 188.—PAINTING WITHOUT A SCULPTURED GROUND
(Museum, Cairo). (Phot. E. Brugsch.)

and what strikes us at once is that they seem to have loosened the bonds which held them together in primitive times; not that the statue or the bas-relief is no longer coloured; but after the Sixth Dynasty, painters were emboldened to suppress the sculptured foundations which had seemed indispensable to their masters of the Memphite age. We must not, however, suppose that the emancipation of painting was complete; the temples did not permit it, and the evidences of it are only to be seen on the walls of tombs (Figs. 187, 188), or in the coarse decorations of certain private houses

FIG. 189.—PAINTED DECORATION OF A PRIVATE HOUSE (After Petrie).

(Fig. 189). It is to be accounted for by purely material causes; the rock in which the hypogea were cut did not offer the sculptor

103

those homogeneous surfaces which mastabas built of blocks of dressed limestone afforded him. But the brush worked

FIG. 190.—WAR DANCE (After Champollion).

with ease where the chisel would have got mediocre results or have failed entirely; a picture without a foundation in relief was also more quickly executed and cheaper. We can understand, therefore, why the Thebans and Heracleopolitans, people of modest means, were often content with painted tombs. Let me hasten to say, that if the execution varied sometimes, the underlying principle remained unchanged, and as in the past, the advantage of the master, god or dead man, was the first consideration; nevertheless, its application was modified, at least in the tombs, under the influence of political circumstances or contemporary ideas. In the neighbourhood of the cataract, where the nobles had no great battalions at their disposal, they repeated the domestic or agricultural themes which had satisfied their ancestors. At Siût, at Bersheh, at Beni-Hasan, where, associated by their geographical position with the struggles

FIG. 191.—SIEGE OF A FORTRESS (After Champollion).

between Heracleopolis and Thebes, they were obliged to keep their troops on a war-footing, preoccupation with military matters

THE FIRST THEBAN AGE

appears more or less insistently in the majority of their hypogea. Tefyeb, Kheti, and Beket, who had been generals of renown in their lifetime, wished to parade in the other world escorted by the soldiers who had made their glory in this, and they demanded to be represented among the bands of vassals whose *double*s they took away with

FIG. 192.—SOLDIERS AT SIÛT. *(Phot. Insinger.)*

them. The drill of recruits, racing, jumping, war-dances (Fig. 190), wrestling, battles, the siege of fortresses (Fig. 191) were introduced into artists' sketch-books, and as in many a tomb there was not space enough for all these novelties, they either ousted an equivalent number of pacific scenes, or reduced them to their simplest expression; agriculture was so indispensable that no one dared to curtail its episodes over-boldly, but there were no such scruples to interfere with the abridgment, upon occasion, of the bringing of offerings, processions of territories, sailors' brawls, and the various handicrafts. For here the evil was very slight, since it was permissible to substitute the wooden groups of the tomb-chamber for the bas-reliefs and paintings of the chapel.

The necropolis of Siût has been so devastated by quarriers that it is hardly possible to appreciate the merits of the artists who decorated it; no doubt also some of their defects are due to the bad quality of the stone. As far as I have been able to judge, they appear to have been inspired by the Memphite School, or the School of Abydos, which, after the end of the Thinite dynasties, was practically an annexe of the Memphite

FIG. 193.—SHOULDER-MOVEMENT, TOMB OF KHNEMU-HETEP (After Champollion).

School. The technical processes are the same in each, as also the proportions of the figures and the distribution of the episodes; the military novelties are treated in accordance with current conventions round Memphis under the Sixth Dynasty, and Kheti's heavy infantry marches along, dragging shields, with no more vivacity than the ancient processions of offering-bearers (Fig. 192). The contrast is very striking when we pass from Siût to Beni-Hasan and Bersheh. These two places and all the surrounding district were indeed under the influence of that School of Hermopolis, which, several centuries earlier, showed such marked originality in the drawing of *the fat* and *the lean*. I think that these masters and their pupils cannot have had a facility with the chisel comparable to that of the Memphites, for they often avoided carving their scenes, and were content to draw and paint them; the use of brush and colour permitted a freedom of action, of which, however, they did not avail themselves equally in all the subjects they had to treat. They followed the old methods for the fundamental themes, those which filled the sketch-books their ancestors had bequeathed to them, save that they occasionally introduced modifications, particularly in perspective. Thus in the tomb of Khnemu-hetep, a good many of the secondary figures have silhouettes more consistent with reality; placed in profile, the bust is sometimes foreshortened accurately, or at least sometimes one

FIG. 194.—SQUATTING PEASANT
(After Champollion).

FIG. 195.—CAT WATCHING FOR PREY
(After H. Carter).

THE FIRST THEBAN AGE

and sometimes the other shoulder is brought forward, according to the gesture to be expressed (Fig. 193). We have seen that the Memphites rarely did as much, save in the later period of the Sixth Dynasty; the Hermopolitans almost transformed what had been the exception hitherto into a current rule. Their attempts of this nature were of the happiest, and it is pleasant to note, in the midst of the conventional poses, attitudes which a painter of our own times would

FIG. 196.—SCENE IN A SIEGE, AT DESHÂSHEH (After Petrie).

not treat otherwise. Such is the action of that peasant, who, in the Tomb of Khnemu-hetep, is about to seat himself on the neck of a gazelle to force it to crouch beside him; the action of the arms, the curve of the loins, the sweep of the back, the effacement of the shoulders, and the protuberance of the breast are all rendered with almost faultless precision (Fig. 194). Even in passages where tradition is rigorously observed, the drawing differs in many respects from that of the Memphites. It is less refined, less sure, less uniformly equal in quality, but also more varied, more expressive, more eager to suggest truth; if the draughtsman respects the general formula and transcribes it in accordance with the consecrated models, he at least strives to

FIG. 197.—WRESTLING, AT BENI-HASAN (After Champollion).

improve the details and to copy nature more faithfully. He is more successful with animals than with human beings; who has ever rendered the cat lying in wait among the reeds at once

ART IN EGYPT

distribution of the episodes; the military novelties are treated in accordance with current conventions round Memphis under the Sixth Dynasty, and Kheti's heavy infantry marches along, dragging shields, with no more vivacity than the ancient processions of offering-bearers (Fig. 192). The contrast is very striking when we pass from Siût to Beni-Hasan and Bersheh. These two places and all the surrounding district were indeed under the influence of that School of Hermopolis, which, several centuries earlier, showed such marked originality in the drawing of *the fat* and *the lean*. I think that these masters and their pupils cannot have had a facility with the chisel comparable to that of the Memphites, for they often avoided carving their scenes, and were content to draw and paint them; the use of brush and colour permitted a freedom of action, of which, however, they did not avail themselves equally in all the subjects they had to treat. They followed the old methods for the fundamental themes, those which filled the sketch-books their ancestors had bequeathed to them, save that they occasionally introduced modifications, particularly in perspective. Thus in the tomb of Khnemu-hetep, a good many of the secondary figures have silhouettes more consistent with reality; placed in profile, the bust is sometimes foreshortened accurately, or at least sometimes one

FIG. 194.—SQUATTING PEASANT
(After Champollion).

FIG. 195.—CAT WATCHING FOR PREY
(After H. Carter).

THE FIRST THEBAN AGE

and sometimes the other shoulder is brought forward, according to the gesture to be expressed (Fig. 193). We have seen that the Memphites rarely did as much, save in the later period of the Sixth Dynasty; the Hermopolitans almost transformed what had been the exception hitherto into a current rule. Their attempts of this nature were of the happiest, and it is pleasant to note, in the midst of the conventional poses, attitudes which a painter of our own times would not treat otherwise.

FIG. 196.—SCENE IN A SIEGE, AT DESHÂSHEH (After *Petrie*).

Such is the action of that peasant, who, in the Tomb of Khnemu-hetep, is about to seat himself on the neck of a gazelle to force it to crouch beside him; the action of the arms, the curve of the loins, the sweep of the back, the effacement of the shoulders, and the protuberance of the breast are all rendered with almost faultless precision (Fig. 194). Even in passages where tradition is rigorously observed, the drawing differs in many respects from that of the Memphites. It is less refined, less sure, less uniformly equal in quality, but also more varied, more expressive, more eager to suggest truth; if the draughtsman respects the general formula and transcribes it in accordance with the consecrated models, he at least strives to

FIG. 197.—WRESTLING, AT BENI-HASAN (After Champollion).

improve the details and to copy nature more faithfully. He is more successful with animals than with human beings; who has ever rendered the cat lying in wait among the reeds at once

ART IN EGYPT

with greater realism and greater brilliance? Every characteristic has been seized, the extension of the neck, the quivering of the spine, the contractions of the tail, the slight recoil of the body before springing upon the prey, and the fixed intensity of gaze which arrests and fascinates the victim. (Fig. 195).

FIG. 198.—PORTRAIT OF SIESIS (Museum, Cairo). *(Phot. E. Brugsch.)*

The merits of the school, however, are nowhere more strikingly shown than in its dealings with martial subjects, for here, indeed, it was not hampered by a long routine. The Memphites had already profited by the liberty due to the absence of religious obligation, to interpret the quarrels and encounters of boatmen upon the canals; in these they showed a knowledge of the human form, and a sense of composition with which we could not have credited them on the evidence of their severely conventional scenes of agriculture and industry. The Hermopolitans commissioned to paint the lives of soldiers, had

FIG. 199.—STATUES OF SESOSTRIS I. (Museum, Cairo). *(Phot. E. Brugsch.)*

models for the actual moment of battle either in the temples, or in certain earlier tombs, such as that at Deshâsheh (Fig. 196), where a prince of the Fifth Dynasty had recorded his exploits; thus the shock of armies, the attack on fortresses, the transport of dead and wounded as treated by them have no characteristic or arresting features. The soldiers who exchange blows with the axe and flights of arrows, show hardly less composure in their approach than do Kheti's soldiers

THE FIRST THEBAN AGE

on the march at Siût. On the other hand, the athletic exercises by which the recruits trained their bodies during their term of

FIG. 200.—ONE OF THE STATUES OF SESOSTRIS (Museum, Cairo). *(Phot. E Brugsch.)*

FIG. 201.—COLOSSAL STATUE OF SESOSTRIS I. (Museum, Cairo). *(Phot. E. Brugsch.)*

instruction show them to us in a variety of attitudes which had never been noted before. In the tomb of Kheti at Beni-Hasan, and in the tomb of Beket there are over 120 of these groups, which reproduce as if in a cinematograph the successive movements of these duels (Fig. 197). In obedience to a somewhat childish convention, the two combatants are not the same colour; one is painted black, the other red, to avoid any confusion in the interlacement of their limbs. We see them approaching, touching, and seizing each other, relaxing or stiffening their muscles alternately, in order to escape the grip of an adversary or to bring him down;

FIG. 202.—WOODEN HEAD FROM LISHT (Museum, Cairo). *(Phot. E. Brugsch.)*

one of them, seized by the middle of the body, is hurled to the ground, but as his shoulders

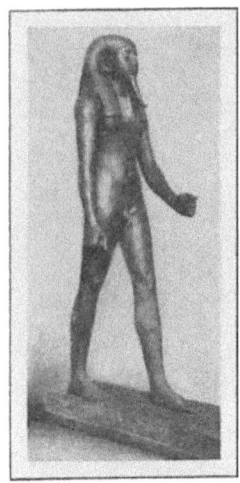

FIG. 203.—PHARAOH HORUS (Museum, Cairo). *(Phot. E. Brugsch.)*

have not touched it, the struggle continues. A professional athlete would easily name the various falls, and he would perhaps also recognise certain tricks of hands or legs which are no longer tolerated in modern arenas; what we can never sufficiently admire is the skill and facility with which the play of the limbs and their interlacement have been analysed, and fixed on the wall. Before achieving such mastery, the draughtsman must have made prolonged studies from life, and have spent much time in the palestra; he could not otherwise have followed the lines and emphasised the decisive moments of each bout. No one familiar with Egyptian monuments would have been surprised to find some ten or even twenty groups well drawn, but what is really amazing is that out of over a hundred and twenty, there are scarcely half a dozen which are incorrect or badly balanced. Not only in bas-relief on the flat stone did contemporary artists venture to combine these violent attitudes; they dared to realise them in the round. The wrestlers of the Munich Museum show the same correctness and animation which characterise those of the hypogea, in spite of a certain rudeness of technique.

FIG. 204.—HEAD OF THE STATUE OF PHARAOH HORUS (Museum, Cairo). *(Phot. E. Brugsch.)*

At Syene, Beni-Hasan, and Siût, workshops depending upon the great nobles flourished during the last years of the Eleventh and the first years of the Twelfth Dynasties. The royal *ateliers* made their appearance, when, the Twelfth Dynasty having firmly established its suzerainty over the great feudal families, the whole country was peacefully united under a single chief. Naturally enough, the Memphite School remained predominant in Middle Egypt, in Abydos, at Heracleopolis and in the Fayûm. Its traditions had not been allowed to fall into decay during the intermediate period; it imposed them on

THE FIRST THEBAN AGE

the Theban kings when, quitting their southern abode, these installed themselves in the palaces of their northern predecessors. We have but a small number of bas-reliefs to attribute to it; but the fragments of the chapel of Amenemhat I. at Lisht and the mastabas of Dahshur are certainly equal to the best works of the Fifth Dynasty. It continued to keep the relief very low on the surface of the stone and aimed more than ever at elegance and delicacy of contour, though this did not prevent it from rendering its sitters with an almost brutal realism upon occasion, as in the portraits of Siesis at Dahshur (Fig. 198). Its statues are penetrated by the same spirit as its bas-reliefs. Those of Sesostris I., which come from Lisht, are marked by great dignity, and they keep the attention of the visitor long fixed upon them, in spite of the sense of monotony induced by the repetition of the same attitude eleven times (Fig. 199). He will soon perceive, however, that their sculptors were swayed by school tradition, when they gave these figures their short, oval

FIG. 205. PAINTED BAS-RELIEF FROM THE TOMB OF MENTHU-HETEP (After Mme. Naville).

FIG. 206.—ONE OF THE SIDES OF PRINCESS KAUÎT'S SARCOPHAGUS
(Museum, Cairo). (Phot. E. Brugsch.)

faces, their smiling, good-humoured expression, their placid eyes (Fig. 200), and broad, plump bodies. They were obsessed

ART IN EGYPT

FIG. 207.—PART OF A STELE OF SESOSTRIS III. (Museum, Cairo). *(Phot. E. Brugsch.)*

by the Memphite type of the Pharaoh fixed by the masters of the Fifth Dynasty. The same convention prevailed in the workshops of Abydos; the colossal Osirian statues of Amenemhat and of Sesostris I. are so commonplace in conception, that even the excellence of their workmanship fails to redeem them (Fig. 201). This languid and impersonal manner persisted under the Thirteenth and Fourteenth Dynasties, and is noticeable even in pieces not devoid of merit, such as the little wooden head at Cairo with its plaster wig (Fig. 202) and the wooden statue of the little King Horus at Dahshur (Fig. 203). He is naked, and walks with a stride, his left arm advanced. He is an agreeable figure enough, but how insipid he seems when compared with the Sheikh-el-beled. The torso is light, the hip slender, the leg long and slight, the features regular (Fig. 204), but the grace is purely superficial, and the first impulse of admiration does not stand the test of careful examination. After this, we shall not be surprised to find in museums many statues and statuettes, manufactur-

FIG. 208.—MENTHU-HETEP IN THE COSTUME OF APOTHEOSIS (Museum, Cairo). *(Phot. E. Brugsch.)*

FIG. 209. ANONYMOUS STATUE (Museum, Cairo). *(Phot. E. Brugsch.)*

THE FIRST THEBAN AGE

ed according to the best receipts, but never rising above the level of commercial imagery; when the inscriptions reveal their origin, we recognise regretfully that they belong for the most part to the inferior Memphite School of the first Theban period, or to its Abydonian branches.

The Theban School, at first hardly distinguishable from the local schools which vegetated obscurely at Denderah, Coptos, Nakadah and Erment during the age of the Great Pyramids, did not repudiate its technique and principles, when the rise of the Antef power roused it from its torpor to interpret the artistic aspirations of a new royalty. Its first known

FIG. 210.—HEAD OF SESOSTRIS I. AT KARNAK. *(Phot. Legrain.)*

works, the stele of Prince Antef and the bas-reliefs of the pyramid-mastaba of Menthu-hetep at Dêr-el-Bahari (Fig. 205) mark an immense advance from the one to the other. The stele is still barbarous in style: figures distributed unsymmetrically in the registers, bodies badly proportioned, attitudes laboured, gestures angular. On the other hand, those of the bas-reliefs which are not so mutilated as to make an appreciation impossible, show drawing as correct and a touch as firm as the good Memphite sculptures of the Fifth Dynasty; the scenes on the sarcophagus of Princess Kauit are good examples (Fig. 206). At the same time, the relief is stronger, the contour bolder and more animated, the man is sturdier, and is planted more solidly on the line of ground, the woman is shorter, and fuller in the hips and bosom. When they had reached this point, the Thebans progressed rapidly. Among the broken blocks which Thothmes III. used at Karnak to raise

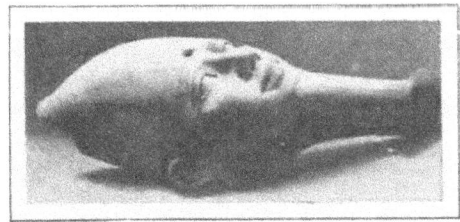

FIG. 211.—HEAD OF A COLOSSAL STATUE OF SESOSTRIS I. (Museum, Cairo). *(Phot. Legrain.)*

the level of one of the courts was a square pillar which came from the limestone temple of Sesostris I. (cf. Fig. 176). On it Pharaoh and the god Ptah, standing, nose to nose, inhale each

ART IN EGYPT

FIG. 212.—HEAD OF A COLOSSAL STATUE OF SESOSTRIS III.
(Phot. Legrain.)

other's breath in accordance with the etiquette observed by persons of rank in salutation. The profiles are vigorously marked, the relief is stronger than at Memphis, and consequently, it throws a stronger shadow, and stands out from the background more decisively than in the pictures of Gizeh or Sakkarah. The scenes of the three other faces reveal an art no less exquisite, and it is much to be regretted that the example is, so far, unique; if all the building was decorated as happily as this fragment, the Twelfth Dynasty must have raised at Thebes a monument comparable to the noblest achievements of the Eighteenth and Nineteenth Dynasties. The only work I can set beside it is the stele of the same king, which he dedicated to the memory of his predecessor Menthu-hetep (Fig. 207) in the pyramid-mastaba of Dêr-el-Bahari. The graving both of picture and inscriptions is marvellous; the figures of the two Pharaohs and of Amon-Rā

FIG. 213.—HEAD OF SESOSTRIS IV.
(Museum, Cairo).
(Phot. Legrain).

are cut with as much delicacy as an intaglio on a precious stone, but the minuteness of the detail does not detract from the breadth of the execution. All this was produced in the royal workshop at Thebes and is the best work of the school; the fairly numerous examples produced in private workshops — stelæ, sarcophagi and bas-reliefs — are by no means on the same level. The most careful of them are disfigured by a stiffness of attitude and a heaviness of chiselling which proclaim them the direct products of the old provincial academies, innocent of Memphite influences. It is probable that the first Antefs, conscious of the defects of their national art, summoned draughtsmen and sculptors from Abydos or some other city to instruct the natives; these assimilated the

THE FIRST THEBAN AGE

more refined processes of their masters, and the fusion of this acquired dexterity with their instinctive rudeness produced the Theban style.

Its characteristics are yet more strongly marked in their statues. When about to undergo the ceremonies of deification which usage prescribed for the Pharaohs after the first years of their reign, Menthu-hetep ordered the statues which were to replace him, or rather, duplicate him, during the mysteries of his identification with Osiris (Fig. 208). They carved one in limestone, a lofty visionary creation with its massive feet and knees, its heavy hands, its perfunctory bust, broadly indicated features, harsh illumination, black flesh, crude white costume, and the dark red cap prescribed by ritual; the whole is savage, but with a deliberate savagery, designed for religious effect. If a Memphite had treated the subject, he would have done his utmost to soften the lines and harmonise the colours; he would unconsciously have approximated his model to the ideal type of humanity which pleased his school, at the risk of robbing him of his native energy. The Theban, on the other hand, strove only to transcribe reality as it presented itself to him, and this preoccupation dominated those who succeeded him to the end. They sought resemblance, with a determination to exaggerate rather than attenuate the characteristic peculiarities of the sitter, and in their pursuit of it, they were not repelled either by harshness of handling or violence of colour. This is well shown in the statue of an unknown person, seated, and wrapped in his mantle, who, with his bold glance, seems still to exhale a breath of intense life, in spite of the

FIG. 214.—STATUETTE OF AMENEMHĀT III. (Museum, Cairo). (Phot. E. Brugsch.)

FIG. 215.—STATUE OF AMENEMHĀT III. (Museum, Cairo) (Phot. E. Brugsch.)

ART IN EGYPT

FIG. 216. SPHINX OF AMENEMHĀT III. (Museum, Cairo). *(Phot. E. Brugsch.)*

mutilations of his face (Fig. 209). Other examples even better are the colossal statues of Sesostris I. (Figs. 210, 211) and of Sesostris III. found by Legrain at Karnak. The body differs from that of the Memphite statues only by its more slender proportions, but what of the head? The artist chosen by Sesostris III. reproduced line by line the long, thin face of the prince, his narrow forehead, his high cheek-bones, his bony, almost bestial jaw. He hollowed the cheeks, enframed the nose and mouth between two furrows, compressed and thrust out the ip in a disdainful out (Fig. 212); he thus fixed the true image of the individual Sesostris where the Memphite and the Abydonian, imbued with the opposite principles, would have evolved from the stone an effigy of Pharaoh, idealised as much as it was possible to idealise without entirely destroying the likeness. Two or three centuries later, at an advanced stage of decadence, the same characteristics persisted in the colossal statue of Sesostris IV. (Fig. 213). This is the only extant portrait of the king, but no one, looking at it, can doubt that he has the man himself before his eyes. The living monarch was certainly what the stone tells us he was, a jovial and sensual rustic. It is not improbable that the will of the sovereign sometimes influenced the manner of the artist I am inclined to believe that this was the case with Amenemhat III. The majority of his statues bear the impress of the school, and are the work of Thebans, whether they originated at Thebes (Fig. 214) or in the Memphite districts; I cannot except even that of Hawara (Fig. 215). The king wears on

FIG. 217.—QUEEN NEFERT (Museum, Cairo). *(Phot. E. Brugsch.)*

THE FIRST THEBAN AGE

his head the *kufieh* and the uraeus, and his face has nothing of the usual conventional cast. The eye is small and prominent, slightly veiled at the extremity, the eyelid heavy, the nose straight and short, the cheek hollow, the cheek-bone very strongly marked, the mouth, with its thin, compressed lips, firm and scornful, the chin hard and obstinate, the neck thin, the chest flat, the leg sinewy, the foot nervous. The whole reveals a very remarkable technique, though certain details of the lower extremities are, as usual, summary. The sovereign must have insisted upon a realistic rendering, and nowhere are the naturalistic tendencies of the school more strongly marked than in this admirable piece of work.

FIG. 218.—HEAD OF A COLOSSAL ROYAL STATUE OF THE THIRTEENTH DYNASTY (Egyptian Museum). *(Phot. E. Brugsch.)*

To him again we undoubtedly owe those sphinxes of Tanis erroneously ascribed by Mariette to the Hyksos Pharaohs (Fig. 216). We can understand, when we see them, that Mariette should have been misled, and that he should have hesitated to believe in their Egyptian origin. There is a superabundant energy in these nervous leonine bodies, which are sturdier and more compact than those of the ordinary sphinxes. The face is bony, the nose aquiline, the nostril slightly flattened; the lower lip is thrust out, a bull's ear emerges from the lion's mane which enframes the face, and drapes the neck and shoulders. The technique is that of the Thebans, and Thebes I believe to be the source of this Tanite School, but we are conscious of an inspiration as yet undisciplined and almost barbarous. The semi-civilised inhabitants of the eastern marshes of the Delta imposed a certain

FIG. 219.—COLOSSAL STATUE OF MIRMASHAU (Museum, Cairo). *(Phot. E. Brugsch.)*

ART IN EGYPT

FIG. 220.
SEBEK-HETEP
(The Louvre, Paris).
(Phot. Gaucher-Gudin.)

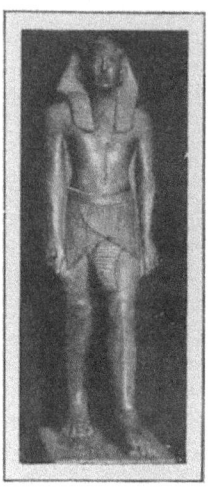

FIG. 221.
SEBEK-EMSAF
(Museum, Cairo).
(Phot. E. Brugsch.)

brutality peculiar to them on the works of their masters. The sphinxes of Amenemhat III. show us plainly enough the ideal they had in view; they produced nothing to surpass these, but we have several remarkable works by them executed under the Twelfth Dynasty, and also between the Twelfth Dynasty and the rise of the second Theban Empire. The black granite statues of Nefert, wife of Sesostris II. (Fig. 217) have a special charm, in spite of the ungraceful Hathorian headdress which makes the face heavy. The colossal head from Bubastis (Fig. 218) and the colossal statues of Mirmashâu (Fig. 219), now in the vestibule of the Cairo Museum, were hewn in broad planes from a recalcitrant granite, and the modelling was not carried very far; it is, however, so correct as to be comparable to the best Theban pieces. The face is mutilated; but on what remains of it we divine a vigour equal to that in the faces of the sphinxes. It would be interesting to see more examples which would throw light on the destinies of this school; but unfortunately the relics of the Thirteenth and Fourteenth Dynasties are so scanty, that it is impossible to deduce even the elements of a history of art from them. As far as we may safely conjeecture, a uniform mediocrity

FIG. 222.—THE TWIN STATUES AT CAIRO.
(Phot. E. Brugsch.)

THE FIRST THEBAN AGE

gradually invaded the whole of Egypt. Neither the Sebek-hetep of the Louvre (Fig. 220) the Sebek-emsaf (Fig. 221), the twin kings of Cairo (Fig. 222) nor the colossal statues usurped by Rameses II. are bad, and yet no one would venture to pronounce them good. The royal workshops whence they came had lost little of their manual facility, but they no longer formed artists capable of competing with those who fashioned the colossal statues of Sesostris. The private workshops were very unequal in their productions. The statues we have from them in the Cairo Museum (Figs. 223, 225), are coarse and heavy, but the majority of their customers ordered only statuettes, many of which are no larger than figurines; these they treated with brilliant dexterity.

FIG. 223.—STATUE OF A PRIVATE PERSON (Museum, Cairo). *(Phot. E. Brugsch.)*

The Sebek-emsaf at Vienna (Fig. 224) owes a rather ridiculous rotundity to his horrible petticoat; his little person is nevertheless, interesting for the knowledge of the human structure it reveals. The dainty walking scribe at Cairo would take his place among the most delicate works of the Twelfth Dynasty, if the inscriptions we read upon him did not compel us to refer him to the Thirteenth. We know scarcely anything of the period, and each time an attempt is made to re-construct it from existing data, new documents come to light, which overthrow systems to all appearance most solidly built up. I have given the results of my examination of all that is known; I refrain from positive conclusions which might be demolished to-morrow.

Furniture, domestic pottery, and table utensils of stone or metal, textiles, embroideries, in a word, the minor arts, all flourished under the Theban Pharaohs,

FIG. 224.—SEBEK-EMSAF (Museum, Vienna). *(Phot. Bergmann.)*

ART IN EGYPT

FIG. 225.—STATUE OF A PRIVATE PERSON (Museum, Cairo). *(Phot. E. Brugsch.)*

although our museums contain but few specimens. The discovery of the treasures of Dahshur has given us so many precious objects that we are able to form a well-grounded opinion of the art of jeweller and goldsmith. Three harems of the Twelfth and Thirteenth Dynasties have combined to bequeathe us almost complete sets of jewels belonging to queens and princesses. Their necklaces, their mirrors, their rings, their bracelets and their crowns are heaped pell-mell beside pectorals bearing the names of their fathers and husbands; he who would wish to give an idea of the elegance of their forms, and the harmonious vivacity of their colours would have to describe everything, or rather reproduce everything in coloured facsimiles. The principal pectoral of Sesostris III. (Fig. 226), simulates a naos in gold with lotus-columns, the field of which is occupied in the centre by a vulture hovering over a cartouche; two griffins, emblems of Mentu, the god of war, strike down Asiatics right and left of the cartouche. The breast-plate of Amenemhat III. (Fig. 227) is also a naos, but the Pharaoh, twice represented upon it, brandishes a club over a kneeling prisoner who begs in vain for mercy. Gold chains, filagree stars, medallions of glass mosaic, necklaces with golden pendants in the form of shells (Fig. 228) we pass from one piece to another, unwearying in admiration. One of the crowns (Fig. 229) is formed of rosettes and lyre-shaped ornaments surmounted by eight upright florets in gold, lapis lazuli, red jasper and green felspar; a vulture of gold and precious stones with outspread wings accompanied this, and an aigrette of gold,

FIG. 226.—PECTORAL OF SESOSTRIS III. (Museum, Cairo). *(Phot. E. Brugsch.)*

THE FIRST THEBAN AGE

representing a spray with golden leaves and trusses of flowers. The other crown (Fig. 230), is an interlacement of delicate threads of gold, on which six Maltese crosses in gold, with centres of cornelian and blue limbs, are set at regular intervals; a handful of little blossoms with red hearts and blue petals arranged in a star is scattered between the florets. Nowhere in Egypt, or throughout the antique world do we find a richer design, a more skilful distribution, a truer sense of colour. The faults that have been pointed out, the superabundance of heavy enamels and the slightness of the mounting are the results of causes which explain and perhaps excuse them. The Egyptians were richly adorned, not only during their lifetime, but after their death; their mummy-jewelry, however, destined for a motionless body, did not need to be so solid as that of a living person, continually shaken by the movements of the wearer. If our crown had adorned the head of Khnemît during the court ceremonies, it would not have lasted more than a few days or perhaps a few hours; the enamelled flowers and crosses weighing on the gold threads, would have broken them promptly. They were designed for the coffin, and the eternal inertia to which

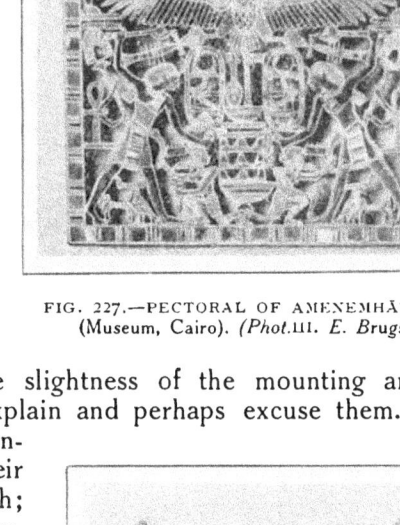

FIG. 227.—PECTORAL OF AMENEMHÂT III. (Museum, Cairo). (Phot.III. E. Brugsch.)

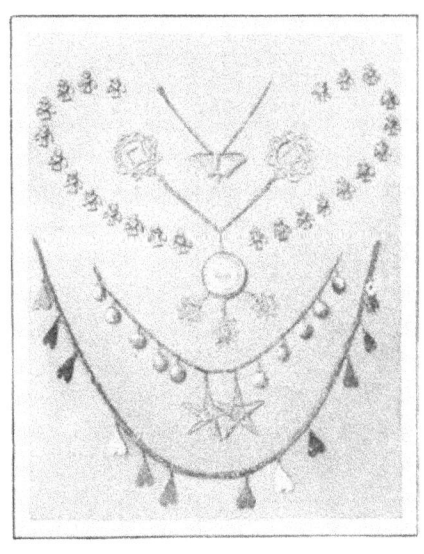

FIG. 228. SELECTION OF JEWELS FROM DAHSHUR (Museum, Cairo). (Phot. E. Brugsch.)

ART IN EGYPT

they were to be consigned encouraged the artist to consider only his own taste and fancy. The Greek goldsmiths reasoned in the same manner, when they worked under similar conditions, and the workmanship of their funerary jewels is as frail as that of the crowns of Dahshur.

FIG. 229.—ONE OF KHNEMÎT'S CROWNS
(Museum, Cairo). *(Phot. E. Brugsch.)*

BIBLIOGRAPHY TO CHAPTER I — PART II

The first Theban age is the one of whose art-history in Egypt we know least, that on which there are fewest books and articles.

Architecture. — For civil architecture, cf. Flinders Petrie, *Hawara Biahmu and Arsinoë*, in quarto, London, 1889, 66 p. and XXIX pl., *Illahun Kahun and Gurob*, in quarto, London, 1891, 55 p. and XXXIII pl., *Kahun, Gurob and Hawara*, 1890, 53 p. and XXVIII pl., and more especially on the decoration of houses: L. Borchardt, *Das ägyptische städtische Wohnhaus mit besonderer Berücksichtigung der inneren Dekoration*, in the Deutsche Bauzeitschrift, vol. XXVII, p. 200; for private hypogea, Mariette, *Voyage de la Haute-Egypte*, vol. I, p. 49-53, and pl. 17; — P. E. Newberry, *Beni-Hassan* (Archæological Survey of Egypt, vol. I, II, V, VII), in quarto, London, I, 1893, 87 p. and XLVII pl., II, 1894, 87 p. and XXXVIII pl., III 1896, 42 p. and X pl., IV 1900, 9 p. and XXVII pl.; *Bersheh* (Archæological Survey of Egypt, vol. III-IV), in quarto, London, I, 1893, 40 p. and XXXIV pl., II 1895, 71 p. and XXIII pl.; — N. de G. Davies, *The Rock-tombs of Deir el Gebrawi* (Archæological Survey of Egypt, vol. XI), in quarto, London, 1902, 43 p. and 26 pl.; — J. de Morgan, *De la frontière d'Egypte à Kom-Ombo*, in quarto, Vienna, 1894, VIII-212 p.; for royal pyramids of the Memphite type: Flinders Petrie, *Kahun Illahun and Hawara*, in quarto, London, 1890, 53 p. and XXVIII pl., and *Illahun, Kahun and Gurob*, 1891, 56 p. and XXXIII pl ; — J. de Morgan, *Fouilles de Dahchour*, in quarto, Vienna, I, 1895, IV-165 p. and 40 pl., II 1903, VIII-119 p. and 27 pl. — J.-E. Gautier and G. Jéquier, *Mémoires sur les fouilles de Licht* (Mémoires de l'Institut français d'archéologie orientale, vol. VI), in quarto, Cairo, 1902, 107 p. and 30 pl.; for pyramid-mastabas: Mariette, *Abydos*, in folio, Paris, 1870, vol. II, p. 38-45 and pl. XLVI-XLVII; — Naville, *The XI*th *Dynasty Temple at Deir el Bahari* (Egypt Exploration Fund, vol. XI-XII), in quarto, London, I, 1907, 75 p. and XXI pl., II, 1910, 29 p. and XXIV pl.; for the points of pyramids: H. Schæfer, *Die Spitze der Pyramide des Königs Amenemhats III.* in the Zeitschrift für Ägyptische Sprache, 1900, vol. XLI, p. 84-85.

THE FIRST THEBAN AGE

Painting and Sculpture. — The history of the Theban School for this and the following period has been established by G. Maspero, *La Cachette de Karnak et l'École de Sculpture thébaine*, in the *Revue de l'Art ancien et moderne*, 1906, vol. XX, p. 241-252, 337-348. For the whole field of artistic activity, cf. in addition to the works of Davies, Gautier-Jéquier, Newberry and Petrie quoted in reference to sculpture, the following: Flinders Petrie, *Tanis* (Egypt Exploration Fund, vol. II and V), in quarto, London, I, 1885, 63 p. and XIX pl., II, 1888, 116 p. and LXIII pl., *Koptos*, in quarto, London, 1896, 38 p. and XXVIII pl.; — Fr. W. v. Bissing, *Denkmäler ägyptischer Skulptur*, pl. 19-35, 40a, 77a; — J. Capart, *Recueil de Monuments égyptiens*, 1902-1905, in quarto, Brussels, pl. XV, XVII, XXIV-XXX-II-LIX-LXII, and the corresponding text; — L. Borchardt, *Kunstwerke aus dem ägyptischen Museum zu Kairo*, pl. 6-7, 23, p. 5, 11; — E. de Rougé, *Album photographique de la Mission*, No. 109-120; — G. Legrain, *Statues et Statuettes de Rois et de particuliers* (Catalogue général du Musée du Caire), in quarto, Cairo I, 1906, p. 1-29, and pl. I-XXVI; — G. Maspero, *Le Musée égyptien*, in quarto, Cairo, 1904, vol. II, p. 25-30, 34-35, 41-45 and pl. IX-X, XIII, XV. *Sur trois Statues du premier Empire thébain*, in the *Annales du Service*, 1902, vol. III, p. 94-95 and 1 pl. — On the special question of the so-called Hyksos Sphinxes of Tanis, cf. W. Golénischeff, *Amenemha III et les Sphinx de San*, in the *Recueil de Travaux*, 1893, vol. XV, p. 131-136 and 5 pl.

For goldsmith's work and the minor arts, see in addition to J. de Morgan's work on the excavations at Dahshur, the treatises of E. Vernier, *La Bijouterie et la Joaillerie égyptiennes* (Mémoires de l'Institut français d'archéologie orientale, vol. II), in quarto, Cairo, 1907, VII-156 p. and XXV pl., and *Bijoux et Orfèvreries* (Catalogue général du Musée du Caire), in quarto, Cairo, 1907-1909, 200 p. and XXXVII pl., also the work of Schæfer, *Ägyptische Goldschmiedearbeiten* (with the collaboration of G. Möller and W. Schubart, forms vol. I of *Mitteilungen aus der Ägyptischen Sammlung)*, in folio, Berlin, 1910, p. 16-19 and pl. 3; — L. Borchardt, Kunstwerke aus dem ägyptischen Museum zu Kairo, pl. 41-42 and p. 17-18.

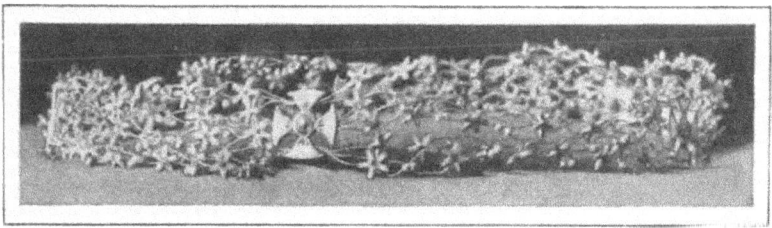

FIG. 230.—DIADEM OF KHNEMIT (Museum, Cairo). *(Phot. E. Brugsch.)*

FIG. 231.—ATLANTES OF THE FORE-COURT AT MEDINET-HABÙ. *(Phot. Beato.)*

CHAPTER II

THE SECOND THEBAN AGE FROM THE EIGHTEENTH TO THE TWENTY-FIRST DYNASTY

Renaissance of Art at the beginning of the Eighteenth Dynasty — The Temple and its various Types — The Hemispeos and the Speos — The royal Workshops of Painting and Sculpture at Thebes and in the Provinces: the decoration of Tombs and Hypogea — Goldsmith's Work, Jewelry, and the minor Arts.

WHEN we compare the works of the Thirteenth and Seventeenth Dynasties, the differences between them appear so slight that we are almost tempted to believe them contemporary. This is more especially true of the statues and statuettes; that of the Shepherd King Khayanu might have been executed for one of the Sebek-heteps, and the mutilated bust which Mariette discovere in the Fayûm (Fig. 232) bears a most deceptive resemblance in technique to the Tanite sphinxes of Amenemhat III. It must be admitted, however, that a judgment based wholly upon these official examples might be unfair. At periods of political abasement, the court workshops were maintained with great difficulty on the scanty resources at the disposal of their masters, and they were reduced to servile reproduction of the

THE SECOND THEBAN AGE

types and technique of happier periods. It seems probable, however, that they did not remain altogether stationary, any more than the private workshops. Uncivilised as the Hyksos are supposed to have been at the beginning of their domination, they had nevertheless brought with them not only material elements of progress, such as the horse, the chariot, the quiver, the bronze squamate cuirass and weapons of a new type, but also habits and modes of thought novel to the Egypt of their day. True, the leaven of originality they introduced into the ancient mass was not so active as to change its

FIG. 232.—BUST OF A STATUE OF THE HYKSOS PERIOD (Museum, Cairo). *(Phot. E. Brugsch.)*

entire nature: but it had strength enough to burst the ancient moulds in many directions. Indications of Asiatic and European influences in furniture, goldsmith's work, and pottery mark their advent; and it is not unlikely that we may be obliged to enlarge very greatly the share assigned to the foreigner in the constitution of Theban art of the second period, when excavations shall have brought to light the monuments of Mesopotamia, Syria, Asia Minor, and the Ægean peoples.

FIG. 233.—THE TWO OBELISKS OF KARNAK. *(Phot. Beato.)*

A. ARCHITECTURE

We are now no longer obliged to judge of architecture by mere fragments: our relics of the earliest periods

ART IN EGYPT

are chiefly sculpture, but thenceforward architecture predominates. Many of the temples built under the second Theban Empire still exist, more or less complete, and reveal to us its conceptions, plans, and methods of execution. It is very possible that the architecture of this period counted several schools, but we do not yet know how to define them. Nearly all of its surviving works are situated at Thebes itself, and in regions under the artistic control of Thebes, i. e. Southern Egypt, and Ethiopia. If any examples of those which embellished Memphis and the cities of the Delta at this time had come down to us, we should no doubt see in them peculiarities which would enable us to settle the question in one way or another; but so far, the fragments which survive are not sufficiently characteristic to give us the right to say that another school, distinct from the Theban School, flourished in the north.

FIG. 234.—RUINS OF THE SECOND PYLON OF HERU-EM-HEB AT KARNAK. *(Phot. Beato.)*

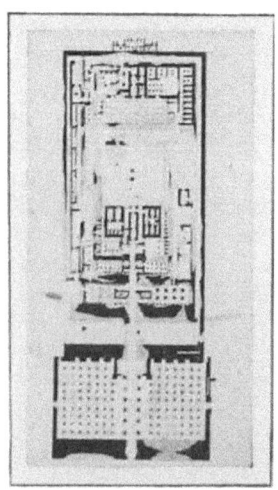

FIG. 235.—PLAN OF THE PRINCIPAL TEMPLE AT KARNAK. *(Phot. Beato.)*

Two elements seem to have been in common use at this period, which were either unknown, or very rarely used in the earlier ages, the pylon with its customary pair of preliminary obelisks (Fig. 233), and the hypostyle hall. The pylon (Fig. 234) is a straight monumental door, surmounted by a massive cornice, and enclosed between two rectangular towers with sloping walls. It is the face which the temple turns to the outer world, and it was through it that Pharaoh and the faithful passed in state, when they went to enter into official relation with the god. Each temple was

THE SECOND THEBAN AGE

supposed to have but one; at Thebes, however, and also, no doubt, at Memphis and other important cities, the kings, anxious to enlarge the divine house, constructed other pylons in front of the principal one, and these were made gradually wider and wider, and higher and higher; as the number was not limited by any law, it increased almost indefinitely, till it was checked only by the poverty or insignificance of the sovereign. At Karnak there are six from west to east (Fig. 235) and four from north to south; they were separated from each other or from the body of the building by a court bordered with a portico on three sides, north, east, and west. A hypostyle hall generally intervened between the last of them and the actual dwelling of the god. It consisted of a central nave upheld by two rows of columns, and two side-aisles, the number of rows in which was variable, two and two at Medinet-Habû, three and three in the western Ramesseum, seven and seven at Karnak. The columns of the central aisle (Fig. 236) are often higher than those of the laterals (Fig. 238) and the architect utilised the resulting difference of levels in the ceilings to light the interior; he pierced

FIG. 236.—CENTRAL AISLE OF THE HYPOSTYLE HALL IN THE RAMESSEUM. *(Phot. Beato.)*

FIG. 237.—ATLANTES OF THE RAMESSEUM AT THEBES. *(Phot. Beato.)*

ART IN EGYPT

FIG. 238.—TRANSVERSE SECTION OF THE HYPOSTYLE HALL AT KARNAK (After Chipiez) (Hist. de l'Art. vol. I, pl. V).

the vertical wall that united them with a stone clerestory, through which the light entered (Fig. 239). The side-aisles were illuminated only by narrow slits in the ceiling; as one receded from the centre, the light diminished, and semi-darkness reigned against the lateral walls, even at the most brilliant hours of the day. Very often, a single chamber not being considered enough, the architect placed two or even three in a line, and in this case he also doubled the sanctuary, which was then composed of a hypostyle hall with four columns for the sacred boat, and beyond this, of one or several rooms where the god received daily worship. For the rest it would seem that the Second Empire added

FIG. 239.—CLERESTORY OF THE HYPOSTYLE HALL AT KARNAK. (Phot. Beato.)

THE SECOND THEBAN AGE

little to what had been in use under the First. Its architects employed pillars, either bare, or with Atlantes against them (Fig. 231, 237), and hexagonal columns of the kind called proto-Doric (Fig. 240), at first lavishly, and then more sparingly, though they were never dispensed with altogether. They persisted, indeed, to a later period, and there are examples at Elephantine dating from Amasis, and in the temple of the Theban Ptah, dating from the Ptolemies. On the other hand, the column with a bell-shaped capital became more frequent, and vied in popularity with the lotus-bud and palm-leaf capitals.

FIG. 240.—PROTO-DORIC COLUMNS AT KARNAK. (Phot. Beato.)

The Hathor column was reserved for the buildings sacred to the goddess Hathor at Bubastis and at Dêr-el-Bahari; the capital was composed of two masks of the goddess set back to back and encircled at the neck by a simple band where they impinge upon the shaft. Once only, in the ambulatory of Thothmes III. at Karnak (Fig. 241), a variation more eccentric than ingenious was tried, in which the bell was reversed, and the thinner end of the shaft was sunk in the base, while the thicker one was set into the mouth of the bell. It would seem that this combination, in which all the elements were transposed, had no success, for we find no trace of it elsewhere. The three usual columns are not found indifferently everywhere; the bell-shaped capital was used preferably for the central aisle of hypostyle halls, while the lotus-bud form was relegated to the exterior porticoes, the interior rooms, or the side aisles of the hypostyle halls, and the palm column reigned in the porticoes. These customs were, however, tenden-

FIG. 241.—ONE OF THE COLUMNS OF THE AMBULATORY AT KARNAK (After Chipiez) (Hist. de l'Art, vol. I, p. 572).

cies rather than a rule; broadly speaking, it may be said that the lotiform order was the one most in favour during the Second Theban Empire.

Some of the temples such as those of Thothmes III. and of Amenophis III. at Elephantine contained only the number of rooms strictly necessary for the wants of the god. One of these (Fig. 242) was merely a sanctuary of sandstone, about 14 feet high, by 40 feet long, and 30 feet wide. It had a basement of masonry with a slight parapet, sustaining a portico composed on each side of five square pillars, enclosed between two large corner-pillars, and on each façade, of two columns with lotus capitals. It was entered on the east, where a flight of ten or twelve steps mounted to the portico and to the cella between the two columns; another door opened at the western extremity (Fig. 243). It was a peripteral temple, and the Pharaohs of the Eighteenth Dynasty had a certain predilection for the plan, for it recurs at Karnak and at Medinet-Habû. That of Medinet-Habû, almost identical with that of Elephantine in dimensions, was founded by Thothmes II. and Queen Hatshepset, but it would seem that before its completion, a second building was added towards the west — perhaps by Thothmes III. — consisting of six rooms arranged in three rows of two each, the sanctuary at the end, and the chapels of the paredri at the sides. Construction and decoration betray negligence, or rather lack of skill, on every hand, and this is not surprising, if we remember that at the time Aat-tcha-Mutet — our Medinet-Habû — was a little provincial town. To give but one instance, the slabs

FIG. 242.—THE EAST TEMPLE AT ELEPHANTINE (After Chipiez' restoration) (Hist. de l'Art, Vol. I, p. 402).

FIG. 243.—LONGITUDINAL SECTION OF THE EAST TEMPLE.

THE SECOND THEBAN AGE

of the roof are so badly adjusted, that it was found necessary to prop up those of the portico by means of columns placed at the angles, regardless of symmetry. They seem to be there more or less by accident, and yet they harmonise so well with the whole, that their presence does not shock the spectator; they appear as a singularity, or a graceful audacity, rather than a constructive error. The temple of Amenophis III at El-Kâb, almost as simple as those of Elephantine and Medinet-Habû, is on a different plan. It has two compartments at present, but the first, which is a portico, was built under the Ptolemies, and formed no part of the original arrangement; only the room of the sacred boat, the sanctuary, dates from the Theban period. It is oblong in shape, and is sustained by four Hathor-pillars; a niche, which was approached by four steps, is hollowed out in the end chamber, and this was the Holy of Holies, the retreat in which the divine statue was concealed. In general, we note two distinct types for the most simple form, the oratory, under the Eighteenth Dynasty: that of the single chamber with or without columns in the interior, and that of the peripteral temple, which, though it does not lend itself to scientific combinations, may, if judiciously treated, produce true masterpieces. The

FIG. 244.—RUINED FAÇADE OF THE TEMPLE OF AMADA. (Phot. Oropesa.)

FIG. 245.—COURT OF THE TEMPLE OF RAMESES III. AT KARNAK. (Phot. Legrain.)

ART IN EGYPT

chapel of Khnum at Elephantine was certainly the most finished example of the latter: the relative proportion of the parts was calculated so scientifically that the artists of the French expedition never wearied in their admiration of its perfection. It is a surprise to those who are accustomed to consider Egyptian architecture a massive and colossal art, to find it producing works positively Greek in their precision and elegance.

FIG. 246.—TEMPLE OF KHONSU AT THEBES; SECTION CUT THROUGH ITS GRAND AXIS (After Chipiez) (Hist. de l'Art, vol. I, p. 355).

There is reason to believe that this peripteral form was unknown in the first Theban period, and that it was invented, or at least brought to perfection, at the beginning of the second. Almost at the same time there appeared a more developed, though as yet restricted model, which I will call the temple of the small town. That of Amada, which dates from the time of Thothmes III. and Amenophis II., consists of three long parallel ducts (Fig. 244), in the centre the sanctuary of Amon-Rā and Rā-Harmachis, and on either side two little rooms in a line. Originally these were disconnected, and access to the further of the two could only be obtained from the Holy of Holies, but later, doors were pierced between the partition-walls, and the rooms were made to communicate. The three aisles lead into a transverse vestibule occupying the entire breadth of the building, and preceded by a portico with four proto-Doric columns. Ending here, the temple was complete, but Thothmes IV., the successor of Amenophis II., interposed, between the portico and the brick enclosing wall, a

FIG. 247.—COLOSSI IN FRONT OF THE TEMPLE OF LUXOR. (Phot. Beato.)

hypostyle hall of twelve square pillars in four rows, the last two of which, right and left, were connected by party walls; later again, Seti I. replaced the plain wall on which the hall abutted towards the east, by a composite pylon, consisting of a sandstone gateway between two brick towers. Even with all these additions, Amada is very small, for it measures barely 30 feet in width by 72 feet in depth, and the height is about

FIG. 248.—NORTH SIDE OF THE AVENUE OF RAMS AT KARNAK DURING THE INUNDATION. *(Phot. Legrain.)*

15 feet, but the execution is very careful, and does credit to the provincial Theban art of the Eighteenth Dynasty. The blocks are accurately adjusted, the sculpture is delicate, and the painting brilliant; the brush has accentuated the work of the chisel, and has expressed the details of figures and hieroglyphics with great elaboration. **The temple of Ptah at Karnak, built by the** the Amenemhāts and reconstructed by Thothmes III., was rebuilt so extensively under the Ptolemies that it would be imprudent to insist upon its original form; I think, however, that the arrangement must have resembled that of Amada. On the other hand, the temple of Rameses III. at Karnak is of a more developed type.

FIG. 249.—COURT OF AMENOPHIS III. AT LUXOR SEEN FROM THE NORTH EAST. *(Phot. Beato.)*

The chevet is here divided into three compartments with the sanctuary in the middle, and just as at Amada, the two rooms which terminate the wings open only into the sanctuary, but the remaining space contains, besides the chapels dedicated to the goddess and the divine son, serving-rooms, one of which, that on the west, does duty as the cage of the staircase which led to the terraces. In addition, the transverse vestibule of Amada has become a hypostyle hall with two rows of columns, and the pronaos is arranged, as is also the pylon, on a new plan which was applied on a larger scale at Medinet-Habû. It is on a higher level than that of the court, and is reached from the latter by an inclined plane; towards the east and the west it adjoins porticoes which terminate against the pylon, and colossal statues of the king as Osiris are set against the pillars which border these porticoes (Fig. 245). It is permissible to suppose that the temple of Mentu, built by Amenophis III., was similar in arrangement, but these ruins have not yet been sufficiently studied to justify an assertion. What we may, however, affirm without rashness is that the temple of the small town, as we see it

FIG. 250.—SOUTH-EAST OF THE TEMPLE OF AMENOPHIS III. AT LUXOR. *(Phot. Beato.)*

FIG. 251.
GREAT COLONNADE OF HERU-EM-HEB AND SETI I. AT THE TEMPLE OF LUXOR.

THE SECOND THEBAN AGE

at Amada, was simply a reduction of the temple of the great city, and that the arrangements were in the main the same in both. The sanctuary was at the end, against the back wall, between two rooms, or two series of rooms, the dwellings of the other gods of the triad, used for the secondary services of worship. A vestibule extending right across the building divided these intimate apartments from those regions accessible to the public, hypostyle halls, courts, monumental gateways flanked by towers; obelisks or a guard of sphinxes rose on the terrace in front.

FIG. 252.—SOUTH-WEST ANGLE OF THE COURT OF RAMESES II. AT THE TEMPLE OF LUXOR. *(Phot. Beato.)*

Well-preserved examples of this type are so rare that we cannot exactly follow its evolution between the Eighteenth and Nineteenth Dynasties. It culminated, towards the end of the Nineteenth Dynasty, in a conception of which the temple of Khonsu at Thebes is the most lucid and complete realisation. (Fig. 246). The distinction between the private dwelling of the god, and the space open to the public is clearly defined. The one is separated from the other by a wall in which two doors are pierced; the first, on the longitudinal axis, was a state portal, for solemn ceremonies, when Khonsu came out of his sanctuary, and for the official visits of the Pharaohs; the second, placed towards the western extremity, was the household postern, by which the priest came and went every day, and

FIG. 253.—ONE OF THE CHAPELS OF GEBEL-SILSILEH. *(Phot. Thédenat.)*

ART IN EGYPT

rooms which terminate the wings open only into the sanctuary, but the remaining space contains, besides the chapels dedicated to the goddess and the divine son, serving-rooms, one of which, that on the west, does duty as the cage of the staircase which led to the terraces. In addition, the transverse vestibule of Amada has become a hypostyle hall with two rows of columns, and the pronaos is arranged, as is also the pylon, on a new plan which was applied on a larger scale at Medinet-Habû. It is on a higher level than that of the court, and is reached from the latter by an inclined plane; towards the east and the west it adjoins porticoes which terminate against the pylon, and colossal statues of the king as Osiris are set against the pillars which border these porticoes (Fig. 245). It is permissible to suppose that the temple of Mentu, built by Amenophis III., was similar in arrangement, but these ruins have not yet been sufficiently studied to justify an assertion. What we may, however, affirm without rashness is that the temple of the small town, as we see it

FIG. 250.—SOUTH-EAST OF THE TEMPLE OF AMENOPHIS III. AT LUXOR. *(Phot. Beato.)*

FIG. 251.
GREAT COLONNADE OF HERU-EM-HEB AND SETI I. AT THE TEMPLE OF LUXOR.

THE SECOND THEBAN AGE

at Amada, was simply a reduction of the temple of the great city, and that the arrangements were in the main the same in both. The sanctuary was at the end, against the back wall, between two rooms, or two series of rooms, the dwellings of the other gods of the triad, used for the secondary services of worship. A vestibule extending right across the building divided these intimate apartments from those regions accessible to the public, hypostyle halls, courts, monumental gateways flanked by towers; obelisks or a guard of sphinxes rose on the terrace in front.

FIG. 252.—SOUTH-WEST ANGLE OF THE COURT OF RAMESES II. AT THE TEMPLE OF LUXOR. *(Phot. Beato.)*

Well-preserved examples of this type are so rare that we cannot exactly follow its evolution between the Eighteenth and Nineteenth Dynasties. It culminated, towards the end of the Nineteenth Dynasty, in a conception of which the temple of Khonsu at Thebes is the most lucid and complete realisation. (Fig. 246). The distinction between the private dwelling of the god, and the space open to the public is clearly defined. The one is separated from the other by a wall in which two doors are pierced; the first, on the longitudinal axis, was a state portal, for solemn ceremonies, when Khonsu came out of his sanctuary, and for the official visits of the Pharaohs; the second, placed towards the western extremity, was the household postern, by which the priest came and went every day, and

FIG. 253.—ONE OF THE CHAPELS OF GEBEL-SILSILEH. *(Phot. Thédenat.)*

135

ART IN EGYPT

was also used by the sovereign when he visited the god informally. Beyond this barrier, we find the tripartite arrangement I have described above; in the middle, the shrine of Khonsu, and on either side, the chapels of the paredri, then the serving-rooms, but with new combinations. In the temple of Rameses III. at Karnak, the Holy of Holies was a single chamber, in which not only the idol was enclosed, but also the *bari* on which the idol was seated when it left its retreat to show itself in public. In the temple of Khonsu, it consisted of three chambers in a line on the axis: first, against the end wall, a dark cabinet which was the mysterious residence of the master, then, in front of this, an anteroom with four columns, and finally, in front of the anteroom, a vast hall in the centre of which rose the pink granite cell which contained the ark. This cell had a back door by which the image was brought out on specified days for embarkation, and a front door from which it emerged in state. The chambers of the side-aisles communicated with one or the other of these three chambers, according to the use for which they were destined, those of the paredri with the ante-room, the others with the shrine of the boat. The staircase which led to the terraces was concealed on the right, in the angle formed by the exterior east wall, and the interior partition wall. Beyond this, the public parts of the building began, and, in the first place, the hypostyle hall which traversed it from east to west. The central aisle was defined by four columns with bell-shaped capitals 23 feet high, and the wings contain two lotus columns 18 feet high; the light is furnished, as at Karnak, by a clerestory between the terrace of the central aisle, and the lateral platforms. The pronaos is supported on twelve columns

FIG. 254.
PLAN OF THE SPEOS OF HERU-EM-HEB AT SILSILEH.

FIG. 255.
FAÇADE OF THE SPEOS OF HERU-EM-HEB. *(Phot. Thédenat.)*

THE SECOND THEBAN AGE

in two rows; an inclined way descends from it into the court, which is bordered south, east, and wes by a double row of lotus columns. Access was freely accorded by four lateral posterns, and by a pylon measuring 104 feet long, 60 high and 33 wide. It is solid, save for the staircase, which runs straight from the northeastern corner of the block to the platform over the door and thence to the summits of the two towers. The façade was grooved with four cavities to hold the masts for pennons. A pair of obelisks, and colossal statues rose in front, their backs to the pylon, their faces to the city (Fig. 247), often precedel by long avenues of sphinxes or rams (Fig. 248), and all these protected the god against evil influences. It is probable that the majority of the Ramesside temples were built on this plan with slight variations; it persisted during the centuries which followed the fall of the Second Theban Empire, and in its main lines, to the end of the pagan period.

FIG. 256.—FAÇADE OF THE HEMI-SPEOS OF BÊT-EL-WALÎ. *(Phot. Oropesa.)*

FIG. 257.—AVENUE OF SPHINXES AT WÂDÎ SABÛ'A. *(Phot. Oropesa.)*

In addition to these regular buildings, the constituents of which were brought together more or less on fixed principles, there

ART IN EGYPT

were some at Thebes, and no doubt in other great cities of Egypt, the arrangement of which does not agree with any recognised type, Luxor, as conceived by Amenophis III., is inspired by the same idea as the temple of Khonsu. It was to have a

FIG. 258.
SECTION OF THE HEMI-SPEOS OF GARF-HUSÊN (After Gau).

pylon turned to the north-east, a court with porticoes, at the end of which was the pronaos with its eight rows of lotus columns (Fig. 249), (almost a hypostyle hall left open in front), then behind this pronaos, the true hypostyle hall, which has lost its columns, and no longer extends right across the building; it is flanked right and left by dark rooms used for the most part as auxiliary chapels. As usual, the hypostyle hall and its annexes terminated the public part of the temple, and a wall, pierced with a state doorway and a service-postern, separated them from the actual abode of Amon. This comprised in its axis two rooms with four columns each, the farther one of which contained the sacred ark, then a second hypostyle hall, and against the back wall, a final room with columns, which was the sanctuary. Right and left of this row of apartments were successive chapels, in one of which, on the east, the marriage of Queen Mutemua with Amon, and the birth of Amenophis III were described and pictured; along the east and west walls little rooms, or rather closets, were ranged, the uses of which are not certainly known, but in which it is probable that clothes, jewels, perfumes, furniture, and gold and silver plate were stored (Fig. 250). The building was almost finished when the king,

FIG. 259.—FAÇADE OF THE LITTLE SPEOS AT ABU SIMBEL. *(Phot. Oropesa.)*

THE SECOND THEBAN AGE

modifying the design, replaced the pylon by a thick wall and laid on the north the foundations of another hypostyle hall, which, had it been completed, would have had no parallel. Only the central aisle with its columns 52 feet high was erected (Fig. 251), and the disturbances in the reign of Amenophis IV. compelled the architect to stop the decoration. When it was resumed, the course of the Nile had deviated eastward, and Heru-em-heb was obliged to deflect the main axis to find room for the new court (Fig. 252) and for a pylon which Rameses II. finished and faced with sculptures. Karnak shows more irregularity and incoherence even than Luxor, and this is not surprising, when we remember that all the Theban Pharaohs from the Seventeenth to the Twentieth Dynasty vied with each other in enlarging it without any definite plan. A big book would not be too much to devote to its history, and even this could not be complete, for lack of evidences bearing on the earlier periods. The original building, that of the Twelfth Dynasty, has disappeared, and we do not know what were its main features. The Ahmessids, from Amenophis I. to Thoth-

FIG. 260.—FAÇADE OF THE GREAT SPEOS OF ABU SIMBEL. *(Phot. Oropesa.)*

FIG. 261.—NORTHERN EXTREMITY OF THE ESPLANADE BEFORE THE GREAT SPEOS OF ABU SIMBEL. *(Phot. Oropesa)*

FIG. 262.
THE PYRAMID-MASTABA OF AN APIS AT SAKKARAH (After Mariette).

mes III., surrounded it with buildings which in some ways repeat the combinations at Luxor, with a room for the boat in the centre, and auxiliary chapels in the side aisles, but also with a perfectly novel element, three pylons rising one behind the other from east to west. Thothmes III., having reached this point, returned to the east, and there re-constructed some old buildings, the most imposing of which, an audience-chamber, bears the traditional, but inaccurate, name of ambulatory; he then enclosed the whole with a stone wall, dug out the lake on the south, and, anxious to provide a triumphal entrance for the god, erected two enormous pylons on the Luxor road, to which Heru-em-heb soon added two others. Thothmes IV. and Amenophis III. erected a still more massive pylon in front of those on the west,

FIG. 263.—A THEBAN TOMB WITH A PYRAMIDAL SUMMIT.

which Rameses I. preceded by another yet more gigantic: between the two he built the famous hypostyle hall which Seti I., Rameses II., and the Rameses of the Twentieth Dynasty finished decorating. Karnak is not, strictly speaking, a single temple; it is a haphazard mass of temples and storehouses (cf. Fig. 172). It must be looked upon in

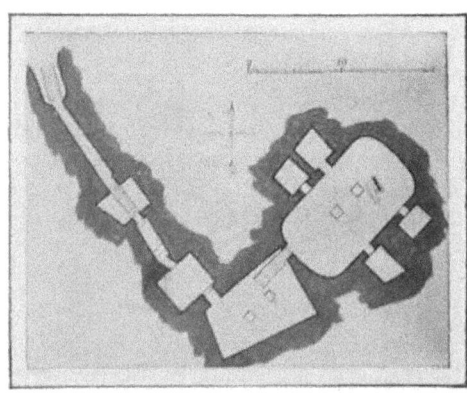

FIG. 264.—TOMB OF THOTHMES III.

140

THE SECOND THEBAN AGE

FIG. 265.—DECORATION OF THE END WALL IN THE TOMB-CHAMBER OF RAMESES V. *(Phot. Golenischeff.)*

the history of Egyptian art, not as a normal creature, long considered, and produced on a preconceived plan but rather as a marvellous monster, whose limbs are grafted on to the original body fortuitously, regardless of logic and symmetry. Taken in detail, the parts are often admirable in execution; when we attempt to coordinate them, we find it impossible to reduce them to unity.

With the ideas which prevailed in Egypt on the nature of the temple and the tomb, it was

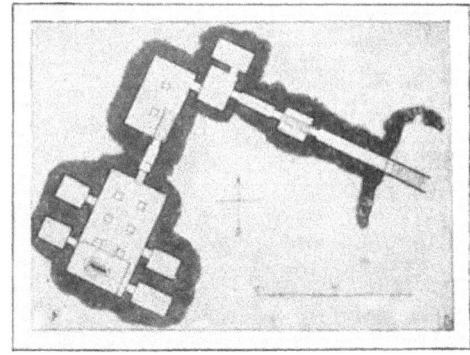

FIG. 266.—PLAN OF THE HYPOGEUM OF AMENOPHIS II.

inevitable that sooner or later it would be proposed to instal the house of the god in the rock. We have as yet no authority

ART IN EGYPT

FIG. 267.—GENERAL VIEW OF DÊR-EL-BAHARI. (Phot. Beato.)

for saying whether this came about under the Memphite or the first Theban Empire; the most ancient subterranean temples known to us, speos and hemi-speos, date from the Eighteenth Dynasty. Queen Hatshepset had a vestibule with eight pillars, a passage and an inner chamber, which was the sanctuary, cut in the rock near Beni-Hasan, in honour of the lioness-goddess Pekhet; two centuries later Seti I. hollowed the chapel of Redesiyeh on the road to the gold mines. When we examine these carefully, we find that the architect took the isolated temple of the small town, and imbedded it in the mountain. Occasionally it is only a single apartment, with a façade set between columns, as at Silsileh (Fig. 253), but the type of El-Kâb prevailed in general, and if the door-way connecting vestibule and sanctuary was elongated, and transformed into a passage, it was partly because the safety of the faithful required a stone partition more solid than an ordinary wall of ma-

FIG. 268.—NORTH-WEST ANGLE OF THE ESPLANADE AT DÊR-EL-BAHARI. (Phot. Beato.)

THE SECOND THEBAN AGE

sonry. Indeed, when we compare the cavern-temple in general with the disengaged temple, we must recognise that the arrangement of the two is in the main identical; the differences are the result of special conditions which the new surroundings imposed on the architect, and are not more marked than those which distinguish the free mastaba from the sepulchral chapel hollowed in the rock. The taste for the speos developed towards the end of the Eighteenth Dynasty, and two, not the least interesting among them, were the work of Heru-em-heb. At Silsileh (Fig. 255) the speos is a long gallery supported by four massive pillars left in the rock, with the sanctuary adjoining it at right angles (Fig. 254). Abahûda, a little to the north of the Second Cataract, has no true façade, but a portion of the cliff was planed vertically, a few steps were cut in

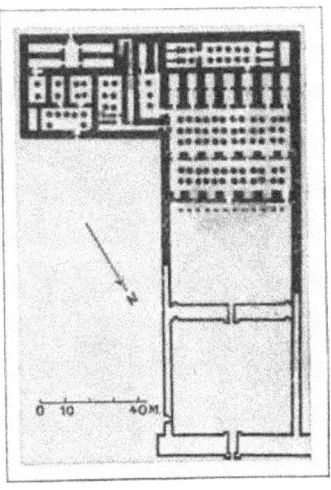

FIG. 269.
PLAN OF THE MEMNONIUM OF SETI I. AT ABYDOS.

front, and a high, narrow door, hardly more than a slit, was pierced in the rock. The hypostyle hall, supported by four polygonal columns, leads to the three usual chapels; these, however, instead of being arranged in a line, parallel one with another, are placed on the three sides, the sanctuary at the end, facing the entrance, the chambers of the mother and son right and left of the hypostyle hall. Rameses II showed a special preference for this type of building, and Nubia is full of those which he dedicated ostensibly to his father Amon, but in reality to his own divinity.

FIG. 270.—ONE OF THE HYPOSTYLE HALLS IN THE MEMNONIUM OF SETI I. *(Phot. Beato.)*

The oldest and the most elegant of all these, the hemi-speos of Bêt-el-Wali, has a deep vestibule,

ART IN EGYPT

FIG. 271.—FAÇADE OF A SEPULCHRAL TEMPLE AT KURNÂH. *(Phot. Beato.)*

suggested on the façade by two square pillars, and covered with a roof not cut in the rock, but vaulted with bricks (Fig. 256). Three doors — those on the sides are later than the central one — lead to the transverse vestibule, where two rather squat proto-Doric pillars have been cut out in the rock; the Holy of Holies contains three statues which represent the three gods of the local triad. At Wadi-es-Sabu'a, at Dêr, at Garf-Husên, the excavation and its outworks of masonry attained the dimensions of the isolated temple of a large town. The propylaea of Sabu'a, recently exhumed, form a magnificent array of colossal figures and sphinxes with human faces or falcons' heads (Fig. 257). Garf-Husên possessed a sanctuary, two hypostyle halls, the larger upheld by pillars adorned with Atlantes, a court with porticoes of the same type as that of the Ramesseum, a pylon, courts, and an avenue of sphinxes (Fig. 258). The little speos of Abu Simbel is less complex in design. Its façade towards the river is decorated with six colossal standing figures in niches, four for Rameses II, two for his wife Nefert-âri (Fig. 259). The hypostyle hall has six polygonal pillars, on the summits of which heads

FIG. 272.—GENERAL VIEW OF THE RAMESSEUM OF THEBES. *(Phot. Beato.)*

THE SECOND THEBAN AGE

of Hathor are placed instead of capitals. It communicates with the vestibule by three doors, and three chapels are connected with the vestibule, the sanctuary in the centre, facing the entrance, the other two at the two extremities. The large adjoining speos (Fig. 260) is a complete temple, built in the spirit which governed the plan of the isolated temples, and containing all the constituent parts of these. First of all there is an esplanade of beaten earth; a short flight of steps connects it with a terrace, bordered by a solid balustrade, behind which rose in a single line twenty figures of alternate Osiris-mummies and falcons (Fig. 261), eight to the right and eight to the left of the central landing. Behind this line,

FIG. 273.—STOREHOUSES WITH BRICK VAULTS IN THE RAMESSEUM. (Phot. Baraize.)

the slanting pylon, cut in the rock, presents its vast surface, the four prescribed colossal statues watching impassibly along it. Beyond the pylon, in the place of the covered court, was a hall 130 feet long, bordered, like the court of Rameses III. at Karnak, by eight square pillars, each with an Osiris set against it.

FIG. 274.—SECOND COURT OF THE TEMPLE OF MEDINET-HABÙ. (Phot. Beato.)

This sort of covered yard was followed by the hypostyle hall, and, at the end of this was the sanctuary between

ART IN EGYPT

the cells of the paredri. Eight crypts, on a lower level than the central nave, were distributed unequally on either side, simulating the accessory chambers.

FIG. 275.—FAÇADE OF THE PALACE OF RAMESES III, TOWARDS THE FIRST COURT OF THE TEMPLE AT MEDINET-HABÛ. (Phot. Beato.)

The differences and inequalities of the arrangement are explained by the necessity imposed upon the builder of choosing the most solid strata in the stone, and of making sure that his work should not be crushed by the mountain.

If the isolated temple thus buried itself in imitation of the old sepulchral chapels, these, by an inverse phenomenon, were often detached from the hypogea to which they belonged, and became isolated temples. Tombs of private persons were of two sorts, as in the first Theban period; one, hollowed out entirely in the cliff, the other in the manner of pyramid-mastabas, but with important modifications in the relative importance of the pyramid and the mastaba. The latter, which at first had been gradually decreased till it became merely an insignificant base, steadily grew until it almost recovered its original size, while the pyramid shrank to the dimensions of the pyramidium on an obelisk. There is only, as far as I know, a single specimen of the kind, the chapel of Apis discovered by Mariette in the Serapeum sixty years ago (Fig. 262). The mastaba is still in existence, a chamber of masonry perched on

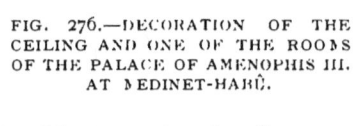

FIG. 276.—DECORATION OF THE CEILING AND ONE OF THE ROOMS OF THE PALACE OF AMENOPHIS III. AT MEDINET-HABÛ.

THE SECOND THEBAN AGE

a solid basement, adorned on the outside, towards the corners, with polygonal engaged columns, and crowned with a cavetto. The pyramidium has disappeared almost entirely, and the vault is under the building, but independent of it; it is approached by an inclined plane which descends into the ground a little way in front of the door of the mastaba. Monuments of this kind abounded at Thebes, but they have

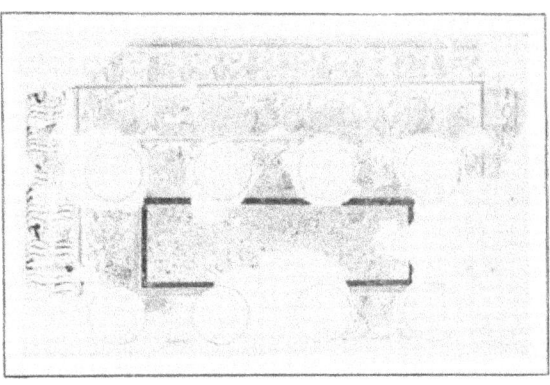

FIG. 277.
PAVEMENT OF ONE OF THE HALLS OF THE PALACE OF AMENOPHIS IV. AT EL-AMARNA.

all been destroyed, and we should not suspect their existence were they not frequently represented in paintings. The pyramidium was more or less pointed, and it was built of brick; a gable-window was occasionally pierced in it which gave light to the interior, and it terminated in a point of black stone, either granite or schist (Fig. 263). The hypogea properly so-called, with which the Theban mountains are riddled, so to say, still followed the tradition of the Twelfth Dynasty in so far as to retain the hypostyle hall behind the façade, but the available space was restricted, and in order to economise this, a less ambitious plan was adopted from the beginning of the Eighteenth Dynasty. It shows generally an open court, roughly quarried in the hillside, where the preliminary rites of burial

FIG. 278.
DETAIL OF A PAVEMENT IN THE PALACE OF AMENOPHIS III. AT MEDINET-HABU.

were performed, then a long, narrow ante-room, to the end of which the stele was often relegated; its decoration included

FIG. 279.—THE MIGDOL AT MEDINET-HABÛ. *(Phot. Thédenat.)*

FIG. 280.—SKETCH IN BLACK ON ONE OF THE PILLARS OF THE HYPOGEUM OF SETI I. *(Phot. Insinger.)*

representations of the various scenes of burial, the funeral banquet, the music, the dances, even the fishing, hunting, and agricultural labours which ensured the nourishment of the deceased. On rare occasions, the form of a Greek cross was admitted for the arrangement of the chapel; but nearly always it was merely an oblong cell, or even a blind alley, at the end of which the deceased and his family sat, carved out in the rock. The vault was concealed somewhere below, sometimes in one place, sometimes in another; it was approached either by a perpendicular shaft, a passage, or a steep staircase. Large fortunes were evidently rarer at Thebes than they had formerly been at Memphis, but competences abounded, and their possessors peopled the cemeteries of Asasif, Sheikh-Abdel-Kurnah, Dêr-el-Medinet, and Kurnet-Murrai; nearly all the gaily painted and delicately carved hypogea which visitors admire in these places were the work of artists paid by these people.

The tombs of the first Pharaohs of the Eighteenth Dynasty, Kames, Aahmes, Amenophis I., were pyramid-mastabas of the same kind as those of Menthu-hetep at Dêr-el-Bahari, but situated near Drahabu'l-Nekkah, on the boundaries of the cultivated land; with Thothmes I. the conception changed, and

THE SECOND THEBAN AGE

a new system was established, which was faithfully observed for nearly five centuries. The parts of the tomb were divided into two groups; the subterranean chambers were exiled to the desert, behind the heights which bounded the plain on the north, in the valley now called Bibân-el-Muluk, the Gate of the Kings; the visible elements remained on the southern slope of the mountains and in the plain, at Dêr-el-Bahari, Sheikh-Abd-el-Kurnah, and Medinet-Habû. Like the main body or subterranean portion of the earlier Memphite pyramid, the Theban hill contains only the vault and the passages leading to it. At first this kind of hypogeum was fairly small; that of Thothmes I. is concealed at the bottom of a hole, in the base of the cliff itself. A steep

FIG. 281.—SKETCH IN THE TOMB OF KHA-EM-HET (After *Prisse* d'Avennes).

staircase brings one down into a square ante-room, where a second staircase leads to the vault. This is an elongated parallelogram, the angles rounded in such a manner as to resemble a cartouche; a cell cut out towards the end, in the left wall, formed a kind of *serdab*. The entrance is on the east, but the axis of the passages and rooms deviates continuously to the left in such a manner as to bring back the coffin to the west by a kind of imperfect arc of a circle, and the same orientation persisted until the end of the dynasty, regulated however in such a manner that the axis, instead of describing a curve, traces two straight lines which join at a more or less acute angle. The passages

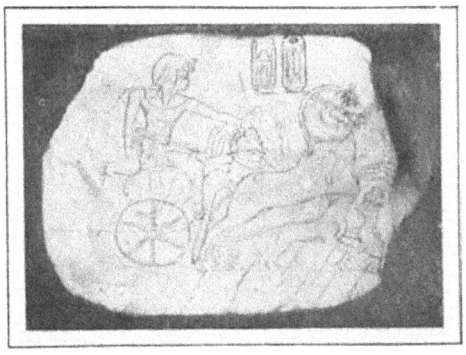

FIG. 282.—THE KING CHARGING (Ostrakon in the Museum, Cairo). *(Phot. E. Brugsch.)*

ART IN EGYPT

FIG. 283.
THE KING BRINGING IN A PRISONER (Ostrakon in the Museum, Cairo).
(Phot. E. Brugsch.)

and the descending staircases led to a square well, generally some 30 feet deep, designed not only to check the advance of the violators of tombs, but to receive water that might invade them during storms. Beyond this obstacle, just opposite the passage of approach, and on a level with it, a door was masked in the wall, giving access to a room with two pillars: it was here, generally speaking, that the axis, turning back upon itself, deviated to the west. Another staircase was set in the left angle of the hypostyle room; it was followed by a slightly inclined passage, leading to the vault; this sometimes has sustaining pillars, and it is flanked by rooms used for depositing offerings, generally four in number. The tombs of Hatshepset, of Thothmes III. (Fig. 264), and IV., of Amenophis II. (Fig. 266) and III., of Heru-em-heb, and later, that of Rameses II., were all on this plan, with variations more or less marked in the number of the

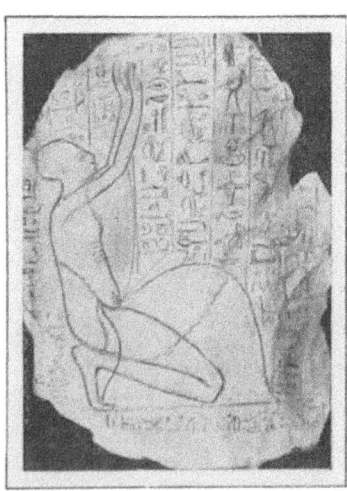

FIG. 284.—A PRIEST PRAYING (Ostrakon in the Museum, Cairo).
(Phot. E. Brugsch.)

FIG. 285.—TWO WRESTLERS (Ostrakon in the Museum, Cairo).
(Phot. E. Brugsch.)

THE SECOND THEBAN AGE

rooms, and the extent of the different parts; the corridor leading to the chambers of Hatshepset is 700 feet long. Towards the beginning of the Nineteenth Dynasty, architects simplified the lines, and straightening the axis, they made it run directly from one end to the other, or with a slight deviation to the side where the well was to be placed. The best known example is the hypogeum of Seti I., with its string of rooms, the last of which, left unfinished, is 325 feet from the outer door. Each Pharaoh made a more or less happy variation on this theme for himself; some, like Rameses III., multiplied the cells right and left of the first passage; others, on the contrary, reduced their number, like the last Rameses of the Twentieth Dynasty. The chief interest does not, however, lie in the architectural arrangements, which are, as we have seen, simple enough, but in the carved and painted decorations, and in the scenes and inscriptions (Fig. 265) which give us definite information as to the mystical doctrines of the Ramesside age.

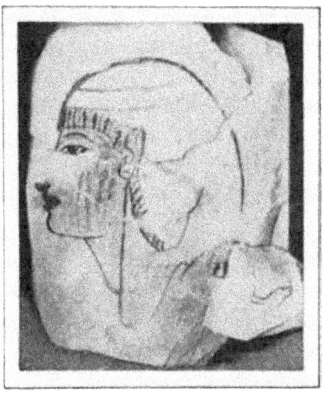

FIG. 286.—HEAD DRAWN IN OUTLINE IN BLACK, HEIGHTENED WITH RED (Ostrakon in the Museum, Cairo). *(Phot. E. Brugsch.)*

The plan of the chapels was so ambitious that they are for the most part temples comparable to those of the right bank. The oldest, that of the two Thothmes and Queen Hatshepset, one of the most original and finished works of Egyptian art, is what is now known as Dêr-el-Bahari, from the Coptic monastery founded among its ruins in the sixth century of our era (Fig. 267). The sanctuaries it contains — the central sanctuary of Amon, of Thothmes and of the Queen,

FIG. 287.—A DANCING GIRL (Ostrakon in the Museum, Turin). *(Phot. Lanzone.)*

151

the sanctuary of Hathor, the sanctuary of Anubis, are cut out in the rock, and give it the character of the hemi-speos; the rest is of detached masonry. Placed beside the pyramid-mastaba of Menthu-hetep, it might be supposed that it would have borrowed certain elements from this; but such is not the case, and never were two buildings more dissimilar. It filled all the northern hollow of the valley, and presented the most imposing appearance to those who approached it by the plain. Three terraces rise in recession one above the other, connected by two gently inclined planes along which ran a serpent with scaly folds sculptured in the limestone. The lower terraces were adorned with porticoes on three sides, those on the west supported by square pillars, and that on the north by polygonal columns of dazzling whiteness: the spirit of the design is so noble, and the contour so pure, that it might almost be a Greek colonnade transported from the Parthenon to the heart of the Thebaïd (Fig. 268). The third terrace was enclosed in front by a straight limestone wall, behind which the sanctuary extended freely. Like the private precincts of the non-funerary temples, it was divided into three compartments parallel one to another. In the centre was the abode of the god, with its hypostyle hall (now destroyed), and its mysterious chambers in the rock. On the

FIG. 288.—A COUPLE OF THEBAN CITIZENS (After a water-colour by H. Carter).

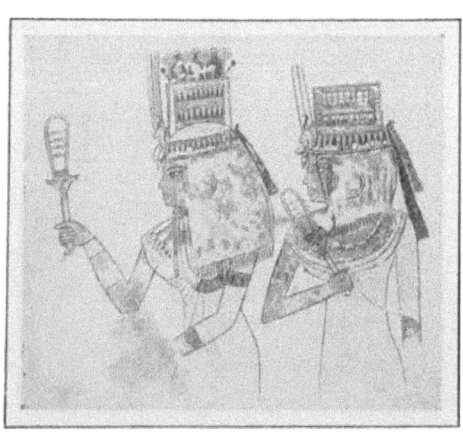

FIG. 289.—TWO MUSICIAN-PRIESTESSES (After a water-colour by H. Carter).

THE SECOND THEBAN AGE

north side, the apartments of the living Horus, identified with Pharaoh, are grouped round a court in which the altar of Harmachis is still standing. In the left aisle, sacred to the divine son, the dead king lodged when he pleased. By a fiction which will not seem strange to those familiar with the Egyptian doctrines, Pharaoh's *double*, when weary of his solitude at Bibân-el-Muluk, left it at will for his sepulchral temple, where he enjoyed the society of the priests who administered his worship.

FIG. 290.—THE TWO YOUNG DAUGHTERS OF AMENOPHIS IV. AT EL-AMARNA.

A kind of temporary lodging was accordingly provided for him, a set of half-a-dozen rooms, one at least of which had an arched ceiling, while in parts its decorations recall those of the Memphite mastabas. The vault was not, indeed, a true vault with a central keystone, but was upheld by corbels. It was no easy task to arrange this corner of the mountain in a manner which, while satisfying all the demands of ritual and doctrine, did not completely rob it of its wild grandeur; here again the Theban architects showed with what technical skill and feeling for nature they adapted the style of their works to the landscape in which they set them.

It is with Dêr-el-Bahari that the Memnonium of Seti I. at Abydos has most analogy (Fig. 269). It is not a hemi-speos, but something intermediate between this and the isolated temple: a temple set against a low hill and partly imbedded in it. Seti had con-

FIG. 291.—SKETCH, WITH AN OUTLINE IMITATING A SCULPTURED CONTOUR IN ONE OF THE TOMBS OF SHEIKH-ABD-EL-KURNÀH. (*Phot. Insinger.*)

153

tented himself for his Theban worship with a place in the building which his father Rameses I. had built at Kûrnah (Fig. 271), but it pleased him to have at Abydos, not exactly a cenotaph, but a resting-place where his *double*, escaping from the darkness of his Theban syrinx, might shelter at leisure under the protection of the tomb of Osiris. He therefore retained the features essential to a temple: pylon, courts, a portico, two hypostyle halls (Fig. 270); then, as there was not room to continue the building to the west without rasing the hill entirely, he reduced the sanctuary and its adjoining chambers to two rows parallel with the façade, the last abutting on the masses of sand. The dividing wall is accordingly pierced with seven doors at equal distances, which lead into as many oblong chambers vaulted on corbels; six of them are closed at the back, but the third on the right is open each end, as befits a chamber for the sacred boat. Passing through it, we come to the little hypostyle hall essential to the plan, and the mysterious chambers, instead of being grouped behind it, are ranged right and left at the sides. And as if this were not enough, the refuge of the deceased sovereign with all its dependencies was thrown out on the left, in a special wing, detached from the main building, and forming a square. Some hundred metres away, Rameses II., choosing a piece of ground which was less uneven, erected a second resting-place on the regular plan, the same used for his funerary chapel at the Ramesseum in the Theban plain (Fig. 272). Chance, which does not always favour the excavator, has preserved for us with this last the crowd of storehouses (Fig. 273), stables, houses of priests or artisans, festival or assembly halls, which clustered round the temples and made each of them the kernel of a veritable city; considerable portions are missing, however, and we should not be able to reconstitute the ar-

FIG. 292.—NORTH WALL OF THE FIRST CHAMBER IN THE TOMB OF NAKHT. *(Phot. Beato.)*

THE SECOND THEBAN AGE

rangement with any certainty, had not Rameses III., that plagiarist of Rameses II., imitated them faithfully at Medinet-Habû (Fig. 274). By combining the two, we are able to see what was the scheme finally adopted by the Ramessids for their mortuary temples. There was first, as in the living temple, a pylon-façade, then a court, the northern portico of which was guarded by Atlantes set against pillars (Fig. 231), a second pylon, a second court with porticoes, and at the end of this, a pronaos on a raised platform, to which access was obtained by a flight of shallow steps. Behind the pronaos was the hypostyle hall, hemmed in between two rows of chapels or store-rooms, and the private apartments of the god began beyond this again, in three parallel lines as usual, the god in the centre with his hypostyle halls and his chamber, the living Horus on the right, the deceased sovereign on the left. Medinet-Habû is the subtlest

FIG. 293.—FRAGMENT OF THE BATTLE OF KADESH IN THE RAMESSEUM AT THEBES. *(Phot. Beato.)*

expression of the conceptions of the Theban priesthood as to the destiny of the royal soul, and the means by which its future was to be ensured. The architect made his art subservient to doctrine, and combining that which was indispensable to the existence of the gods with that which was essential for the perpetuity of the *double*, he welded the whole into a grandiose and harmonious creation. Would he have done better still later? Rameses III. was the last of the great conquerors, and his successors, lacking the resources provided by foreign warfare, undertook no such vast structural enterprises as his. They usurped more or less successfully a corner of the temples their ancestors had prepared, and, graving their names upon them, appropriated their revenues.

Just as the Memphite Pharaohs of an earlier age and the first Thebans had lived in sight of and in daily contact with their pyramids, so the second Thebans did not shrink from attaching their dwellings to their sepulchral temples. Even in the Ramesseum, we find on the left of the first court the levelling courses of a building, the arrangement of the rooms in which show it to have been a habitation, one of the houses of Rameses II. At Medinet-Habû, we find similar ruins in the same situation; the south porch of the first court, with its eight bell-shaped columns, was, as it were, the religious face of a palace of Rameses III., now destroyed (Fig. 275). Three doors opened into it, and from a sort of tribune the balcony of which projected from the centre of the wall, Pharaoh took part in the ceremonial of worship without having to mingle with the crowd. The building was in brick, with details of stone and enamelled earthenware; it has been ravaged by antiquity-hunters, and collectors of manure, but the remains of a villa of Amenophis III., still visible

FIG. 294.—THE MENEPTAH WITH TWO ENSIGNS (Museum, Cairo). (Phot. E. Brugsch.)

FIG. 295. RAMESES II. BETWEEN AMON AND MUT (Museum, Cairo). (Phot. E. Brugsch.)

FIG. 296.—CROUCHING FIGURE HOLDING A DIVINITY (Museum, Cairo). (Phot. Legrain.)

about 1200 yards further south, give us an idea of what it was. Like the feudal castle of our own past, the Theban palace was

FIG. 297.—KNEELING FIGURE CARRYING A TRIAD (Museum, Cairo). *(Phot E. Brugsch.).*

FIG. 298.—A PERSON SEATED ON THE GROUND WITH ONE LEG FLAT (Museum, Cairo). *(Phot. E. Brugsch.)*

rectangular on plan, and a solid wall, almost without doors or windows, enclosed it. When this was passed, one entered a labyrinth of little courts, columned rooms, alcoves, and dark cells leading one into the other and often ending in a blind alley. The main parts of the structure are of sun-dried bricks, some of them stamped with the royal cartouche. The floor is of beaten clay, so firmly pounded that it is almost as hard as stone. The walls were plastered with a coating of mud similar to that still used in Egyptian villages. The appearance of the various places does not everywhere suggest how domestic life was carried on in these interiors. We may, however, surmise that two oblong halls, upheld by two parallel lines of wooden columns with limestone bases,

FIG. 299. SURVEYOR WITH HIS LINE (Museum, Cairo). *(Phot. E. Brugsch.)*

were guard-rooms; courtiers and officers of the crown no doubt thronged them, taking up their positions in hierarchical order on audience-days. A modest ante-room led thence into the

FIG. 300.—RAMESES PUSHING A BOAT (DESTROYED) (Museum, Cairo). *(Phot. E. Brugsch.)*

private apartment, where persons honoured by admission to the royal presence saw before them, enframed between two painted wooden columns, the daïs on which Pharaoh deigned to show himself. Bath-rooms were numerous; three of these still contain the water-conduits and the stone slabs on which the bather crouched or lay to be dried or massaged. Several bedrooms follow one another close by, with the platform on which the bed was raised. Other rooms, small and bare, seem to have been for the use of servants; it is not known where the kitchens and store-rooms were situated. To sum up, we have here one of those princely residences of which there are so many not very comprehensible sketches in the tombs of El-Amarna. They were slight in structure like the houses of modern Egypt, but covered with paintings which disguised the poverty of the material. Vultures with outspread wings hovered on the ceilings, together with flights of pigeons (Fig. 276), or ducks imprisoned in frames of undulating lines or many-coloured spirals. On the pavements fountains were traced,

FIG. 301.—AMENOPHIS II. AND THE SERPENT MARITSAKRO (Museum, Cairo). *(Phot. E. Brugsch.)*

THE SECOND THEBAN AGE

or thickets of aquatic plants, where oxen graze and frolic (Fig. 277); fish swim under the water, ducks cruise among the lotuses (Fig. 278), and captives bound in constrained attitudes are ranged in lines along the banks.

Civil architecture seems therefore to have progressed, and perhaps if we knew more of the palaces of the Memphite age, comparison would show those of the Thebans to have been richer in treatment, and more complex in arrangement; military architecture had not been modified in any way, and the reason of its immobility is obvious. The conditions of war on the banks of the Nile had not changed since the old days, and since the expulsion of the Shepherds, conquering Egypt had never experienced a reverse serious enough to cause her to reconstruct the walls of her towns on a new plan. Not that the Pharaohs had not, in Syria, attacked stone citadels built on the most scientific principles; only one of them, however, Rameses III., gave himself the pleasure of showing his good Thebans what he had seen in Syria, by way of commemorating his victories. Across the eastern front of

FIG. 302.—TWO PRISONERS TIED BACK TO BACK (Museum, Cairo). *(Phot. E. Brugsch).*

A JAR (Museum, Cairo). *(Phot. E. Brugsch.)*
FIG. 303.—SLAVE BEARING

FIG. 304.—GROTESQUE SLAVE BEARING A JAR (Museum, Cairo). *(Phot. E. Brugsch.)*

159

ART IN EGYPT

FIG. 305.—QUEEN TUITISHERE (British Museum). *(Phot. Perrin.)*

FIG. 306.—STATUE OF AMENOPHIS I. (Museum, Turin). *(Phot. Petrie.)*

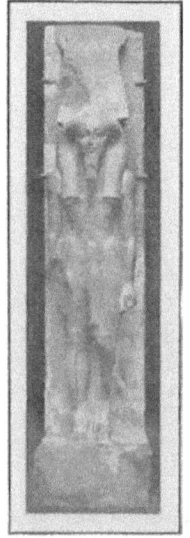

FIG. 307.—STATUE OF AMENOPHIS I. (Museum, Cairo). *(Phot. E. Brugsch.)*

his sepulchral chapel at Medinet-Habû, he raised a battlemented wall of sandstone, averaging about 13 feet in height. This was the equivalent of the brick screen of the old Egyptian fortresses, and the rampart it covered was of brick, but the first gateway has the appearance of a veritable *migdol*, a pair of pincers in masonry, gripping a parade-ground which diminishes sharply; the two branches are reunited at the end by a building of two storeys where the real entrance appears (Fig. 279). The towers are about 70 feet high. The base is sloping, to prevent sappers from approaching the foot of the wall, and to cause the projectiles thrown by the defenders from the curtain to ricochet against their assailants. This is a solitary example, and here again the Egyptians, having proved themselves skilful imitators of the foreigner, returned to their secular habits. Thus, during these centuries of prosperity, all their natural talents and all their faculties of invention seem to have been concentrated on a single object, the perpetual aggrandisement and embellishment of the temple, whether as the lodging of the gods, or the refuge of dead

THE SECOND THEBAN AGE

kings whose souls wearied of the darkness of the hypogeum. They did not at once realise the ideal they had set before themselves, and so many monuments have perished that we are no longer able to reconstitute the series of forms through which they passed, before reaching the complex types of Luxor and Medinet-Habû. I have tried to note a few, but there are others to study. Actual results impress us most strongly with the richness of inspiration to which these buildings bear witness, and the vigour with which

FIG. 308.
HEAD OF AN ATLAS OF THOTHMES I.
(Museum, Cairo). *(Phot. Legrain.)*

their builders realised their boldest inventions *in situ;* no architects have ever rivalled them in the treatment of mass, and the Pharaohs made no vain boast when they declared in their inscriptions that they had erected imperishable stones. True, these admirable unknown artists did not all show equal talent, and the mediocre is not entirely absent in the work, but many of them proved themselves true men of genius, and their names, had they been transmitted to us by their contemporaries, would deserve to be inscribed side by side with those of the artists to whom we owe the noblest monuments of Greece and Rome. The temple as created by them is one of the most original and mighty conceptions of the human intellect, not only in Egypt under the Theban dynasties, but among all peoples and in all ages.

B. PAINTING AND SCULPTURE.

In painting and sculpture, as in architecture, relics are almost innumerable, and they follow in such strict chronological order that we may study the

FIG. 309.—QUEEN ISIS (Museum, Cairo). *(Phot. E. Brugsch.)*

ART IN EGYPT

FIG. 310.—HEAD OF A STATUE OF THOTHMES III. (Museum, Cairo). *(Phot. E. Brugsch.)*

development of one of the great schools, the Theban, if not from year to year, at least from reign to reign. This is not the case of the others, save perhaps that of Abydos; at Hermopolis and Memphis, and in the Delta, our lack of knowledge is such that we cannot as yet discern the progress of art. If, however, we compare and co-ordinate the data we have gained, we are enabled to deduce from them a number of facts and conclusions applicable not only to Thebes, but to the whole of Egypt.

In the first place, the principles and methods of decorative art underwent such serious modification, that it is impossible to confound certain series of bas-reliefs and funerary or martial pictures of the second Theban Empire with similar pictures of the Twelfth Dynasty and the Memphite age. The design remains just as pure (Fig. 280) and the sketches in black in the tomb of Seti I. and certain Theban hypogea (Fig. 281) will bear comparison with the best of those which abound in the mastabas of Sakkarah or Gizeh. But the boldness of the artist has grown with the practice of centuries, and he attacks compositions and movements which would have discouraged his ancestors. The rough sketches drawn upon fragments of stone by the band who decorated the syrinx of Rameses IV. bear witness to amazing firmness of touch and an inexhaustible variety of imagination. Whether the king charges at the utmost speed of his horses (Fig. 282), or walking sedately, brings a minute prisoner to the gods (Fig. 283); whether the kneeling priest raises his hands to heaven in prayer (Fig. 284), or

FIG. 311. THOTHMES IV. AND HIS MOTHER (Museum, Cairo). *(Phot. E. Brugsch.)*

THE SECOND THEBAN AGE

two wrestlers close before seizing each other (Fig. 285), the line is always equally flexible and boldly touched; a certain head of a man heightened with a few dashes of red (Fig. 286) is a marvel of swift precision, and few of our contemporaries could have given a more realistic rendering of the girl-acrobat, throwing herself back for a somersault, on the ostrakon at Turin (Fig. 287). We find the same freedom, combined with a greater delicacy of line, in the finished pictures at Sheikh-Abd-el-Kurnah, a couple of citizens (Fig. 288), a pair of musician-priestesses (Fig. 289), and, at El-Amarna, the two little nude princesses on their cushion, caressing one another with gentle and ingenuous gestures (Fig. 290). The composition, too, has matured, and is almost equal to the drawing. The Memphite artist had been wont to resolve the simultaneous operations of an agricultural scene or of a battle into their simple elements, which he superposed in independent rows. The Theban, under the Ahmessids and their successors, did not discard the artifice of the various registers; he even adhered to it strictly in the treatment of religious subjects;

FIG. 312.—THE GODDESS SEKHET AT KARNAK. *(Phot. Legrain.)*

neither in a temple nor in a tomb did he cease to observe the tradition bequeathed to him by antiquity. But it was no longer the same when he passed from pictures of the divine to those of civil or military life, and this greater liberty is explained at least in part by the constant progress made by painting from the preceding age onwards. Without entirely abandoning its part as the auxiliary of sculpture, it had learned to separate itself from it, and to dispense with its collaboration upon occasion. As I have already indicated, the nature of the Theban mountains had a good deal to do with this. They consist of a very fine limestone, the strata of which were dislocated by some

FIG. 313.—STATUE OF A MONKEY (Museum, Cairo). *(Phot. E. Brugsch.)*

ART IN EGYPT

remote cataclysm, in such a manner that it does not lend themselves everywhere to the work of the chisel with the same facility. Though solid enough in the Valley of the Kings, it cracks in every direction at Sheikh-Abd-el-Kûrnah, and is full of huge flints, which had first to be removed, and then replaced by inserted fragments. Hence, inm any cases the decorators of tombs were content to cover the surface with a plaster which hid the defects, and to paint on this in distemper what they would have carved under more favourable conditions. Seduced by the facilities of the brush, they became even more emancipated than their precursors of the Twelfth Dynasty. They multiplied the motives on their ceilings, and added to the stars and geometrical designs which had hitherto predominated, elements borrowed from nature, single florets, bouquets of lotus, bulls' heads, flying birds, groups of hieroglyphs of the happiest effect. They continued, from a lingering respect for the traditions of the past, to surround their figures with a line which recalled the effects of the primitive reliefs (Fig. 291), but they grouped them in attitudes increasingly natural, and they broke down the tyranny of the superposed registers. Thenceforth, if, wishing to represent work in the fields, they chose to

FIG. 314.
ONE OF THE LIONS OF GEBEL-BARKAL
(British Museum, London).

FIG. 315.—CHAPEL OF THE COW HATHOR
(Museum, Cairo). *(Phot. E. Brugsch.)*

express it, as we do, by the normal methods of perspective, they were free to do so. As in the tomb of Nakht, they set upon the walls, at various heights, according to distance, the persons who play a part in the action: the dead man superintending his workmen, ploughmen turning the furrow, the sower scattering seed, labourers breaking the sod with pickaxes, a woodman cutting down a tree, the thirsty toiler taking a draught from his leather jar (Fig. 292). The experiment is a clumsy one, more akin to the scenes on a Chinese screen than to our landscapes, but it is an essay in perspective, and this is no isolated example; we find several others in the painted hypogea of Sheikh-Abd-el-Kûrnah. From fresco, the method passed rapidly to bas-relief, and we find it on pylons; here the artist gives us, not offerings and sacrifices, but battles, as at Luxor and the Ramesseum, where the entire surface is one vast composition, in which the actors assemble and disperse without any separation of the planes by lines (Fig. 293). There is no unity of action, but a complete narrative is set forth, some of the incidents of which are historical, as, for instance, the battle of Kadesh, the council of war held by the Egyptian generals, and the report of the spies, the surprise of the camp by the Hittites, Rameses II. charging, the arrival of the reinforcements, the battle on the banks of the Orontes, the sortie of the Amorrhaeans who saved the remnant of the Asiatic army. As we

FIG. 316.—BAS-RELIEF OF THE COW HATHOR (Museum, Cairo). *(Phot. E. Brugsch.)*

FIG. 317.—THE COW OF DÊR-EL-BAHARI (Museum, Cairo). *(Phot. E. Brugsch.)*

ART IN EGYPT

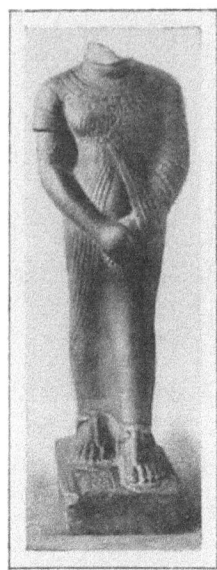

FIG. 318.—STATUE OF AMENOPHIS III. CLOTHED IN THE ASSYRIAN MANNER. *(Phot. Chassinat.)*

know the main theme from literary texts, we do not find any great difficulty in interpreting the artistic developments of it, but it must be admitted that if we had only the picture, it would be very difficult for us to establish the chronology of events and distinguish their progress with any certainty. The Ramesside artist was as yet incapable of discerning the decisive moments and seizing the critical point of a battle; he piled up his incidents in a more or less haphazard fashion, without troubling about the time when they happened, and their influence upon the final result. His chief concern was to make the presence of Pharaoh conspicuous, and to rivet attention upon him. In every crisis, he grouped the secondary personages round the king, and the better to draw the eye of the spectator to this figure, he made him of heroic size. At Luxor as in the Ramesseum. Rameses II., standing in his chariot, and piercing the flying Asiatics with his shafts, is the centre of the action. The artifice which consists in attributing colossal proportions to the prince, is puerile in itself; but in a huge "machine" such as the illustrated record of a battle, it is, after all, the only means of giving a kind of unity to the decoration.

Progress in less apparent in sculpture, and it was long supposed that here artists had merely carried on the Memphite tradition, while falsifying and degrading it. We so often recognise the formulæ of the age of the Pyramids in their works, that we get the impression that nothing had been changed; but as soon as we examine their details, we find that novelties abound. Let us take, for instance,

FIG. 319.—COLOSSAL GROUP OF AMENOPHIS III. AND THI (Museum, Cairo). *(Phot. E. Brugsch.)*

THE SECOND THEBAN AGE

the erect figure, sovereign or subject, receiving homage. He stands straight and firm, one foot advanced, but his hands, which formerly were either empty, or grasped a fragment of a sceptre or a handkerchief, are now loaded with gigantic emblems. These are in general sacred ensigns, stout halberds surmounted by the head of a human or animal divinity; sometimes he is content with one, sometimes he demands two (Fig. 294), the lower extremities of which rest on the ground beside his feet, while their faces enframe his head right and left. Groups of two seated persons, or triads incorporated with a supporting slab at the back, like the Rameses II. between Amon and Mut (Fig. 295), are conceived entirely in the ancient taste, but in the isolated figures, the sitter does not merely lay his right hand on his breast, like the Rahetep at Mêdûm; he grasps an Osirian crook, a scourge, a scroll, or, if a woman, a handkerchief, a spray of blossom, a sistrum. The kneeling or crouching figure, which has become frequent, bears in front of it an altar, a naos, a triad (Fig. 297), a statuette of a divinity (Fig. 296); a roll of rope, surmounted by a ram's head, denotes the calling of land-surveyor exercised by the model (Fig. 299). Other types present themselves which never occurred among the earlier works, such as that of a person seated with one knee drawn up,

FIG 320.—THE TWO COLOSSAL FIGURES OF MEMNON AT THEBES. *(Phot. Beato.)*

FIG. 321.
AMENOPHIS, SON OF HAPU
(Museum, Cairo). *(Phot. Legrain.)*

ART IN EGYPT

FIG. 322.
AMENOPHIS, THE CROUCHING SCRIBE
(Museum, Cairo). *(Phot. E. Brugsch.)*

the other flat against the ground under him (Fig. 298), and that of the kneeling king who drags himself along the ground in front of the god, pushing an object of worship or an offering, an altar, a jar, or a sacred boat (Fig. 300). In like manner, scenes which existed only in bas-reliefs on the walls, are detached from it, and become stone groups; the king standing between Horus and Set, and receiving from them the waves of the water of life, the king escorted by his lion and conducting a chained barbarian to the god, a lion devouring a captive, a seated scribe reading a book and carrying a little monkey on his neck, (an incarnation of the god Thoth), a foster father squatting on his haunches and holding to his breast the royal child whose education is confided to him.

FIG. 323.—SENNEFER, HIS WIFE AND DAUGHTER (Museum, Cairo). *(Phot. E. Brugsch.)*

The Asiatic or negro prisoners bound back to back are treated with an amazing realism, sometimes verging on caricature (Fig. 302). The beasts themselves play their part, and the cow Hathor or the serpent Maritsakro attach themselves to a Pharaoh in order to protect him (Fig. 301). All these are in stone, sometimes lifesize, and show a facility of invention and a flexibility of execution we should hardly look for in the second Theban period. Wood was less in favour for statues than formerly, save for those ritual figures of which only fragments remain, but it was commonly used for the statuettes which took the place of the *double*-statues in the tombs of the lower middle class, and for certain objects of

168

THE SECOND THEBAN AGE

industrial art which demanded the human figure, such, for instance, as the bearers of jars of kohol; here, the number of new forms is considerable: foreign slaves bowed beneath a sack or a jar (Figs. 303, 304), children gathering flowers, young girls swimming and pushing a duck or a goose before them. There was the same variety in metal-work, but the majority of the gold and silver statues have disappeared, and only s small number of bronze examples remain. Statuary, whether in stone, wood, or metal, may be said to have developed in every direction; far from being inferior to that of preceding ages, it surpasses it, as we have just seen, in variety of motive, and very often equals it in beauty of handling. The first monuments we possess of the time of the Ahmessids are still fairly faithful to the style of the preceding schools. This is notably the case in the figure of Queen Tuitishere, in London (Fig. 305), and in the two statues of Amenophis I. at Turin

FIG. 324.—HEAD OF A MAN
(Museum, Cairo).
(Phot. E. Brugsch).

FIG. 325.—TORSO AND HEAD
OF A WOMAN (Museum, Cairo).
(Phot. E. Brugsch.)

FIG. 326.—BOND'S STATUETTE.
(Museum, Cairo).
(Phot. E. Brugsch.)

ART IN EGYPT

FIG. 327.—THE EGYPTIAN FLEET, AT DÊR-EL-BAHARI. *(Phot. Beato.)*

and Cairo. That at Turin (Fig. 305) is an admirably preserved work in white limestone; the king is seated, confronting the spectator, in the hieratic attitude, and but for the cartouches, we might well take it for a work of the Twelfth Dynasty. The Cairo statue (Fig. 307) is mutilated, but the face and bust are intact; the king was invested with the insignia of Ta-Tenen and his flesh was painted. It has all the delicacy of the ancient Memphite schools, together with the firmness of chisel and the virile air which are characteristic of the Thebans. The head of one of the Atlantes now at Cairo, erected by Thothmes I. in the court of the obelisk at Karnak, establishes, I think, the transition from the ancient to the modern style. As it retains the red colouring, it is very life-like in appearance, in spite of the loss of the head-dress (Fig. 308). The Pharaoh himself seems to be welcoming the visitor, and his round face, his smiling eyes, his dimpled cheeks and amiable mouth, recall the features of the Sesostris at Lisht; it is further characterised by a firmness of touch

FIG. 328.—QUEEN AAHMES AT DÊR-EL-BAHARI. *(Phot. Beato.)*

THE SECOND THEBAN AGE

and an individuality of expression lacking in the others. When once the royal workshop was organised, the multiplicity of orders that flowed in soon awoke in it qualities quiescent since the invasion of the Shepherds, to which it added new elements, derived, I think, from influences coming from other parts of the valley. The Thebans alone would not have sufficed for the decoration of monuments, temples, or tombs. They received provincial auxiliaries, and borrowed from them something of the traditions and temperament these brought with them from their native cities. Thus reinforced, the school subdivided into several branches, each of which soon assumed its personal physiognomy.

FIG. 329.—QUEEN THI, AT SHEIKH-ABD-EL-KURNAH. *(Phot. Weigall.)*

I should, for instance, attribute a good proportion of the royal statues at Turin, and others recently brought to light in the *favissa*, the Isis, the Thothmes III. and the Senmut, to a single workshop, probably established at Karnak. The statuette of the queen Isis (Fig. 309) reveals the initiator of the facial type which prevailed under the Ahmessids for three generations, the hooked nose, the large prominent eyes, the fleshy mouth, the round face. The heavy wig which encases the head was not calculated to make the sculptor's task easier; he managed, however, to minimise its disastrous effect. Thothmes III. has his mother's face, but the type is less hard (Fig. 310). The statue is of fine schist, and no reproduction could do justice to the delicacy of the

FIG. 330.—HEAD OF A STATUETTE OF QUEEN THI (Museum, Cairo). *(Phot. E. Brugsch.)*

modelling; the play of the muscles is noted discreetly, with extraordinary felicity, and as the imperceptible shadows it produces vary as we pass round the figure, the expression of the features seems to change every moment. The kneeling statues of Amenophis II. offering wine or water, are not unworthy of the series; although they show less individuality than the Thothmes III. and the couple, Thothmes IV. and his mother, they are not wanting in natural grace (Fig. 311). The touch of the chisel is identical in all, and reveals a common origin. I may say the same of the group representing the little princess Neferu-Ra and her guardian Senmut. Nothing could be less conventional than the free gesture with which the worthy man clasps the child, and the confident self-abandonment with which it nestles against his breast. The natural movement harmonises well with the intellectual benevolence of the face and the smile in the eyes and on the thick lips. We have here further a direct proof that the Thebans, like the Memphite artists, were concerned above all things to get likeness in their portraits. The mummy of Thothmes III. has certainly suffered; the face shrivelled in the course of embalming, and the shrinking of the flesh, the sinking of the eyes, the discoloration of the skin, the flattening of the nose, make it very different to what it was in life. Nevertheless, if superficial relief has been lost, that of the substructure has endured; when we compare it with the modelling of the statue, we are obliged to admit that they are alike, and that the sculptor has perpetuated the expression of life which has passed away from the mummy.

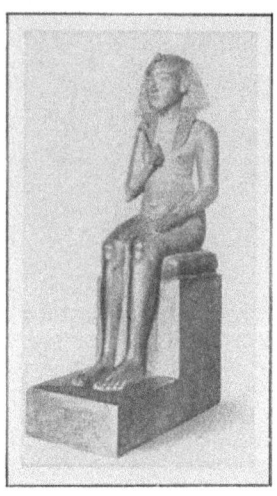

FIG. 331.—STATUETTE OF AMENOPHIS IV.
(The Louvre, Paris).

FIG. 332.—HEAD OF ONE OF THE CANOPIC JARS OF AMENOPHIS IV.
(Museum, Cairo). (Phot. E. Brugsch.)

THE SECOND THEBAN AGE

It would have been strange if people so skilful in rendering the human form had not been masters of the treatment of animals. The lion and its offspring the sphinx, the ram, the monkey (Fig. 313), the falcon, the vulture, inspired the Thebans in admirable works. Never was the faculty of welding the members of different beings into a single body carried further than in such creations as the sphinx of Queen Hatshepset at Rome, the sphinx of Thothmes III. at Cairo, the Sekhet with the lion's head, standing (Fig. 312) or sitting, the various hieracocephalous (falcon-headed) and criocephalous (ram-headed) sphinxes, and rams. The lions of Amenophis III. at Gebel-Barkal (Fig. 314), have a nobility of attitude and a truth of physiognomy which was always lacking in the lions of the Greek and Roman sculptors. They were products of the royal workshops, and to one of these, no doubt, we must also attribute the Amenophis II. in black granite, standing and leaning against the swelling neck of the goddess of the dead, the serpent Maritsakro, who is thus in-

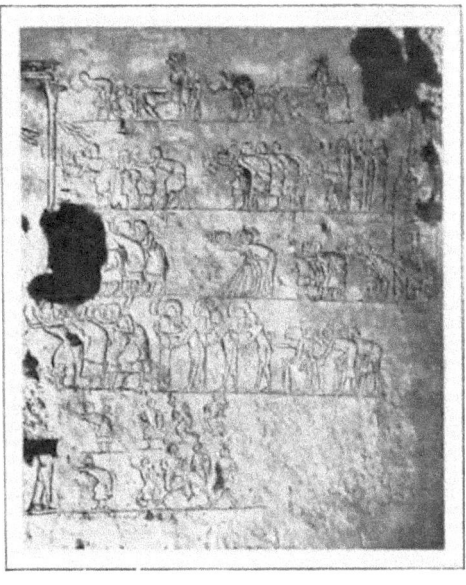

FIG. 333.—WALL IN ONE OF THE TOMBS OF EL-AMARNA. *(Phot. Bouriant.)*

FIG. 334.—AMENOPHIS IV. AND THE QUEEN (Museum, Berlin).

ART IN EGYPT

FIG. 335.
A)ENOPHIS IV., THE QUEEN, AND THEIR CHILDREN
(Museum, Berlin).

dicated as his protector. The execution here is minute and trivial; the work is faithfully rendered mythology and nothing more. But the cow discovered by Naville in an almost perfect chapel at Dêr-el-Bahari (Fig. 315), is a work of a very different order. This is equal, if not superior to the best achievements of Greece and Rome in this *genre*, and we have to come down through the ages to the greatest animal sculptors of our own days before we find a work of such striking reality. She is encumbered with mystic emblems, the head-dress of discs and feathers between

FIG. 336.
CAST OF THE HEAD OF A)ENO-
PHIS IV. (Museum, Cairo).
(Phot. E. Brugsch.)

FIG. 337.—STUDY WITH THE POINT
FOR THE PORTRAIT OF A PERSON OF
THE TIME OF A)ENOPHIS IV.
(Museum, Berlin).

THE SECOND THEBAN AGE

her horns, and two tufts of lotus, springing from the ground at her feet, rise to her shoulders (Fig. 317). In her the faithful adored Hathor, posted at the edge of the western marsh to intercept those who had lately died, and inifiate them into the life beyond the tomb; nevertheless, the sculptor reduced the religious paraphernalia to their simplest expression. Was it he who created the theme, or who, in other words, detached it from the bas-reliefs (Fig. 316) to translate it into the round? His goddess is no conventional cow modelled upon a traditional form; she is an individual creature chosen for her beauty from among the sacred flock. In spite of her trappings and her Pharaoh, we recognise in her the kindly maternal beast, gentle, strong, vigorous, and natural. The master she inspired modelled

FIG. 338.—BUST OF AMON AT KARNAK. *(Phot. Legrain.)*

the relief of sides and hind-quarters lovingly, and we almost see the quivering of the skin under the caresses of the light. In the head he even had recourse to technical artifices which appear for the first time in this example, as far as I know; he treated the nostrils and cheeks with a fine rasp or file, and the furrows left by the tool express in a very curious manner the perpetual tremor that agitates the face. Life has been

FIG. 339.—TRIUMPHAL BAS-RELIEF OF SETI I. AT KARNAK.

breathed into the stone; the nostrils quiver with the breath that passes through them, and the eyes are half closed in indolent

ART IN EGYPT

reverie. The figure of Pharaoh does not rise above the average; I am nevertheless inclined to think that the group, taken as a whole, is the finest achievement of the Theban School under the Ahmessids. The mutilated statue of Amenophis III. in Assyrian dress (Fig. 318) is an eccentricity. The gigantic group of Amenophis III. and Thi or Ti, in the Cairo Museum (Fig. 319) is a marvel of purely material dexterity, but it is nothing more, and it has no merit save the immensity of its proportions. The colossal figures in red sandstone which this same Pharaoh placed at the entrance of his sepulchral temple on the left bank of Thebes, the two Memnons, measure 65 feet in height (Fig. 320). They are correct in style, and highly elaborated; in their present mutilated condition, they are chiefly effective as mass, and they impress by their isolation in the middle of the plain rather than by their beauty.

FIG. 340.—FRAGMENT OF A STATUETTE OF PERTRIFIED WOOD (Museum, Cairo). *(Phot. E. Brugsch.)*

The art of the private workshops is perhaps less familiar to us than that of the royal studios, but it was far from inferior to this. The high priest Amenophis, son of Hapu, is a very happy creation, in spite of those retouches of the Ptolemaic period which have modified the expression of the face (Fig. 321). His namesake provides us with a good example of the type of the seated scribe treated in the new manner (Fig. 322). Let us turn to the trio in black granite from Karnak (Fig. 323), the husband and wife seated on the same seat, the child standing between the two. They are Theban notables, heavy of form and insignificant of feature.

FIG. 341.—BUST OF KHONSU (Museum, Cairo). *(Phot. E. Brugsch.)*

THE SECOND THEBAN AGE

Sennefer is well pleased with himself, and not without reason; he is commandant of the Thebaid; he wears round his neck the necklace of four rows, and on his breast the two circular ornaments, the insignia of his rank; his wife was the king's foster-mother, and their daughter appears to be well married. The artist has fixed on the stone, perhaps with a touch of irony, the expression of gratified vanity that irradiated their persons. The handling is very searching, and the only touch of convention is to be found in the torso of the man, where the loose folds caused by age and soft living are noted with an excess of symmetry. It is a pity that only fragments have survived of a couple contemporary with the last Ahmessids, who were buried at Sheikh-Abd-el-Kûrnah. The head only (Fig. 324) of the man has come down to us, and even this has lost the nose, the chin, and part of the mouth, but the woman has suffered less (Fig. 325). In spite

FIG. 342.—THE SO-CALLED THI (Museum, Cairo). *(Phot. E. Brugsch.)*

of the mutilation of the nose, the face is charming, with the low forehead almost concealed by the wig, the narrow eyes slanting upwards towards the temples, the slightly prominent cheek-bones, and the full mouth, the corners of which melt into dimples. The cape and the pleated robe in which she is draped reveal a well modelled arm and define the contours of the body; we divine beneath the veil healthy hips, a slender waist, and round, firm breasts. The details of the dress and ornaments, which were laid on with the brush, have worn away, but the material, a close, crystalline limestone resembling alabaster, is

FIG. 343.—TUTANKHAMEN. *(Phot. E. Brugsch.)*

of a most agreeable creamy tone. The unknown woman whose portrait, half the size of life (Fig. 326), was discovered by Mond

in 1906, has the same attitude and a similar costume, an almost transparent drapery from which the left hand emerges, holding
a lotus-flower to the breast. The bust is not fully developed, and the breasts are so small that they hardly swell the drapery that veils them. The artist has seized the characteristics of the first dawn of womanhood with much truth and penetration, and the discreet manner in which he suggests the over-slender grace of the model under the dress is masterly. The wig is so ingeniously arranged that instead of crushing the face, it forms a frame round it, and gives it importance. This face changes in character, and almost seems to change its century, according to the angle at which we study it. Confronting us, it is round and full, without superabundance or looseness of flesh, that of a pleasant little Theban girl, pretty, but vulgar in structure and expression. In profile, between the wings of her wig, which fall upon her shoulders

FIG. 344.—HEAD OF A STATUE OF HERU-EM-HEB (Museum, Cairo). *(Phot. E. Brugsch.)*

FIG. 345.—ZAI AND NAI (Museum, Cairo). *(Phot. E. Brugsch.)*

FIG. 346.—AMON AND MUT (Museum, Cairo). *(Phot. E. Brugsch.)*

THE SECOND THEBAN AGE

like two long side-curls, she has a malicious and mutinous subtlety very uncommon among Egyptian women; she might well pass for a contemporary of our own, who had donned an antique headdress and costume out of caprice, or a refinement of coquetry.

Great as was the activity of the statuary, that of the mural sculptor was not inferior to it. The decoration of the innumerable temples which were built at this period, not only at Thebes, but in the provinces, admitted of very little novelty in the dogmatic portions, and the scenes depicting the bringing of offerings or ritual solemnities, differ but slightly from such representations in earlier ages. They seem, however, to be crowded together more closely, and to be more numerous; perhaps some of them, such as the issuing forth in procession with the divine *bari*, are much later than the rest; they have less stiffness than the ancient pictures, and greater richness and variety in the accessories. In the majority, however, the hieratic element persists, and they do not impress the spectator by rapidity of movement, nor by the grouping of the figures, but by correctness of line and perfection of modelling. Go to Karnak, or to Dêr-el-Bahari; the basreliefs of Thothmes, of Queen Hatshepset and of Amenophis are masterpieces of skilled graving and harmonious colour. Study, at Dêr-el-Bahari, the Queen Aahmes-Nefertari, who has come to the end of her pregnancy, and is being conducted to her bed of labour by the divinities who protect women in travail; the expression of pain and

FIG. 347.—BAS-RELIEF OF SETI I. AT KARNAK. *(Phot. Banville.)*

FIG. 348.—PAINTED BAS-RELIEF IN THE TOMB OF SETI I. *(Phot. Beato.)*

weariness on her face, and the languor and self-abandonment of her whole person, make this figure a most accomplished piece of sculpture (Fig. 328). Or take the highly entertaining expedition to Punt as a contrast to the gentle sentiment of the above. The artist was not content to give a general impression of the voyage of an Egyptian fleet (Fig. 327); he has noted in detail the local scenery, the conical huts perched on piles above the level of inundation, the fat women, the giraffes, the monkeys, the oddly-shaped fish.

FIG. 349.—BAS-RELIEF IN THE MEMNONIUM OF SETI I. AT ABYDOS. *(Phot. Beato.)*

If, as I imagine, the workshop which carved this fragment of a maritime epic in the limestone was the same to which we owe the cow, we need feel no surprise at the mastery displayed. The sculptors of Karnak were not so successful with the triumph of Amenophis II. on his return from Syria; from this they only extracted the material for a series of vignettes, skilfully combined, but without charm or originality. The private workshops surpassed the royal ones, indeed, in many cases, and the tombs of Sheikh-Abd-el-Kûrnah contain the finest paintings and bas-reliefs of the Eighteenth Dynasty. The soft and ductile limestone of the hill lent itself to all the subtleties and even to all the fantasies of the chisel; thanks to it, the Thebans of Amenophis III. had attained a mastery far greater than that of the Memphites. Their relief is rather higher

FIG. 350.—SETI I. AT ABYDOS. *(Phot. Beato.)*

THE SECOND THEBAN AGE

and rounder, and consequently less dry than that of the Fifth Dynasty; at the same time the arrangement of the episodes is richer and less immutable. The hypogea of Iuâa, Kha-emhet, and a score of others, shattered, ravaged and mutilated though they are, contain, to my mind, some of the best, perhaps indeed the best, of the Egyptian bas-reliefs. The touch in these is fat, long, and bold, the drawing free and flowing; we seem to behold Amenophis III., Queen Thi (Fig. 329) and Iuâa themselves. Artists of a later period may have equalled these works, but they never surpassed them.

FIG. 351.—PRINCE RAMESES, AFTERWARDS RAMESES II. AT ABYDOS. (Phot. Beato)

Then suddenly, at the moment when Thebes had reached its apogee, the semi-religious, semi-political madness of Amenophis IV. compromised the existence of its art, and drawing out a provincial school from the obscurity in which it was vegetating, sought to substitute it for that of Thebes. When he transferred his capital to El-Amarna, he might have taken with him the whole or a part of the artistic staff of Karnak; the men who had worked so valiantly for his father, had lost nothing of their vigour; the little portrait of Thi at Cairo (Fig. 330), the statuette which one of them made of him, now in the Louvre (Fig. 331), are only to be equalled by the marvellous heads of his Canopic jars (Fig. 332); and the decorators of the tomb of his minister Ramosis, if they were not the same who worked

FIG. 352.—SETI I. AND THE THREE GODDESSES IN THE MEMNONIUM AT ABYDOS. (Phot. Beato.)

ART IN EGYPT

on that of Iuâa, were fully equal to these. At El-Amarna, the manner of attacking the stone differs entirely from the Theban method, and is rather clumsy; it betrays an old-fashioned technique, which still persisted at Hermopolis, the largest town in the region; the ancient hypogea of Beni-Hasân revealed its character in the works of the Twelfth Dynasty. If we place the works of the two periods side by side, it will sufficiently prove that they are the outcome of the same teaching and the same practice. In both cases, the isolated figures are often drawn with a clumsy hand, but they are grouped well; they act, they overflow with movement and life. The episodes are taken from the lives of actual persons, and record their great events with a spirit quite untrammelled by convention. Of course, the world had progressed since the days of the Twelfth Dynasty, and the composition had become more scientific; whereas the artist of Beni-Hasân arranged his wrestlers in symmetrical groups, his *confrère* at El-Amarna mingles his persons, and makes a seething crowd of them. The king, accompanied by the queen and one of his daughters, goes in his chariot to pray in the temple of Aton, or he summons one of his favourites to the palace, to recompense him for his services by the gift of gold necklaces. He hands them to the favourite from the tribune, and the little princesses, amused by the spectacle, throw down others with ingenuous gestures; behind the decorated favourite, servants indicate their joy by bows or capers, âccording to their social rank and their education. The private life of royalty is treated with a familiarity hitherto unknown among

FIG. 353.—SETI II. IN HIS TOMB. *(Phot. Insinger.)*

FIG. 354.—SEPTAH-MENEPTAH IN HIS TOMB. *(Phot. Weigall.)*

THE SECOND THEBAN AGE

the Thebans; Pharaoh is seated at table with his family, and they are all gnawing bones covered with meat; or he lingers in the harem to play with his daughters (Fig. 335) and the queen offers him a bouquet to smell (Fig. 334), or, seated upon his knees, nestles lovingly against him, while his children caress each other on a cushion before him, in all the innocence of their age. The equivalent of such motives is to be found elsewhere, but they are arranged and raised to the dignity of sacramental themes; the novelty here is the realism with which they are treated. The artists of El-Amarna worked from nature even more closely than those of Thebes; we have proof of this in the casts they took (Fig. 336), the studies with brush and point by them which have come down to us (Fig. 337), and the manner in which they rendered the type of the sovereign. Whereas the Thebans idealised this, they transcribed it as they saw it, reproducing the low forehead, the projecting face, the pointed chin,

FIG. 355.—SCENE FROM THE TOMB OF SEPTAH-MENEPTAH. *(Phot. Weigall.)*

FIG. 356.
SESOSTRIS FIGHTING, AT ABÛ SIMBEL.
(Phot. Oropesa.)

ART IN EGYPT

FIG. 357.—ONE OF THE DAUGHTERS OF RAMESES II. (Museum, Cairo). *(Phot. E. Brugsch.)*

the thin neck, the puffy belly and the puny limbs. The king took this in good part, and his courtiers, adopting the type themselves in order to flatter, did their best to resemble it. The result of these tendencies was a very individual style, less independent than that which prevailed in the rest of Egypt, and, above all, more paradoxical; just as the religion of Aton was nothing but an ancient worship suddenly raised to the first rank in order to check the disquieting importance of Amon, so the school of El-Amarna was but an ancient school drawn forth from its obscurity by the will of the master, and unexpectedly transformed by him into a royal workshop.

If the enterprise of Amenophis IV. had succeeded, would the influence of these Hermopolitans have supplanted that of the Thebans? It is highly improbable; the Thebans were too skilfully organised, and possessed too numerous a *clientèle* for a rapid eclipse of their prosperity. When, after some ten or fifteen years, the city of El-Amarna was abandoned, and the artists who had shed lustre upon it relapsed into obscurity, the Theban School easily resumed its place as the official school of royalty. They did not, however, take up things again at the precise point where they had been left at the death of Amenophis III., at least as far as the bas-relief was concerned. We have only to study the pictures with which Tutankhamen and Heru-em-heb adorned the lateral walls of the great colonnade at Luxor to recognise the influence of Hermopolitan ideas. Amon comes forth from Luxor towards Karnak through the streets of the city

FIG. 358.—ALABASTER STATUE OF RAMESES II. (Museum, Turin). *(Phot. Alinari.)*

FOUR OF THE ENAMELLED PLAQUES
From the Palace of Rameses III. at Medinet-Habû
(Museum, Cairo)

THE SECOND THEBAN AGE

and upon the Nile, and the population rejoices round him; the composition has the regularity and balance of Theban art, but many of the accessory scenes, feasts in the houses, singing, dancing, military ballets, seem to have been borrowed from that of El-Amarna. Heru-em-heb's master draughtsman had studied the work of his provincial brethren, and had gleaned from it certain ideas for the rejuvenation of the traditional designs. Some touch of this inspiration seems to have passed into the triumphal reliefs of Seti I. (Fig. 339) and Rameses II., but it vanishes almost immediately after these, and, in any case, it had no influence at all upon sculpture. This art, hampered

FIG. 359.—REPLICA OF THE RAMESES II. AT TURIN (Museum, Cairo). *(Phot. E. Brugsch.)*

for some years by persecution, recovered its vigour as soon as the heresy died out, and the royal statuaries of Karnak produced a series of works comparable to the finest of their earlier achievements. They comprise, besides the bas-reliefs of Heru-em-heb on one of his pylons, the Amon (Fig. 338), which is a portrait of this Pharaoh, the Khonsu and the Tutānkhamen, the so-called head of Thi at Cairo, the group of Heru-em-heb and Amon at Turin, perhaps the Cairo bust of petrified wood (Fig. 340), and a few pieces of less interest. I think it evident that the Khonsu (Fig. 341) and the Tutankhamen (Fig. 343) are by the same hand. The two figures might almost be superposed;

FIG. 360.—THE TWO COLOSSI ON THE SOUTH SIDE AT ABÙ SIMBEL. *(Phot. Beato.)*

FIG. 361.—COLOSSAL HEAD OF RAMESES II. (Museum, Cairo).
(Phot. E. Brugsch.)

the hollow of the eye is of the same depth in each, the junction of the nose is identical, as are the slight inflation of the nostrils, the pout of the lips, and the constriction of the corners of the mouth. The expression of suffering is common to both faces, but the indications of ill-health, the obliquity and sunkenness of the eyes, the thinness of the cheeks and neck, and the projecting shoulder-blades are more marked in the Khonsu than in the Tutankhamen; they betray consumptive tendencies which the artist has noted with sufficient realism to justify, the diagnosis of a modern physician. The group of Heru-em-heb and Amon is less personal in sentiment; but the two faces have a beautiful expression, and the technique resembles that of the others. Its affinities with the so-called Teye are perhaps less obvious to those who know this only by drawings or photographs (Fig. 342), but they become evident enough to a student of the originals, and the peculiarities of the Khonsu and the Tutankhamen re-appear here in a modified form. The queen is not a consumptive, but the various parts of her face indicate great delicacy, and the hand which modelled them is certainly that which treated with so much subtlety the contemporary images of the god and the Pharaoh. The Turin group has the solemn impress suitable to the subject, the adoption of the sovereign by his father Amon, and his enthronement; the two heads are marked, nevertheless, by that air of somewhat sickly gentleness which characterises the others. I should be inclined for the same reason to class with these the personage called by Mariette Meneptah, who is in reality Heru-em-heb (Fig. 344). Here, as with the Khonsu and the Tutankhamen,

FIG. 362.—RAMESES IV. AND A LIBYAN PRISONER (Museum, Cairo).
(Phot. E. Brugsch.)

THE SECOND THEBAN AGE

the hardness of the material, a close-grained granite, offered serious difficulties to the sculptor. He overcame them with almost insolent success, and this anxious, refined face is an unforgettable creation.

Seti I. then received from the Eighteenth Dynasty the Theban School in the full tide of its prosperity, and he kept it at this high level. The few statues of his period that we have, the group of Amon and Mut in the Cairo Museum (Fig. 346), and that of Zaï and Naï (Fig. 345), are charming works, marked by a sentiment and distinction which were never surpassed in the sequel. It was indeed characteristic of Theban art under this prince, that, refining still more

FIG. 363.—BUST OF A STATUE OF MENEPTAH (Museum, Cairo). (Phot. E. Brugsch.)

upon the tendency of Heru-em-heb, it sought grace and elegance rather than grandeur and energy. True, the religious and triumphal bas-reliefs (Fig. 347) of the temple of Karnak show that on occasion it did not lack breadth and vigour, but these are, after all, mere bravura pieces without any personal accent, while the character of the period is revealed in all its purity at the temple of Kûrnah, the hypogeum of Bibân-el-Mulûk (Fig. 348) and the Memnonium of Abydos. The pictures in the hypogeum are not all finished, and entire halls where the designer has finished his task while the sculptor has never begun his, are decorated simply with sketches in red and black inks. These show very vividly the great practical dexterity of the ordinary workmen, and it would be difficult to appreciate too highly the skill with which the director, revising the labour of his assistants,

FIG. 364.—HEAD OF PHARAOH (Museum, Cairo). (Phot. E. Brugsch.)

laid the impress of his own talent upon it by means of a few discreet re-touches (Fig. 349). The general effect, however, is sad and solemn, as befits a tomb; it is only at Abydos that we get the full measure of the genius of the school. Study the original *in situ*, and you will not doubt that the same master designed the decorations both of temple and hypogeum, nor that some at least of the same assistants collaborated in the two. The relief is at once flexible and precise (Fig. 349), a surface which the chisel lingered over lovingly, giving a kind of colour to the epidermis by a multitude of almost imperceptible strokes. The gods and goddesses have the features of the sovereign, and this oft-repeated profile is differentiated each time by a new shade of melancholy languor. To have seen the Pharaoh and the three goddesses his companions (Fig. 352), about ten o'clock on a fine February morning, is to understand to what a degree Egyptian art, so mournful superficially, may kindle with life and exquisite tenderness. The funerary workshop, as distinguished from that of Karnak, persisted under the successors of Seti I. We owe to it the Memnonium of Rameses II. at Abydos, now half destroyed, and what remains of the battle-scenes of Kadesh prove to us that upon occasion it was capable of boldness. After the completion of the Memnonium, the workshop was removed to the left bank, and devoted itself to the decoration of the royal hypogea; that of Rameses II. is almost

FIG. 365.—THE PRIEST WITH THE MONKEY (Museum, Cairo). *(Phot. E. Brugsch.)*

FIG. 366.—A WALL OF THE HYPOGEUM OF PAHERI AT EL-KAB. *(Phot. Insinger.)*

THE SECOND THEBAN AGE

equal to that of Seti I., and in those of Meneptah, Seti II. (Fig. 353) and Septah Meneptah, we find isolated figures (Fig. 354) and scenes (Fig. 355) which prove that it had long possessed gifted artists. After Septah, all traces of it are lost, and it is probable that it had ceased to exist at the time of Rameses III, at the beginning of the Twentieth Dynasty.

The period of Rameses II. has often been pronounced the beginning of the artistic decadence. No opinion could be less justifiable. Rameses II. built enormously during his reign of sixty-seven years, and he was no doubt obliged to employ all available artists, good and bad alike, to satisfy the exigencies of his monumental mania: wherever the traveller goes in Egypt, he will almost certainly encounter a stele which bears his name, a statue, a votive bas-relief, a chapel, a temple of his period. For the most part, these are the works of local artists, and are no more important than their authors; in Nubia, for instance, it is difficult to imagine the depths of barbaric clumsiness into which the artisans who worked on the hemispeos of Dêr and that of es-Sabua descended. Yet it would be incorrect to say that even here, we recognise decadence, for there can be no decadence where there is no art, and such is the case in these two temples. If we wish to form a just idea of art under Rameses II., we must study it where he maintained a duly organised body of craftsmen, at Thebes and in its dependencies, at Abydos, Memphis and Tanis; we shall see then that it compares favourably with that of preceding ages. The triumphal bas-reliefs of Luxor, Karnak, the Ramesseum, and Abu Simbel, all of which represent the battle of Kadesh, are masterly in their general treatment, and the artists who composed them showed great fecundity of imagination when they had to adapt this single subject to the

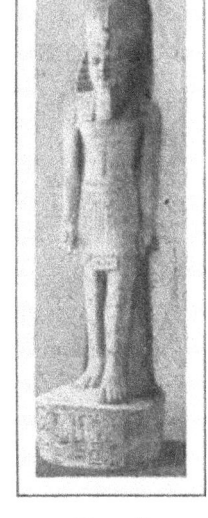

FIG. 367.
COLOSSAL FIGURE
OF RAMESES II.
(Museum, Cairo).
(Phot. E. Brugsch.)

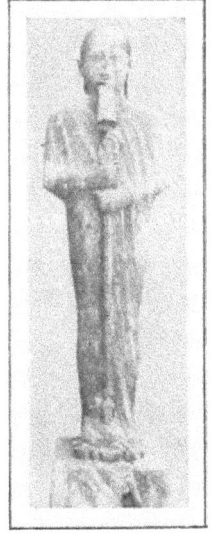

FIG. 368.— MEMPHITE PTAH (Museum, Cairo).
(Phot. E. Brugsch.)

ART IN EGYPT

FIG. 369.—THE TRIAD OF HERACLEOPOLIS (Museum, Cairo). *(Phot. E. Brugsch.)*

varying conditions in each locality, resulting from the shape and size of the panels they had to cover. The religious bas-reliefs are more strictly conventional; at Thebes, however, they are of excellent quality. If they become feebler in certain portions of the Memnonium at Abydos, it was because, after having re-established the workshops of Seti I. in the capital, Rameses II. was forced to make use of local craftsmen of an inferior type. In Nubia, at Abu Simbel and Bet-el-Walî, whither he deported Theban artists, the suulpture retains its sterling character. Abu Simbel possesses the work which Champollion pronounced, not without reason, the masterpiece of Egyptian bas-relief, the Sesostris fighting (Fig. 356). It is somewhat harsh of aspect, owing to the coarse texture of the sandstone, but the composition and design are extraordinarily perfect. The king has already struck down one Libyan chief, and trampling him underfoot, he seizes another by the arm, to thrust him through with his spear; every muscle is strained by the movement, and his whole body shoots forward to participate in the effort by which he throws himself upon the enemy. His opponent is no longer to be numbered among the living. His eyelids quiver, his mouth relaxes, his head sinks and droops, his legs give way under him. The remnant of life in him is concentrated in the bust, and flutters feebly under the sharp point that pierces the flesh; as soon as the conqueror releases him, he will fall in a heap, and

FIG. 370. FRAGMENT OF A MEMPHITE BAS-RELIEF (Museum, Cairo). *(Phot. Quibell.)*

190

will move no more. Never has the drama of violent death, which disintegrates the whole man at a stroke, and stretches him inert on the ground, been analysed with such knowledge, or realised with such energy.

The statuary is not perhaps equal to the bas-reliefs, although it has bequeathed us several very agreeable examples, such as the portrait of one of the daughters of Pharaoh (Fig. 357).

FIG. 371.—MOURNERS CRYING ALOUD IN A FUNERAL PROCESSION IN THE TOMB OF HARMIN (Museum, Cairo). (Phot. E. Brugsch.)

In general it is marked by a paradoxical double tendency, on the one hand to the puerile, on the other to the gigantic. The alabaster Rameses of the Turin Museum (Fig. 358), with its softly rounded contours, is still governed by the tradition of Seti I., and it belongs to the Theban School, as is proved by the discovery of a replica in granite (Fig. 359) which Legrain found in the *favissa* at Karnak. The same is undoubtedly the case of the colossal figures of the Ramesseum and Abu Simbel. Those of the Ramesseum have suffered so much that the only sentiment they evoke is astonishment at their immensity, but those at Abu Simbel fully deserve the enthusiasm they inspire in travellers. I have studied them by day and by night, from every angle, and under every play of light (Fig. 360).

FIG. 372.—CONVEYANCE OF OFFERINGS IN THE TOMB OF HARMIN (Museum, Cairo). (Phot. E. Brugsch.)

At morning, in the pale light of dawn, they seem to be sounding the distant horizon with a hard, sombre gaze; but soon, when the sun,

ART IN EGYPT

gliding over the mountain-slope, reaches their faces, their eyes light up, their lips tremble and smile, and for a moment it seems as if a quiver of life ran through their bodies. We ask ourselves how the master who created them managed to give them such perfect proportions, on an incline where it was impossible for him to stand back, and where he could only begin to judge of his work when it was already far advanced. The most remarkable thing about these figures is the manner in which they harmonise with the landscape; it is impossible to conceive of them elsewhere, or, being here, that they should be other than they are. We find it difficult to imagine the colossal figures of Memphis or Tanis; placed in the court of the temple, like those of the Ramesseum, they must have been out of proportion with the statues and buildings that surrounded them, and they cannot have blended harmoniously with the general structure as do those of Abu Simbel. They were distinguished, nevertheless, by technical qualities which make it impossible to forget them; the most famous of them, the *Abu'l-hôl* of Mitrahineh, and the figure from which the colossal head in the Cairo Museum (Fig. 361) was detached, show no signs of decadence. The decline, indeed, first declared itself after the the death of Rameses II., during the civil wars and foreign invasions which darkened the last years of the Nineteenth Dynasty. It was already manifest under Meneptah (Fig. 363), and more emphatically under Rameses III., who copied his illustrious ancestor heavily and clumsily. The sculptures of Medinet-Habû will not bear comparison with those of Abu Simbel or Luxor, although some of the pictures, those of the lion-hunt

FIG. 373.—FRAGMENT FROM THE TOMB OF MAIPTAH (Museum, Cairo). *(Phot. E. Brugsch.)*

THE SECOND THEBAN AGE

and the aurochs-hunt, for instance, are very spirited; it is probable that the king's individual taste militated against the revival of the school. After him, under the Twentieth Dynasty, some respectable works were produced, which do not rise greatly above the average; among the best are a head of Pharaoh in a helmet, with thick lips, an enormous nose, and heavy eyes (Fig. 364), and a little group in granite of Rameses IV. conducting a Libyan prisoner to the god Amon (Fig. 362). There is pride in Pharaoh's bearing, the barbarian's constrained attitude is skilfully observed, and the movement of the miniature lion which slips in between the two is rendered with the naturalism proper to the Egyptian artist in the treatment of animals.

FIG. 374.—THE TWO NILE FIGURES (Museum, Cairo). *(Phot. E. Brugsch.)*

The priest with the monkey (Fig. 365), or, to call him by his name, Rameses-nakht, it seated on the ground, studying with an abstracted air the contents of a scroll spread across his legs. A little hairy monkey-headed creature, the god Thoth, perches on his shoulder, and reads with him. It was difficult to co-ordinate the man and the animal in a manner not ungraceful; the sculptor solved the problem very creditably. The priest bends his neck a little, but we feel that the monkey-god, who is partly concealed by the head-dress, does not weigh heavily upon him. The style is Theban, but there is greater freedom than in the Rameses IV.; the latter was no doubt a product of one of the royal workshops, while the man with the monkey came from one of the private workshops at Karnak.

The Theban school, which had enjoyed such brilliant opportunities while Thebes maintained its ascendancy in Egypt, declined rapidly when the political and military power devolved on the cities of the north.

FIG. 375.—PIECE OF INCRUSTATION IN GREEN ENAMEL (Museum, Cairo). *(Phot. E. Brugsch.)*

ART IN EGYPT

FIG. 376.—ONE OF THE COFFINS OF THUÂA (Museum Cairo). *(Phot. Quibell.)*

In what particular forms art was manifested in the provinces during these long centuries it is not possible to say with any certainty, in view of the scarcity of survivals. The bas-reliefs of the hypogea of El-Kâb (Fig. 366) and of the temples of Elephantine, seem to indicate that those of the south were under Theban influences, and also those of the centre, if we may judge by the colossal figure of Rameses II. from Hermopolis (Fig. 367) and the triad of Heracleopolis (Fig. 369). The Memphite School prospered, as we know by the inscriptions, which tell us how many temples the Ahmessids and Ramessids built or restored in the second of their capitals, but, with the exception of certain colossal figures of Rameses II. of which I have already spoken, and the two great Ptahs in the Cairo Museum, (Fig. 368), we possess hardly anything which can be ascribed to it with certainty. It has been thought that Theban influences are to be recognised in several statues, and this in indubitable

FIG. 377.—BUST ON THE COFFIN OF RAMESES II. (Museum, Cairo). *(Phot. E. Brugsch.)*

FIG. 378. SANDSTONE BUST OF RAMESES IV. (Museum, Cairo). *(Phot. E. Brugsch.)*

THE SECOND THEBAN AGE

in the bas-reliefs from contemporary tombs preserved at Cairo. Might we not suppose that the personage of Fig. 370 came from the tomb of Iuâa or Khaemhet? The scenes of domestic life and of funerary rites are no longer arranged in the antique fashion, in decorously co-ordinated registers, with persons walking one behind the other. The composition and perspective are distinctly Theban, and this is especially noticeable in the tomb of Harmin (Fig. 372), in the picture of the farewell to the dead (Fig. 371); the weepers and the women of the family defile before the mummy, jumping, dancing, tearing their hair, beating tambourines, while the men run to and fro, waving long reeds to keep away evil spirits; the excited throng has all the realism of the times that followed immediately after Amenophis IV. The same may be said of the fragments of the tomb of Maiptah (Fig. 373); the dancer of the first register and the carpenter of the second would not be out of place in the finest tombs of Sheikh-Abd-el-Kurnah or El-Amarna. The artists of the Delta, with the exception of the Tanites,

FIG. 379.—STATUETTE OF AMENOPHIS II. IN BLACKENED WOOD (Museum, Cairo). *(Phot. E. Brugsch.)*

FIG. 380.—STATUETTE OF HERU-EM-HEB IN BLACKENED WOOD (Museum, Cairo). *(Phot. E. Brugsch.)*

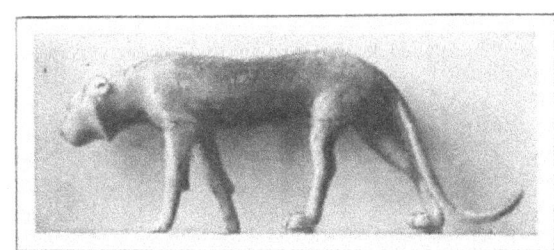

FIG. 381.—ARM OF A CHAIR IN THE FORM OF A FELINE ANIMAL (Museum, Cairo). *(Phot. E. Brugsch.)*

ART IN EGYPT

FIG. 382.
JEWEL CASKET OF AMENOPHIS III.
(Museum, Cairo). *(Phot. E Brugsch.)*

have left us almost nothing; and here the perpetual usurpation of the statues of the first Theban period by Rameses II. is very perplexing, when we attempt to show what they owed to the Nineteenth Dynasty. It is only after the accession of Smendes that we find a few pieces of a well-marked style, notably the twin figures of Nilus in the Cairo Museum (Fig. 374), which bring symmetrically arranged offerings of flowers and fish to the gods. They resemble the sphinx of Amenemhat III. in technique, but the handling is softer; none the less, they demonstrate the persistence of the ancient local art, and only some happy accident is needed to reveal even more characteristic works. Such as they are, they justify the belief that the north of Egypt was not behind the south artistically, and that her masters, if they did not produce so many remarkable works as those of Thebes, were capable of carrying on the tradition of their founders, and of transmitting it, with undiminished lustre, to future generations.

C. THE MINOR ARTS.

The minor arts, like the major, had achieved perfection, and alone would furnish materials for a history. Pottery, domestic and funerary furniture, arms, jewels and goldsmiths' work, are all the natural development of what had existed in earlier ages, and yet we find on every hand combinations formerly unused, and elements many of which are foreign. The Shepherds had

FIG. 383.—THE EMPIRE ARM-CHAIR (Museum, Cairo). *(Phot. E. Brugsch.)*

THE SECOND THEBAN AGE

brought from Asia objects of common use and of martial equipment hitherto unknown, among them the chariot and the quiver; conquest and trade introduced others, and fashion favouring their adoption, the Egyptians of the Eighteenth and Nineteenth Dynasties ended by assimilating table-utensils, arms, and ornaments, a certain number of which were direct copies of Amorrhæan, Assyrian, Asiatic and Ægean models, while the rest betray more or less markedly the influence of the Eastern Mediterranean races. When we compare the Mycenæan daggers and dishes with the Egyptian, and note their obvious affinity, it is very difficult to decide which was modelled on, or simply inspired by the other; to assert, as has been done, that the Egyptians were the plagiarists, is to make a statement which cannot be proved, while study tends to indicate the exact opposite. We must further take into account those reactions and evolutions by means of which motives and forms long since sent forth to foreign lands, often return to their original homes with new arrangements. If we consider the prestige enjoyed by Egypt among barbarous peoples, and her supremacy over them, we are obliged to admit *a priori* that she was likely to have given them at least as much as she borrowed from them; though, on the other hand, it is not to be denied that entire branches of her industry, such as ceramics, were borrowed. She took possession of the various forms of the Mycenæan vases, their double lips, their twin bodies, their handles, their necks, but she decorated them by processes of her own, notably by covering them with enamel, that vivid blue enamel, so pure and so grateful to the eye, which her potters had recently invented. Even here, her inventive spirit did not fail her, and her adaptation

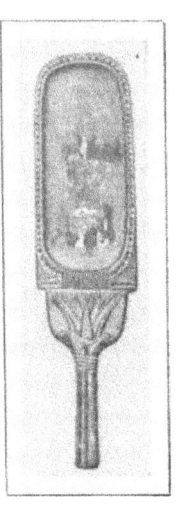

FIG. 384.—WOODEN SPOON FOR COSMETICS (The Louvre, Paris).

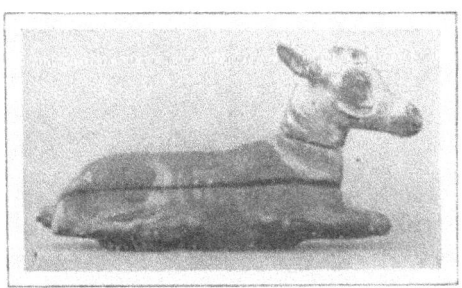

FIG. 385.—BOX FOR COSMETICS (Museum, Cairo). *(Phot. E. Brugsch.)*

ART IN EGYPT

of foreign forms did not prevent her from creating some that were peculiarly her own. I need only instance those polished saucers, and beautiful cups of blue pottery in the form of lotus-flowers, or those red and green glazed kohol-pots, some of which are in the forms of mitred falcons, hedgehogs, monkeys and the god Bes. The doors and façades of the palaces of Amenophis I. and of Rameses III. were ornamented with polychrome plaques of pottery incrusted in the walls, showing Pharaoh himself adoring the gods (Fig. 375), friezes of flowers and birds, and rows of prisoners (Pl. IV). We have further a whole array of peculiarly Egyptian ornament in those necklaces and bracelets of glazed earth or coloured glass pastes, florets, discs, rings, beads, pendants, cartouches, little plaques covered with figures or hieroglyphs, which were the luxury of the poor, and objects of common use among the middle classes. This again was the period when the vast family of amulets began to make their appearance, scarabs, girdle-knots, little columns, mystic eyes, hawks, frogs, and twenty other forms which fill the glass-cases of our museums. Many of these are perfect marvels. The funerary figurines, the *ushebtis*, which took the place of the deceased for the performance of irksome tasks in the paradise of Osiris, were often as carefully executed as the large statues; there are some of enamelled porcelain, such as those of Thothmes IV. and Ptahmes, which modern industry down to the present despairs of copying to perfection, and it would be difficult to say too much in praise of those made of limestone, painted wood, green or blue composition, and in some rare cases, of bronze, which come from private tombs. The Theban craftsmen were neither less skilful nor less inventive than the artists strictly so-called.

FIG. 386.—BOX FOR COSMETICS (Museum, Cairo).
(Phot. E. Brugsch.)

This is most evident among the wood-carvers. The particular idea the Egyptians had of death gave rise to various artistic forms among them, which no longer exist among us, or which have become purely utilitarian. Among these were sleighs for conveying mummies to the tomb, boxes and chests for Canopic

THE SECOND THEBAN AGE

jars and figurines, black sarcophagi with gilded figures, and, above all, the mummy-shaped coffins. On these, in many cases,

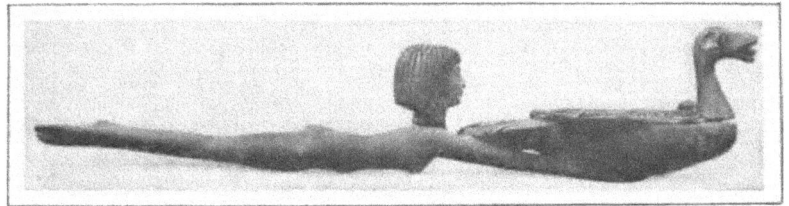

FIG. 387.—PERFUME-SPOON IN THE FORM OF A WOMAN SWIMMING (Museum, Cairo). *(Phot. E. Brugsch.)*

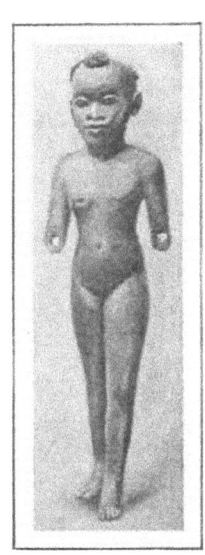

FIG. 388.
STATUETTE OF A NEGRESS
(Petrie Collection).
(Phot. Petrie.)

the artisan reproduced in the mask the features of the corpse within; some of them may be compared for truth of modelling and richness of ornament to the best productions of the royal schools; among the finest are the coffins of Thuâa and Iuâa (Fig. 376), the father and mother of Queen Thi, gilded and incrusted with stones or glass paste, and that of Rameses II. (Fig. 377) executed at the end of the Twentieth Dynasty to replace the original destroyed by robbers. These show all the qualities of great sculpture, vigour, expression and grace, qualities which persisted among the Theban funeral-furnishers after they had begun to die out in the ordinary workshops; we cannot but admit this when we compare the coffin of Rameses II. with the stone statue of Rameses IV. (Fig. 378), which is earlier by some years. The images of gods and kings which were placed in the hypogea after serving for the rites of sepulture, were less carefully executed than the coffins, but they retained a certain grandeur of appearance, if we may judge by the fragments preserved in the Cairo Museum. Among these are figures of Thothmes III., Amenophis II. (Fig. 379) and Heru-em-heb (Fig. 380) carved in cedar or pine-wood, then coated with pitch or bitumen in preparation for the ceremonial of *Opening of the Mouth*. They amaze us, in spite of the mutilations they have undergone. And the furniture which accompanied them was produced by the hands

199

ART IN EGYPT

of workmen; I do not think that the walk of the great feline animals, slow, supple, and restrained, has ever been more perfectly rendered than in the figures of the leopards which adorned the funerary chairs of Amenophis II. (Fig. 381). Nor was furniture ever more elegant or better adapted to the requirements of daily life. What could be more ingenious or more charming in their way than the three arm-chairs, or the jewel-boxes (Fig. 382), deposited by Amenophis III. and his children in the hypogeum of the parents of Queen Thi? The chairs have an extraordinary air of modern comfort; one of them, that in which the front feet are surmounted by human heads, has been christened by visitors the *Empire Chair* (Fig. 383); another might be aptly described as the *Louis XVI. Chair.*

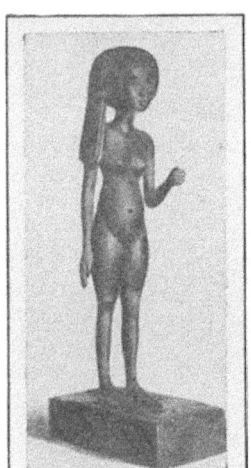

FIG. 389.—STATUETTE OF A WOMAN
(Phot. Chassinat).

The *genre* in which technical skill is manifested in its most original and fertile form is that of the manufacture of toilette utensils, and especially of those which are incorrectly called perfume-spoons. These consisted of a slight handle, and a receptacle for cosmetics and essences (Fig. 384); the variety of invention displayed in design and proportions is amazing; a couchant calf whose back is the lid (Fig. 385); a fox running away, carrying off a large fish whose body forms the spoon; a lotus seed hollowed out as a bowl on a bouquet of flowers (Fig. 386); a young girl, gathering flowers, or passing along the marsh playing a guitar; a nude servant bearing offerings; a grotesque slave bowed beneath the weight of a sack, a leather jar, a vase (Fig. 303) or a boiler out of proportion to his size (Fig. 304). The favourite type, and also the most graceful one, is that of the woman swimming (Fig. 387), her outstretched arms holding up on the water a hollow duck, whose wings fold back and form a lid. Certain statuettes, which look to our modern eyes like drawing-room ornaments, are *double*-statues for persons of modest means, either to represent the master of the house, or to ensure his domestic comfort and the services of slaves. As they were not very expensive, they were much in request, and their manufacturers had acquired inimitable skill in executing them. The ethnical type is rendered with the utmost

THE SECOND THEBAN AGE

fidelity, as in the little negress of the Flinders Petrie collection; rarely has the expression of careless gaiety and good humour proper to the black races been more happily rendered (Fig. 388). The figure of the princess described by Chassinat (Fig. 389), and that in the James Simon collection, emphasise, without exaggerating, the characteristics of the family of Khu-en-Aton, the straight, pointed face, the long, thin body, the curved hip and full thigh. The Lady Naï in the Louvre is a gem, with her roguish face, her young bust, chastely modelled under her gauze robe, the lotus-bud nestling between her breasts. The little maiden at Turin (Fig. 392), adjusting her earring, is naked, and quite unabashed; she is at that indeterminate age when the forms seem to hesitate between those of boy and woman. Male models were less decorative as material. Several who belonged to the priesthood, insisted upon being reproduced in all the splendour of their sacred insignia, and have gained nothing by the process.

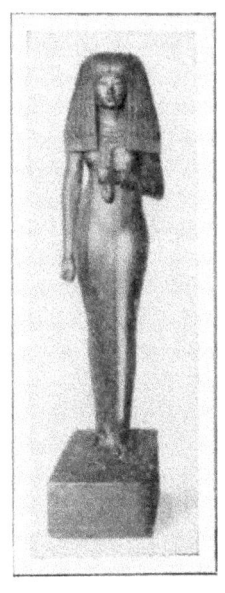

FIG. 390.
THE LADY NAÏ
(The Louvre, Paris).

Those, whose statues are in the Louvre and at Cairo (Fig. 391), would have made a better impression if they had not encumbered themselves with the ensigns of their gods, statuettes of Amon and of Ptah (Fig. 391), and a great ram's head surmounted by a solar disc. The three little fellows at Cairo, with their deceptively Japanese appearance, and the statuettes of officers at Berlin (Fig. 394) and in the Louvre, are not unworthy of a place beside the Lady Naï; their short wigs show the shape of head and neck, their tunics hardly veil the bust, and their shapely, muscular legs emerge robustly from their turned-up petticoats. These are but the wreckage of a flourishing industry, and for the twenty odd specimens that have survived, how many must have perished from antiquity onwards, as fuel! They show us that towards the close of the second Theban age there was a semi-popular art, marked by a variety of aspect and a freedom of

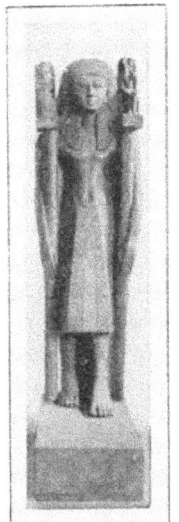

FIG. 391.
STATUETTE OF
A PRIEST.

ART IN EGYPT

technique very disconcerting to those who still hold the immobility of the Egyptian civilisation as an article of belief.

It would seem that the processes of casting metal must have been perfected in the centuries which divide the two Theban periods; thenceforth we find no more of those examples which are partly cast, partly hammered, like the statue of Pepi I.; instead, we have life-size cast bronze statues, like that to which the bust of Rameses IV. in the Pelizaeus collection must have belonged. They were not at first cast all in one piece, but the various parts were prepared separately, and then put together with tenons imbedded in the mass. Scarcely anything has come down to us of the metal statuary, bronze, copper, silver, or gold, and only statuettes have escaped the general destruction; but the goldsmith's work and the jewelry are known to us even better than those of the Twelfth Dynasty. Examples of bronze and copper are not lacking, and there are some very fine specimens in our museum, such as the two gilded bowls found by Newberry in the dust of the tomb of Rakhmiriya, with a little ox in relief at the bottom, or the dish which Daressy brought back from the hypogeum of Hatiyai (Fig. 393); this had a central boss of gold or silver (now lost), and round it a thicket of lotus, among which flocks are pasturing, unconscious that one of their bulls has just been pulled down by a lion. The Louvre possesses some remains of the plate owned by Thuti, the legate of Thothmes III.: a perfect gold cup, and a fragment of a silver cup, but the treasure discovered a few years ago at Zakazik, among the ruins of the ancient Bubastis, dates from the time of Rameses II.

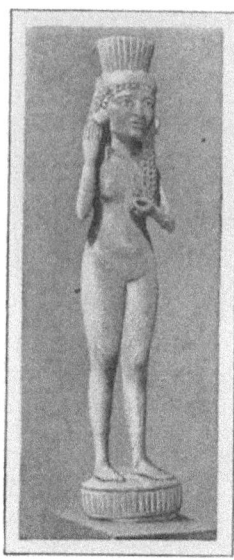

FIG. 392.—YOUNG GIRL (Museum, Turin). (Phot. Lanzone.)

FIG. 393.—DISH OF HATIYAI (Museum, Cairo). (Phot. E. Brugsch.)

THE SECOND THEBAN AGE

and his successors. A golden drinking-vessel, in the form of a half-open lotus mounted upon its stem, bears the cartouche of his granddaughter Tuosret. I would not propose it as a model to our contemporaries, but some twenty shallow silver cups, with flat bases found with it are very delicately ornamented. At the bottom of one of these (Fig. 395), is a lake, well stocked with fish, on which a little papyrus boat with a shepherd and calf as its crew floats idly; a little further on, two young women are swimming side by side. On the bank, four conventional palm-trees grow at equal distances; winged sphinxes with female heads prowl in the interstices, and animals run about distractedly: a wild bull flying from a leopard, hares and gazelles pursued by foxes, dogs and wolves. The figures of the middle register are so low in relief that one would declare them to be incised; those at the edge were *repoussé* more boldly, then worked over and finished with the burin. Two golden jugs accompanied the dishes (Fig. 396); one has a smooth body, and a neck encircled with foliage and figures in outline; the body of the other is symmetrically studded with ears of maize, and

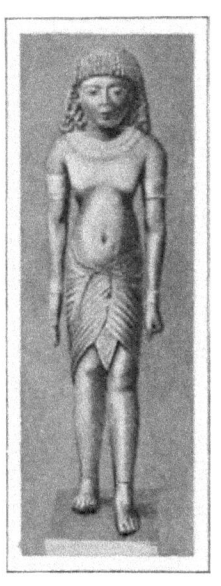

FIG. 394.—STATUETTE OF AN OFFICER (Museum, Berlin).

FIG. 395.—GOBLET FROM ZAKAZIK (Museum, Cairo). *(Phot. E. Brugsch.)*

has a hanging ring fixed to the edge of the neck by a couchant calf most exquisitely worked. The masterpiece of the collection, however, is a ewer, the body of which is covered for three-quarters of its height by longitudinal lines of ovoli, overlying one another like the scales of a pine-cone. The feature that makes it unique is its handle (Fig. 397). A kid, attracted by the aroma of the wine it contains, has climbed up the body, and looks over the brim, standing boldly upon her hind legs, her shins tense, her spine rigid, her knees pressed against two golden flower-calyces, which spring horizontally from the silver surface, her muzzle quivering; a ring inserted in her nostrils served to hang up the jug. The technique is excellent, but here the conception surpasses the technique; nothing could be better than the eagerness of the little animal, and the expression of greedy desire expressed in her whole body.

FIG. 396.—THE TWO GOLD JARS FROM ZAKAZIK (Museum, Cairo). *(Phot. E. Brugsch.)*

Personal ornament, whether arms or jewels, was never treated more solicitously, and on the whole with greater success than at this period. Rings both for fingers and toes, bracelets, chains, mirrors, are all perfect in taste and exquisitely finished. I may instance the mirror-handle, the astounding ivory Bes in our museum (Fig. 398); even certain cases for mirrors are little short of masterpieces, such, for instance, as the one found in the tomb of Amenophis II. (Fig. 399), on which the king's daughter is seen naked among the flowers. And it is not only isolated specimens turned out of the soil by the accidents of research, but whole collections which show us what were the jewel-caskets of persons of high rank, men or women. Queen Aah-hetep, whose mummy received a present from each of her husbands and children, alone possessed enough to enable us to judge. What has not already been said about the dagger and axe bestowed on her by Amasis? (Fig. 400.) The dagger in particular (Fig. 401) excites curiosity, with its blade of dark bronze set in massive gold, on the surfaces of which a lion pursues a

FIG. 397.—THE JUG WITH THE GOAT FROM ZAKAZIK (Museum, Cairo). *(Phot. E. Brugsch.)*

THE SECOND THEBAN AGE

FIG. 398.—IVORY HANDLE OF A MIRROR (Museum, Cairo). *(Phot. E. Brugsch.)*

bull in the presence of four great grasshoppers, and fifteen flowers unfold their petals in a delicate damascened gold pattern. It recalls the Achæan daggers of Mycenæ; but did the dawning civilisations of Europe borrow from Egypt, or did Egypt find inspiration in one of their creations? If the motive be foreign, which is by no means proved, the handling and

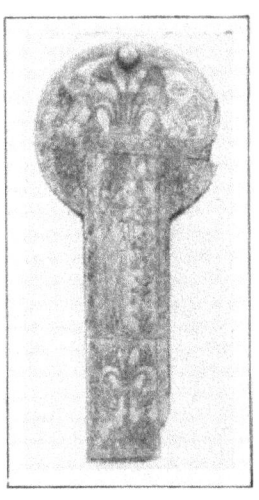

FIG. 399.—MIRROR-CASE (Museum, Cairo). *(Phot. E. Brugsch.)*

composition are purely Theban. The same may be said of the ornaments found with it, necklaces, chains, bracelets, toe and finger rings. Only on the banks of the Nile would mourning relatives have conceived the idea of placing among the plenishings of her they bewailed, boats and their crews in gold or silver (Fig. 402) that she might be able to embark at will upon the western sea or on the ponds of her sepulchral domain. Again, if we examine the various parts of the large necklace which hung round the queen's neck (Fig. 403), we shall see that it had golden falcons' heads enamelled with blue, to fix the ends to her shoulders, a motive in favour among the goldsmiths of the Twelfth Dynasty, as among their predecessors of the Memphite age. The spirals, the flowers with four petals forming a Greek cross, the roundels, the small bell-pendants which form seven of

FIG. 400.—SELECTION OF THE JEWELRY OF AAH-HETEP (Museum, Cairo). *(Phot. E. Brugsch.)*

ART IN EGYPT

the eleven rows, abound on the scarabs and archaic ornaments, and what could be more distinctively Egyptian than the flying falcons, the seated cats, the gazelles turning their heads as they flee, the kids pursued by lionesses?

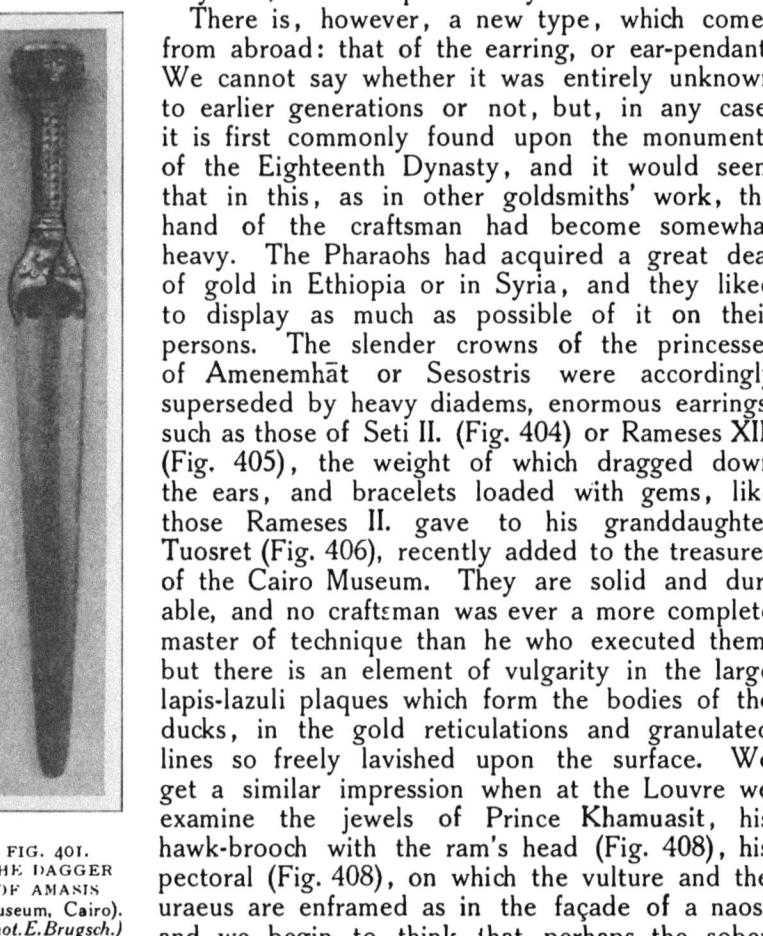

FIG. 401.
THE DAGGER
OF AMASIS
(Museum, Cairo).
(Phot. E. Brugsch.)

There is, however, a new type, which comes from abroad: that of the earring, or ear-pendant. We cannot say whether it was entirely unknown to earlier generations or not, but, in any case, it is first commonly found upon the monuments of the Eighteenth Dynasty, and it would seem that in this, as in other goldsmiths' work, the hand of the craftsman had become somewhat heavy. The Pharaohs had acquired a great deal of gold in Ethiopia or in Syria, and they liked to display as much as possible of it on their persons. The slender crowns of the princesses of Amenemhāt or Sesostris were accordingly superseded by heavy diadems, enormous earrings, such as those of Seti II. (Fig. 404) or Rameses XII. (Fig. 405), the weight of which dragged down the ears, and bracelets loaded with gems, like those Rameses II. gave to his granddaughter Tuosret (Fig. 406), recently added to the treasures of the Cairo Museum. They are solid and durable, and no craftsman was ever a more complete master of technique than he who executed them, but there is an element of vulgarity in the large lapis-lazuli plaques which form the bodies of the ducks, in the gold reticulations and granulated lines so freely lavished upon the surface. We get a similar impression when at the Louvre we examine the jewels of Prince Khamuasit, his hawk-brooch with the ram's head (Fig. 408), his pectoral (Fig. 408), on which the vulture and the uraeus are enframed as in the façade of a naos, and we begin to think that perhaps the sober and delicate taste of the old goldsmiths had been perverted by the models which war or commerce had imported from Asia; it would, however, be going too far to affirm this, before excavation has given us the equivalents in Mesopotamia and Assyria of the treasures gathered together on the banks of the Nile. A great many Asiatics and Europeans established themselves in Thebes and other great cities during

THE SECOND THEBAN AGE

the centuries while the Egyptian hegemony lasted. They modified the habits of the nation to some extent, suggesting new needs to them, and it certainly seems that the passion for very elaborate jewelry came in with them. Here and there, however, the natural temperament still prevailed, and pieces of exquisite simplicity were produced; the high priest Pinotem wore as bracelet a simple gold reed, ornamented with a network of polychrome enamel, and this is one of our finest specimens in the Cairo Museum.

FIG. 402.—ONE OF THE BOATS OF QUEEN AAH-HETEP (Museum, Cairo). *(Phot. E. Brugsch.)*

In these narrow domains of industrial art as in the vaster field of architecture, the second Theban Age showed itself capable of evolving new forms, although it adhered for the most part to the old, and manifested a vigour of creation and production which equalled, if it did not surpass, that of the Memphite Age. The ideal of its artists was less pure and less serene, but it came closer to reality. The impulse which had carried Pharaoh and his armies beyond the isthmus, had moved the whole people, and even those who took no part in the conquests, theologians, men of letters, merchants and artists, feeling the boundaries of their world enlarged, had extended the circle of their knowledge and inspiration, each in his own calling. Seeing things on a great scale, they sought

FIG. 403.—GOLD NECKLACE WITH HEADS OF FALCONS (Museum, Cairo). *(Phot. E. Brugsch.)*

to create greatness, no longer, after the manner of their ancestors the Pyramid-builders, by the exaggerated bulk of their material, but by the reasoned immensity of their conceptions; thus architects had arrived at the gigantic colonnades of Luxor and Karnak, and sculptors at the colossi of the Theban plain and Abû Simbel. When they had reached this point, which they could not surpass, they did not long maintain themselves at its level; exhausted by the very effort they had made, their artistic vigour declined no less rapidly than their military prowess after the reign of Rameses III. Their work is not perhaps the most uniformly beautiful produced by Egypt, and some may rank that of the Memphite times above it; to me it seems, nevertheless, the most vital, the most varied, the most complete, that which is most characteristic of the people, its defects and its qualities. It is certainly that which does most honour to Egypt, and secures for her one of the highest places in the artistic history of the world.

FIG. 404.
GOLD EARRINGS OF SETI I.
(Museum, Cairo).
(Phot. E. Brugsch.)

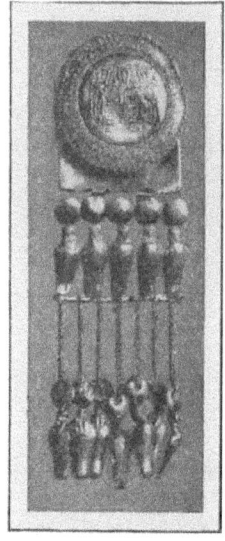

FIG. 405.—EARRING OF RAMESES XII.
(Museum, Cairo).
(Phot. E. Brugsch.)

THE SECOND THEBAN AGE

BIBLIOGRAPHY TO CHAPTER II — PART II

Second Theban Age. Here the monuments are so numerous, aud so much has been written about them, that it has been necessary to make a selection of books. For a general survey, we may recommend Mariette, *Voyage dans la Haute Egypte*, vol. I, p. 55-81, 90-98, and pl. 18-34, 37-38, vol. II, p. 1-82, 107-109, and pl. 39-65, 74, and E. de Rougé, *Album photographique de la Mission*, nos. 47-48, 125.133, 138-141, 151-155, with the portions of text corresponding to these numbers.

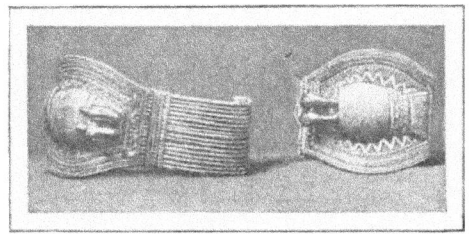

FIG. 406.—BRACELETS OF RAMESES II.
(Museum, Cairo)   *(Phot. E Brugsch.)*

Architecture. — A. *Temples.* — For the temples of the Second Theban Empire, see Perrot-Chipiez, *Histoire de l'Art dans l'Antiquité: I, Egyp*te, 1882, LXXVI-879 p.; — G. Maspero, *Archéologie égyp*tienne, 1st ed., 1888, p. 66-87; W. Spiegelberg, *Geschichte der ägyptischen Kunst*, 1903, p. 40-51. — For the history of the principal temples of Thebes and Nubia, see for Luxor: L. Borchardt, *Zur Geschichte des Luqsortempels*, in the *Zeitschrift für ägyptische Sprache*, 1896, vol. XXXIV, p. 122-138; — Gayet, *Le Temple de Louxor* (Mémoires de la Mission du Caire, vol. XVIII), 1894, Vienne 4to, 174 p. and LIV pl.; — G. Daressy, *La Procession d'Ammon dans le Temple de Louxor* (Mémoires de la Mission française, vol. VIII), p. 380-391 and XVI pl., and the *Notice explicative des ruines du Temple de Louxor*, 1893, Cairo, 8vo, IX-81 p.; — for Karnak: Mariette, *Karnak*, Paris, 1875, Text 4to, 88 p., and *Atlas* fol., LVI pl.; — G. Legrain, *Rapports sur les travaux de Karnak*, in the *Annales du Service des Antiquites*, I 1900, p. 193-200, II 1901, p. 184-189, 265-280, IV 1903, p. 1-40 and 6 pl., V 1904, p. 1-43 and 6 pl.; — L. Borchardt, *Zur Baugeschichte des Amonstempels von Karnak*, 4to, Leipzig 1905, 47 p. and 1 pl.; — for Dêr-el-Bahari; Naville, *The Temple of Deir el Bahari* (Egypt Exploration Fund, vol. XII—XIV, XVI, XIX, XXVI, XXIX); *Introductory Memoir*, 4to, London, 1894, 31 p. and XIV pl., fol., I 1896, 15 p. and XXXI pl., II 1897, 17 p. and XXXII-LV pl., III 1898, 21 p. and LVI-LXXXVI pl., IV 1901, 11 p. and LXXXVII-CXVIII pl., V 1906, 12 p. and CXIX-CL pl., VI 1908, 31 p. and CLI-CLXXIV pl.; — for the Ramesseum: J. E. Quibell, *The Ramesseum (Egyptian Research Account*, vol. II), 4to, London 1898, 21 p. and XXXI pl.; — E. Baraize, *Déblaiement du Ramesséum*, in the *Annales du Service des Antiquités*, 1907, vol. VIII, p. 193-200; — for the temple of Thothmes III and other ruined sepulchral temples: Grébaut-Maspero, *Le Musée égypti*en, vol. I, 1890-1900, p. 3-9 and pl. XVI-XVII; Daressy, *La Chapelle d'Uazmès*, in the *Annales du Service des Antiquités*, 1900, vol. I, p. 97-108; Flinders Petrie, *Six Temples at Thebes*, 1897, 4to, London, 33 p. and XXVI pl.; Weigall, *A Report on the Excavation of the funeral Temple of Thutmosis III at Gurneh*, in the *Annales du Service des Antiquités*, 1906, vol. VII, p. 121—141 and vol. VIII, p. 286; — for Médinet-Habû; G. Daressy, *Notice explicative des ruines de Médinét-Abou*, 8vo, Cairo, 1897, VII-120 p.; Uvo Hölscher, *Das Hohe Tor von Medinet-Habu, eine baugeschichtliche Untersuchung*, 4to, Leipzig 1910,

ART IN EGYPT

to create greatness, no longer, after the manner of their ancestors the Pyramid-builders, by the exaggerated bulk of their material, but by the reasoned immensity of their conceptions; thus architects had arrived at the gigantic colonnades of Luxor and Karnak, and sculptors at the colossi of the Theban plain and Abû Simbel. When they had reached this point, which they could not surpass, they did not long maintain themselves at its level; exhausted by the very effort they had made, their artistic vigour declined no less rapidly than their military prowess after the reign of Rameses III. Their work is not perhaps the most uniformly beautiful produced by Egypt, and some may rank that of the Memphite times above it; to me it seems, nevertheless, the most vital, the most varied, the most complete, that which is most characteristic of the people, its defects and its qualities. It is certainly that which does most honour to Egypt, and secures for her one of the highest places in the artistic history of the world.

FIG. 404.
GOLD EARRINGS OF SETI I.
(Museum, Cairo).
(Phot. E. Brugsch.)

FIG. 405.—EARRING
OF RAMESES XII.
(Museum, Cairo).
(Phot. E. Brugsch.)

THE SECOND THEBAN AGE

BIBLIOGRAPHY TO CHAPTER II — PART II

Second Theban Age. Here the monuments are so numerous, aud so much has been written about them, that it has been necessary to make a selection of books. For a g a survey, we may recommend Mariette, *Voyage dans la Haute Egypte*, vol. I, p. 55-81, 90-98, and pl. 18-34, 37-38, vol. II, p. 1-82, 107-109, and pl. 39-65, 74, and E. de Rougé, *Album photographique de la Mission*, nos. 47-48, 125-133, 138-141, 151-155, with the portions of text corresponding to these numbers.

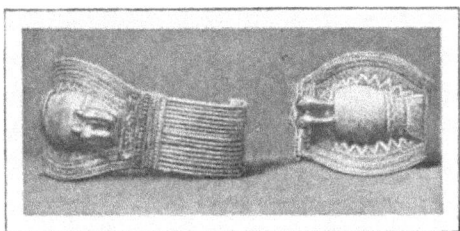

FIG. 406.—BRACELETS OF RAMESES II.
(Museum, Cairo) *(Phot. E Brugsch.)*

Architecture. — A. *Temples.* — For the temples of the Second Theban Empire, see Perrot-Chipiez, *Histoire de l'Art dans l'Antiquité: I, Egypte*, 1882, LXXVI-879 p.; — G. Maspero, *Archéologie égyptienne*, 1st ed., 1888, p. 66-87; W. Spiegelberg, *Geschichte der ägyptischen Kunst*, 1903, p. 40-51. — For the history of the principal temples of Thebes and Nubia, see for Luxor: L. Borchardt, *Zur Geschichte des Luqsortempels*, in the *Zeitschrift für ägyptische Sprache*, 1896, vol. XXXIV, p. 122-138; — Gayet, *Le Temple de Louxor* (Mémoires de la Mission du Caire, vol. XVIII), 1894, Vienne 4to, 174 p. and LIV pl.; — G. Daressy, *La Procession d'Ammon dans le Temple de Louxor* (Mémoires de la Mission française, vol. VIII), p. 380.391 and XVI pl., and the *Notice explicative des ruines du Temple de Louxor*, 1893, Cairo, 8vo, IX-81 p.; — for Karnak: Mariette, *Karnak*, Paris, 1875, Text 4to, 88 p., and *Atlas* fol., LVI pl.; — G. Legrain, *Rapports sur les travaux de Karnak*, in the *Annales du Service des Antiquites*, I 1900, p. 193-200, II 1901, p. 184-189, 265-280, IV 1903, p. 1-40 and 6 pl., V 1904, p. 1-43 and 6 pl.; — L. Borchardt, *Zur Baugeschichte des Amonstempels von Karnak*, 4to, Leipzig 1905, 47 p. and 1 pl.; — for Dêr-el-Bahari; Naville, *The Temple of Deir el Bahari* (Egypt Exploration Fund, vol. XII—XIV, XVI, XIX, XXVI, XXIX); *Introductory Memoir*, 4to, London, 1894, 31 p. and XIV pl., fol., I 1896, 15 p. and XXXI pl., II 1897, 17 p. and I XXXII-LV pl., III 1898, 21 p. and LVI-LXXXVI pl., IV 1901, 11 p. and LXXXVII-CXVIII p., V 1906, 12 p. and CXIX-CL pl., VI 1908, 31 p. and CLI-CLXXIV pl.; — for the Ramesseum: J. E. Quibell, *The Ramesseum* (Egyptian Research Account, vol. II), 4to, London 1898, 21 p. and XXXI pl.; — E. Baraize, *Déblaiement du Ramesséum*, in the *Annales du Service des Antiquités*, 1907, vol. VIII, p. 193-200; — for the temple of Thothmes III and other ruined sepulchral temples: Grébaut-Maspero, *Le Musée égyptien*, vol. I, 1890-1900, p. 3-9 and pl. XVI-XVII; Daressy, *La Chapelle d'Uazmès*, in the *Annales du Service des Antiquités*, 1900, vol. I, p. 97-108; Flinders Petrie, *Six Temples at Thebes*, 1897, 4to, London, 33 p. and XXVI pl.; Weigall, *A Report on the Excavation of the funeral Temple of Thutmosis III at Gurneh*, in the *Annales du Service des Antiquités*, 1906, vol. VII, p. 121—141 and vol. VIII, p. 286; — for Médinet-Habû; G. Daressy, *Notice explicative des ruines de Médinét-Abou*, 8vo, Cairo, 1897, VII-120 p.; Uvo Hölscher, *Das Hohe Tor von Medinet-Habu, eine baugeschichtliche Untersuchung*, 4to, Leipzig 1910,

ART IN EGYPT

IV.68 p. and 10 pl.; — for Bêt-Wali, Garf-Husên, Wadi-es-Sabuâ, Amada, Derr, Abu Simbel, Abahuda: Gau, *Monuments de la Nubie*, Stuttgart Paris 1822, pl. 12-14, 27-32, 42-63; Maspero - Barsanti, *Les Temples immergés de la Nubie.* ' *Rapports*, p. 60-61, 87-89, 106-168 and pl. LIII, LXXXV-LXXXVII, CX-CXL, CXI IV-CLXIX. — B. *The tombs*. — For Ethiopia: Cailliaud, *Voyage à Méroé*, atlas, fol., Paris, 1828, vol. II, pl. VII-XV; — for the royal tombs, see in addition to the works quoted in connection with the temples of Thebes: Mariette, *Abydos*, fol., Paris, I 1868, 86 p., and 53 pl., 1 pl., II 1879, 51 p. and pl. 1-21; Caulfield-Petrie, *The Temple of the Kings at Abydos (Egyptian Research Account*, vol. VIII), 4to, London 1902, 23 p. an I XXVI pl.; — E. Lefébure, *Les Hypogées Royaux de Thèbes (Mémoires de la Mission du Caire*, vol. II-III), 4to, Paris, vol. I 1886, 31 p. and LXIV pl., II 1887-1888, VIII and 191 p. and 74-XLI pl.; — V. Loret, *Les Tombeaux de Thoutmès III et d'Aménophis II et la Cachette royale de Biban el-Molouk*, in the *Bulletin de l'Institut égyptien*, 1899, III d series, vol. IX, p. 91-112 and 15 pl.; — Fr. Guîlmant, *Le Tombeau de Ramsès IX* (Mémoires de l'Institut français du Caire, vol. XV), square 4to, 1907, 96 l.; — Theodore M. Davis, *The Tomb of Thutmes IV*, 4to, London, 1905, XI V-150 p. and XXVIII pl., *The Tomb of Hatshepsitou*, 4to, London 1906, XV-112 p., *The Tomb of Jouîya and Touîyou*, 4to, London 1907, X-48 p. and XLIV pl, *The Tomb of Siphtah*, 4to, Lo don 1908, 45 p. and XXIX pl., *The Tomb of Queen Tiyi*, 4to, London 1910, 45 p. and XXXV l₁., *The Tomb of Haremheb*, 4to, London 1911 (in the press); — for the private tombs; Bénédite - Bouriant - Chassinat - Maspero - Scheil - Virey, *Tombeaux thébains (Mémoires de la Mission du Caire*, vol. V), 4to, Vienne 1899-1894, 657 p.; — Boussac, *Le Tombeau d'Anna (Mémoires de la Mission du Caire*, vol. XVIII), fol., Paris 1896, IV p. and XVI pl.; — Taylor-Griffith, *The Tomb of Paheri at El-Kab*, fol., London 1894, 34 p. and 10 pl.; — N. de G. Davies, *The Rock-tombs of el-Amarna (Archæological Survey of Egypt*, vol. XII-XVIII), 4to, I ondon I 1902, 56 p. and XLI pl., II 1905, 48 p and XLVII pl., III 1905, 41 p. and XXXIX pl., IV 1906, 36 p. and XLV pl., V 1907, 37 p. and XLIV pl., VI 1908, 44 p. and XLIV pl. — C. *The Palaces*. — In addition to Flinders Petrie's work quoted above on Tell - el - Amarna, see G. Daressy, *Le Palais d'Aménophis III à Médinêt-Abou*, in the *Annales du Service des Antiquités*, vol. IV, p. 165-170 and 1 pl. — Robb de P. Tytus, *A preliminary Report on the Re-Excavation of the Palace of Amenhetep III*, 4to, New York 1904, 25 p. and 4 pl.; — Maspero, *Causeries d'Egypte*, 8vo, Paris 1907, p. 257-264.

FIG. 407.—BROOCH OF KHAMUASIT
(The Louvre, Paris).

Painting and Sculpture. — A. *Painting*. — In addition to the works quoted in connection with royal and private tombs, see Fr. W. de Pissing and Reach, *Bericht über die malerische Technik der Hawata-Fresken von Kairo*, in the *Annales du Service des Antiquités*, 1906, vol. VII, p. 64-70; — Flinders Petrie, *Egyptian decorative Art*, 8vo, London 1895; — G. Jéquier, *La Décoration égyptienne*, 4to, Paris 1910/1911, 28 pages and XI. planches — B. *Sculpture*. — For the sculpture of the Second Theban Empire, see, in addition to. the general works: Mariette, *Album du Musée de Boulak*, fol., Cairo 1874, pl. 32, 34, 37; — E. de Rougé, *Album photographique*, fol., Paris 1867, nos. 55-56, 64, 70, 72-74, 77, 80-85, 125-135; — Fr. W. de Bissing, *Denkmäler der ägyptischen Skulptur*, pl. 36-59, 76-97, and the corresponding portions of text; — L. Borchardt, *Kunstwerke aus dem ägyptischen*

THE SECOND THEBAN AGE

Museum zu Kairo, fol., Cairo 1908, pl. 8-15, 24-38, 33 and p. 6-8, 11-13, 14; — J. Capart, *L'Art égyptien*. 4to, Brussels 1909, pl. 61-74, and the article by Maspero, *La Cachette de Karnak et l'École de Sculpture thébaine*, in the *Revue de l'Art ancien et moderne*, 1906, and XX, p. 337-348; the following books, pamphlets and articles: G. Legrain, *Statues et Statuettes de Rois et de particuliers* (Catalogue général du Musée du Cairo), 4to, Cairo, I 1906, p. 30-89, and pl. XXVII-LXXIX, II 1909, 40 p. and LIII pl.; — R. Lepsius, *Eine Sphinx*, in the *Zeitschrift für ägyptische Sprache*, 1882, vol. XX, p. 117-120; — G. Maspero, in O. Rayet, *Monuments de l'Art antique*, fol., Paris 1880-1884, vol. I; *la Statue de Khonsou*, in the *Annales du Service des Antiquités*, 1902, vol. III, p. 181 and I pl.; *Sur un fragment de Statuaire Thébaine*, in the *Revue de l'Art ancien et moderne*, vol. XVII, p. 401-404 and 1 pl.; *La Vache de Déïr el-Bahari*, in the *Revue de l'Art ancien et moderne*, 1907, vol. XVII, p. 5-18 and 3 pl.; *Les Quatre Têtes de Canopes du Musée du Caire*, in the *Revue de l'Art ancien et moderne*, 1910, vol. XXVIII, p. 241-252 and 1 pl.; *Le Musée égyptien*, vol. I, 1890-1900, pl. I, XLIV, and p. 3-4, 39-40, t. II, 1901-1907, pl. V-VI and p. 15-20; — Legrain, *Le Musée Egyptien*, vol. II, pl. I-IX and p. 2-14; — G. Bénédite, *A propos d'un buste égyptien récemment acquis par le Musée du Louvre*, in the *Monuments et Mémoires de la Fondation Piot*, 1905, vol. XIII, p. 3-25; — J. Capart, *Tête égyptienne du Musée de Bruxelles*, in the *Monuments et Mémoires de la fondation Piot*, 1906, vol. XIII, p. 27–34; *Une importante donation d'Antiquités égyptiennes*, in the *Bulletin des Musées royaux du Cinquantenaire*, Brussels 1908, 2nd series, vol. I, p. 84-86; — L. Borchardt, *Der Porträtkopf der Königin Teje im Besitz von Dr. James Simon*, Leipzig 1911, 30 p. and 5 plates.

FIG. 408.—PECTORAL OF RAMESES II.
(The Louvre, Paris).

The minor Arts — A. *Ceramics*. — For household pottery and objects in terra-cotta or glazed and enamelled stone ware, see Fr. W. de Bissing, *Fayencegefässe* (Catalogue général du Musée du Caire), 4to, Vienna 1902, XXXI-114 p.; — Henry Wallis, *Egyptian Ceramic Art*, the *Macgregor Collection*, 4to, London 1898, IV-85 p. and 30 pl.; *Egyptian Ceramic Art*., 4to, London 1900 p. and 12 pl.; — for the enamelled earthenware decoration of palaces and temples: G. Daressy, *Plaquettes émaillées de Medinet-Habou*, in the *Annales du Service des Antiquités*, 1910, vol. XI, p. 49-63. — B. *Wood-work*. For funerery objects, see Theodore M. Davis, *The Tomb of Jouiya and Touiyou*, 4to, London 1907, pl. VI-X, XII-XVI, XXXIII-XLI; — E. Quibell, *Tomb of Yuaa and Thuiu* (Catalogue général du Musée du Caire), 4to, Cairo, 1908, 80 p. and LX pl.; — for toilet utensils, see: G. Maspero, in O. Rayet, *Monuments de l'Art antique*, vol. I; — J. Capart, *L'Art et la Parure féminine dans l'ancienne Egypte*, in the *Annales de la Société d'archéologie de Bruxelles*, 1907, vol. XXI,

ART IN EGYPT

p. 303-334; *Figurine egyptienne en bois au Musce de Liverpool*, in the *Revue archeologique*, 1907, vol. II, p. 369-372 and 1 pl.; — for wooden *double*-statuettes: G. Maspero, in A. Rayet, *Monuments de l'Art* antique, vol. I; — Chassinat, *Une Tombe inviolée de la XVIII*c *Dynastie*, in the *Bulletin de l'Institut français d'archéologie orientale*, 1901, vol. I, p. 225-234; — Flinders Petrie, *An Egyptian Ebony Statuette of a Negress*, in *Man*, 1901, no. 157; — G. Bénédite, *La Statuette de la dame Touï*, in the *Monuments et Mémoires de la Fondation Piot*, 1895, vol. II, p. 29-37 and pl. II-IV, — C. *Goldsmith's work and jewelry:* In addition to the two works by Vernier quoted above, in connection with the jewels of the first Theban period, consult his article: *Notes sur les boucles d'oreilles égyptiennes*, in the *Bulletin de l'Institut français d'Archéologie Orientale*, 1911, vol. VIII, p. 15-41 and pl. I-VII, also: Mark Rosenberg, *Ægyptische Einlage in Gold und Silber*, 4to, Frankfort-on-the-Main 1905, 12 p.; — Fr. W. de Bissing, *Eine Bronzeschale Mykenischer Zeit*, in the *Jahrbuch des Deutschen Archæologischen Instituts*, 1898, vol. XIII, p. 28 - 56, *Ein Thebanischer Grabfund aus dem Anfange des Neuen Reiches*, fol., Berlin 1890—1909 (unfinished); — Daressy, *Un Poignard du temps des Rois Pasteurs*, in the *Annales du Service des Antiquités*, 1906, vol. VII, p. 115-120 and 1 pl.; — C. C. Edgar, *The Treasure of Tell Basta*, in the *Musce égyptien*, vol. II, p. 93-108 and pl. XLIII-LV; — G. Maspero, *Causeries d'Égypte*, 8vo, Paris 1907, p. 335-341, *Le Trésor de Zagazig*, in the *Revue de l'Art* ancien et moderne, 1908, vol. XXIII, p. 401-412 and vol. XXIV, p. 29 38; — Mariette, *Le Sérapéum de Memphis*, fol., Paris 1857, 3rd part., pl. 9, 11-12, 20; — L. Borchardt, *Kunstwerke aus dem ägyptischen Museum zu Kairo*, pl. 43-44 and p. 18.

FIG. 409.—THE ISLAND OF PHILAE AND ITS MONUMENTS SEEN FROM THE SOUTH-WEST BEFORE THE COMPLETION OF THE BARRAGE AT ASSUÂN. *(Phot. Beato.)*

PART III
THE SAÏTE AGE AND THE END OF EGYPTIAN ART

Architecture among the Saïtes: the Theban temple is transformed, and resolved into the Ptolemaic and Roman type — Painting and Sculpture — The Minor Arts: their Development under the Influence of Greek Conceptions — The Death of Egyptian Art.

THE political decadence of Thebes and the fall of the Egyptian Empire hampered the progress of art, but did not interrupt it altogether, as some have supposed. The schools of architecture, sculpture and painting which existed under the Ramessids continued to produce, some even brilliantly, and the entry into public life of certain cities of the Delta, which had hitherto dragged out an obscure existence, led to the tardy development of new schools. It must indeed be admitted that none of these, even in their best moments, displayed that sovereign activity which had characterised the Theban and Memphite Schools. There are, further, some among them, the Saïte, for instance, which are hardly more than names for us as yet. Saïs has

ART IN EGYPT

disappeared, her temples are laid low, and their ruins have perished so completely that we can no longer even trace their plan on the ground; while such of her statues and bas-reliefs as have escaped destruction, are scattered indiscriminately in museums, and we are unable to distinguish them from other relics of the same period. Herodotus speaks of her buildings and their colossi in terms which show that he considered them equal to those of Memphis. I may, however, be allowed to say, after having visited the site on which they stood, that all the temples put together cannot have made up a whole comparable in extent to that formed by the buildings, I will not say of Karnak, but of Luxor. It must be remembered that the Pharaohs who devised them did not command the almost inexhaustible resources of the conquering dynasties, Asia no longer poured a steady stream of gold and silver into their treasury; the fortune they spent in building was drawn from the valley itself, or the regions nearest to the African desert. They had no lack of precious metals, as we know from the enumeration of the sums which Osorkon II. devoted to the restoration of one of the sanctuaries of Bubastis; but what did these represent when compared with those of which Thothmes III. and Rameses II. had formerly disposed? The grandiose enterprises which their predecessors had carried on for centuries were denied to them, but, reduced though their wealth was in comparison with the riches of the past, it was sufficient to make them the boldest architects in the world of their day.

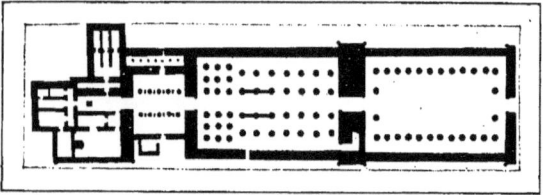

FIG. 410.—THE MOST ANCIENT TEMPLE OF NAPATA.

FIG. 411.—SANCTUARY OF THE TEMPLE OF TIRHAKAH AT NAPATA
(After Cailliaud).

THE SAÏTE AGE

They worked so assiduously, from the Cataracts to the Mediterranean, that they not only preserved the tradition of great art, but transmitted it intact to their foreign successors, Greek or Roman. The majority of the temples we admire in the Saïd are the work of the Ptolemies or the Caesars.

A. ARCHITECTURE.

The various types of the house, the palace and the tomb, had been so ingeniously perfected in the course of the second Theban age, that they changed very little subsequently, and it is extremely difficult to distinguish the Græco-Roman house from that of the Nineteenth or Twentieth Dynasty among the ruins. The former was, in fact, very often nothing but the latter, rebuilt on the same plan, and partly with the same materials. Mastabas, whether of the Theban age with their pyramidal crowns, or of the Memphite age with their flat roofs, were no longer in favour; they had been superseded everywhere by hypogea with or without external chapels. At Thebes it was rarely thought worthwhile to cut new ones, so numerous were those which had been rifled and abandoned after the extinction of the families who had founded them. These were requisitioned, or bought cheaply from the

FIG. 412.—RUINS OF THE PROPYLAEA OF TIRHAKAH AT KARNAK. *(Phot. Beato.)*

FIG. 413.—EAST FAÇADE OF THE TEMPLE OF HEBT. *(Phot. Baraize.)*

ART IN EGYPT

corporations of priests, and one or two of the rooms were adapted, together with the well; after two or three generations, the second-hand owners suffered the fate they had inflicted on their predecessors, and usurpers in the third degree were in like manner despoiled by new intruders. It was different at Memphis, where the sand, covering up the mastabas of previous centuries, generally preserved them from attack by those who coveted ready-made sepulchres. Violations were, however, sufficiently frequent to induce the invention of a type which had some chance of escaping it. At Sakkarah and at Gizeh, accordingly, the following system was adopted: a cavity, some 40 to 50 feet wide, and from 70 to 90 feet deep, was dug out in the plateau, and beside it, on the south, a little square well, from 4 to 6 feet wide, which communicated with it at the bottom. A huge compact block of limestone was then lowered into it to serve for a sarcophagus, covered with mystical scenes and inscriptions; in this a basalt coffin of anthropoid form was imbedded, and round it a vaulted chamber was raised, built of small dressed limestone blocks, the inner walls decorated with written prayers, and sometimes with figures borrowed for the most part from the *Book of the Dead,* or the *Ritual of the Pyramids;* a narrow rectangular window was left in the middle of the vault. On the day of burial, when the mummy had been laid in its bed, the two covers of basalt and limestone were adjusted, then the passage which led to the little well was walled up, and the two cavities were filled in

FIG. 414.—THE TEMPLE OF DAKHLEH. *(Phot. Lythgoe.)*

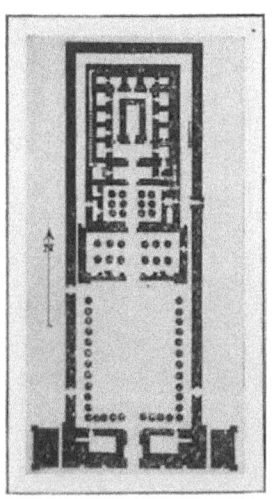

FIG. 415.—PLAN OF THE TEMPLE OF HORUS AT EDFÛ.

THE SAÏTE AGE

with sand and fragments of stone. Thieves attacked the little well at all hazards; when they got into the passage, they began to clear it, but the sand which the masonry had kept in place fell in upon them, and prevented them from advancing. I myself, every time I have attempted to enter by this way, have been stopped just as were the marauders of old, and have had to resign myself to digging out the principal cavity. As it contains from 6000 to 16000 cubic feet of soil, this is generally the work of about three months, with gangs of 100 workmen. We can understand that persons obliged to work furtively and in small numbers, in perpetual fear of surprise, should have respected such well-defended sepulchres; nearly all of those we discover at Sakkarah are virgin tombs.

FIG. 416.—PYLON OF THE TEMPLE OF HORUS AT EDFÛ. *(Phot. Beato.)*

The plan of the temples, like that of the tombs, was very gradually modified. The Tanite and Bubastite Pharaohs built a great many in Lower Egypt, only shapeless fragments of which remain to us at Tanis and Bubastis. In Upper Egypt, the priest-

FIG. 417.—COURT AND PORTICOES OF THE TEMPLE OF HORUS AT EDFÛ. *(Phot. Beato.)*

ART IN EGYPT

kings of the Theban Amon, less wealthy than their rivals of the north, confined themselves to repairing or completing the work of the Ahmessids and Ramessids; it was all they could do to save enough money to complete the decoration of the temple of Khonsu, or to build chapels in a vicious style, such as that of Osiris, Master of Eternity, in the eastern quarter of Karnak. The foundation of the Kingdom of Napata, which separated Ethiopia from the Saïd shortly after the accession of Shashank I., had cut off one of their chief sources of revenue, the gold they had obtained from the rivers and placers of the Upper Nile. Some of the artists employed by the successors of Her-Heru followed their descendants into their new country, and the Theban School was thus divided into two branches; one of these dragged out a languid existence in its ancient workshops, while the other started on a new career in the far south. Ethiopia has not been sufficiently explored to enable us to judge its art equitably. The temples of Napata do not seem to have differed much from those of Thebes in plan and decoration. The most ancient of them (Fig. 410), that which the victorious Piankhi erected about the middle of the eighth century before Christ at the foot of the Holy Mountain, recalls the plan adopted by

FIG. 418.—PRONAOS AND TERRACES OF THE TEMPLE OF HORUS AT EDFÛ FROM THE TOP OF THE PYLON. *(Phot. Insinger.)*

FIG. 419.—THE NAOS OF NECTANEBUS AT EDFÛ. *(Phot. Beato.)*

THE SAÏTE AGE

Amenophis III. at Luxor. It is entered by a court some 150 feet long bordered by porticoes, the twenty-six columns of which are about 6 feet in diameter; next comes a kind of pronaos with forty-six columns, then a hypostyle hall with ten columns, and behind it, the three chapels of the Theban triad, that of Amon in the centre, those of Mut and Khonsu right and left. The temple of Tirhakah, which is later by about forty years, belongs to the category of the hemi-speos, and we might suppose it to have been copied from one built by Rameses II., Dêrr or Wâdi-es-Sabû'a, were it not for certain original features.

FIG. 420.—ÆDICULA ON THE TERRACE OF THE TEMPLE OF HATHOR AT DENDERAH. (Phot. Beato.)

A portico of eight columns gives access to a court of greater length than breadth, with porticoes of eight square pillars, on the outer faces of which were colossal figures of the god Bes. The sanctuary is completely imbedded in the rock, and the approach to it is guarded by two pillars of Bes (Fig. 411). It is improbable that this type was invented by the Ethiopian architects, and indeed it is derived from the Osirian pillar used at Medinet-Habû; we should no doubt find it in Egypt, if all the monuments built after the disappearance of the Ramessids still existed. The distinguishing peculiarity of the examples at Napata is a certain fury of execution which gives this essentially savage god a character even more savage than that

FIG. 421.—HATHOR COLUMNS OF THE PRONAOS AT DENDERAH. (Phot. Beato.)

ART IN EGYPT

bestowed on him by the pure Thebans; a strain of Sudanese barbarism was already manifesting itself in the exiled branch of the Theban school.

FIG. 422.—DOUBLE COURT AND PRONAOS AT KOM-OMBO. *(Phot. Beato.)*

In Egypt, on the other hand, the Ethiopian Pharaohs, transformed into the masters of their former masters by an unimaginable turn of fortune, made no changes in local methods. The chapel commemorating his accession which Tirhakah interpolated more or less successfully to the north west of the holy lake at Karnak, between the wall of Meneptah and the rampart of Rameses II., is built and decorated in a deplorable manner, but wholly without any traces of exoticism. Though the huge column of the great court (Fig. 412), the only fragment still erect of the triumphal propylæa he had designed to build in front of the pylon of Rameses in place of the avenue of rams, belongs to a new order of conception, that conception is purely Egyptian, and marks the terminal point of that slow evolution which had been accomplished in the course of several centuries in the workshops of the Thebaïd and the Delta.

FIG. 423.—THE KASR-KARÛN (After Lepsius).

For indeed this little known period which lasted from the Twenty-first Dynasty to the end of the Persian Period, coincided with a rich aftermath of developments and transformations in architecture. Elements it had previously neglected, and combinations of which it had not thought, were suddenly manifested to it, and the uses it learned to make of them, though they did not modify the

THE SAÏTE AGE

FIG. 424.—ROMAN TEMPLE AT MEDÎNET-HABÛ (After Beato).

main principles of its doctrine, led it to regulate its practice more strictly, and to vary it. Thus the open portico which formed the façade of the hypostyle hall in many of the Theban temples, at Luxor, in the temple of Khonsu, in the Ramesseum, and at Medînet-Habû, sometimes on a level with the court of honour, sometimes from 6 to 10 feet higher, with a low balustrade right and left of the central staircase leading up to it, grew in depth and breadth to the proportions of a monumental vestibule, a pronaos of three or four rows, closed in front by a party wall half-way up the columns of the outer row, pierced by a single door on the longitudinal axis of the building. Again, architects conceived the idea of placing normally in front of the pylon, propylæa more or less imposing, conducting the faithful to the true entrance of the house of the god,

FIG. 425.—FAÇADE OF THE TEMPLE OF DÊR-EL-MEDÎNET. *(Phot. Baraize.)*

FIG. 426.—PRONAOS OF THE TEMPLE OF DÊR-EL-MEDÎNET. *(Phot. Beato.)*

by a kind of triumphal way analogous on a small scale to that which connected Luxor and Karnak, several doors rather near one another; these had two massive jambs surmounted by the usual cavetto, and then an oblong hall open to the sky, enclosed by a variable number of columns in pairs, connected by low walls with the uraeus cornice; instead of an architrave there was a series of divine emblems, probably the falcons or hawks of Horus, for which the cubes on the columns served as bases. As I have just said, the columns of Tirhakah at Karnak belonged to propylæa of this kind, the most ancient known to me; it had nine sisters, of which only the lower courses now exist. In the interior, the arrangement of the chapels had been regularised, and the result was a very sensible amelioration in the disposition of the sanctuary. The Hall of the Sacred Boat, formerly a room open at either end, lost its four colums, and was closed up at the back, so that it could only be entered by a single door facing the pylon. The other rooms were ranged hierarchically round it, the Hall of the Statues, which was the actual sanctuary, immediately behind it, and the rooms of the *paredri* right and left of the Hall of Statues, on three sides of the passage which isolated the Hall of the Boat. This was no abrupt

FIG. 427.—THE MAMMISI AT EDFÛ. *(Phot. Oropesa.)*

THE SAÏTE AGE

metamorphosis; we note its gradual evolution in several temples of the Saite period which escaped destruction or restoration under the Ptolemies. The earliest example of a sanctuary whit a single door, encircled by an ambulatory, is furnished by the chapel of Amenârtâs at Medinet-Habû, but 350 years later, Alexander II. and Philip Arrhidæus built at Luxor and Karnak, sanctuaries with two doors in the long axis of the room. We are rather better informed as to these matters since the temple of Hebt (Fig. 413) in the Great Oasis, has been more closely studied. Founded by Darius I. and finished by Nectanebus II, it has both the successive doors and the preliminary hall, but the three sanctuaries are still side by side as in temples of the purely Theban order (Fig. 414), and the central shrine is a veritable naos, the walls of which are covered with sacred pictures on a small scale.

FIG. 428.—A WALL IN THE TEMPLE OF ISIS AT PHILÆ. *(Phot. Beato.)*

It is, to tell the truth, a second-rate building, relegated to one of the poorest and most distant provinces, and it can give us but little idea of the true temple of the Saïd; nevertheless, when we compare it with the *débris* of the same period which has survived, and then with the complete temples of the Ptolemies, we are easily convinced that from the time of Psammetihus I. to the Macedonian conquest, archi-

ART IN EGYPT

teets produced far more than was supposed when Egyptology was in its infancy. We can hardly assert as yet that they showed any strong inventive faculty, but it is clear that they strove to get new results from the elements they had inherited from their predecessors, and that they employed them more rigorously and logically, if i ⁱ a less grandiose manner. Egypt owes them the magnificent and harmonious plan she applied in her closing centuries at Philæ, Denderah, Edfû and Kom-Ombo; if they did not create masterpieces, as to which it is difficult to form an opinion, at least they taught their pupils how to produce them.

FIG. 429.—THE LONG WESTERN PORTICO AT PHILÆ.
(Phot. Beato.)

Let us take the best preserved of their temples now remaining, the only complete one indeed, that of Horus at Edfû (Fig. 415). It is in the form of a much elongated rectangle, running from north to south on its main axis, and with its façade to the south (Fig. 416). Roughly speaking, the arrangement is the same as in the temple of Khonsu, but the differences in detail are very great. In the first place, in the temple of Khonsu, as in that of Rameses III., and all the known temples of the Theban age, the exterior wall, which starts from one of the towers of the pylon, turns twice at a right angle, and comes back symmetrically to the other tower, is not a free wall, forming an enclosure for the body of the building; it is bound up indissolubly with it, in such a

FIG. 430.
MIXED HATHOR
CAPITAL AT PHILÆ.

manner that the rooms which surround the sanctuary abut upon it, and forms their back wall. In the temple of Horus, on the other hand, it is independent, save at the extremities, where it joins the pylon, and it envelopes the temple without touching it at any point; it interposed like a screen between the external world and the domain of the god, and prevented the profane from seeing anything that was going on inside. Sometimes it was dispensed with, when time or money was lacking, and this was the case at Denderah, and probably also at Esneh. The Saïte and Ptolemaic plan had then, as an addition to the main features of the Ramesside plan, what I may call an isolating barrier, and as soon as the gateway is passed, the differences become more marked. The Ramesside colonnade ran along the two lateral walls, and joined the façade or the second pylon, as in the Ramesseum, or, if the façade had its own raised portico with a balustrade between the columns, as in the temple of

FIG. 431.—THE KIOSK OF NECTANEBUS AT PHILÆ. *(Phot. Fiorelli.)*

FIG. 432.—EAST FAÇADE OF THE MAMMISI AT PHILÆ. *(Phot. Fiorelli.)*

Khonsu and at Medînet-Habû, it was merged more or less adroitly into the colonnade. In the temple of Horus the portico is set into the back of the pylon on either side of the door (Fig. 417); it then follows the lateral isolating walls, and remains as distinct from the main building as these; it stops a short distance from their two angles, and leaves a narrow space between them and itself. The pronaos here has three rows of columns, but the balustrade of the Ramessids was raised between the columns of the first row, and its panels acted as an effectual screen for the more intimate rites (Fig. 418). The court was the only part of the divine house which was really public; only those privileged by their religious calling or social rank penetrated beyond it, and, the better to emphasise the division, a partition-wall, the postern of which was carefully closed in general, barred the ambulatory between the enclosing wall and the sanctuary to the height of the pronaos; the vulgar were never, it would seem, admitted to view the scenes from the life and wars of Horus with which the inner walls were adorned. When the pronaos had been passed through, the sort of forecourt into which one entered, consisting of a hypostyle hall, a vestibule, and its adjacent chambers, was more or less on the ancient plan, but the private apartments of the god were arranged in the new manner. Passing through an anteroom common to both staircases of the

FIG. 433.—CAPITALS OF THE COLUMNS OF THE PRONAOS AT PHILÆ. *(Phot. Beato.)*

FIG. 434. PTOLEMAIC DOORWAY BEFORE THE TEMPLE OF KHONSU. *(Phot. Beato.)*

THE SAÏTE AGE

terrace, the little court giving access to the Chapel of the New Year, several dark chapels, and finally the tabernacle of the sacred boat were reached. In this the Bubastites had replaced the wooden naos of antiquity, by a naos of chased and polished stone; under the Saites, each temple contained at least one of these, sometimes of considerable size, which was much more the real home of the god than the boat. That at Edfû (Fig. 419) has only three lines of inscriptions on the door-jambs, but it is the best of those we

FIG. 435.—THE PROPYLAEA AND FAÇADE OF THE ORATORY OF THE THEBAN PTAH.
(Phot. Legrain.)

know as regards beauty of material and finish of workmanship. The passage which encloses the naos-chamber on three sides is bordered by chapels assigned to the gods of the Enneas; that at the end, where the rites of worship were carried on while the chamber of the boat remained closed, was here called the Forge, in memory of the blacksmiths who helped Horus to conquer Egypt, and who were supposed to have been his first priests. I may add in conclusion that the terraces, formerly forsaken, or given up to the sacred astronomers, had acquired considerable importance, thanks to the expansion of the Osirian myths. On appointed days the mysteries of the passion and resurrection of Osiris were celebrated here in shrines (Fig. 420), or before stelæ designed for this purpose; the parapets, which were made very

FIG. 436.—THE KIOSK OF TRAJAN AT PHILÆ.
(Phot. Beato.)

high, prevented the people from seeing anything of the spectacle offered to the priests and their associates.

ART IN EGYPT

Such was the final type of the Egyptian temple. It had already taken form under Alexander, and it persisted throughout the last centuries of paganism, subject to the slight variations which local worship imposed on its architects. As Denderah, for instance, was the palace of Hathor, the columns of the pronaos had the Hathor-capital with four faces, and the ceiling rested on a forest of immense sistra (Fig. 421). At Kom-Ombo, where the worship of a single divinity had given way, under the Theban Pharaohs, to that of the twin gods Horus and Set, and afterwards, when Set was proscribed for the murder of Osiris, that of Horus and Sobek, a single dwelling would not have sufficed for the habitation of two beings so diverse as the falcon and the crocodile; the temple was accordingly divided into two parallel aisles joined together in the longer axis, but it cannot be described as two adjoining temples; though there are two separate rooms for the boats, the whole forms but a single block encompassed by a corridor, along which are the rooms of the Enneas, those on the south for Sobek, those on the north for Horus. In the same manner the other constituents are not doubled, but are divided each into two sectors belonging respectively to the hawk and the crocodile according as to whether they are situated north or south of the diameter drawn

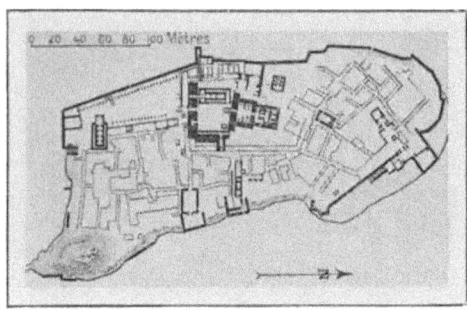

FIG. 437.—PLAN OF THE ISLAND OF PHILÆ (After Cne. Lyons).

FIG. 438.—SOUTH FRONT OF THE TEMPLE OF ISIS AT PHILÆ DURING THE INUNDATION. *(Phot. Fiorelli.)*

THE SAÏTE AGE

from east to west. Neither are there two pylons, but between the towers of the usual pylon are twin doors, the openings of which correspond to those giving access to the two chambers of the sacred boats. We have thus a pronaos, a hypostyle hall, three bi-lobate rooms, if I may so express it, and at their sides the usual closets and staircases. Two stone walls with two ambulatories ran round these; the exterior wall abutted on the pylon as at Edfû, but the interior wall formed a prolongation of the pronaos north and south; it was furnished on the east with a row of cells, probably to lodge the officiating priests, three for Horus on the northeast, three for Sobek on the south-east; in the centre, on the line of junction, a staircase led to upper storeys now demolished. The plan, drawn on paper, shows us a monument too wide for its length, the disproportion of which must have emphasised the heaviness for which Egyptian architects are blamed. We ask, indeed, with some uneasiness if the effect of that gaping double void between the towers of the pylon can have failed to be disastrous; perhaps, however, there was no pylon, but merely a wall like that which encloses the court of Amenophis III. at Luxor. Apart from this point, as to which there is no certainty, the scholars and travellers who visit Kom-Ombo find nothing to offend the eye (Fig. 422); the master who conceived and executed it under the Ptolemies reconciled the general traditions of the school and the exigencies of religion with a great deal of tact.

FIG. 439.—EAST BLOCK OF THE SECOND PYLON AT PHILÆ. (Phot. Beato.)

Temples on a smaller scale, such as I have called the temple of the small town, lent themselves less readily to changes than the others. Although they remained faithful to the Ramesside

ART IN EGYPT

tradition, the examples at Sanhur, at El-Kalaa, near Coptos, of Assuân, of Dakhlâh in the Great Oasis, of Kasr-Karûn (Fig. 423) and even that at Medînet-Habû (Fig. 424), all dating from the Roman period, have not proved sufficiently attractive to engage the attention of archaeologists. Others are but the accessory features of a greater building, such as the delicate chapel of Hathor at Philæ with its dainty court and single chamber. The best specimen of these is the charming temple of Hathor and Amenophis at Dêr-el-Medînet, which fascinated the artists of the French Commission, but has been unduly neglected since their time. It stands like a sentry towards the entrance of the savage gorge which leads from the base of Kurnet-Murrai to the Valley of the Queens, and the Coptic monks who occupied it for a long time rebuilt the brick rampart bestowed on it by the Ptolemies almost on the original foundations. It

FIG. 440.—PRONAOS AND HYPOSTYLE HALL OF THE TEMPLE OF ISIS AT PHILÆ. *(Phot. Beato.)*

forms a rectangle, the façade of which looks to the south-east, and it is quite bare on the outside, the only ornaments being the torus and cavetto which crown the walls (Fig. 425). Inside is a vestibule supported by two columns with floriated capitals, separated from the pronaos by the usual partition-wall (Fig. 426);

FIG. 441.—SOUTH-WESTERN ANGLE OF THE MAMMISI AND GREAT DOOR OF THE TEMPLE OF ISIS AT PHILÆ. *(Phot. Fiorelli.)*

THE SAÏTE AGE

the three sanctuaries adjoin the pronaos, side by side, and a staircase against the western wall led to the terraces. The proportions, the colour, the illumination, are all of extraordinary refinement, and even the sculpture is good for the period; the seven masks of Hathor in a line over the door on the front wall of the pronaos, form an unexpectedly agreeable frieze.

FIG. 442.—TEMPLE OF DÂBÛD BEFORE RESTORATION. *(Phot. E. Brugsch.)*

The two other chapels in the plain on the left bank, south of Medînet-Habû, are far from possessing the same attraction for the traveller. The nearer of the two, called by the natives Kasr-el-Aguz, which was dedicated to a local saint by the Ptolemies, was preceded by a portico, but it consists only of a wide vestibule, and three dark chambers in a line one behind the other. The other, the Kasr-el-Shalauit, was built for the Isis of Hermonthis under Otho, Vespasian and Domitian, and finished by Hadrian and Antoninus Pius; it contains an isolated sanctuary in the middle, two little rooms on the north-west, three on the south-west, and in the last of these, the narrow staircase leading to the roof-terraces. These little temples must not be confused with the *Mammisi*, the house of retreat to which the goddess retired every year to spend in ritual solitude the unclean weeks of travail and convalescence. We know by the scenes depicted at Luxor and Dêr-el-Bahari, that the queens or mother-divinities were placed in

FIG. 443.—TEMPLE OF TAFEH BEFORE RESTORATION. *(Phot. E. Brugsch.)*

ART IN EGYPT

a kind of quarantine at the birth of their children, but their usual prison was concealed in the interior of their houses. Complete isolation and retirement became obligatory under the Ethiopians or the Saïtes. and the first indubitable examples of it are contemporary with the Ptolemies. The Mammisi stood at a short distance from the principal temple, in front of the façade and to the right on coming out of the pylon at Edfû (Fig. 427), at Kom-Ombo, at Philae, and to the left at Denderah; only in one instance, at the temple of Khonsu at Karnak, was it placed behind the facade, almost in the shadow of the western wall of the hypostyle hall. In general, it was built in the form of the hypæthral temple, which had been abandoned since the Eighteenth Dynasty, and it consisted almost everywhere of a single room, surrounded by a colonnade, and preceded sometimes by a court and a monumental doorway; the columns are of the Hathoric order at Edfû, images of the god Bes being applied to them at Denderah, with the complication of a floriated capital at Philæ. The Mammisi of Opet at Karnak is conceived in a totally different spirit, which I attribute to a purely local cause. Popular piety had enshrined the most deeply venerated of Theban relics, the head of Osiris, in the very building where it was supposed the god was born of Opet and the shrine had been placed against the ordinary Mammisi. New arrangements were necessitated by a new use; the chamber of travail with its Hathor-columns was accompanied by corridors and rooms, the most remote of which, a sort of sculptured crypt, was the tabernacle, or rather the cenotaph of the god.

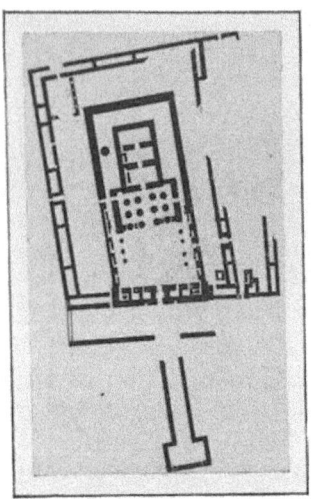

FIG. 444.—PLAN OF THE TEMPLE OF KALABSHAH (After Barsanti).

FIG. 445.—TEMPLE OF DAKKEH (After a drawing by Burton).

THE SAÏTE AGE

Like the plan, the elements of construction and decoration were directly derived from those of the Ramesside age, but the use of them had been systematised and defined. The idea that not only the whole temple, but each of its chambers, was an image of the world, predominates more and more, and manifests itself even in minute details of ornamentation. Thus the lower part of the walls was covered with a flora and a fauna the variety of which increased from century to century, from Edfû to Kom-Ombo, Denderah and Philæ. Bouquets of field and river flowers, buds and blossoms of lotus, thickets and marshes in the midst of which oxen wander and birds nestle, processions of Niles and Nomes bearing the customary tribute in great profusion, all that land and river produce was figured by the Ptolemaic and Roman architects, in places where the Ramessids had prescribed a plain, smooth band, painted black, and separated from the carved panels of the wall by superposed lines of red, yellow and white. This rustic decoration admitted, in addition to natural forms, conventional motives, flowers united into artificial bouquets with interlacements, divine emblems such as the lily crowned with feathers

FIG. 446.—KIOSK OF KARTASSI.
(Phot. E. Brugsch.)

of Nefer-temu, even prisoners bound together in couples at the stake. The decoration of ceilings was no longer restricted to a sprinkling of yellow stars on a dark blue ground, or a flight of vultures; they exhibit the constellations of the Egyptian heavens with their protecting divinities or their conventional animal silhouettes; in certain chambers in the Chapels of the New Year and the Osirian processional altars on the terraces at Denderah, zodiacs composed in imitation of those of the Greeks, replace the stellar imagery of purely Egyptian origin. Between plinth and cornice, that is to say, according to doctrine, between heaven and earth, there was a like profusion of pictures. There are no longer only two or three registers upon the walls, but five or six or more, and their multiplication was the natural consequence of the auxiliary virtue attributed to divine figures and their actions. If two or three scattered divinities preserved a chapel from destruction, twenty or more would necessarily increase the security. Moreover, the empty spaces between the figures were like so many breaches, through which evil influences might penetrate; artists did their best to reduce them by increasing the number and length of formulae and explanatory texts. Thus the Ptolemaic and Roman temples are literally peppered with scenes and inscriptions, the closer and more minute as the date of construction advances; a hall of medium size at Edfû, Denderah, Ombo or Philæ (Fig. 428) contains more than the great hypostyle hall of Karnak. And in many cases, the magic of this external defence was doubled by an internal defence known only to the initiated. In Pharaonic buildings there are few examples of secret chambers, corridors or cabinets concealed in the thickness of the walls. I know of one at Abydos in the Memnonium of Seti I., another at Medinet-Habu in the cenotaph of Rameses III., and finally, one in the temple of Khonsu to the left of the sanctuary. The last is a veritable crypt near the ceiling, 13 feet from the ground, in the space between two accessible chapels, and was perhaps the hiding-place of the priest who pronounced the oracles. On the other hand, the Ptolemaic and Roman temples always contain a number more or less great, which are group-

FIG. 447.—CHAPEL IN THE QUARRIES OF KARTASSI. *(Phot. Thédenat.)*

FIG. 448.—THE EAST GATE OF KASR-IBRÎM. *(Phot. Oropesa.)*

THE SAÏTE AGE

ed in general round the sanctuary of the boat. They seem to have been built after the downfall of the national dynasties to

FIG. 449.—FIELD OF THE PYRAMIDS OF MEROE
(After Lepsius).

receive the sacred treasures, the precious utensils, the jewels, statues, and mystic emblems, all the material used by Pharaoh in the rites he alone could celebrate, which naturally fell into disuse when foreign monarchs ascended the throne; it was stored in subterranean cells, in the hope that the day would come when the ancient sovereignty would be restored, and the antique rites would reappear in all their splendour. Edfû possesses at least two, and Denderah more than a dozen, some of which are bare, while others are ornamented with bas-reliefs which indicate the uses to which they were destined. Although they were entered only by a few priests, their sculptures are as carefully executed and as delicate in style as those of the public rooms; the god, who could see everything, would not have tolerated mediocrity in his secret places, any more than in his public domain. Such a room was entered by an aperture, sometimes on a level with the floor, sometimes placed so high that it could not be entered without a ladder; a movable stone, concealed in the decoration, masked this ingress, known only to the priests, who transmitted the secret from generation to generation.

Pillars and columns were modified by the same influences as mural decoration, not in the base and the shaft, which remained essen-

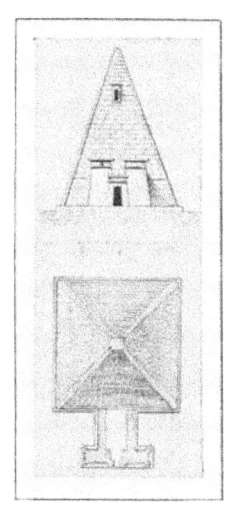

FIG. 450.—PLAN AND ELEVATION OF AN ETHIOPIAN PYRAMID
(After Lepsius).

tially identical with those of the Ramesside age, but in the capital. The pillar was used much less than in earlier times; or at least we rarely see it in the temples which have survived. On the other hand, the evolution of columns and their capitals, once initiated, continued rapidly, and a hasty survey of some of the most famous temples, those of Edfû or Philæ, show what a variety of forms it engendered; the number was so great as to suggest to architects a highly ingenious combination. Whereas their Ramesside predecessors had, as a rule, allowed only a single kind in any one part of a building, and even when they introduced two, as in their hypostyle halls, rigorously restricted each to the special place assigned to it, these later architects mingled them all, but in such a manner that each kind was represented by two symmetrical examples in the general scheme; thus at Edfû, the dactyliform or papyriform capitals which succeed each other in the west portico of the great court have their counterpart at the same height and in the corresponding row in the east portico. When once this principle had been laid down, it was applied assiduously, and its effect was to co-ordinate the somewhat vague sensations evoked in the spectator's mind by the infinite diversity of types. When we enter the court at Edfû, or the long porticoes of Tiberius at Philæ (Fig. 429), we are struck instinctively by the impression of unity they give, and on reflection we perceive that this unity arises from the symmetry observed between one side and the other in the use of capitals. In the beginning, the Saites were content to utilise the styles

FIG. 451.—THE TEMPLE OF MESAURÂT (After Lepsius).

FIG. 452.—STATUE OF A SQUATTING FIGURE (Museum, Cairo). (Phot. Legrain.)

THE SAÏTE AGE

for which the monuments of the past furnished models, even those which might have been supposed to have been entirely discredited. Thus at Elephantine we find polygonal columns with sixteen faces erected by Amasis and bearing his name. This, however, was exceptional, and the so-called proto-Doric order was never used after his time, save in those cases where the Ptolemies deliberately imitated the fashions of the Eighteenth Dynasty, as in the chapel of the Theban Ptah, which they aspired to pass off as a work of Thothmes III. Everywhere else, they adhered to the styles preferred by the Ramessids, the lotus, papyrus, and dactyliform columns, and in the places where religion demanded them, Hathor-columns, but so modified as to be almost unrecognisable. It even happened sometimes that their new

FIG. 453.—PETUBASTIS
(Museum, Cairo). *(Phot, E. Brugsch.)*

conception of an order so far triumphed over the old that the Hathor capital no longer consisted merely of two female masks welded together at the nape of the neck, not always with a very happy effect, even at Dêr-el-Bahari; it was expanded into four faces, united by the folds of the headdress, and the square cube which crowned them showed over each a naos between two volutes (Fig. 430). The column thus terminated has the form of a gigantic sistrum, and in spite of the want of proportion between the shaft and the head, it has a grand appearance; there is nothing more impressive in Egypt than the Hathor-portico at

FIG. 454.—OSORKON II. PUSHING A BOAT
(Museum, Cairo). *(Phot. E. Brugsch.)*

ART IN EGYPT

FIG. 455.—AMENARTĀS (Museum, Cairo). *(Phot. E. Brugsch.)*

Denderah. At Philæ, in the kiosk of Nectanebus (Fig. 431) and in the colonnade of the Mammisi (Fig. 432), the architect has introduced the Hathorian motive as a sort of abacus or cube between the architrave and other capitals with floriated decorations. The combination has a certain bizarre grace not unpleasing; the art with which the sistrum is incorporated with the bouquet from which it rises is truly admirable. The modifications to which the papyriform column was subjected are no less happy. The first step was to apply four or more bunches of flowers to the edges of the open corolla, which clothed its nudity; the details of this addition, conventionalised more and more, soon gave the whole the appearance of a heraldic lily. This same ornament laid upon the lotus or palm-leaf capitals, reduced them by degrees to identity with the papyriform capital; towards the end of the Ptolemaic age and under the Caesars, the original forms of the three orders had become hardly more than an almost invisible support on which motives borrowed from the flora of the country, leaves, flowers, buds, grasses, clusters of dates and bunches of grapes, rose in vigorous profusion. All these were not heaped up or applied haphazard; the various elements were gradually combined with an exquisite sense of arrangement and proportion; designers did not create them all at once, and we can follow the development of their ideas from the relatively simple essays of Edfû to the more cunning complexities of Philæ and Esneh. The hypostyle hall of the great temple of Isis at Philæ undoubtedly contains their most perfect achievement (Fig. 433). Not only are the motives they carved on each of the capitals inconceivably rich and tasteful; they heightened the effect

FIG. 456. ANKHNASNUFIABRI (Museum, Cairo). *(Phot. E. Brugsch.)*

THE SAÏTE AGE

of these by shades of green, blue, red, and yellow incomparably soft and harmonious; those painted columns, which the enlargement of the barrage at Assuân will soon destroy, are among the purest and most delicate creations not only of Egyptian, but of any art. It would seem that in Upper Egypt, at any rate, the first Ptolemies merely cleaned and restored the buildings of the Theban Pharaohs. Thus Ptolemy Soter, under the name of Philip Arrhidæus and Alexander Aigos, transformed the columned chapels in which Thothmes III. and Amenophis III. had kept the sacred boat at Karnak and Luxor respectively, into dark sanctuaries; he retained the two doors of the original plan, one of which, however, that at the back, soon disappeared. The great temple of Amon was encumbered with ex-voto offerings and statues, and the ruins which the Ethiopian and Assyrian invasions had accumulated here, had never been restored completely. All this rubbish, which was of no interest to contemporaries, was buried in an immense *favissa* dug out between the hypostyle hall and the seventh pylon; then the eastern walls of the hypostyle hall were consolidated, the level of the floor was raised a little, the pavement was replaced, and the bases of the columns, already eaten away by saltpetre, were restored. The monumental doorway in front of the temple of Khonsu was entirely rebuilt (Fig. 434). The oratory of the Theban Ptah (Fig. 435) was restored, and a last pylon, more immense than any of the others, was being built in front of the pylon of Rameses II., when, the town having revolted, Ptolemy Soter II. destroyed it

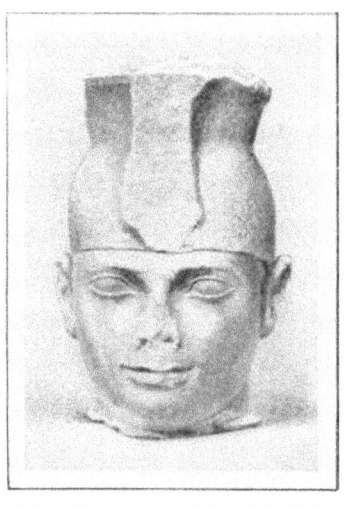

FIG. 457.—HEAD OF A STATUE OF TIRHAKAH (Museum, Cairo). *(Phot. E. Brugsch.)*

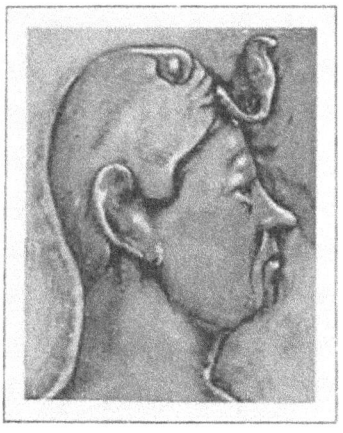

FIG. 458.—PSAMMETICHUS I. (British Museum, London).

ART IN EGYPT

FIG. 459.—PSAMMETICHUS III.
(The Louvre, Paris).

in the year 87 B. C. On the other bank of the river Ptolemy IV. Philopator and Ptolemy Euergetes founded, in the place of a ruined shrine of Amenophis III., the little temple of Dêr-el-Medînet, dedicated, as I have already said, to the goddess Hathor and the magician Amenophis, son of Hapu, whose worship was then so popular. Their activity was not confined to the limits of the ancient capital; wherever we go in Middle Egypt and in the Delta, we find grandiose traces of it, at Sebennythos, at Xois, at Bubastis, at Heracleopolis, at Oxyrrhynchos, at Hermopolis, at Kau-el-Kebir, at Akhmîm, and chaotic though the remains of their work are, we are obliged to admit that in dimensions at least they bear comparison with the most important monuments of the Theban age. We should, however, have some difficulty in determining what was its general character, if the Saïd had not preserved certain temples, intact, or nearly so, at Esneh, Edfû, Kom-Ombo, Assuân, and Philæ (Fig. 409). The Romans continued the work of the Ptolemies; the few buildings or fragments of buildings which date from their domination, such as the pronaos of Esneh and the kiosk at Philæ (Fig. 436), show that the schools of architecture had not degenerated under their rule. Philæ was to the later centuries what Karnak had been to the earlier ages, the favoured spot where all the sovereigns had worked uninterruptedly, and consequently where the successive phases of the evolution of art may be most clearly observed (Fig. 437), Amasis had built a chapel there, and in front of this Nectanebus had put up first a gateway and then a pavilion which marked the southern landing-stage for travellers coming from the south. Ptolemy Philadelphus demolished the building of Amasis, and devised the present temple (Fig. 438), pylons (Fig. 439), courts, hypostyle

FIG. 460.
STATUETTE OF A QUEEN
(Museum, Cairo).
(Phot. E. Brugsch.)

THE SAÏTE AGE

hall (Fig. 440), sanctuary, and mammisi (Fig. 441), which where decorated by his Macedonian or Ethiopian successors. Towards the northern end of the island, Augustus erected a chapel in the Roman style, as if to emphasise the rights of the Empire, but having accomplished this act of annexation, he returned to the native tradition in the great southern colonnade and the unfinished kiosk, incorrectly called the Kiosk of Trajan. It was also purely on the Egyptian system that Claudius built the sanctuary and Hadrian the propylæa of the west.

FIG. 461.—MENTEMHÊT (Museum, Cairo). *(Phot. E. Brugsch.)*

The town occupied all the space not filled by the temple; towards the close of the third century of our era, it was

FIG. 462.—NSIPTAH (Museum, Cairo). *(Phot. Legrain.)*

FIG. 463.—MENTEMHÊT (Museum, Cairo). *(Phot. E. Brugsch.)*

a kind of museum, in which the later manifestations of Egyptian art could be studied almost reign by reign.

ART IN EGYPT

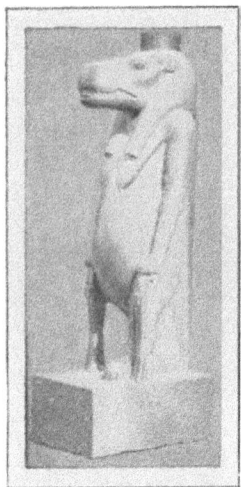

FIG. 464.—THOUÊRIS
(Museum, Cairo).
(Phot. E. Brugsch.)

Beyond lay what was still Egypt for a time, but an Egypt which had relapsed into a semi-barbarous state, and in which artistic life was only maintained by the effort of a foreign will. The kings of Ethiopia, who disputed the possession of the Nubian marches first with the Ptolemies and then with the Caesars, have left few traces of their supremacy there. They founded two temples, however, at least, one near Dâbûd (Fig. 442), some half dozen miles south of Philæ. the other at Dakkeh, on what was probably the site of an oratory of Thothmes III.; the Ptolemies completed the first, the Romans enlarged the second, and when they had thoroughly colonised the country, they built small chapels here and there; at Tafeh (Fig. 443), at Kartassi, at Dendûr, at Maharraka, and a great temple at Kalâbshah. The plan (Fig. 444) is that used in Egypt proper at the same period, but the execution is less careful. Kalâbshah is not unlike Edfû, and is imposing in spite of the obliquity of its pylon and the disproportion between its depth on the main axis and the breadth of its façade; but Dakkeh (Fig. 445) when it was intact, made a far more favourable impression. The Ethiopian king Ergamenes first raised a small shrine to Thoth-Paotnuphis, to commemorate the taking of Dodecaschoenus, (i. e. the territory of the Cataract between Philæ and Syene), from the Macedonians. Ptolemy Philopator and Ptolemy Physcon successively added to it a sêkos, a pronaos with two columns in the façade, and a pylon; less than a century later, Augustus surrounded the primitive chapel with a number of new buildings; on the east, an

FIG. 465.
HEAD OF A SAÏTE KING
(Museum, Cairo). *(Phot. E. Brugsch.)*

THE SAÏTE AGE

aedicula dedicated to the two lions of the Heliopolitan Enneas, Shû and Tefnut, on the south a sanctuary with its naos in

FIG. 466.—STATUE OF A PRIEST (Museum, Cairo). *(Phot. E. Brugsch.)*

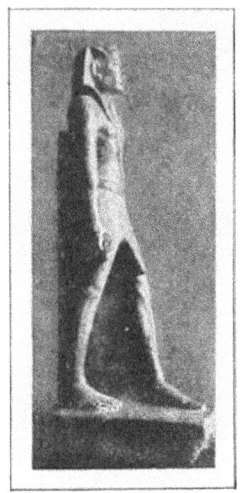

FIG. 467. STATUE OF PSAMMETICHUS I. (Museum, Turin).

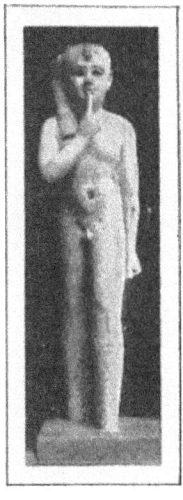

FIG. 468.—STATUE OF HORUS AS A CHILD (Mus., Cairo). *(Phot. E. Brugsch.)*

granite, on the west a flight of steps leading to the terrace of the sanctuary, and finally, a double stone wall, which made the whole a kind of donjon destined to protect the village of Pselchis against the barbarians. Dendûr is set against the mountain, in front of the grotto in which lies the local saint who was worshipped here, and its quay, the triumphal gate which precedes the pronaos, and the pronaos itself are agreeable in design. The chapel hewn in the sandstone of the quarries of Kartassi in the first century of our era is happy in its effect (Fig. 447). The kiosk (Fig. 446), which is all that remains of the local temple, recalls the kiosk of Trajan at Philæ

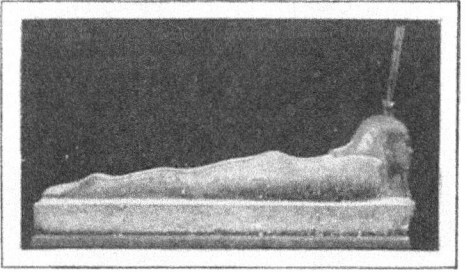

FIG. 469.—STATUETTE OF RECUMBENT OSIRIS (Museum, Cairo). *(Phot. E. Brugsch.)*

ART IN EGYPT

FIG. 470.—STATUE OF ISIS (Museum, Cairo). *(Phot. E. Brugsch.)*

FIG. 471.—STATUE OF OSIRIS (Museum, Cairo). *(Phot. E. Brugsch.)*

from a distance, but it owes its more picturesque charm to its position on a kind of rocky spur on the river-bank. Maharraka, the southernmost temple built by the Emperors, is also the latest. Seen from outside, it is a rectangular box, dull and heavy in appearance; inside, it is a court bordered by colonnades on the south, west, and north, and towards the north-east angle, a block of masonry in the thickness of which is a spiral staircase, the only one of its kind in the southern regions. Beyond Maharraka, there are no memorials of the Latin domination save at Ibrîm, where the eastern door of the wall still exists (Fig. 448), while towards the northern extremity of the plateau there is a nondescript building, half temple, half barrack, which certainly dates from the time of Septimius Severus. This outpost of the Empire

FIG. 472.—THE COW HATHOR OF SAKKARAH (Museum, Cairo). *(Phot. E. Brugsch.)*

THE SAÏTE AGE

evidently remained its artistic, as well as its political dependency, but did its influence extend further south, to the territories connected with the kingdom of Meroë? We know so little of the history of Ethiopia after the time of Tirhakah and his immediate successors, that it is difficult to say anything definite on this head. The tombs of the Ethiopian Pharaohs, the plans and designs of which have survived, are obviously derived from the pyramid-mastabas of the Theban age. (Fig. 449). They include a pyramid, in fact, but it rests on a low base, has a sharper point than the Memphite pyramids, and tori dividing its faces; a monumental door, or even a pylon, marks the entrance of the chambers, which are frequently decorated with bas-reliefs (Fig. 450). Long after Tirhakah, the temples continued to be purely Egyptian in type, though they show a slovenliness of execution which betrays the unskilfulness of their architects and stone-cutters, but towards the close of the first century after Christ, Greek elements began to mingle with the Pharaonic, and a hybrid style was formed, of which the temple of Messaurât is the best known example so far (Fig. 451). It dates from the third century of our era, that is to say, from the last days of the monarchy. Meroitic art may have long survived the downfall of the dynasties of Egyptian origin; I am inclined to recognise its influence in what we know of Axumitan art.

FIG. 473. STATUE ROUGHLY BLOCKED OUT (Museum, Cairo). (Phot. E. Brugsch.)

FIG. 474.—STATUE FINISHED BUT FOR THE HEAD (Museum, Cairo). (Phot. E. Brugsch.)

Architecture then had been dead for some time in Egypt proper, when the last and most obscure of its progeny perished on foreign soil. It was still so vital and so magnificent in the third century, when it produced Ombos and Esneh, that we cannot explain its sudden downfall by inherent causes. Up to its supreme moment, its masters knew their craft thoroughly, and applied its principles with incontestable superiority; it would surely have subsisted for

ART IN EGYPT

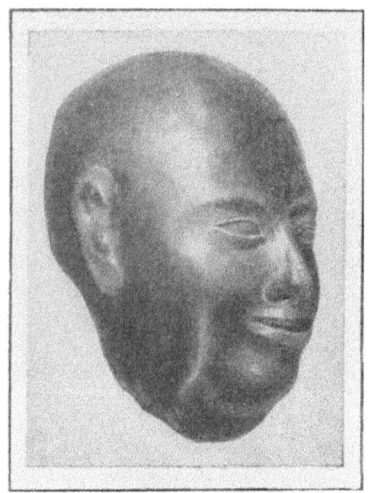

FIG. 475.—HEAD OF A STATUE
(Museum, Berlin).

centuries longer, if it had not been so thoroughly impregnated with the religious conceptions to which it owed its inspirations, that it could not survive them. The Roman basilica, and even the Greek temple, had hardly any constituent elements which were exclusively pagan; at the price of certain modifications of no great importance, they lent themselves to the requirements of triumphant Christianity, and furnished it with suitable churches. But the arrangements which made the Egyptian temple the mysterious abode of Amon, Horus, or Isis and their court, had no longer any reason for existence in relation to the new God. What need was there for the chambers of the boat, the shrine of statues, the chambers of the Enneas, the hypostyle halls, the pronaos, in a religion the whole ritual of which was performed in public, and in which

FIG. 476.—HEAD OF A STATUE
(The Louvre, Paris).

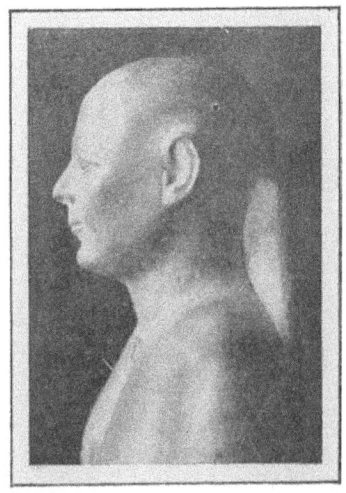

FIG. 477.—BUST OF A STATUE
(Museum, Cairo). *(Phot. E. Brugsch.)*

THE SAITE AGE

the paraphernalia of images and vases was reduced almost to nothing? Christ and his saints did not hide in dim recesses, and did not rigorously exclude certain categories of the faithful; they flung wide their doors, and allowed all who joined their community to approach them freely. Those of the Egyptians who rallied to them could not help renouncing their national architecture, as they had renounced their national writing; both were too close a reflection of the antique religion to survive it.

B. SCULPTURE.

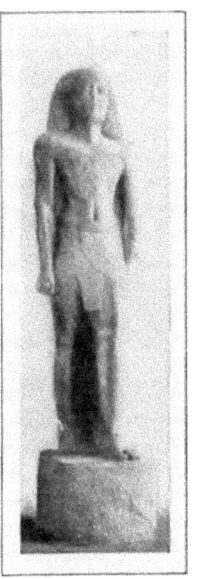

FIG. 478.—COLOSSAL STATUE OF AMENOPHIS, SON OF HAPU (Museum, Cairo). (Phot. E. Brugsch.)

Sculpture did not offer such a vigorous resistance to the action of centuries as architecture; yet it had its happy seasons, and at various times produced works which deserve to rank very highly in the estimation of our contemporaries.

Many of these works were still of the Theban school. We know how, rather more than a century after the death of Rameses III., the priests of Amon usurped authority and ruled over the Thebaïd, sometimes under the title of High Priest, sometimes under that of King. They allowed their relatives to set up statues in the temples, and this privilege, continuing throughout five or six centuries, ended by encumbering the halls with works, many of which, if not actually bad, lack originality. The favourite attitude was inelegant. It represents the sitter swathed in the closely fitting mantle from which only the hands emerge, squatting on the ground, the thighs drawn up to the chest, the arms crossed on the knees (Fig. 452). How was it possible to get any effect out of an attitude which condemned the model to be nothing but a bundle with a head? It had been popular since the Twelfth Dynasty, and there are good examples of it of the time of Thothmes III., in the Senmut of Cairo and that of Berlin; but under the High Priests and the Saïtes, it became almost obligatory for the ex-votoes of the temples. All the merit of these figures lies in the head, which is often very delicate, as in the Pedishashi at Berlin, in which an expression of joyous youth and good-nature atones for the clumsiness of the whole, and the Petubastis at Cairo (Fig. 453). In cases where the model

ART IN EGYPT

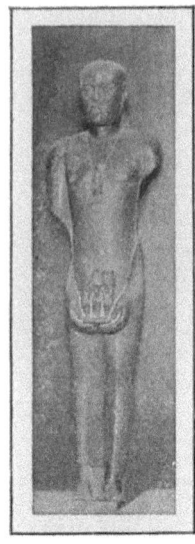

FIG. 479.
TANITE STATUE
(Museum, Cairo).
(Phot. E. Brugsch.)

consented to adopt a less irksome position, our admiration is no longer confined to the head, and the fine qualities of the school are revealed. They proclaim themselves in the limestone statuette of Osorkon II., dragging himself along the ground, and pushing before him a boat (now mutilated), as an offering to his god (Fig. 454); and again, though in a lesser degree, in the alabaster Amenartas so much admired by Mariette (Fig. 455); the face is doleful and lifeless, but the modelling of the bust and abdomen is chaste and delicate. The Ankhnasnufiabri (Fig. 456) of Cairo might almost bear comparison with the Amenartas, but for the headdress which weighs down her head, and the heavy pillar against which she is set; the features have a somewhat affected delicacy, but the rest is poor in design. This, indeed, is characteristic of the works of this period: the limbs are often neglected, while the face is very carefully treated. For every one or two passable bodies, we shall find some twenty fine heads, such as the energetic head of the Ethiopian Tirhakah (Fig. 457), with his almost negroid face, the intelligent head of that crafty old peasant, Psammetichus I. (Fig. 458), the melancholy head of Psammetichus III. (Fig. 459). The mutilated queen at Cairo, which dates from the Ethiopian period (Fig. 460) is a little rough, perhaps because of the material in which it is carved, the pink granite of the cataract, but it does not lack decision and nobility. The portrait of Mentemhēt (Fig. 461), who ruled at Thebes at the end of the Twenty-fifth Dynasty, is the most vigorous example known to us of this last Theban school. The man was common, even brutal in appearance, and the singular wig with

FIG. 480.—ALEXANDER AIGOS (Museum, Cairo).
(Phot. E. Brugsch.)

THE SAÏTE AGE

which he thought well to crown himself on this occasion, was not calculated to temper the mulish vulgarity of his countenance; all the more credit is due to the artist for having built up a work of such power that it remains superb in spite of mutilation, on such an unpromising foundation. The statues of Nsiptah (Fig. 462 and 463) son of Mentemhēt and his heir in the administration of the principality of Amen, are not marked by the same almost excessive realism; nevertheless, the sculptor has faithfully reproduced the expression of self-sufficiency and aristocratic inanity which differentiates this personage from his father. I might enumerate some nine or ten examples which, though not equal to this, will bear comparison with it; one among them, the Thouêris at Cairo, demands special mention for its monstrosity of conception. It represents neither a human being nor a normal animal (Fig. 464), but a hippopotamus with a huge muzzle, smiling jaws, flabby breasts, and swollen abdomen, the form in which the Egyptians incarnated one of the divine protectresses of maternity. Rising elegantly upon her hind legs, her two forepaws resting upon symbolical knots of rope, she is cut out of a block of green breccia with a precision which somewhat redeems the strangeness of her appearance, but all the skill of the technique fails to mask her hideousness; one cannot but pity the master-craftsman whose religion obliged him to treat a motive so unfavourable to art seriously.

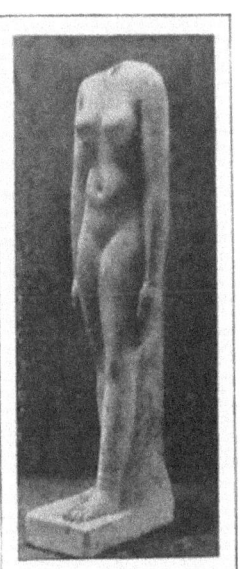

FIG. 481.—STATUETTE OF A WOMAN
(Museum, Alexandria).
(Phot. Breccia.)

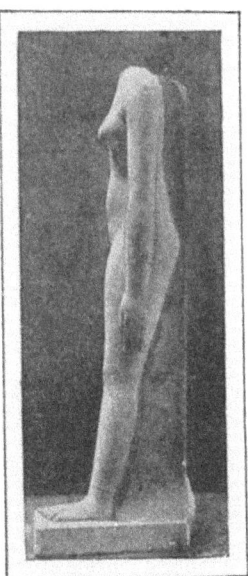

FIG. 482.—THE SAME IN PROFILE
(Museum, Alexandria).
(Phot. Breccia.)

All the schools of Northern Egypt put together have not given us one half of that which has been bequeathed us by

ART IN EGYPT

FIG. 483.—THE ALEXANDRIAN HORUS (Museum, Cairo). *(Phot. E. Brugsch.)*

the Theban School. The Memphite School has left us a few busts of kings, Saïte or Ptolemaic, (Fig. 465) and certain rare statues, distinguished by that characteristically soft and delicate execution which has made it possible for us to recognise its existence: these are, a full-length statue of Psammetichus I. (Fig. 467), a statue of a priest holding an Osiris before him (Fig. 466), a statue of a youthful Horus, naked, his finger to his lip, the plait over his ear, the uraeus on his forehead (Fig. 468), a statuette of an Osiris mummy, lying face downwards on his base, and raising his head in the first spasm of resurrection. The four monuments of Psammetichus in green breccia preserved in the Cairo Museum, which belong to the beginning of the Persian period, are the most remarkable. I deliberately pass over the table of offerings, which is merely a good piece of work by the marble-cutter of some necropolis; the Isis (Fig. 470), and the Osiris (Fig. 471), at whose feet it originally stood, are marked, it must be admitted, by a flatness of inspiration in painful contrast to the supreme skill of their technique. The modelling is correct, but soft and nerveless, the eyes empty, the smiles inane, the faces inanimate; they are, in fact, a perfect anticipation of those religious figures which abound in our modern ecclesiastical warehouses. The cow which accompanied them (Fig. 472) is posed in the same manner as that of Naville, and also wears the two huge feathers of Hathor; Psammetichus is standing in the shadow of her head, in the attitude of Amenophis II. The Saïte sculptor, like his Theban predecessor, was unable to disengage the legs of his beast, and has retained a stone partition between her belly and the ground; nevertheless, he was determined to show her complete on either side, so to her one head, she has two chests in profile, two bodies and two sets of legs. The contours have an unpleasant dryness due to the hardness of

FIG. 484. MEMPHITE STATUE (Museum, Cairo). *(Phot. E. Brugsch.)*

THE SAÏTE AGE

the stone, but the modelling is extraordinarily fine and the faces both of man and goddess are marked by a serenity touched with melancholy. It is, in fact, an excellent example, and one we greatly admired before seeing the group of Dêr-el-Bahari. The mythological convention is perhaps less embarrassing than in the latter, but the formula of the workshop manifests itself more aggressively. Hathor is a conventionalised heifer which has lost the natural grace and freedom of the good Egyptian milch-cow; she has all the elegance and all the insipidity of the Isis and Osiris. Beyond these pieces, I know of none which deserve mention, but there are so many statues of the Saïte age scattered in museums with no indication of their origin, that we may be sure some of these will have to be assigned to the Memphite School, when we are better acquainted with its characteristics at this period. The other schools of the Delta are no more familiar to us, and for the same reason; we must be content for the present to recognise the general features of the period, without attempting to distinguish local peeuliarities.

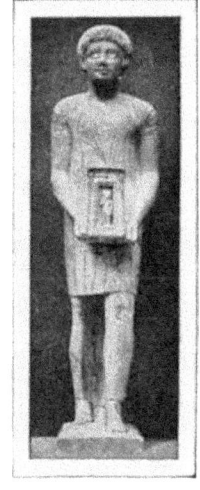

FIG. 485.—MEMPHITE STATUETTE (Museum, Cairo). (Phot. E. Brugsch.)

Saite artists did not forsake either granite or the softer materials, limestone and sandstone; they showed, however, a marked preference for hard, close-grained stones such as basalt, breccia, and serpentine, and excelled in the art of rendering them supple. Their fine works may therefore be recognised generally at a glance by the beauty of the substance, and the pellucid polish with which they clothed it; but in addition to these material indications, there are others more subtle which result from the manner in which they interpreted the human form. On the one hand, they tended to conventionalise it more and more, and they modelled it from the drawings of masters, and the pattern-books of the workshop rather than from

FIG. 486. MEMPHITE STATUE (Museum, Cairo). (Phot. E. Brugsch.)

FIG. 487.—HEAD AND BUST OF A WOMAN (Museum, Cairo).
(Phot. E. Brugsch.)

nature; excavators have found, and are still finding in the ruins, what may be described as ready-made statues, some entirely blocked out in the rough (Fig. 473), others with the bodies finished, and a shapeless block of stone left for the head (Fig. 474), to await the client whose likeness it was to receive; also feet, hands, arms and heads in different stages of preparation, which were used for the instruction of pupils, or were the products of their experiments. Under the influence of this method, the science of anatomy languished, contours became soft, the muscles relaxed and were incorrectly placed, the planes of the flesh were merged one into the other and became perfectly smooth. On the other hand, great pains were taken to make the head as exact a reproduction of the original as possible, and in order to succeed in this, sculptors were no longer content to render the features of the face very faithfully in the stone; they gave much attention to the modelling of the neck and skull, which had hitherto been neglected. Our museums contain examples of these disconcerting statues, in which the feebleness of the body is in such striking contrast to the truth of the face. The wrinkles of the forehead are emphasised with scrupulous insistence, the sunken eyes and the crows' feet at the corners, the muscles which encircle the nostrils, the laughing lines of the mouth, the curve or the flatness of the nostrils; the *double*-statues no longer represent their master as uniformly young; if he is mature or old they show the stigmata of age. The head at Berlin (Fig. 475) like that in the Louvre (Fig. 476), is the unflattered portrait of a Memphite

FIG. 488.—HEAD AND BUST OF A WOMAN (Barracco Collection).
(Phot. Bissing.)

THE SAÏTE AGE

citizen, whose ugliness has been transferred to green schist or serpentine with the mechanical precision of a photographic plate. The skull of the shaven priest at Cairo (Fig. 477) is as minutely modelled as if the sculptor had been commissioned to make an anatomical model for a medical school; it shows every bump, every depression, all the asymmetries, and a doctor could tell at a glance if there were congenital defects in the original.

This recrudescence of realism is not to be attributed to the appearance of the Greeks on the scene; the Greeks of the fifth and fourth centuries B. C. did not carry this almost painful striving after resemblance so far. It was the natural development, and as it were the consequence of the ancient theory of the *double*, and was produced

FIG. 489.—HEAD AND BUST OF A MAN (Museum, Cairo). *(Phot. E. Brugsch.)*

under the influence of the changes introduced into costume by the fashion of the period. After the Twenty-sixth Dynasty it would seem that the use of the wig gradually became less general, and that it disappeared entirely under the Persians. The priests, who kept their skulls bare for reasons of professional cleanliness, lived, it may be said, with uncovered heads, and those members of the other upper classes who were not affiliated in some way to the priesthood, acquired the habit of wearing short hair. Once again it was religious dogma which drew art

FIG. 490.—SPHINX OF THE ROMAN PERIOD (Museum, Alexandria). *(Phot. Breccia.)*

ART IN EGYPT

into a new path, and when artists copied the head so exactly, it was in the hope of securing for the *double* all the benefits

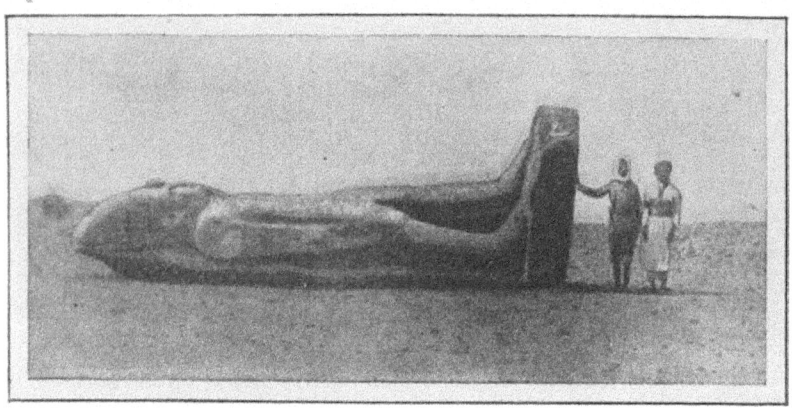

FIG. 491.—CROWNED COLOSSUS IN THE ISLAND OF ARGO.

he had enjoyed on earth. It is not surprising, therefore, that the example thus set by the Memphite School should have been followed by all the others. The few Theban statues of Ptolemies which have survived betray a like interest in the accidents of the face. Those of the princes of Asyût, which seem to be related to the Hermopolitan School, show traces of the same influence, and those of the Tanite School which we find at Cairo (Fig. 479) have not escaped it, a fact which will surprise no one, seeing that an analogous tendency makes itself felt in the earliest of its productions, the sphinxes of Amenemhāt III. Nevertheless, in the cities colonised by the Macedonians, at Alexandria, at Memphis, and even at Thebes, the sight of Greek statues, and perhaps contact with the masters who executed them, had finally made some impression on the natives, and though they never entirely abandoned their ancestral traditions, they hellenised them to some extent. The Theban Colossus of Amenophis, son of Hapu (Fig. 478), is purely

FIG. 492.
THE GOD AMON AND AN ETHIOPIAN CANDACE
(Museum, Cairo).
(*Phot. E. Brugsch.*)

THE SAÏTE AGE

Egyptian, and that which represents an Alexander Aigos (Fig. 480) has no exotic elements save the arrangement of the hair and the cast of the face. In the Alexandrian statuette (Figs. 481, 482), the attitude and costume are, on the other hand, purely Egyptian, but the Greek afflatus has passed over the body, animating every part of it, the rounded bust, the small, firm breasts, the closely modelled belly, the well-developed hip, the slender, nervous leg. The priest Horus (Fig. 483),

FIG. 493.—ETHIOPIAN STATUES OF SOULS (Museum, Cairo). *(Phot. E. Brugsch.)*

less delicate in handling, is much more advanced in evolution; it looks like a Greek work executed by an Egyptian rather than a purely Egyptian creation. Here again the body is open to criticism; the shoulders are not broad enough, the chest is too narrow, and the artist had a difficulty in rendering both the fall of the arms and the folds of the chlamys. The head is not bad; the nose is thin and straight, the chin square, the jaw obstinate, and the whole has a certain general resemblance to the portraits of the young Augustus. These hybrid statues were also produced at Memphis at this period. One, which is of basalt (Fig. 484), is not unlike our Horus in costume and attitude, while the other (Fig. 485), in limestone, represents a priest walking and holding a naos in both hands; the eyes are inserted, and the eyebrows have been blackened with kohol; the whole work is uninteresting. There is the same unskilfulness in the large limestone figure of our museum (Fig. 486), and although the heads, male (Fig. 489) and female (Figs. 487, 488), near it give the impression of faithful likenesses, the dryness of the chisel has played the excellent intentions of the sculptor false.

FIG. 494.—STATUE RE-CARVED AS A CÆSAR (Museum, Cairo). *(Phot. E. Brugsch.)*

255

ART IN EGYPT

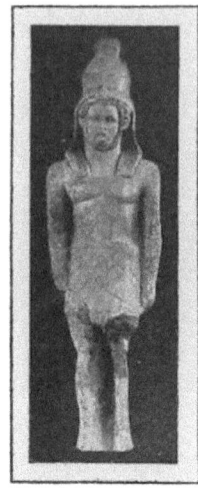

FIG. 495.
COLOSSUS OF THE
ROMAN PERIOD
(Museum, Cairo).
(Phot. E. Brugsch.)

Certain ancient types were modified in this last stage of sculpture; that, for instance, of the female sphinx, who began to lean her head to one side and to cross her forepaws (Fig. 490). No original type was born of this belated alliance between the Greek and the Egyptian spirit; the remnant of creative vigour which the old tradition kept alive, had taken refuge in Ethiopia. It is not manifested in the crowned Colossus of the island of Argo (Fig. 491), nor in the few royal statues which have come down to us from Argo, Napata, and Meroë; the Cairo group (Fig. 492), in which a Queen Candace stands beside an Amon, has some pride and spirit, in spite of the imperfection of the execution, but it has no elements which are not purely Egyptian. And yet recent excavations have revealed a new conception of the soul among this people which was relapsing into barbarism (Fig. 493). Taking as their point of departure the bird with a human head which had in all times served to express it, they substituted a human body for that of the falcon, at first without altering the proportions; but soon, enlarging the miniature body to normal dimensions, they produced what I have called the *soul-statue* in contradistinction to the *double-statue*, the figure of a man or woman over whose shoulders the falcon's skin hangs like a cloak. It does not seem that this type ever penetrated into Egypt proper. Indeed, soon after its appearance, the purely indigenous schools of sculpture were either closed, or, all along the valley, merely produced artisans incapable of a passable work; when, about the beginning of the third century, certain towns of the Fayûm or the Delta wished to erect monuments in honour of the Caesars, Commodus or Caracalla, they were reduced to borrowing an antique statue and re-carving the face (Fig. 494), or, if they demanded an original, the artist gave them the caricature of a

FIG. 496.—STATUE OF A MONKEY (Museum of the Vatican). *(Phot. Petrie.)*

THE SAÏTE AGE

Colossus in the antique style (Fig. 495). The hybrid art of Alexandria was on a higher level, as we learn from the two statues of a man and woman of the tomb of Kom-es-Shugafa, and the animal-sculptors were able for some time yet to produce figures of monkeys (Fig. 496), sphinxes (Fig. 498), and lions passant or seated (Figs. 497, 499), which may be taken for living animals at a first glance. The pacific lion of Fig. 500,

FIG. 497.—LION PASSANT
(Museum of the Vatican). *(Phot. Petrie.)*

and the Kom-Ombo statue, of which only the crowned head has survived (Fig. 501), were probably among the last efforts of Egyptian or Egyptianistic art; none of the monuments I have met with so far seem to me later than the second half of the third century after Christ.

The history of the Saite and Græco-Roman bas-relief is analogous to that of the statues. It had its glorious moments from the eighth to the third century before Christ; it then passed through a long period of decadence, and closed towards the middle of the third century of our era. A few stelæ, the rescript of Nectanebus on Naucratis, and the Horus with the crocodiles (Fig. 502) in the Cairo Museum, will bear comparison with the best works of the Ahmesside age, and the fragment of a decree of Ptolemy Euergetes has a motive unknown in earlier periods, that of a Pharaoh on horseback charging the enemy, sarissa in hand (Fig. 503). The bas-reliefs of buildings anterior to the Greek conquest are of a very pure style in the Delta, at Beh-bêt, for instance, where Nectanebus I. restored the temple of Isis; even certain fragments of a temple of Akoris,

FIG. 498.—SPHINX OF THE PTOLEMAIC PERIOD
(Museum, Cairo). *(Phot. E. Brugsch.)*

ART IN EGYPT

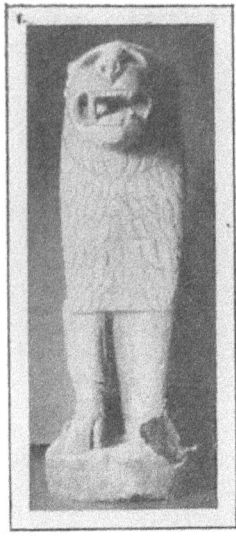

FIG. 499.—SEATED LION (Museum, Cairo). *(Phot. E. Brugsch.)*

found at Sakkarah, would be almost equal to those of Seti I. at Abydos, if their delicacy were not marred by a certain insipidity. Over-roundness of modelling, and softness of contours are indeed the defects we note in the decoration, defects which became more and more marked towards the end. They make themselves felt even in the experimental pieces, and the collection of models which every studio possessed, relics which are found in quantities in the ruins of the great towns, from Tanis to Edfû and Philæ. Figures of kings and queens are the most frequent (Fig. 504), and this is natural, for the reigning Pharaoh and the women of his family had an immemorial right to be represented on the walls of the temples, and it was also customary to lend their features to the gods and goddesses with whom they consorted; animals and hybrid forms of godhead, half man, half beast, also abound, and this again is not surprising, for sculptors were perpetually called upon to execute them, both in pictures and inscriptions. One of the masters would trace on thin slabs of limestone, sometimes squared on the surface, the better to instruct the tyro in the proper relation

FIG. 500.—THE LION OF KOM-OMBO (Museum, Cairo). *(Phot. E. Brugsch.)*

of parts, the portrait of a Ptolemy or a Cleopatra (Fig. 505), in various skilfully graduated stages, from the moment of sketching in the silhouette and the relief (Fig. 506), until that when they are finished in their slightest details (Fig. 507). Several of these examples are masterpieces, and there are things in the Cairo Museum, such as the head of a lioness and the image of a bull, no whit inferior in delicacy of touch to the best in the temple of Abydos or the tomb of Seti I. Yet even in these we discern

THE SAÏTE AGE

the tendencies which, becoming more and more pronounced, brought about irremediable decline. It is not good for an apprentice to be kept exclusively at the reproduction of models, however perfect. He loses touch with reality, he becomes a machine, and soon he prides himself on being nothing but the servile copyist of antique forms. Plato, no doubt, reflected the state of mind of his Egyptian contemporaries when he praised as admirable the persistence with which they had produced the same types without change for thousands of years. If, thanks to the beauty of its stereotyped designs, late Saite art retained a certain elegance, it soon had nothing of its primitive originality and creative vigour left. Its figures had become mere puppets without any anatomical basis; the nose became rounder, the lips more pouting, the chin thicker, the cheeks heavier, the mouth was set in a smile which lifts it at the corners and draws up the nostrils towards the eyes. This contraction of the whole countenance, slight under the first Ptolemies, degenerates under their successors and the Caesars into a grimace, which gives the person represented a distressingly silly expression.

FIG. 501.—HEAD OF A STATUE
(Museum, Cairo). *(Phot. E. Brugsch.)*

Thebes and Philæ are almost the sole places where we may trace the progress of this decadence. The bas-reliefs of the gate of Nectanebus on the east of the great temple of Amon are dignified and agreeable, if they have no claim to supreme excellence, and the same qualities reappear at Luxor in the sanctuary of Alexander II., at Karnak, on the walls of the granite chamber constructed by Philip Arrhidæus in the shrine of the sacred boat of the time of Thothmes III. They begin to die out in the little temple of Ptah (Fig. 508), and the decoration of the large door built by Ptolemy Physcon for the hypostyle hall is frankly detestable; above all, in the places where sculptors presumed to fabricate bas-reliefs in the names of Thothmes (Fig. 509) or

ART IN EGYPT

FIG. 502.—STELE OF HORUS ON THE CROCODILES (Museum, Cairo). *(Phot. E. Brugsch.)*

Rameses (Fig. 511), the handling is so feeble that the imposture is obvious to the most ignorant eye. The material in which they are carved is in part responsible for their shortcomings. Whereas the architects of the Saïte period used a close, durable sandstone, capable of keeping the play of the chisel firm, those of the Ptolemaic age were content, no doubt for economical reasons, with a soft, coarse-grained sandstone which did not lend itself to precise lines or delicate transitions in relief. Sculptors were accordingly obliged to suppress in the contours and the modelling of their figures minutiae for which the stone was unsuitable, and as, even by avoiding these as much as possible, they did not altogether escape such accidents as the splitting or crumbling of the work, they substituted for relief on a sunk surface *(relief en creux)*, which had been almost obligatory in former centuries relief on the normal surface of the wall, which they applied even to inscriptions. It thus became easier for them to complete their decoration without endangering their figures and hieroglyphics unduly; but, on the other hand, they secured integrity at the cost of flexibility; their works, reduced to the utmost simplicity of modelling for fear of accidents during execution, look as if they had lost their skin, and were presenting hastily flayed figures to view. At Philæ the decadence, though slower, was not less sure, and was brought about by

FIG. 503. PTOLEMY EUERGETES CHARGING (Museum, Cairo). *(Phot. E. Brugsch.)*

THE SAITE AGE

the same causes as at Karnak; we follow it step by step, from the pavilion of the doorway of Nectanebus II. to the shrine of Euergetes II., the porticoes of Augustus and Tiberius, the doors of Hadrian and Trajan. In such of the temples as were decorated on a homogeneous plan, without too long a period between the dates of beginning and completing the work, Edfû, for instance, there is no distressing contrast between room and room, and the unity of the decoration conceals its feebleness to a certain extent. No very keen study is needed, however, to perceive that the sculptor here was a workman, who mechanically transferred a stereotyped design to the wall, and was no longer capable of giving it a personal impress (Fig. 510); his main preoccupation was the correct reproduction of costume and liturgical accessories (Fig. 512). For the great Theban School, which had inspired all the provincial schools of the Saïd for centuries, was dying, if indeed it was not already dead at the moment when Edfû and Denderah were decorated, and the local workshops could only reproduce mechanically the motives the architect ordered, as in those pictures where the Emperor Domitian comes to worship the gods of Thebes; where architecture, a mathematical art, had retained its vitality for centuries, a few years had sufficed to cause sculpture to degenerate and bring it to the point of death. The

FIG. 504.—MODELS OF HEADS AT DIFFERENT STAGES
(Museum, Cairo).
(Phot. E. Brugsch.)

stelae of the Fayûm (Fig. 514) and the bas-reliefs of Macrinus and Diadumenianus at Kom-Obos (Fig. 515), the last which bear a date, have neither life nor style, nor anything else; they are mere hieratic lumber, timidly manufactured by an ignorant workman. Ethiopia was no better equipped than Egypt proper. The heads of some of her kings (Figs. 516—517) look like caricatures, so clumsy is their execution. Even in Nubia, where, it might have been thought, the domination first of the Ptolemies and then of the Caesars would have tended to preserve the Theban

ART IN EGYPT

tradition, the bad taste characteristic of Meroë prevailed. The sculptures at Dakkeh (Fig. 518) and Kalâbshah, which are for the most part of the time of Augustus, are worse than those of Ombo, later by over 200 years. The temple of Dakkeh, as we know (cf. p. 242) received its final form under Augustus, who added the sanctuary and pylon. The pylon-towers have a few reliefs on the outside. The sanctuary reliefs show an unknown Emperor doing homage to various deities. Among the reliefs of a chamber built by the Ethiopian Ergamenes (contemporary with Ptolemy II.), is one of the king pouring a libation. The reliefs in the temple of Kalabshâh were never completed, and the crudity of those which were executed is such as to obviate any regrets on this score. They decorate the pronaos and the three following rooms, and represent Augustus sacrificing to the gods of Egypt. At Maharrakah, the ancient Hierasycaminos, side by side with certain execrable bas-reliefs purely Egyptian in style, I must instance a last attempt to fuse the Alexandrian and Pharaonic styles, Isis and Horus in Greek draperies, sitting or moving after the manner of Roman deities (Fig. 519). The intention was praiseworthy, but no more barbaric work ever disgraced an Egyptian chisel.

FIG. 505.—FIGURE OF A QUEEN OR GODDESS AT TWO DIFFERENT STAGES (Museum, Cairo). (Phot. E. Brugsch.)

The funerary bas-relief of the Saïte age is considered by archæologists an evidence of the renascence of ancient Memphite art, and the purity and tenderness which characterise it are readily attributed to direct imitation of the Ancient Empire. It cannot be denied that the Egyptians of this period must often have penetrated into the earlier hypogea, but if, after pillaging and demolishing them to make fresh use of their materials, they derived texts and magic formulæ from them, they had no need to borrow school motives. The designs prescribed for use in the mastabas had never been completely abandoned, although, under the Ahmessids and the Ramessids, the imitation of Theban

THE SAÏTE AGE

processes had loaded them with details alien to the primitive conception. When the political hegemony of Thebes was overthrown, its artistic influence vanished rapidly, and soon, towards the end of the Bubastite age, or under the Ethiopians, local inspiration, casting off these adventitious elements, returned to an almost primitive simplicity. Thus, in the tomb of Patanafi or that of Psammetiknufisashmu, the general scheme is that of the bas-reliefs of the Fifth and Sixth Dynasties, for the bearers of offerings walk in single file, separated and juxtaposed (Fig. 520), not superposed in profile; but as soon as we give more than a superficial attention to the work, we note combinations which we had not perceived at first. The primitive fiction of the *wakf*, indicating a number of domains, each with its geographical individuality, had been replaced by the idea of a tribute levied once for all upon the entire patrimony; the procession of the domains is therefore merely an artistic survival, a motive of earlier times, used to symbolise the rendering of dues to the dead man, but no longer corresponding to rites performed round the tomb. An indifferent staff of priests, professional mourners, musicians and dancers was now employed for the ceremonies, in place of the deceased's own servants. It is not surprising that this perversion of the original idea should have entailed modifications in the treatment of the scenes. On the bas-relief of Zanufi in the Cairo Museum, the women are not drawn from a uniform pattern. The artist has made them young, in accordance with the ancient tradition, but they have no longer the dainty roundness and the virginal appearance which pleased in earlier ages; he has given them the heavy breasts,

FIG. 506.—SKETCH FIGURE OF A KING (Museum, Cairo). *(Phot. E. Brugsch.)*

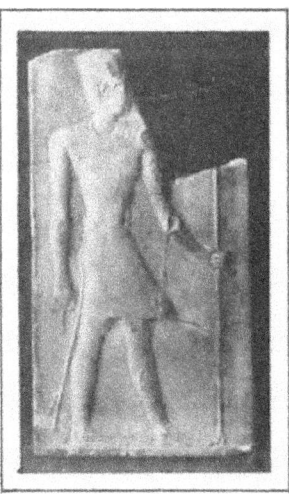

FIG. 507.—FINISHED FIGURE OF A KING (Museum, Cairo). *(Phot. E. Brugsch.)*

thick waist, full abdomen, wide hips, and firm gait of married women, and often of mothers (Fig. 521). As was natural, the men are little changed, but their attitudes are less conventional than formerly, and one of them, the man in the middle, brings his left shoulder forward with an attempt at perspective of which no one seems to have thought before the Theban period. The desire for variety is even more strongly marked in the animals; not a single one of the eight bullocks the men are leading is in the same attitude as its fellows. It is, however, in a bas-relief in the Museum of Alexandria that the difference between the old style and the new is most pronounced (Fig. 522). Here, every head of a man or a woman has been studied separately, as in a modern bas-relief, and the rendering has been carried very far; I doubt if we shall ever find in any example of the time of the Pyramids an equivalent for the player of the triangle or the female musician who is striking the drum. Not only have the figures each a different physiognomy, suggesting the probability of portraiture, but their gestures, their costumes, their draperies and accessories are all diversified. The painter, too, came to the aid of the sculptor with a daring impossible to an artist of the Fifth or Sixth Dynasty. His brush supplied the portions of the dresses which the chisel could not have expressed clearly enough; he even added shades which his colleague was accustomed to neglect entirely, so that where the colour has disappeared the work is incomplete. It is for this reason that we are puzzled at first by the cut of the wrapper worn by one of the wives of Psammetiknusashmu, a curious garment, which though drawn up round the neck and fitting closely to the limbs, seems to leave the bust, abdomen and thighs bare, while draping the shoulders,

FIG. 508.—A BAS-RELIEF IN THE TEMPLE OF THE THEBAN PTAH.
(Phot. Legrain.)

THE SAÏTE AGE

back, and loins. This peculiarity did not exist originally; the painter had supplied the sculptor's omissions by a few discreet touches, and, thanks to him, the body, revealing its contours under a wash of red or blue, was clothed in a semi-transparent robe.

At this period there was no longer much question of local schools, but this particular style spread throughout Egypt, and even penetrated to Thebes; we find it in several of the hypogea of Asasif, notably that of Abai, where it has the same character-

FIG. 509.—PASTICCIO OF EIGH-
TEENTH DYNASTY RELIEF; TEMPLE
OF THE THEBAN PTAH. *(Phot. Legrain.)*

FIG. 510.—BAS-RELIEF IN THE
TEMPLE OF EDFÛ.
(Phot. Beato.)

istics as at Memphis, and this is not surprising, since the "divine spouses of Amon" of the Twenty-sixth Dynasty were Saïte princesses who brought their households with them; the persons of their suite either prepared their tombs in accordance with the usages of their own country, or imposed its fashions on the Thebans. Here, at least, no foreign influence intervened at first, and we have to come down to the first Cæsars to find hybrid works, in which the Egyptian manner is wedded to the Greek, as in the figures of Antæus and Isis in the Cairo Museum (Fig. 523), At Memphis, the case was very different, and as we gradually advance, under the Persians, under the last Saïtes, under the Ptolemies, we feel that by living in contact with the Greeks, first those of Naucratis, and then those of Alexandria, the people of the Delta had ended by drawing inspiration from them. The ample pallium cut into battlements below in which Psammetiknufisashmu, his scribe, and the musician with the triangle, are draped, was a garment borrowed from neighbouring Greece. The mantle of the woman playing the drum is also Greek; she herself bears a strong likeness to her companions on painted Alexandrian stelæ. Such, however, was the strength of tradition among this singular people, that, although they consented to disguise a sculptured relief by painting over it, they declined to modify the foundation itself; the silhouette of the figures remained archaic, even when colour had modernised their superficial detail. The foreign influence, was moreover, very slow in its action; the fragments of the tomb of Psammetiknufisashmu, in which it is incontestable, are not earlier than the Twenty-ninth or Thirtieth Dynasty, and I do not hesitate to assign the two bas-reliefs of the tomb of Zanufi to the reign of one of the first Ptolemies. This would make them the latest, as they are certainly the finest that we know. With these may be classed those admirable Memphite sarcophagi of the families of Tchaho and Ankh-Hàpi at Cairo, on which every little figure and even every hieroglyph, is carved as conscientiously as if it were a motive on a cameo; their artistic merit is very slight, but they are the perfection of craftsmanship. After them not only art but craftsmanship declined suddenly, save perhaps in the neighbourhood of Alexandria, where bas-reliefs in a mixed style analogous to that of the statues of Horus are occasionally excavated. At Kom-es-Shugafa, the

FIG. 511.—PTOLEMAIC PASTICCIO OF THE STYLE OF THE EIGHTEENTH DYNASTY.
(Phot. Legrain.)

THE SAÏTE AGE

piety of a great family suggested the construction of a Pharaonic hypogeum, at the beginning of the third century of our era (Fig. 524). The principal scenes of ancient times were reconstituted, the mummy on its lion-footed couch given over to the care of Horus, Anubis and Thoth (Fig. 525), the sovereign before an Apis bull which an Isis shelters under her wings, priests reciting the office of the dead, or offering sacrifice to Isis, but the whole is bedaubed with crude colours and the technique

FIG. 512.—A BAS-RELIEF OF THE TEMPLE OF OMBOS. *(Phot. Beato.)*

shows how utterly the Egyptian style was forgotten; even our own artists of the seventeenth and eighteenth centuries were not more remote from their originals, when they published so-called facsimiles of the Ramesside stelæ and bas-reliefs.

C. PAINTING AND THE MINOR ARTS.

Independent painting played an increasingly important part as the antique artistic conception of the Egyptians declined. This could hardly have been otherwise, seeing that they had been brought into daily contact with a people like the Hellenes, among whom painting had emancipated itself from sculpture to become an art in itself; but their works, executed upon non-durable materials, wood or canvas, have perished for the most part. The remnant is chiefly made up of papyri, the panels of funerary

FIG. 513.—THEBAN BAS-RELIEF OF THE TIME OF DOMITIAN. *(Phot. E. Brugsch.)*

FIG. 514.—STELE OF THE FAYÛM (Museum, Cairo). *(Phot. E. Brugsch.)*

caskets, stelæ, coffins or cartonnages of mummies, the most ancient of which, those of the priests of Amon or Mentu, carry on the tradition of the Ramesside workshops. The vignettes of the papyri are often veritable miniatures, perfect in line and fresh in colour; the best of them are unquestionably those of the *Ritual* of Queen Māt-ka-Rā, wife of one of the king-priests of the Twenty-first Dynasty (Pl. III). The panels are less carefully executed, but they lack neither vigour nor harmony, as is shown by that of Pakheri in the Cairo Museum (Fig. 526), where we see the deceased bringing offerings to Hathor the cow, who is emerging from the western mountain. The stelæ generally represent the dead man or woman adoring Amon or Mut, or, from the Twenty-first and Twenty-second Dynasties onward, more frequently Harmachis. They are generally speaking the work of some scrupulous artisan who executed them conscientiously according to the principles of the school, but several were painted by artists of talent, and bear comparison with the best miniatures of the Theban School. I may instance that of the priestess Zadamonefonukhu (Pl. II) in the Cairo Museum; half naked under her flowing robe, she raises

FIG. 515.—BAS-RELIEF OF MACRINUS AND DIADUMENIANUS AT KOM-OMBO. *(Phot. Thédenat.)*

THE SAÏTE AGE

her hands to the god, claiming her share of the offerings heaped before him. She is charming in the deliberate rigidity of her hieratic pose, and never did a more supple line envelope a young body more gracefully slender. The colour, at once rich and tender, relieves the melancholy proper to a funerary monument by its gaiety, and the gray-blue background against which the figures and inscriptions are set modifies their vivacity. Under the principal scene, in the midst of a landscape almost unique so far, the corner of the burial ground where the deceased rests is indicated very effectively. A sandy mountain, yellow streaked with red, descends from left to right. The façades of three tombs are set against it, and before them a kneeling woman smites her forehead with her hands, bewailing the priestess; a *nabeca* and three date-trees loaded with fruit rise on the right, and between the two latter is the table of offerings on which the soul will presently alight to take its meal. The composition is not badly balanced, and the solitary mourner in the middle commands the spectator's attention. If we compare it with other stelæ of the same category, we shall recognise in it a desire to renew the expression of the religious idea they set forth, and to bring it closer to reality than had hitherto been done. In the earlier conception, the lowest register represented the scenes that passed on earth, the rites performed by survivors in honour of the relative they lamented, while in the upper register the deceased was seen arriving in the other world and receiving from the gods his share of the sacrifice. The artist commissioned to execute the stelæ of Zadamonefonukhu, conscious of the absurdity of associating as in contemporary life persons some

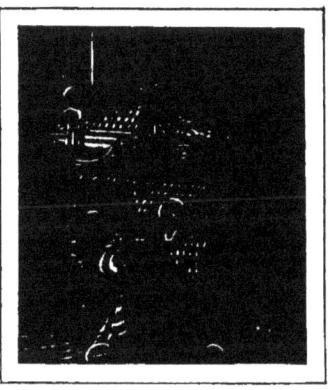

FIG. 516.
HEAD OF AN ETHIOPIAN KING
(Museum, Cairo). *(Phot. E. Brugsch.)*

FIG. 517.—HEAD OF AN ETHIOPIAN KING (After Lepsius).

of whom were still living on the earth, while others had left it, and thinking further that the distinction between the terrestrial ceremony and the apotheosis in the abode of the gods was not sufficiently marked, took upon himself to accentuate the contrast to the eye as strongly as to the spirit. Retaining the upper picture unaltered, he replaced the fictitious *tête-à-tête* of the lower register by an episode of real life, one that might have been seen any day in cemeteries. The dead woman is invisible, but one of the women of the family has come to bring her the homage of her relatives, and to weep for her; the antique idea persisted under a rejuvenated form, better adapted to the tendencies of contemporary art.

FIG. 518.—BAS-RELIEF AT DAKKEH. (*Phot. Oropesa.*)

Like all the other attacks upon tradition, this one failed. Three stelæ of the same period and origin show that the Cairo example was no solitary caprice; in these the landscape is less elaborate and the lower register contains only a conventional sketch, either of the mountain (Fig. 527) or of the garden where the soul was supposed to shelter during the heat of the day, a group of date-palms and sycamores very hastily painted. It was the same with the coffins and cartonnages. For these the Theban artists continued to invent,

FIG. 519.—BAS-RELIEF OF MAHARRAKAH (Museum, Cairo). (*Phot. E. Brugsch.*)

THE SAÏTE AGE

if not new forms, at least new beauties. In some cases the lid reproduced not only the mask, but the contours and relief of

FIG. 520.-BAS-RELIEF OF PSAMMETIKNUFISASHMU (Museum, Cairo). *(Phot. E. Brugsch.)*

the whole body, with all the details of the costume, the wig, the plain or pleated skirt, the gauze robe, the sandals, so that it has the appearance of a statue of the defunct, lying in state. Towards the end of the Twentieth Dynasty and under those that followed, it was sometimes as carefully executed as a real statue; the work is comparable to work in limestone, but it is more sincere and less in bondage to a school convention. The subject, of course, admitted of no fancy in the attitude; the model had to lie flat on his back, his head straight, his chest expanded, his legs and his feet joined; the only variation was in the position of the arms, which sometimes lie along the sides, sometimes are crossed on the breast. The whole is, however, so true in its proportion, the colours which heighten each part are so happily har-
monised, that we get almost an illusion of life. These cartonnages, especially those of women, almost attained to perfection towards the Twenty-second Dynasty. Thus the Princess Tantkalashiri, who died in the reign, of Osorkon II., is wrapped in a dra-

FIG. 521.—BAS-RELIEF OF ZANUFI (Museum, Cairo). *(Phot. E. Brugsch.)*

pery of pale pink which defines the contours without indiscreet emphasis. Her arms are free, and one of them is laid upon

ART IN EGYPT

her bosom under the breasts; some half dozen amulets, the sign of life, the buckle, the altar with four tablets, hang from her

FIG. 522.—BAS-RELIEF OF PSAMMETIKNUFISASHMU (Museum, Alexandria).
(Phot. E. Brugsch.)

wrist and protect her. The face, enframed by the puffed wig, is a rather flat oval, with small but merry eyes, a thick mouth, a short nose, and an expression of gaiety and good humour. Even on inferior coffins, the carved wooden mask is often excellent down to the beginning of the Persian era, after which the decadence of Thebes was complete, and her funeral-furnishers produced nothing but commercial articles, barbarous both in colour and modelling. The workshops of Lower Egypt held their own better, and participated in the revival of Saïte art. Under the first Ptolemies, when they were relieved from the necessity of copying in wood the uncouth masses of green schist or granite coffins, they executed works comparable to the best Theban examples; such are the coffin of Psammetichus, discovered at Wardân (Fig. 528)

FIG. 523.—ANTÆUS AND ISIS (Museum, Cairo).
(Phot. E. Brugsch.)

THE SAÏTE AGE

and that of the lady Tataharsiasi, which belongs to the Berlin Museum (Fig. 529). The Greek influence is supreme here in the arrangement of the headdress, but the technique is Egyptian; the sculptor belonged to one of those mixed schools whose existence at Memphis and Alexandria towards the end of the Ptolemaic age I have already noted.

The Egyptian palette had enriched itself; it included at least two kinds of pink, five or six shades of green, blue, and yellow, violets, lilacs, and mauves, notably in the regions colonised by the Greeks, round Alexandria, in the Fayûm, at Ptolemaïs in the Thebaïd.

FIG. 524.
A ROOM IN THE HYPOGEUM OF KOM-ES-SHUGAFA.

The Egyptian painters promptly yielded to the temptation to paint portraits or decorate walls in the manner of the works they saw in the Hellenic villas. We must go to the Oases to find in the temples or the hypogea some fragments of these mural paintings, in which the drawing is incorrect and the touch unskilful (Fig. 530).

FIG. 525.
DECORATION ON THE TOMB OF KOM-ES-SHUGAFA.

Portraits, on the other hand, have come down to us in considerable numbers, thanks to a caprice of fashion. Towards the middle of the last

her bosom under the breasts; some half dozen amulets, the sign of life, the buckle, the altar with four tablets, hang from her

FIG. 522.—BAS-RELIEF OF PSAMMETIKNUFISASHMU (Museum, Alexandria).
(Phot. E. Brugsch.)

wrist and protect her. The face, enframed by the puffed wig, is a rather flat oval, with small but merry eyes, a thick mouth, a short nose, and an expression of gaiety and good humour. Even on inferior coffins, the carved wooden mask is often excellent down to the beginning of the Persian era, after which the decadence of Thebes was complete, and her funeral-furnishers produced nothing but commercial articles, barbarous both in colour and modelling. The workshops of Lower Egypt held their own better, and participated in the revival of Saïte art. Under the first Ptolemies, when they were relieved from the necessity of copying in wood the uncouth masses of green schist or granite coffins, they executed works comparable to the best Theban examples; such are the coffin of Psammetichus, discovered at Wardân (Fig. 528)

FIG. 523.—ANTÆUS AND ISIS (Museum, Cairo).
(Phot. E. Brugsch.)

THE SAÏTE AGE

and that of the lady Tataharsiasi, which belongs to the Berlin Museum (Fig. 529). The Greek influence is supreme here in the arrangement of the headdress, but the technique is Egyptian; the sculptor belonged to one of those mixed schools whose existence at Memphis and Alexandria towards the end of the Ptolemaic age I have already noted.

FIG. 524.
A ROOM IN THE HYPOGEUM OF KOM-ES-SHUGAFA.

The Egyptian palette had enriched itself; it included at least two kinds of pink, five or six shades of green, blue, and yellow, violets, lilacs, and mauves, notably in the regions colonised by the Greeks, round Alexandria, in the Fayûm, at Ptolemais in the Thebaïd. The Egyptian painters promptly yielded to the temptation to paint portraits or decorate walls in the manner of the works they saw in the Hellenic villas. We must go to the Oases to find in the temples or the hypogea some fragments of these mural paintings, in which the drawing is incorrect and the touch unskilful (Fig. 530).

FIG. 525.
DECORATION ON THE TOMB OF KOM-ES-SHUGAFA.

Portraits, on the other hand, have come down to us in considerable numbers, thanks to a caprice of fashion. Towards the middle of the last

273

ART IN EGYPT

century before our era, the rich families of the Fayûm and Upper Egypt, disgusted by the heaviness and coarseness of the wooden coffins, conceived the idea of substituting for carved masks some equivalent in which their artistic tastes would be more respected, and likeness better observed. They had recourse to two different methods. The first, that of which we have the oldest examples, consisted in replacing the face in relief by a panel painted with wax and slightly re-touched with distemper, or even painted entirely in distemper; it was set into the cartonnage, above the mummified head, and the deceased seemed to be looking through a window to see what was going on in the world of the living, just as his ancestors had done by means of the eyes formerly painted on the sides of the coffin. The majority of these portrait-coffins were found in the burial grounds of Dimeh or Hawara, and date from the century before or the first century after Christ; several, now in the Louvre, come from Thebes and represent members of the noble clan of the Soters, who flourished under the Antonines. Some of them are so excellent in design and colour that they might almost be ascribed to a good Italian master of the fifteenth century, but though painted by native Egyptians, they have nothing in common with Pharaonic art; their source of inspiration is Alexandrian. The second method is less completely exotic (Fig. 531); it required, instead of the wooden mask, a plaster bust, in the hollow of which the veiled head of the mummy was encased, and the lower edges

FIG. 526.—PAINTED PANEL OF PAKHERI
(Museum, Kairo). *(Phot. E. Brugsch.)*

FIG. 527.—PAINTED STELE
(Museum, Cairo). *(Phot. E. Brugsch.)*

of which disappeared beneath the bandages of the chest. The design as a whole was Greek; but certain details remained specially Egyptian, such as the custom of inserting the eyes, and imitating their natural effect by incrustations of talc or glass. This fashion obtained towards the second century of our era among the higher classes of Heptanomis (Middle Egypt) from the Fayûm to the confines of the Thebaïd. Even in the Fayûm it did not exclude the use of cartonnage masks modelled in the semblance of the dead, but treated in the Greek manner, with indications of the upper part of the clothing, faces enlivened by paint, jewels, curled locks and wreaths of flowers; seeing them in our glass cases, we might take them for busts of coloured wax (Fig. 532). At Akhmîm and in its outskirts, the custom of laying the dead in their outdoor costumes upon their tombs came into favour again towards the times of Severus, but instead of giving them the loin-cloth and archaic wig, they were dressed in their modern costume, tunics, peplums, mantles made by some fashionâble *modiste*, whose inventions were probably some months behind the latest creations of Alexandria or Rome (Fig. 533). The box is made of Nile mud, plastered on a framework of cardboard or stuccoed cloth; it was given a form approximating to that of the person for whom it was destined, and over the modelling was painted, in distemper or tempera, the face, the flower-crowned head, the hands, jewels, and multi-coloured stuffs.

FIG. 528.—COFFIN FROM WARDAN (Museum, Cairo). *(Phot. E. Brugsch.)*

FIG. 529. COFFIN OF TATAHARSIASI (Museum, Berlin).

This was the last effort towards originality of the artists who worked for the burial-grounds. Mummy-painting and sculpture ceased towards the middle of the third century, at the same time as ordinary sculpture and painting, and for the same reasons; the civil wars, the effects of which were felt in Egypt, and then the invasion of Christianity, destroyed all the arts which depended for their existence on the maintenance of the antique religions. Sculpture in metal and ceramics were also affected. As they overcame the technical difficulties of casting, the Saïte masters were emboldened to increase the size of their works until at last they succeeded in casting figures larger than life in a single piece. Not one of these metal colossi has come down to us intact, but we possess fragments which enable us to reconstitute their appearance, such as the hand grasping the hydra, now in the Cairo Museum, which Daninos found among the ruins of Memphis: it is terminated at the wrist by a rectangular tenon which held it to the arm, and the effigy of the kneeling king to which it belonged must have been about $6\frac{1}{2}$ feet in height. But this is exceptional. The statue of Petukhanu, the torso of which was in the Stroganoff collection, was barely life-size, and the most important pieces we have of the Bubastite or Saïte ages are rarely as much as 3 feet in height. Several of them are finer than the best contemporary examples in limestone or granite, notably the little sphinx of Apries in the Louvre (Fig. 534) and the kneeling Tirhakah at Cairo (Fig. 535). The Karomama in the Louvre (Fig. 537) bought by Champollion of a dealer who had himself bought it at Luxor, is Theban in handling. The queen is standing, dressed in a long, closely-fitting gown with flowing sleeves, her head crowned with a ceremonial wig, the forelocks of which overhang her brow; the eyes are inserted, and the divisions of the wig, as well as the folds of

FIG. 530.—PAINTING OF A HYPOGEUM IN THE OASIS OF BAHRIYAH. *(Phot. Moritz Bey.)*

THE SAÏTE AGE

the dress, were incrusted with gold. The body is finely modelled under the stuff, but the head is above praise. Karomama was certainly no beauty, with her long, beak-like nose, her sunken nostrils, her dry mouth and bony chin. But as she had a lofty bearing, the artist, unable to make her attractive, concentrated all his powers on the pride and energy of the face; his Karomama is the incarnation of what he conceived the wife of Pharaoh and Queen of Egypt should be. The Takushit of the Athens Museum (Fig. 536) on the other hand is a woman of the middle class, a worthy lady of Bubastis, and her statuette, probably the product of a local workshop, is a contrast in the somewhat flaccid roundness of its contours to the nervous spareness of the Karomama.

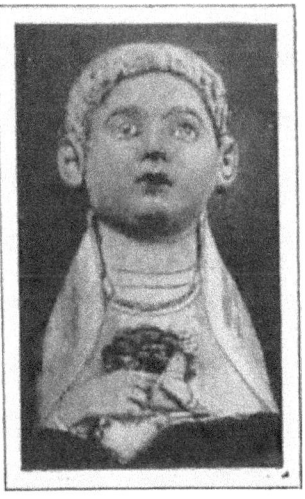

FIG. 531.—PLASTER MASK OF A MUMMY (Museum, Cairo). *(Phot. E. Brugsch.)*

The good dame has started off with the left foot, and she walks without haste, her right arm hanging, her left held against her breast; her drapery moulds while affecting to conceal her full hips and abdomen, and her round, heavy breasts. The face is broad and fat under the wig of short locks rising in tiers one above the other, and her narrow eyes, her short nose, her fleshy lips and rounded cheeks are those of a fellah woman without any touch of race. The bronze with its mixture of gold and silver, is irradiated by soft reflections which seem to animate the forms; the dress is covered as with an embroidery by religious scenes and inscriptions incised and filled in with a silver line.

We can hardly say whether the activity of the Theban foundries relaxed from the beginning of the Saïte period, or whether the lack of Theban bronzes is due merely to the perversity

FIG. 532.—MASK OF A MUMMY IN PAINTED CARTON (Museum, Cairo). *(Phot. E. Brugsch.)*

ART IN EGYPT

of chance. But with the exception of an enormous Osiris found in the *favissa* at Karnak, the finest and most important bronzes of our collections all come from Memphis or the Delta. Bubastis was the home of the four bronzes bought by the Louvre at the Posno sale. The first, one Masu, whose name is tattooed on his breast (Fig. 538) near the heart, advances towards the spectator with a proud, confident movement; the face, somewhat disfigured by the loss of the eyes, which were of enamel encircled with silver, breathes energy and arrogance. The second is less vigorous in bearing, but the third (Fig. 539), a Horus who originally lifted up a jar from which he poured water over a king kneeling before him, is harsher and drier, and was perhaps cast in the same workshop as the kneeling Horus at Cairo; the composition of the metal seems to be identical in each, the handling is similar, and the manner in which the bird's head is adjusted to the human bust is marked by the same exactness. It must, indeed, be allowed that these divine monsters, in whom the human and animal natures are allied, inspired the makers of bronzes more happily than the statuaries. The Basts and Sekhets discovered by Barsanti at Saïs (Fig. 540) are not only comparable to the black granite Sekhets of Amenophis III., but superior to them in dignity of attitude, and the suggestion of restrained vitality. Their cat or lion heads rest more easily on their feminine shoulders, and they are less in the nature of a defiance to the laws which rule the division of species. The lions of Thmuis and Tell-es-Sab are no earlier than the first Ptolemies. Those of Horbêt were cast under Apries (Fig. 541). They were part of a mechanical contrivance for closing the doors of a temple, and they had a wooden beam prosaically inserted in their hind-quarters, but the artist turned the conditions imposed by their functions to excellent decorative account; he imagined them lying flat on the ground, in an oblong cage, the lateral walls of which were pierced to show their bodies, while their heads and forepaws emerged from the open trap in front. He simplified the lines, but in the manner of which the Egyptians were masters, neither suppressing nor weakening any of those

FIG. 533.—COFFIN OF AKHMÎM (Museum, Cairo). (Phot. E. Brugsch.)

THE SAÏTE AGE

which give the animal its character; the face is calm and soberly majestic. The cat is treated no less happily than the lion, and it may be said without exaggeration that among the thousands, either whole cats or heads of cats, brought out in 1878 from the *favissa* of Bubastis, very few were bad, or even mediocre (Fig. 542); no people ever showed more skill in seizing the undulating grace of the beast, the treacherous softness of its attitudes, and the expression of its mask, now dreamy, now mutinous.

FIG. 534.—LITTLE BRONZE SPHINX OF APRIES (The Louvre, Paris).

The other animals — rams, Apis or Mnevis bulls (Fig. 543), crocodiles, cynocephali, the innumerable figurines of Amon (Fig. 544), Osiris, Isis, Horus, Nît, Anubis with a dog's muzzle (Fig. 545), Sekhet with a lion's face (Fig. 546), Thoth with the head of a monkey or an ibis, do not bear comparision with the cats and lions; though many of them are remarkable for the perfection of their casting, or the delicacy of their chasing, the majority are the prosaic reproductions of non-artistic types devised for the edification of the faithful. They bear the same relation to the splendid bronzes at Cairo and in the Louvre as do the gilded and painted saints of the St. Sulpice quarter to the works of the great Christian sculptors of France and Italy.

And here we are confronted by a problem the solution of which we can only divine at present. Among the innumerable bronzes found in the same places, where they seem to have been deposited at the same time, we find

FIG. 535.—BRONZE STATUETTE OF TIRHAKAH (Museum, Cairo). *(Phot. E. Brugsch.)*

some so different from the rest in style, that were we not certain of their origin, we should be disposed to attribute them to very

ART IN EGYPT

FIG. 536.—THE LADY TAKUSHÎT (Museum, Athens). (Phot. E. Brugsch.)

diverse periods and localities. It is in the cats above all that these divergences are most strongly marked. Some are vigorous and realistic after the manner of the best Theban sculptors; their silhouettes have a certain harsh abruptness of contour which is not the result of any lack of skill in the artist, but the effect of a determination to express the energy and strength rather than the grace and ease of the animal's movements. With others, however, the desire for elegance gets the mastery, and the contours are softened to the verge of flaccidity; we recognise the Memphite technique in its most trivial aspect. Noting these contrasts, we are inclined to ask whether the fact that such dissimilar works were all buried together in the *favissa* of the temple of Bast is sufficient evidence that they were all manufactured at Bubastis. May not the pilgrims who dedicated them to the goddess have brought them from their native towns? Their dissimilarity would be comprehensible enough in this case; those in which we seem to distinguish the impress of Theban or Memphite art would then have made their way hither from Thebes or Memphis. But even if we accept this hypothesis, we shall not have resolved the difficulties entirely. Carefully examined, these groups do not present a homogeneous appearance, for whereas some of the examples really reveal the characteristics of the Saïte age, many others would seem from their treatment to be earlier by several centuries: and yet the circumstances of the find and the nature of the bronze hardly permit us to doubt that they were all cast within the space of a few years. An observation I made in the ruins of a pottery workshop discovered last winter behind one of the mounds of Eshmûnen, may help to explain this anomaly. The majority of the moulds for lamps and of the kiln-refuse it still contained, belonged to the Christian

FIG. 537.—QUEEN KAROMAMA (The Louvre, Paris).

JUDGMENT BEFORE OSIRIS
(Vignette from the funerary Papyrus of Queen Mat-ka-Ra. Twenty-first Dynasty)

THE SAÏTE AGE

FIG. 538.—BRONZE STATUETTE OF MASU (The Louvre, Paris).

FIG. 539. BRONZE HORUS (The Louvre, Paris).

era, as we learn from the crosses and inscriptions, but others are decorated with pagan figures and legends, and cannot be later than the second or third century of our era; the potter must have had in the back of his shop old models which came from his distant predecessors, and these, slightly altered to suit the requirements of the new religion, were still sold occcasionally. It is probable that founders also preserved old-fashioned moulds, and continued to cast with them from time to time for their clients. Thus some Theban devotee of Bast might, before starting for Bubastis, have provided himself with ex-votoes, cats, or cat-headed statuettes, or other figures of divinities which, though of new metal and fresh from the furnace, were none the less the work of older generations by virtue of the moulds used.

FIG. 540.—BRONZE SEKHET (Museum, Cairo). (Phot. E. Brugsch.)

The same may be said of the countless divinities made of different compositions or of terra-cotta, which swarm in the tombs and cities of the Saïte period and of the Græco-Roman epoch. The last centuries of paganism were above all centuries of pious imagery for the use of dead and living, at least in the Delta and the northern part of Middle Egypt, for the Saïd never fell into these excesses, and the use of amulets was not much more general here than in

ART IN EGYPT

in the glorious days of the second Theban Empire. It was inevitable that manufacturers and dealers should spare themselves the trouble of inventing new types and sacrificing their old models, so long as these could be made to suffice for the demand and content their customers. And, naturally, objects prepared by the hundred, and even by the thousand, for daily sale, could not fail to be mediocre and lacking in originality. There are many of which we can only say that they faithfully express the hieratic attitude, the gesture, costume, head-dress, and exterior attributes of the god they represented; this was all the devout asked, and it was the same with the *Ushabtiu (substitutes)*. Provided they vaguely suggested the mummy by their forms, and the name of their master had been traced on them, together with the opening words of the consecrated prayer, they served for the rite, and this was all-sufficient; at the beginning of the Roman period many were sold which are hardly more than pieces of clay or paste lengthened out, with a vague indication of the head and the feet, things more barbarous than the most barbarous Polynesian idols. Here and there, however, we meet with examples which stand out from the general level of ugliness, and are almost finer than those of the great period. They come generally from the wells of Sakkarah, and belong to the time of the Persian domination, or to the early reigns of the Macedonian dynasty. The

FIG. 541.—BRONZE LION OF AFRIES (Museum, Cairo). *(Phot. E. Brugsch.)*

FIG. 542.
BRONZE CAT (Museum, Cairo). *(Phot. E. Brugsch.)*

THE SAÏTE AGE

best, those of a certain Admiral Patanesis, varied in size from 4 to 10 inches. Modelled in a very pure paste, and fired with extraordinary skill, they were glazed with a non-lustrous clear, vivid blue, the freshness and evenness of which are unimaginable; I have seen nothing to approach them in modern porcelain. The head is a gentle, melancholy portrait; the only thing comparable to it in its own *genre* is the little blue porcelain head at Cairo (Fig. 547), perhaps an Apries or Necho II. Others, though not so beautiful as these, show a laudable effort to produce something new; I may instance the little group of green enamelled frit, which, inspired perhaps by a motive of the time of Amenophis IV., represents queen Amenartas seated on Amon's lap and passing her arms lovingly round his neck (Fig. 548); the kohol jar, the body of which is formed by a head of Apries in a Greek helmet (Fig. 549), and the votive

FIG. 543.
STATUETTE OF APIS
(Museum, Cairo).
(Phot. E. Brugsch.)

statue in green paste of Nufiabres, standing on a high pedestal and holding the naos of the Osiris-mummy in front of him with both hands. Some twenty of the Nîts, Râs, Horuses, Ptahs and Nefer-Atmus in porcelain preserved in the Cairo Museum, were executed by workmen brought up in the good school. Whereas their neighbours in the glass cases show the rounded, flaccid forms which pleased the Ptolemaic sculptors, we note in them the nervous, and sometimes rather dry handling of an earlier age. Of course it was not very easy to mark the play of muscles in works barely ten or twelve inches high, sometimes considerably less. Artists accordingly adopted the plan of enclosing the limbs in a series of frankly cut planes with sharp angles, and exag-

FIG. 544.
HARPOCRATES, OSIRIS, AND AMON. BRONZE STATUETTES
(Museum, Cairo).
(Phot. E. Brugsch.)

ART IN EGYPT

gerating the proportions of the anatomical details which they preserved in the knees, feet, arms and face, but with such an intelligent sense of effect that we have to examine them a second time, if we have not been already informed of the device, before we notice the exaggeration. If they had respected the true dimensions, certain elements of the human body would have been so attenuated as to become almost invisible, and the general impression of truth would have suffered. Several of these figurines are treated so skilfully that instead of appearing what they are, miniatures of men or animals, we feel when we examine them as if we were looking at colossal figures from the wrong end of a field-glass.

FIG. 545.—BRONZE STATUETTE OF ANUBIS (Museum, Cairo). (Phot. E. Brugsch.)

FIG. 546.—BRONZE SEKHET (Museum, Cairo). (Phot. E. Brugsch.)

The Egyptians of the Pharaonic age had used plain earthenware, neither glazed nor coloured, only for the manufacture of coarse domestic utensils and amulets, chiefly articles intended for the poor, *ubshabti*, beads, figures of the gods, more especially Bes; it is only exceptionally that we find, towards the close of the second Theban age, heads of Canopic vases in clay as delicately executed as if they had been in stone or enamelled ware. From the accession of the Ptolemies, and probably under the influence of Greece, taste developed. We know what masterpieces were bequeathed to us by the potters of Alexandria; several of the statuettes found in

FIG. 547.—ROYAL HEAD IN BLUE ENAMEL (Museum, Cairo). (Phot. E. Brugsch.)

THE SAÏTE AGE

the burial grounds of Meks equal those of Tanagra. The natives imitated their foreign comrades, and gradually the use of earthenware, baked or unbaked, but always painted in bright colours, became general from one end of the valley to the other. It found favour more especially in localities where there were colonies of Hellenes, in the Delta, at Memphis, in the Fayûm, at Hermopolis, at Akhmim, at Syene, but it also made its way into places that had remained purely Egyptian. Its manifestations are innumerable, from the decorative plaques in temples and public buildings to household utensils, lamps, domestic lares, groups representing episodes in private life, grotesque and sometimes obscene figurines, camels (Fig. 551), elephants (Fig. 550), birds, and the majority are industrial rather than artistic creations (Fig. 552). Nevertheless, some of the subjects are treated with a most amusing dexterity (Fig. 553), and bronze was even used

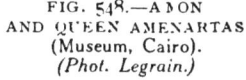

FIG. 548.—A DON AND QUEEN AMENARTAS (Museum, Cairo). (Phot. Legrain.)

in some cases (Fig. 555). A study of Perichon Bey's collection is particularly instructive for this *genre*. It all came from the *tells* of Eshmunên, the ancient city of Thoth, and the majority of the pieces composing it do not go back further than the second century of our era. Yet at Cairo there are heads of dwarfs and idiots of surprising truth (Fig. 554). Sugar-loaf skulls, narrow retreating foreheads, eyes overhung with bushy eyebrows, crooked noses, bony cheeks, hanging lips, minute chins, enormous ears set on each side of the head like the handles of an ill-made pitcher — no feature is lacking of all that makes up well-observed human deformity; two or three strokes of the thumb lengthened and kneaded the paste

FIG. 549.—VASE IN THE FORM OF A HEAD IN A HELMET (The Louvre, Paris).

ART IN EGYPT

to the desired module; then a pinch here and another there to bring out the protuberances of the face, a stroke of the graver for the mouth, two pellets for the eyes, and there it was, as ugly as nature, but more amusing. Animals are treated with no less spirit, dogs especially, not the thin greyhound, the prototype of the so-called jackal Anubis, but the pug, with the angry muzzle, pointed ears, long waving hair and curly tail, or the good fellow of no particular breed (Fig. 556), who thinks his constant barking protects the house, but whose true function is to be tormented by the children in it. Here

FIG. 550.—TERRA-COTTA ELEPHANT
(Museum, Cairo). *(Phot. E. Brugsch.)*

and there are feminine heads so graceful that they would not disgrace the Alexandrian series; they are purely Greek. The only persons who have not entirely forsworn their Egyptian character are the fashionable divinities. Harpocrates chubby as a Pompeian Cupid, but adorned with a minute *pschent*, Agathodemons with a uraeus body and an Isis head (Fig. 557), Isis chastely draped (Fig. 558), and others destined to serve as wives to the dead, their tunics rolled up on their breasts; these replaced the statuettes of blue and green porcelain towards the close of the first century after Christ, and until the definitive triumph of Christianity they sufficed for popular devotion.

The same transformation took place in the other minor arts, though we are not yet in a position to note its successive stages. Furniture retained the ancient forms in its essentials, at least among the poor and

,FIG. 551.—TERRA-COTTA CAMEL
(Museum, Cairo). *(Phot. E. Brugsch.)*

THE SAÏTE AGE

the lower middle classes; the domination of the foreigner had, in fact, altered nothing, or almost nothing, in the habits of the fellahîn and the artisan, and even the introduction of a current coinage had not affected the conditions of their domestic life as might have been expected. They did not want a single piece of furniture more than their ancestors had used under the Pharaohs, and the little they required they continued to make on the consecrated models, beds and arm-chairs with lion's feet incrusted with ivory, bone or ebony, stools and benches with leather seats and many-coloured cushions, linen-chests, bread-bins, jewel-caskets, kohol-pots, perfume-boxes; they admitted innovations only in certain funerary articles. The catafalque in which the mummy journeyed to the tomb, under the Tanites of the Twenty-first Dynasty, an enormous rectangular case laid

FIG. 552.
TERRA-COTTA GROTESQUE
(Museum, Cairo). *(Phot. E. Brugsch.)*

upon a sleigh, became under the Ptolemies a carved wooden bed with a canopy. The one in the Edinburgh Museum, which Rhind got at Sheik-Abd-el-Kurnah, simulates a kiosk with a

FIG. 553.—GROTESQUE HEAD IN TERRA-COTTA (Museum, Cairo). *(Phot. E. Brugsch.)*

FIG. 554.—GROTESQUE HEAD IN TERRA-COTTA (Museum, Cairo). *(Phot. E. Brugsch.)*

ART IN EGYPT

barrel-vault, three sides of which are upheld by little columns of coloured wood. The fourth, that of the head, has a façade with three superposed cornices, each decorated with its winged disc, the whole bordered by a row of rampant uræi; a door between two columns, guarded by serpents, was supposed to give access to the interior. The mummy within was, as it were, in a peripteral temple the sanctuary of which was his coffin. The catafalque in our Museum (Fig. 559) which I found at Akhmîm in 1885, is conceived in a spirit more attuned to its funereal function. Its lateral columns are replaced by cut out pieces of painted wood representing the goddess Maat, the Truth who protected the *doubles* at the tribunal of Osiris; she crouches on her haunches, her pen on her lap, and beside her the winged Isis and Nephthys of the ordinary sarcophagi fill up the space at the short ends. The vault is of open-work, and on each of the seven curves which compose it are painted vultures, spreading out their wings above the mummy; two statuettes of Isis and Nephthys, posted at the two extremities, lament as prescribed by ritual. The work is agreeable to the eye, and if provincial artisans were capable of productions so tasteful, we may imagine what those of Memphis could do; here again, the cult of the dead prevented art from falling too low, when it sank into decadence in civil life. There is reason to believe that Hellenism made way among the rich, and that the same class who under the first Cæsars substituted their wax portraits for wooden coffin-masks, furnished their houses in the western fashion, like modern Egyptians, who buy the furniture for their dining, reception, and bed-rooms in Venice, Paris, and London. None of these Hellenistic pieces of furniture have come down to us, but in 1901 Daninos found at Memphis fragments of several carrying-chairs which had belonged to one of the last Saïte Pharaohs. The wood, which was in bad condition, was profusely decorated with small bronze plaques, some in very low relief, others cut out flat in the metal and incised the designs being Niles (Fig. 560) and Osirises bringing offerings (Fig. 562), or helmeted kings (Fig. 561), Thothmes III., Osorkon III.

FIG. 555.
GROTESQUE FIGURINE IN BRONZE
(Museum, Cairo).
(Phot. E. Brugsch.)

THE SAÏTE AGE

Psammetichus II, Amasis. It is possible that they came from Thebes, in the trousseau of some princess married at Memphis; whatever their origin, they are mediocre in design and even more so in execution.

Goldsmith's work and jewelry alone flourished to the end, and were transmitted, by a complete cycle of transformations, to the Byzantines and then to the Arabs, thus escaping to some extent the destruction of the Pharaonic civilisation. In the beginning, under the Twenty-second and Twenty-sixth Dynasties, these productions differed only by almost imperceptible shades from those of the Theban age. The shallow goblets, some Egyptian, others Cypriot, but in the Egyptian style, discovered in the palaces of the Sargonids in Assyria, resemble those in the treasure of Bubastis; nevertheless, martial scenes occur frequently in them, and the progress of military art complicates them with incidents unknown to the strategy of earlier generations, cavalry charges side by side with chariot charges.

FIG. 556.
TERRA-COTTA DOG (Museum, Cairo).
(Phot. E. Brugsch.)

But for this, the composition is very little changed; as formerly, it is arranged in concentric bands, in which the incidents are separated by florets or trees. The influence of Greece began to make itself felt towards the end of the Saïte period, and several of the pieces from Tukh-el-Karamus are importations from Ionia, as, for instance, the bracelet with the Eros, the rhyton, the two perfume-burners in the form of altars; but others were manufactured in Egypt by Egyptians, and these are not the least remarkable. The oxide from which we have not been able to free them mars their purity of contour and delicacy of ornamentation; but it does not prevent us from recognising that they are covered with true Egyptian motives, treated in the Egyptian manner, lotus-flowers or buds, running ornament, foliage, and clusters of aquatic plants. We distinguish these still more plainly on the silver vessels of Thmuis,

ART IN EGYPT

where no extraneous matter clogs the surfaces (Fig. 563). They are deep libation-cups, rounded at the bases, the bodies of which, slightly compressed towards the top, open out widely at the lip. A rosette enclosed in a circle marks the centre of gravity, and focusses the external decoration, lotus-blossoms alternately in bloom and in bud, then narrow leaflets laid closely together, their points separated by ovæ in relief. The handle of the cover is formed by two lotus-flowers laid flat upon the surface and united by the stems. Some of the pieces were beaten out in a mould of hard stone, or *repoussé*, and then retouched with the point; others were chased solidly upon the silver; in several cases the most salient parts of the decoration, the ovæ, for instance, were cast and worked separately, and then soldered to the surface. It is hard to say which is more admirable in the majority,

FIG. 557.
SERPENT-ISIS
(Museum, Cairo).
(Phot. E. Brugsch.)

FIG. 558.
TERRA-COTTA ISIS
(Museum, Cairo).
(Phot. E. Brugsch.)

FIG. 559.—CATAFALQUE OF AKHMÎM (Museum, Cairo). *(Phot. E. Brugsch.)*

THE SAÏTE AGE

the mastery of the technique or the perfection of the taste displayed in the composition. When we compare them with the treasure of Bosco Reale, we cannot but think that the Egyptian goldsmiths' work of the Saïte and Ptolemaic periods must have sometimes furnished models for the metal-workers of imperial Rome.

The jewelry of the Bubastite and Tanite dynasties carries on the tradition of preceding ages almost without a break, in the

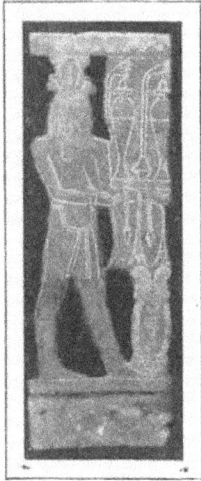

FIG. 560.
NILE IN PIERCED BRONZE

FIG. 561.—FIGURE OF PHARAOH IN PIERCED BRONZE
(Museum, Cairo). (Phot. E. Brugsch.)

FIG. 562.—FIGURE OF AN OSIRIS-NILE IN PIERCED BRONZE

form of bracelets, rings, earrings, broad necklaces and slender chains. We have to come down to the Psammetichan kings to find new designs among them. I have said elsewhere that the vessels made by the Ionians for Necho II. probably inspired the craftsman who chased the clasps of the necklace in the Louvre (Fig. 564); these are imitations of galleys, with their flat chamber, their spur, their swan or goose-necked poop. The little amulets which served as a kind of magic cuirass to the mummies of the great Saïte dignitaries entombed at Sakkarah, owe nothing to the foreigner, and the original types to be met with among them are exclusively national — the tiny gold palm-trees, with scaly trunks and heavy clusters of dates, and the cynocephalous figures worshipping before a cartouche crowned with feathers (Fig. 565).

ART IN EGYPT

Some are composed of thin flakes of gold hammered out and soldered together; others are worked upon miniature ingots to which the accessories have been added, and we admire the dexterity of the chasing. The seated cat, the two cynocephalous figures standing on each side of the Osirian fetich, the Isis suckling Horus, the boat of Sokaris resting upon its cradle, with its crew of tiny fish and falcons, lose nothing on close examination through a microscope. And the most surprising thing is, that the patient work of the tool has not produced dryness or awkwardness: the proportions of the parts are calculated as skilfully as those of the faïence or lapis-lazuli figurines, and nowhere do we see better how completely the Egyptians had mastered human and animal forms than in these infinitesimal objects. Some of the figures of Osiris, of Isis, of Thoth and of Amon discovered by Edgar with the treasure of Tukh-el-Karamus, suggest decadence only by a touch of affectation and over-refinement. Soon, however, the Greek models, so free and so various in conception, spread throughout the country, to the detriment of the Pharaonic types. From the accession of the first Caesars, only jewels and amulets in the Italian or Hellenic style were sold in the towns, or bestowed on mummies. These were twisted serpents with emerald or garnet eyes, for bracelets, keepsake-rings for hair, the bezel composed of a massive gold plaque or a cameo, chains with heavy links, earrings in the form of bunches of grapes, crescents, shells, diadems of Gorgons' heads with crinkled hair, the entire jewel-case of the Roman or Byzantine lady. The mania for western jewelry obtained even at the court of the last Meroitic Pharaohs, and the jewels Ferlini stripped from the mummy of a Candace a century ago, came from a workshop more than half Greek. The exotic designs executed in gold for the rich, were transferred to silver for the benefit of the poor, and, interpreted by rustic goldsmiths, they regained something of the ancient technique under their hands. In the more modern examples of the treasure of Ben-ha there are bracelets with checkered

FIG. 563.—SILVER PLATE OF THMUIS (Museum, Cairo). *(Phot. E. Brugsch.)*

THE SAÏTE AGE

ends or twists which recall the old types of the Ramessids: if we compare them with contemporary Egyptian ornaments, we shall find that they differ from them only in insignificant details, and if they were offered for sale in a village shop, the fellahin would buy them without suspecting their antiquity.

FIG. 564.—CLASP FOR A NECKLACE IN THE FORM OF A BOAT (The Louvre).

BIBLIOGRAPHY TO PART III

Saïte Age. — The Saïte and Græco-Roman ages have been neglected by most of the writers who have treated the history of art in Egypt They have been content for the most part to describe a few of the monuments, without attempting to sum up their general character.

Architecture. — A. *Tombs* — For the tombs of the Saïte and Ptolemaic period, see Barsanti-Maspero, *Fouilles autour de la pyramide d'Ounas* (Extract from *Annales du Service des Antiquités*, vol. I, 99), p. 36-174, 8vo, Cairo 1900-1909 (unfinished); — Rhind, *Thebes, its Tombs and their Tenants*, 8vo, London 1862. — B *Temples.* — For the manner in which the style of columns developed from the time of the Ramessids to thatiof the Saïtes, see A. Kœster, *Die ägyptische Pflanzensäule der Spätzeit.* in the *Recueil de Travaux*, 1901, vol. XXV, p. 86-119. — The temples of Ethiopia are only imperfectly known to us by Cailliaud, *Voyage à Méroé*, 8vo, Paris 1823, atlas fol., pl. IX-LXXXV. — Lepsius, *Denkmaler aus Ägypten und Äthiopien*, I, pl. 120, 126-130, 135-139, 144; — E. Wallis Budge, *The Egyptian Sudan*, 1907, 8vo, London, vol. I, p. 337-435, vol. II, p. 1—184; the same may be said of those of the Saïte period: Cailliaud, *Voyage à l'Oasis de Thèbes*, fol., Paris 182-186; — H. Brugsch, *Reise nach der grossen Oase El-Khargeh*, 4to, Leipzig 1878, VI-93 p. and XXVII pl.; — Honroth-Rubensohn-Zucker, *Bericht über die Ausgrabungen auf Elephantine*, in the *Zeitschrift für ägyptische Sprache*, 1907, p. 14-61 and 9 pl. — The principal temples of the Græeo-Roman age have been the subject of some fairly exhaustive monographs: Philæ: G. Bénédite, *Le Temple de Philæ (Mémoires de la Mission permanente du Caire*, vol. XIII, XVII), 4to, I 1895, 388 p. and vignettes, II 1909, 356 p.; Kom-Ombo J. de Morgan, *Kom-Ombo* 4to, Vienne, 2 vols. 1895-1909; Edfû: J. Dümichen, *Bauurkunde der Tempelanlagen von Edfu*, in the *Zeitschrift für ägyptische Sprache*, 1870, p. 1-14, 1871, p. 25-32, 88-89, 105-111, 1872, p. 33-42, 1873, p. 109-130; — M. de Rochemonteix, *Le Temple d'Édfou*, 4to (*Mémoires de la Mission française*, vol. X-XI), Vienne, 1892-1899

ART IN EGYPT

(unfinished); — E. Chassinat et Piéron, *Le Mammisi d'Edfou (Mémoires de l'Institut français d'Archéologie*. vol. XVI), 4to, Cairo, 1909, 208 p. and LII pl.; le Kasr-el-Agouz, à Thébes: D. Mallet, *Le Kasr-el-Agoûz (Mémoires de l'Institut français d'Archéologie*, vol. XI), 4to, Cairo 1909, 103 p. and I pl.; the temple of Opet at Karnak: — M. de Rochemonteix, *Œuvres diverses*, 8vo, Paris 1894, p. 167-318, and pl. I-XVI; the temple of the Theban Ptah, at Karnak: G. Legrain, *Le Temple de Ptah-Ris-anbouf, à Thèbes*, in the *Annales du Service des Antiquités*, vol. III, p. 38-56, 97-115; the temple of Dêr-el-Médinét, in the *Commission d'Égypte*, Ant. vol. II, p. 317-340 and plates, vol. II, pl. 34-37; — the temple of Denderah: J. Dümichen, *Baugeschichte der Tempelanlagen von Denderah*, 4to, Leipzig, 1865, 46 p. and XIX pl.; — Mariette, *Denderah*, text 4to, Paris 1875, VI-347 p., atlas fol., Paris 1873, I-IV, *Supplément* 1874, 9 pl. — For the temples of Nubia, see Gau, *Les Monuments de la Nubie*, fol., Paris, Stuttgart, 1823, pl. 1-11-15-26, 33-41; — Maspero-Barsanti, *Les Temples immergés de la Nubie, Rapports*, 4to, Cairo, 1909-1911, XXIII-215 p. and CLIX plates, with plans in addition.

Sculpture. — For the general character of sculpture in Saïte and Græco-Roman times see Maspero, *Le Musée égyptien*, 4to, Cairo, 1906, vol. II, p. 74-92 and pl. XXXII-XLII, — Mariette, *Album du Musée de Boulag*, fol, Cairo, 1872, pl. 33-35; — Fr. W. de Bissing, *Denkmäler ägyptischer Skulptur*, fol., Munich, 1906-1911, pl. 60-75, 98-119, and the corresponding portions of the text; — L. Borchardt, *Kunstwerke aus dem ägyptischen Museum zu Kairo*, fol., Cairo, 1908, pl. 16, 24-30, 48 and p. 8-9, 13-14, 19; — C. C. Edgar, *Sculptor's Studies and unfinished Works* (Catalogue général du Musée du Caire), 4to, Cairo, 1906, XII-91 p. and 43 pl. Various questions of detail and several isolated monuments have been studied by Gourlay-Newberry, *Mentu-em-hat*, in the *Recueil de Travaux*, 1896, vol. XX. p. 188-192; — G. Bénédite, *Une Tête de Statue royale*, in the *Gazette des Beaux-Arts*, 1897, vol. XVIII, p. 35-42; — W. Golénischeff, *Eine neue Darstellung des Gottes Antæus*, in the *Zeitschrift für ägyptischen Sprache*, 1894, vol. XXXII, p. 1-2; — Fr W. de Bissing, *Les Bas-Reliefs de Kom-el-Chougafa*, Munich, 1902, text 8vo, 9 p. and atlas fol., 13 pl.; *Sur une Statue de la Collection Barracco*, in the *Recueil de Travaux*, 1895, vol. XVII, p. 105-113, with three plates; — C. C. Edgar, *Remarks on Egyptian Sculpture Models*, in the *Recueil de Travaux*, 1905, vol. XXVII, p. 137-150; — Maspero, *la Vache de Déir-el-Bahari*, in the *Revue de l'Art* ancien et moderne, 1907, vol. XXII, p. 5-18, with a photogravure plate.

Painting and the minor Arts. — This is the section in art-history in which the bibliography is most scanty. A. *Painting*. The only general work is: C. C. Edgar, *Græco-Egyptian Coffins, Masks and Portraits* (Catalogue général du Musée du Caire, 4to, Cairo, 1895, XIX-136 p. and XLVIII pl.; for details see Maspero, *Mélanges de Mythologie et d'Archéologie égyptiennes*, 8vo, Paris, vol. IV, p. 241-248 and 1 pl.; — C. Watzinger, *Griechische Holzsarkophagen aus der Zeit Alexanders des Grossen, Abusier III* (*Wissenschaftliche Veröffentlichungen der Deutschen Orient-Gesellschaft*, vol. VI), 4to Leipzig, 1905, 96 p. and 4 pl.; — H. Schäfer, *Priestergräber und andere Grabfunde vom Ende des alten Reiches bis zur griechischen Zeit vom Totentempel des Ne-user-Rê* (*Wissenschaftliche Veröffentlichungen der Deutschen Orient-Gesellschaft*, vol. VIII), 4to, Leipzig, 1908, VIII-185 p. and 13 pl. — B *Work in bronze*. — Only one general treatise: Edgar, *Greek Bronzes* (Catalogue général du Musée du Caire), 4to, Cairo, 1904, XI-99 p. and XIX pl.; various studies on points of detail: G. Daressy, *Une Trouvaille de bronzes à Mitrahinéh*, in the *Annales du Service des Antiquités*. 1902, vol. III, p. 139-150 and 3 pl.; *Statuette grotesque égyptienne*, in the *Annales*, 1903, vol. IV, p. 124-125; — G. Bénédite, *Une Statuette de reine de la Dynastie Bubastite au Musée du Louvre*, in the *Gazette des Beaux-Arts*, 1896, vol. XV. p. 447-485 and 1 pl.; *Un Guerrier Libyen, figure égyptienne en bronze incrusté d'argent, conservée au Musée du Louvre*, in the *Mémoires et Monuments de la fondation Piot*, 1902, vol. IX, p. 123-133; — E. Chassinat, *Une Statuette en bronze de la reine Karomama*, in the *Mémoires et Monuments de la fondation Piot*, 1897, vol. IV, p. 15-25 and pl. III; — G. Maspero, *Mélanges de Mythologie et d'Archéologie égyptiennes*, 8vo Paris, vol. IV, p. 259—266 and 2 pl. and *Sur une chatte de bronze égyptienne*, in the *Revue de l'Art* ancien et moderne, 1902, vol. XI, p. 377-380; — Mariette, *Monuments divers*, folio, Paris, pl. 41; *Album du Musée de Boulaq*, pl. 5, 9. — C. *Ceramics*. — Two collections of Egypto-Grecian figurines, that of C. C. Edgar, *Greek Moulds* (Catalogue général du Musée du Caire), 4to, Cairo 1903 XVII-89 p. and XXXIII pl., and that of Valdemar Schmidt, *De Græsk-Ægyptiske Terrakote i Ny Carberg Glyptothek*, 1911, Copenhagen 94, p. and LXIII-VII pl.; — For certain isolated monuments cfr. G. Legrain, *Sur un groupe d'Amon et d'Améniritis I.*, in the *Recueil de Travaux*, 1909, vol. XXXI, p. 139-142; — On porcelain and pottery in general down to the Græco-Roman period cf. Fr. W. de Bissing, *Fayencegefässe* (Catalogue général du Musée du Caire), 4to, Vienna, 1902, XXI-114 p. —

THE SAÏTE AGE

D. *Joinery*. — For carved and painted w d catafalques, see Rhind, *Thebes, its Tombs and their Tenants*, 8vo, London 1862, p. 111,112 and frontispiece. — Maspero, *Archéologie égyptienne*, 1ˢᵗ ed., 1888, p. 278-279 and fig. 256-257. — E. *Goldsmith's Work and Jewelry*. In addition tosthe two works by Vernier quoted above, see, f the treasure of Tukh-el-Karamus: Maspero, *Causeries d'Egypte*, 8vo, Paris, 1907, p. 305-310; — C. C. Edgar, *Report on an Excavation at Toukh el-Garamous*, in the *Annales du Service des Antiquités*, 1906, vol. VII, p. 205-212; for Saïte goldsmith's work, Maspero, *Lettre sur une trouvaille de bijoux égyptiens faite à Sakkarah*, in the *Revue de l'Art ancien et moderne*, 1900, vol. VIII, p. 353-358; — for Meroitic goldsmith's work, Schäfer-Möller-Schubart, *Ægyptische Goldschmiedearbeiten* (in the *Mitteilungen aus der ägyptischen Sammlung*), II, 8vo Berlin, 1910, 243 p. and 36 pl., where also we shall find the jewels and goldsmith's work of earlier ages owned by the Berlin Museum.

FIG. 565.—GOLDEN AMULETS OF THE SAITE PERIOD (Museum, Cairo).
(*Phot. E. Brugsch.*)

CONCLUSION

SUCH, in its main lines, is the history of Egyptian Art. Its first pages, those which deal with its origin are completely lacking; and if several chapters of its more recent ages have been reconstituted, others are still full of lacunæ, or break off abruptly. We know not how long it lasted, but more than forty centuries intervene between the moment when it begins for us and that at which it ends. Up to the present, this is the longest period through which it has been given to us to follow more or less continuously the evolution of one of the great artistic nations of antiquity.

Is it possible for us to discern already some of the causes which made Egyptian art what it was, and preserved its character? I have shown more than once in these pages that it did not seek to create or to record beauty for its own sake. It was originally one of the means employed by religion to secure eternal life and happiness for the dwellers upon earth. This end attained, if beauty resulted in addition, it was received with joy, though it was by no means looked upon as indispensable to the perfection of the work undertaken; no effort was made to ensure it, if such effort could be held in any way to interfere with the desired consummation. As art owed to the gods and the dead dwellings secure against destruction, it was concerned from the beginning to choose among materials and forms those which seemed to it best fitted to secure the longevity of temples and tombs. It therefore invented, from purely utilitarian motives, that prodigious architecture, the colossal masses and powerful lines of which leave on the mind of the spectator the strongest impression of indestructibility that any works by human hands have ever produced. And since bas-reliefs and statues had at first no reason for existence beyond that of affording an imperishable lodging for the souls of divinities, and the *doubles* of the incarnate, art in the beginning aspired only to express faithfully the idea of divine types formed by the people, and to perpetuate in stone, in metal, or in wood, the features of persons

CONCLUSION

whose rank or fortune had secured for them the privilege of immortality. Soon, however, the same interested motive which had induced it to carve faithful portraits, led it to disregard this exactitude in certain points. It was, of course, necessary that the *doubles* should find their fictitious bodies sufficiently like their actual ones to feel at ease in them; but their second existence would hardly have seemed a blessing to them, had they been condemned to spend it with limbs weakened by all the infirmities of age. By substituting for the sickly or decrepit reality the figure of the individual as he was in his youth or in the vigour of his maturity, the artist conferred on him more certainly the full enjoyment of his strength and faculties. This is why there are so few statues of old men before the Saïte period; even when a centenarian was represented, Amenophis, son of Hapu, or Rameses II, their portraits are not very different to what they must have been in their youth. And if we go further into details, was it not an analogous scruple which caused the rarity of nude statues? Nudity was a sign of low condition for all but children, and persons of good family, inflicting it on their statues, would have risked finding themselves confounded with the proletariat, and losing caste in the next world. If there are some few exceptions to this rule, it was because some superior interest made the model's singularity of advantage to him. The Anisakha at Cairo showed, by laying aside his loincloth, that he was circumcised, and thus gained the advantages due to the faithful who bore this mark of ritual initiation; otherwise would he have given his *double* a body naked as that of a labourer, with loins and thighs exposed?

It was then the desire for utility which gave Egyptian sculpture that combination of hieratic idealism and realism to which it owes its most personal charm. This was not without disadvantages to it, since it robbed it of some part of its liberty, but what it gained, if it did not entirely compensate for this loss, at least went far to minimise it. The case was very different with painting. I have said that it played an honourable part in the civilisation of archaic times, whether it was charged with the ornamentation of the house or the tomb, or whether — though of this we have no certain proof as yet — it had its allotted task in palaces and temples. It had, in short, this advantage over the other arts, that its apparatus was simpler, and its processes less expensive. Nevertheless, as the fragility of its methods left the gods and the dead ill protected against supreme dissolution, it yielded to sculpture as soon as the latter had acquired

ART IN EGYPT

facility in its technique, and became a secondary art almost everywhere; where a certainty of immortality was insisted on, it was no more than the humble servant of its comrade. When it was laid down that the gods could only become imperishable in a medium itself imperishable, it could not serve them independently, and was reduced to being a mere play of artificial tones without any form but those of the sculptured reliefs over which it was spread. It succeeded nevertheless in emancipating itself by degrees in the tombs, but this was not the result of a spontaneous effort of development; it was simply because the conceptions of the afterlife were modified and enlarged. As long as universal belief tied the *double* to the spot where the corpse rested, care for its well-being demanded that it should be surrounded by indestructible scenes; colour remained an accessory, and it was only tolerated by itself in places where the nature of the rock was recalcitrant to the chisel. From the day when it began to be imagined that the soul, no longer inhabiting the vault, could dispense with an eternal decoration, the number of painted hypogea increased. It might have been supposed that the painter, left to himself, would speedily have discovered the resources of his craft, and would have developed them in directions where the sculptor was powerless to follow him. But this was by no means the case; the traditions and routines to which it had been subjected for centuries had obtained such mastery over him, that he had no longer the energy to cast them off. He discarded some of the stereotyped forms bequeathed to him by his predecessors, he treated others with greater breadth and liberty, he intermingled his lines more harmoniously, he gained greater flexibility in his processes, but on the whole he remained what ages of subjection had made him. He utilised all the ingenuity and the experience of centuries to copy with his brush the silhouettes the sculptor had cut out with his chisel, and persisted in filling them in artlessly with uniform planes, without any effort to model their reliefs by combinations of shade and half-tones scientifically opposed or graduated. The fatality of utilitarianism continued to enslave him, when it had long ceased to have any *raison d'être*.

It will be readily understood that a people among whom the manifestations of art were so strictly subordinated to the material advantage of those who evoked them, was very little concerned to preserve the names of their authors. Thus many of the masterpieces which are anonymous for us were equally so for their contemporaries. The temple raised at Luxor by Amen-

CONCLUSION

ophis III. in honour of his father Amon, the statue which the Sheikh-el-beled had hidden in his tomb, the bas-relief on which Sesostris struck down the Libyan heroes — in all these the interest of the person they immortalised would not have tolerated that the merit of their execution should have been claimed in any degree by their creators. If the name of the artist had been associated with that of the master, the former would have participated in the benefits they conferred, and by so much would the bliss to which the *double* or the god had a right have been diminished. It happened sometimes, when the artist belonged to the household of a great personage, that the master would associate him by special favour with his posthumous destiny, and we owe our knowledge of one or two sculptors to this unusual condescension; but the exception is one of those which prove the rule. In a general way we shall not be mistaken if we assume that the principle of utility forbade all those who praetised an art to sign their works, and consequently condemned them to oblivion. We should like, indeed, to know what they were called, what was their native city or their condition of life, who had been their first teachers, and by what efforts those geniuses who made the plans of Dêr-el-Bahari or the Hypostyle Hall, raised the Pyramid of Chephren, and carved the Seated Scribe in the Louvre, the Thothmes III. and the Amenartas at Cairo, the Seti I. and the goddesses of Abydos, outstripped the crowd of their competitors. The choice that fell on them to undertake these great tasks proves sufficiently that they did not pass unnoticed among their immediate circle, and that they enjoyed in their day the reputation of being the most skilful and the most gifted in their craft. Fame was not lacking to them, at least in their lifetime, and among those who surrounded them, but when their generation had passed away, the admiration of the new races was poured out on the Pharaohs or the rich men who had employed them; the memory of the bold craftsman who dared to design and execute the speos of Abu Simbel was not handed down with his work as was that of Ictinus with the Parthenon. It was thus that, ignorant of the ambition of immortality by fame, the action of which is so powerful among the moderns, the Egyptian masters were for the most part content to observe conscientiously, as they would have done in any ordinary calling, the rules which the teachings of their predecessors had assured them were necessary to the well-being of souls human and divine. When by chance any were born whose inventive minds rebelled against the half technical, half religious education of the workshop, their efforts towards progress or reform had no serious results. Might it not well be that by changing something in the recognised processes, they would compromise the salvation of their models? In doubt, the crowd stood aloof from them, and held prudently to the old customs; I have described above how an attempt at picturesque painting failed in the Theban necropolis under the Twenty-first or Twenty-second Dynasty, and yet painting was of all the arts that which tended at the time to dissociate itself most from the useful. By refusing thus to modify the themes and types of an earlier age save in details, Egypt gave her art that character of uniformity which strikes us. The personal temperament of the individual is revealed only by almost imperceptible shades of handling, and the majority of visitors carry away with them from museums and ruins the sense of a collective impersonality, slightly varied here and there according to time and place by the greater or lesser degree of skill in the executant. They do not understand what an amount of natural talent and acquired science the unknown authors of great temples and fine sculpture expended, to make themselves more than mere skilful craftsmen.

I am far from asserting that religious utility was the sole consideration here; it was the main one, that which after having inspired the dawning arts, governed their developments to the last, and had I leisure, I should like to show how its influence appears in every direction, not only in the major arts but in industry. Not that the Egyptians were conscious of it each time that it determined a momentary progress or decadence among them, but that, by instinct and by routine, they followed the incline on which they had been launched at the beginning of their history. Other antique nations were influenced by it as well as they, and throughout the world, in Assyria, in Chaldæa, in Asia Minor, in Syria, architecture, sculpture, and painting were, as in Egypt, means for ensuring to gods and men together with eternal life, prosperity before and after death; but whereas in Greece the desire for pure beauty soon triumphed, Egypt, falling behind more and more in her archaic methods of thought, ended by becoming incapable, I will not say of adopting the nobler conceptions that were growing up around her, but of realising their value. The divorce between her inveterate routine and the enterprising spirit of the new world was so profound when Christianity rose before her, that she could offer it nothing it could adapt to its needs, even with many alterations of artistic expression. The western arts lent it their basilicas, their statues,

CONCLUSION

their bas-reliefs, their frescoes, and it readily evolved from these forms suitable to its ideas and its beliefs. But as for Egypt, how could the Christ find an abode in those dark and massive temples, where every line, every chamber, every decorative motive, every accessory of furniture, would have recalled dogmas and practices he reprobated? How could his priests and people have metamorphosed into images of their saints and prophets, or reconciled with their hopes of immortality those bestial or half-human statues, and those pictures, the elements and composition of which they declared to have been governed throughout antiquity by the most impure of demons? There was in a Jupiter enough beauty, independent of all religious faith, to enable an artist, stripping it of its heathen trappings, to make it the Christian conception of the one God; but to what person or what incarnation would it have been possible to assimilate the cold, inanimate figures of an Amon, a Ptah, an Osiris, even when their characteristic insignia and attitudes were taken from them? The demands of utility, which had made them what they were, had riveted them by bonds so numerous and so solid to the dying creed, that they had no choice but to depart with it. The art of Egypt, like its literature, its science, its current civilisation, was one with its religion; the blow which struck at the one struck at the others and crushed them.

It died completely, and the world lost sight of it; for some fifteen centuries, nothing was known of it, save that classical writers described it as marvellous, and that rare travellers had seen some gigantic remains of it in the neighbourhood of Cairo, or in the deserts of the Thebaïd. The draughtsmen and scholars of the French expedition having brought it to light again some hundred years ago, it has reconquered that place in the esteem of the present generation from which the neglect of former ages had dethroned it. To tell the truth, it is not, and I fear it never will be, one of those arts which fire the student at first sight. Some of the works it has bequeathed us command instant admiration, and a first glance suffices to enable us to understand them as easily as the finest works of Greece or Rome. The merits of the rest are not at once apparent; we can only grasp them after patient study, and they must be pointed out to people who have not time to discover them for themselves. Is not this the same in literature, and are there not poets, Pindar, for instance, whose verses are the delight only of a chosen few? Their beauty is as real as when they were first composed, but the long commentary they require before yielding their charm

ART IN EGYPT

has obscured it to the eyes of the multitude. Artists and men of letters, who were disconcerted at first by Egyptian sculpture and painting, have recovered from their stupefaction; they take an extreme pleasure in appreciating them, and it is primarily of them I have been thinking in writing these pages. It is not to be supposed that professional Egyptologists and critics will endorse without considerable reserve all the opinions and judgments they will have read in them; but should they reject them all, they will nevertheless, I hope, have gained something. For is not this, in fact, the first time that an attempt has been made to relate in a consecutive fashion the history of an art as extinct as the races of monsters we find imbedded in the lower strata of our globe? By studying closely the vicissitudes of its existence, its hesitations, its progress, its failures, its recoveries, and its long agony, they will learn to recognise more precisely than they have hitherto done some of the principles which regulate the incubation, the birth, the efflorescence and the death of the arts of other nations.

INDEX

INDEX

References to Illustrations are indicated by an *.

A.

Aah-hetep, 204.
Aahmes, 148, 170*.
Aahmes-Nefert-ari, 179.
Aat-tcha-Munt, see Medinet-Habu.
Abai, 265.
Abahuda, 143.
Abu'l-hol, 192.
Abuni, the soldier, 20, 20*.
Abu-Roash, 38, 83.
Abu-Simbel, 144, 189, 190, 191, 208, 299; Esplanade before great Speos at, 139*; Façade of great Speos at, 139*; Façade of little Speos at, 138*.
Abusir, 45, 48, 57, 62.
Abydos, 3, 4, 6, 7, 19, 60, 77, 91, 99, 101, 102, 110, 112, 114, 153, 154, 162, 187-190, 239; School of, 24, 105.
Ædicula on Terrace of Temple of Hathor, 219*.
Ægean peoples, 125.
Afai, Hypogeum of, 37.
African mud architecture, 28, 28*.
Agathodemons, 286.
Aha, Tablet of, 3.
Ahmessids, 139, 163, 169, 171, 176, 177, 194, 218, 262.
Akhmim, 37, 60, 240, 275, 285.

Akoris, Temple of, 257.
Alexander the Great, 228.
Alexander II., 223, 259.
Alexander Aigos, 239, 248*, 255.
Alexandria, 254, 257, 265, 266, 273, 275, 284.
Alexandria Museum, 264.
Amada, 132-135; Façade of Temple of, 131*.
Amasis, 129, 204, 237, 240, 289.
Amelineau, 7.
Amenemhāt III., 116, 118, 120; Statue of, 115*; Statuette of, 115*.
Amenartas, 223, 238*, 248, 299; and Amon, 283, 285*.
Amenemhāt, 100, 110, 124, 133, 205, 254.
Ameni, 101.
Amenophis the Scribe, 168*, 176.
Amenophis, son of Hapu, 167*, 176, 240, 254, 297; Colossal Statue of, 247*.
Amenophis I., 139, 150; Statue of, 160*.
Amenophis II., 150, 172, 173, 180, 199, 204; and the Serpent Maritsakro, 158*; Wooden Statuette of, 195*.
Amenophis III., 130, 131, 134, 140, 150, 156, 173, 176, 180, 181, 184, 200, 219, 239, 240, 278, 299; Statue of Amenophis III. in Assyrian

Dress, 166*; and Queen Thi, 166*.
Amenophis IV., 139, 181, 184, 195, 283; Cast of Head of, 174*; Head of Canopic Jar of, 172*, 181; and his Queen, 173*; with the Queen and their Children, 174*, 183; Statuette of, 172*.
Amentit, 57.
Amon or Amen, 138, 151, 167, 184-187, 201, 218, 219, 239, 246, 247, 249, 256, 265, 268, 279, 292, 299, 301; Bust of, 175*; Temple of, 259; with Amenartas, 283, 285*; with Candace, 254*; with Mut, 178*.
Amon-Ra, 114.
Amorrhæans, 165.
Amulets, 198, 281, 291, 292; golden, 295*.
Animals in Egyptian Art, 173-175, 278.
Anisakha, 84, 304.
Ankh-Hapi, 266.
Ankhmara, 71; Dancers in Tomb of, 69*.
Ankhnasnufiabri, 238*, 248.
Anonymity of Egyptian artists, 66, 298-300.
Anonymous Statue, 112*.
Antæus and Isis, 265, 272*.
Antef dynasty, 113, 114.

305

INDEX

Antef, Prince, 113.
Antonines, the, 55, 274.
Antoninus Pius, 231.
Anubis, 152, 267, 279, 286; Bronze Statuette of, 284*.
Apis, 267, 279; Statuette of, 283*.
Apries, 278, 283; Sphinx of, 276.
Arabs, 289.
Archaic Statuette, 78*.
Architecture, 125.
Argo Isle of, 256.
Arm of a Chair in form of a feline Animal, 195*.
Asasif, 143, 265
Ashu, 57.
Asia, 206; Minor, 125, 300.
Assuân, 27, 230, 239, 240.
Assyria, 206, 289, 300.
Asyût, 254.
Athens Museum, 277.
Atlantes, 155; at Medinet-Habu, 124*; of the Ramesseum, 127*.
Atlas of Thothmes I., Head of, 161*, 170.
Aton or Aten, 182, 184.
Augustus, 241, 242, 261, 262.

B.

Bakers, 88*.
Barsanti, 278.
Bas-relief, 179-181; at Abusir, 57; in Alexandria Museum, 264; from Chapel of Sahu-Râ, 59*; of the Cow Hathor, 165*; at Dakkeh, 270; at Edfû, 265*; of Macrinus and Diadumenianus, 261, 268*; of Maharrakah, 270*; Memphite, 190*; in the Memnonium of Seti I. at Abydos, 180*; of Psammetiknufisashmu, 263, 266, 271*, 272*; of Seneferu, 58*; of Seti I., 179*; at Sinai, 22*; in the Temple of Ombos, 267*; in the Temple of the Theban Ptah, 264*; in the Tomb of Mekhu, 61*; from Tomb of Menthuhetep, 111*; of the time of Domitian, 267*; of Zanufi, 271*.
Bast (goddess), 278; temple of, 280.

Battle of Kadesh, in Ramesseum, 155*, 165.
Beh-bêt, 257.
Beket, 105, 109.
Ben-ha, 292.
Beni-hasan, 101, 103, 106, 108, 110, 182.
Beni-Mohammed, 60.
Berlin Museum, 87, 201, 247, 252.
Bersheh, 101, 106.
Bes (god), 202, 219, 232.
Betchau, see Neter-baiu.
Bêt-el-Wâli, 113, 190; Hemispeos of, 137*.
Bêt-Khallaf, 7, 38, 39; Plan of Tomb at, 8*; Tomb, 8*.
Birket-el-Kurun, 96.
Biban-el-Muluk, 149, 153.
Blue enamel Head, 284*.
Blunted Pyramid, 100.
Boat, sacred or solar, 46.
Boat of Queen Aah-hetep, 207.
Book of the Dead, 66, 216.
Bosco Reale, 291.
Box for Cosmetics, 197*, 198*.
Bracelets from Abydos, 2*.
Bracelets of Rameses II., 209*.
Brawl on the Water, 68*.
Brewer, 71*.
Brick Boat of Râ-en-user, 46, 50*.
Bronze Statues, Two, 75*.
Brooch of Khamuasit, 210*.
Brussels Museum, 80.
Bubastis, 118, 129, 202, 214, 217, 240, 278-281.
Bull lassoed by the King, 56*.
Bust of a Statue, 246.
Byzantines, 289.

C.

Cæsar, 215, 239, 242, 256, 259, 261, 265, 288; Statue recarved as a, 255*.
Cairo, Museum of, 22, 51, 71, 79, 81, 86, 87, 88, 90, 92, 118, 119, 170, 173, 176, 181, 185, 187, 192, 194, 199, 201, 206, 247-250, 254, 256, 258, 265, 266, 268, 276, 278, 279, 283, 285, 289, 297, 299.
Camel, terra-cotta, 286*.
Candace, Queen, 256, 292.
Canopic jars, 181.

Capitals, 97, 103, 232; bell-shaped, 129; lotus, 129; palm-leaf, 129; Hathor, 97, 224*, 228, 237; irregular, 129.
Caracalla, 256.
Caramania, 77, 273.
Cartonnages, 270-273.
Cat, Bronze, 282*.
Cat watching for Prey, 106*.
Catafalque, 287, 288; of Akhmim, 290.
Cataracts, 143, 215.
Chairs, 200; "Empire" Chair, 196*.
Chaldæa, 300.
Champollion, 103, 190, 276.
Chapel of Apis, 146; of Cheops, 44; of Chephren, plan, 48*; of the Cow Hathor, 164*; of Mekhu, 38, 43*; of Râ-en-user, 49*; of Sabni, 38, 43*; of Sahu-Ra, plan, 49*.
Chapels, sepulchral, 146, 147.
Chassinat, 83, 201.
Cheops, 26, 41, 62, 77; in ivory, 74*.
Chephren, 47; the aged, 70*; alabaster, 79*; the Great, 79*; Pyramid of, 41, 299; Statue of, 81-84.
Chinese artists, 69.
Christianity destructive to Egyptian Art, 246, 276, 286, 301.
Claudius, 241.
Clasp for Necklace in form of a Boat, 293*.
Cleopatra, 258.
Coffin of Akhmim, 278*; of Tataharsiasi, 275; of Wardan, 275.
Coffins, 199, 271, 272.
Column of the Ambulatory at Karnak, 129*; of Râ-en-user, 54*; of Shepses-Ptah, 53*.
Colossi, 191, 192, 256, 257, 276; at Abu Simbel, 185*, 191; of the Ramesseum, 192; of Luxor, 132*.
Colossus of Argo, Crowned, 254*; of the Roman period, 256*.
Columns, 127, 235-238; lotiform, 49; palmiform, 53.
Commodus, 256.
Concert, 90*.
Cook, 87.

306

INDEX

Coptic Monastery, 151.
Coptos, 113.
Copts, 230.
Cow of Dêr-el-Bahari, 165*, 174, 175; of Sakkarah, 244*, 250, 251; turning to her Calf, 66*. See also Hathor.
Crouching Figure holding a Divinity, 156*.

D.

Dabud, Temple of, 231*, 242.
Dagger of Amasis, 206*.
Dahshur, 26, 33, 38, 41, 62, 100, 111, 120, 122.
Dakhleh, Temple of, 216*, 230.
Dakkeh, Temple of, 232*, 242, 262.
Daninos, 276, 288.
Daressy, 202.
Darius I., 223.
Daughter of Rameses II., 184*.
Daughters of Amenophis IV., 153*, 163.
Decadence of Egyptian Art, 259.
Decoration of Interiors, 50-56; in Palace at Medinet-Habu, 146*; of tombs and temples, 51-73; in Tomb-chamber of Rameses V., 141*; in Tomb of Kom-es-Shugafa, 273*.
Decorative Art in Egypt, 162-166.
Delta, 19, 24, 36, 162, 195, 213, 220, 240 256, 251, 265, 278, 281, 285; School of the, 54.
Denderah, 36, 60, 113, 224, 225, 228, 229, 232-234, 238, 261.
Dendûr, 242, 243.
Dêr-el-Bahari, 99, 113, 114, 129, 148, 149, 151-153, 174, 179, 231, 237, 299; Esplanade at, 142*; General View of, 142*.
Dêr-el-Medinet, 148, 230, 240; Façade of Temple at, 221*; Pronaos of Temple at, 222*.
Dêr-el-Melak, 37.
Derr, 144, 189, 219.
Deshasheh, Scene in a Siege at, 107*, 108.
Diadem of Khnemit, 123*.

Diadumenianus, 261, 268*.
Didufriya, Statue of, 81*, 83.
Dimeh, 274.
Dish of Hatiyai, 202*.
Dodecaschœnus, 242.
Dog, terra-cotta, 289*.
Domitian, 231, 261.
Double or Ka, 10, 17, 20, 31, 32, 37, 38, 41, 73, 77, 86, 89, 253, 254.
Double-Statues, 168, 200, 201, 250.
Drah-Abu'l-Nekkah, 148.
Dukaf (appanage), 15.
Dwarf of Gizeh, 82*.
Dwarf Khnemu-hetep, 82*.

E.

Earring of Rameses XII., 208*.
Earrings of Seti I., 208*.
Edfû, 15, 224, 227, 228, 233, 236, 238, 240, 242, 258, 261; Nomes bringing offerings, 14*.
Edgar, 292.
Edinburgh Museum, 287.
Egypt, Lower, 53, 272; Middle, 96, 100, 101, 240, 281; Upper, 36, 38, 53, 96, 239, 274.
Egyptian Fleet, at Dêr-el-Bahari, 170.
El-Amarna, 158, 163, 181-185.
El-Armarna, 195; Wall in Tomb at, 173*.
El-Kab, 36, 131, 194.
El-Kalaa, 230.
Ellahun, 100.
Enamelled Chamber of King Zoser, 92*.
Enneas, 227, 228, 243, 246.
Ergamenes, 242.
Erment, 113.
Eshmunên, 280, 285.
Esneh, 225, 238, 240, 245.
Ethiopia, 24, 126, 206, 218, 242, 245, 261.
Ethiopian King, Head of an, 269*.

Ethiopian Pyramid, plan and elevation, 235.
Ethiopian Statues of Souls, 255.
Euergetes II., 261.

F.

False Doors, 31-33; of Atoti, 37*; of Mereruka, 37*; of Neferseshem-Ptah, 38*.
False Pyramid at MêJûm, 44*.
Fayum, the, 36, 100, 110, 124, 261, 273-275, 285.
Female Figure, 58*.
Ferlini, 292.
Figure of a Queen or Goddess at two different Stages, 262*.
Figurines of Animals, 3*.
Finished Figure of a King, 263*.
Fortress of Kom-el-Ahmar (plan), 4*.
Fortresses, 159, 160.
France, 2, 279.
French Expedition, 230, 301.
Frontality, Law of, 73.
Furniture, 286, 287.

G.

Garf-Husên, 138*, 144.
Garstang, 7; Hemi-speos.
Gebel-Barkal, 173.
Gebel-Silsileh, Chapel at, 135*, 142.
Geese of MêJûm, 51, 55*.
German excavations, 45.
Gizeh, 33, 38, 45, 62, 80, 114, 216; corner of Necropolis at, 30*.
Goblet of Zakazik, 203*.
Gold Jars of Zakazik, 204*.
Græco-Egyptian Sculpture, 255, 262, 265.
Greece, 161, 174, 301.
Greeks, 253, 273, 289.
Grooved Façade of Thinite Fortresses, 4*.
Grotesque Figures in Bronze, 288*.
Grotesque Head, Terra-cotta, 287*.
Grotesque, Terra-cotta, 287.
Grotesque Slave bearing a Jar, 159.

INDEX

Grotesques, 285.
Group of *Persons* standing or sitting, 17*.

H.

Habi Sadu (festival), 79.
Hadrian, 231, 241, 261.
Hapu, 240, 297; the dwarf, 19*, 20.
Hapsefai, 101.
Harmachis, 268.
Harmin, 195; Mourners in Tomb of, 191*; Offering-bearers in Tomb of, 191*.
Harpocrates, 286; with Osiris and Amon, 283*.
Hathor, 22, 83, 152, 168, 174-175, 228, 240; and Amenophis, Temple of, 221*, 230; Chapel of, 230; Columns, 219*; Cow, 250, 251, 268; Cow at Sakkarah, 244*; heads, 145, 231; Pillars, 131. See also under Capita's *and* Cow.
Hatiyai, 202.
Hatshepset, Queen, 130, 150, 151, 173, 179.
Hawara, 100, 116, 274.
Hawk's Head, Golden, 94*.
Head in the Louvre, 85*.
Head of a Colossal royal Statue, 117*.
Head of a Man, 169*.
Head of a Statue, 246*, 259*.
Hebt, 223; East Façade of Temple, 215.
Heliopolis, 19, 44, 54, 61, 97.
Heptanomis, 275.
Heracleopolis, 60, 104, 110, 194, 240.
Hermonthis, 231.
Hermopolis, 60, 96, 162, 182, 194, 240, 285; School of, 24, 106-109.
Heru-em-heb, 139, 143, 150, 184-187, 199; Head of a Statue of, 178*; Wooden Statuette of, 195*.
Her-Heru, 218.
Hesi, Wooden panels of, 59, 60*.
Hieraconpolis, 4, 6, 7, 78.
Hierasycaminos, 262.
Hittites, 165.
Holy Mountain, 218.

Horbêt, 278.
Horus, 21, 32, 112, 153, 155, 168, 222, 227-229, 246, 250, 266, 267, 278, 279, 283, 292; Alexandrian, 250*; Bronze, 281*; as a Child, 243*; with the Crocodiles, 257*; Temple of, at Edfû (plan), 216*, 224, 225; Court and porticoes of Temple of, 217*; Pronaos and Terraces of Temple of, 218*; Pylon of Temple of, 217.
Humorous Episode, 65*.
Husband and Wife seated, 72*; standing, 72*; of unequal Height, 73*.
Hyksos or Shepherd Kings, 117, 124, 125, 159, 171, 196.
Hypogea, 36, 37, 147-150, 215-217.
Hypogeum of Ameni, 102*; of Amenophis II., 141*; of Khnemu-hetep, 101*; of Kom-es-Shugafa (room in), 273*; of Paheri wall in, 188*; of Seti I. Sketch in, 148*.
Hypostylè Hall, the, 127, 128; at Karnak, Clerestory, 118*, and Transverse Section, 128*; in the Memnonium of Seti I.*, 143; in the Ramesseum, 127*.

Ibrim, 244.
Ictinus, 299.
Incrustation in green Enamel, 193*.
Infantry from Meir, 91*.
Influences, foreign, in Egyptian minor arts, 197, 289.
Ionia, 289.
Isis (goddess), 231, 246, 251, 267, 279, 288, 292; and Horus (relief), 262, 270; statue of, 244*; in terracotta, 290*; Temple of, 14*, 257*.
Isis, Queen, 161*, 171.
Italy, 279.
Iuaa, 181, 182, 195, 199; and Thuaa, 200*.

Ivory, use of, 77; bas-relief, 74*; Feet of Bed and Stool, 2*; Mirror-handle, 205*.

Japanese Artists, 69.
Jewel-casket of Amenophis III., 196*.
Jewelry, 92, 120-122, 200, 204-206, 289-293; of Aah-hetep, 205*; from Dahshur, 121*.
Jug with Goat from Zakazik, 204*.

K.

Ka-apiru, 32; see also Sheikh-el-beled.
Kadesh, Battle of, 165, 166; reliefs, 155*, 189.
Kalabshah, 242, 262; plan of temple, 232*.
Kames, 148.
Karnak, 97, 113, 116, 127, 129, 130, 133, 136, 139-141, 145, 171, 176, 179, 180, 187, 188, 208, 214, 218, 220, 222, 223, 232, 234, 239, 240, 260; Avenue of Rams at, 133*; Court of the Temple of Rameses III. at, 131*; Favissa, 191; Great Temple of Amon, 95*; Ruins of Propylæa of Tirhakah, 215; Workshops at, 193.
Karomama, Queen, 276, 277, 280*.
Kartassi, 242, 243; Chapel in Quarries of, 234*; Kiosk of, 233*.
Kasr-el-Aguz, 231.
Kasr-el-Shalauit, 231.
Kasr-es-Sayâd, 37, 60.
Kasr-Ibrim, East Gate, 234*.
Kasr-Karun, 220*, 230.
Kau-el-Kebir, 37, 60, 240.
Kauit, Princess, 113.
Kha-emhet, 181, 195.
Khamuasit, Prince, 200.
Khasakhmui, 76*.
Khayanu, 124.
Kheti, 105, 108, 109.

INDEX

Khnemit, 121; Crown of, 122*; Diadem of, 123*.
Khnemu, Chapel of, 132.
Khnemu-hetep, 101; hypogeum of, 101*, 106, 107.
Khonsu (god), 15, 185, 186, 218, 219; Bust of, 176*; Temple of, 11*, 221, 224, 226, 232; Temple at Thebes (section), 132*, 135-137.
Khonsu, Temple of, 239.
Khu-en-Aton, 201.
Khufu-enekh, 27; Sarcophagus, of, 27*.
Kiblah, 52, 53.
Kitchen, 89*.
Kneeling Figure carrying a Triad, 157*.
Kneeling Man, 77*.
Kokome, 40.
Kom-el-Ahmar, 11*, 37, 79, 92; Door-jamb in Temple of, 7*.
Kom-es-Sagha, 96; Temple of, 96*; Interior of Temple of 96*.
Kom-es-Shugafa, 257, 266.
Kom-Ombo, 55, 224, 228, 229, 232, 233, 240, 257; Double Court and Pronaos at, 220*.
Koseir-el-Amarna, 37.
Kurnah, 187; Façade of sepulchral Temple, 144*.
Kurnet-Murrai, 148, 230.

Legrain, 116, 191.
Libyan Chief struck down by Sahu-Rā, 56*.
Libyan Desert, 38.
Lion passant, 257*; seated, 258*.
Lion at Gebel-Barkal, 164*; Bronze, time of Apries, 282*; of Kom-Ombo, 258*; of Sakkarah, 52*.
Lisht, 97, 100, 111, 170.
London (British Museum), 22, 169, 288.
Louvre, The, 57, 75, 80, 87, 119, 181, 201, 202, 206, 252, 274, 276, 279.
Luxor, 138-140, 161, 165, 166, 192, 208, 214, 219, 220, 221, 223, 231, 239, 259, 276; Court of Amenophis III, at, 133*; Court of Rameses II. at, 135*; Temple of Amenophis III. at, 137*.

M.

Maat (goddess), 288.
Macrinus, 261; Bas-relief of, 268*.
Maharrakah, 242, 244, 262.
Maiptah, 195; Fragment from Tomb of, 192*.
Mammisi, or Birth-house, 231, 232, 233, 241; at Edfû, 222*.
Man, Head and Bust of a, 253*.
Mariette, 81, 117, 124, 180, 248.
Maritsakro, 168, 173.
Mastaba, the, 29, 30, 31, 36, 37, 38, 41, 45, 62, 98-100, 102, 215, 216; with hollow Chamber and discharging Arch, 42*; at Gizeh, 30*, and Shaft in same, 29*; of Ka-apiru, Cell and Forecourt, 34*; of Khabeuptah, 35*; of Menefer, Façade, 34*; of Mcreruka, 33, 36*, 37, 65, 73; of Ne er-hetep, Forecourt, 35*; of Ti, Portico of, 36*; of Zazamenekh, 35*.
Masu, 278; Bronze Statuette of, 281*.
Mat-ka-Rā, Queen, 268.
Medinet-Habû, 127, 130, 131, 134, 149, 155, 160, 161, 192, 219, 221, 223, 226, 230; Façade of Temple of Rameses III. at, 146*; Migdol of, 148*; Roman Temple at, 221*; Second Court in Temple of, 145*.
Mediterranean, 215.
Médûm, 25, 33, 38, 45, 62, 80, 167; False Pyramid at, 40; Geese of, 51, 72; Tomb at, 51; Statues of, 81.
Meir, 37; decorations at, 61; Fat Men of, 62*; Lean Men of, 62*; Soldiers of, 90, 91*.
Mekhu, 38.
Meks, 285.
Memnon-Colossi at Thebes, 167*, 176.

Memnonium, 153, 187, 188, 190; of Seti I. at Abydos, plan, 143*.
Memphis, 19, 29, 37, 38, 95, 106, 114, 126, 148, 162, 189, 192, 216, 254, 265, 273, 276, 278, 280, 285, 288, 289.
Memphite Dynasties, 23.
Memphite School, 24, 26, 61, 79, 81, 105, 107, 108, 110, 113, 213, 251, 254; contrasted with Theban School, 115.
Memphite Statue, 250*; Statuette, 251.
Meneptah, 186, 189, 192, 220; Bust of a Statue of, 187*; with two Ensigns, 156*.
Menes, 6, 23.
Menkhau-Heru, 57; Statue of, 57*; Statuette of, 82.
Mentemhet, 241*, 248.
Menthu-hetep, 99, 114, 115, 149, 152; in the Costume of Apotheosis, 112*; Tomb of, 113.
Mentu (god), 120, 268; Temple f, 134.
Merenka, 33, 37, 65, 73. See also under Tomb.
Meroë, 245, 256, 262.
Mesaurat, Temple of, 245; 236*.
Mesopotamia, 125, 206.
Metal, casting, 202, 276; use of, 77, 78; utensils, 92.
Migdol, 160.
Mirmashau, 118; Colossal Statue of, 117*.
Mirror-case, 205*.
Mitrahineh, 192.
Mnevis, 279.
Models of Heads at different Stages, 261*.
Mond's Statuette, 169*, 177, 178.
Monkey, Statue of a, 163*, 255*.
Mummy, Mask of a, 277*.
Munich Museum, 80, 110.
Mural Decorations, 18.
Musician-priestesses, 152*.
Mut (god), 167, 187, 219, 268.
Mut-emua, Queen, 139.
Mycenæ, 205.
Mycerinus, 27; Pyramid of, 41; Sarcophagus of, 27*; Statue of, 16*, 83; Statuette of, 82; Triad of, 81*; and his Wife, 80*.
Myers' Bust, 85; Statuette, 83*.

309

INDEX

N.

Naī, 187; the Lady, 201*.
Nakadah, 7, 26, 27, 113; Plan of Tomb, 7*.
Nakht, 165.
Name Horus of Chephreu, 32*.
Napata, 218, 219, 256; most ancient Temple at, 214*; Sanctuary of Tirhakah at, 214*.
Naples Museum, 80.
Napriti, 58.
Nasi, The Lady, 77*, 80.
Naucratis, 257, 265.
Naville, 174, 250.
Necklace with Heads of Falcons, Gold, 207*.
Necho II., 291.
Nectanebus, 238, 240, 257, 259; Naos of, 218*.
Nectanebus II., 223, 261.
Nefer-Atmu, 283.
Nefer-hetep, 32.
Nefer-ka-Rā, 43, 48.
Nefer-ka-Rā-Huni, 26.
Neferseshemptah, 34, 68*.
Nefert, 80; Queen, 116*, 118.
Nefert-ari, Queen, 144.
Nefer-temu, 233.
Neferu, 85*; Statuette of, 86.
Neferu-Rā, 172.
Negress, Statuette of, 199*, 200.
Nephthys, 288.
Neter-baiu, 22; Tablet of (obverse), 23*; (reverse), 24.
Newberry, 202.
Nibū, the Dog, 18*, 20.
Nile, 38, 90, 139, 159, 185, 218; Figure of the, 196, 233, 288; in pierced Bronze, 291*; Twin Figures of, 193*.
Nit (goddess), 279, 283.
No. I. Statue at Cairo, 77*, 79.
Nomes (divisions of Egypt), 8, 16, 63, 233.
Nsiptah, 241, 249.
Nubia, 24, 143, 189, 190, 261.
Nufiabres, 283.
Nutir, the Lady, 19*, 20.

O.

Oases, 273.
Obelisks, 97; at Karnak, 125*; of Ptah-hetep and Maiti, 41*; of Heliopolis, 98*.
Obelisk-worship, 46.
Offering-bearers, 89*.
Officers, Statuettes of, 201, 203*.
Ombos, 234, 245, 262.
Opening of the Mouth, 199*.
Opet (goddess), 232.
Orontes, 165.
Osiris, 79, 115, 134, 145, 154, 218, 227, 228, 232, 250, 251, 279, 288, 292, 301; Bronze, 278; Osiris-Nile in pierced bronze, 291*; Recumbent, 243*; Statue of, 244*.
Osorkon II., 214, 248; pushing a boat, 237.
Osorkon III., 288.
Ostraka at Cairo and Turin, 149*-151*, 163.
Otho, 231.
Oxford, 79
Oxyrrhynchos, 240.

P.

Painted bas-relief in Tomb of Seti I., 179*.
Painted Decoration of a Private House, 103*.
Painted Stele, 274*.
Painting, Egyptian, 50, 51, 267-270.
Painting of a Hypogeum at Bahriyeh, 276*.
Painting and Sculpture, combination of, 103.
Painting without sculptured Background, 103*.
Fakheri, 269; Painted Panel of, 274*.
Paris, 22, 288.
Parthenon, 152, 299.
Pasticcio Ptolemaic, 266*; in Temple of Theban Ptah, 265*.
Patanafi, 263.
Patanesis, 283.
Pavement in Palace at El Amarna, 147.
Peasant Squatting, 106*.
Pectoral of Amenemhāt, 111, 121*; of Rameses II.; of Sesostris III., 120*.
Pedishashi, Statue of, 247*.

Pelizæus Collection, 202.
Pepi I., 202; Bust of, 76*; Head of Statuette of, 76*; Statue of, 78*.
Pepi II., 95.
Perfume-spoon in Form of Woman swimming, 199*.
Perichon Bey, 285.
Persians, 253.
Person seated with one Leg flat, 157*.
Person of the time of Amenophis IV, 174*
Petrie, Flinders, 3, 77, 91, 96, 201.
Petubastis, 237*; Statue of, 247*.
Petukhanu, 276.
Pharaoh in a Helmet, Head of, 187*, 193; Horus, 110*; Khasakhmui, 76*, 79; in pierced Bronze, 291*.
Pharaohs, 9, 10, 16, 17, 18, 21, 27, 52, 55, 57, 62, 95, 96, 100, 112, 113, 114, 119, 130, 135, 151, 156, 158, 159, 175, 176, 183, 207, 217, 228, 239, 257, 288; Ethiopian, 220, 245; Palaces of, 156-159; Tombs of, 38.
Philæ, 224, 230, 232, 233, 236-240, 242, 243, 258-260; General View of, 213* Capitals of Pronaos, 226*; East Block of second Pylon, 229*; Kiosk of Nectanebus, 225*, 238; Kiosk of Trajan, 227*, 240; Mammisi, 225*; Mammisi and Great Door, 230*; Plan of Island of, 228*; Pronaos and Hypostyle Hall, 230*; Temple of Isis during Inundation, 228*; Wall in Temple of Isis, 223*; Western Portico, 224*.
Philip Arrhidæus, 223, 239, 259.
Piankhi, 218.
Pillar at Karnak, 97*.
Pillars, 235-238.
Pinotchem, 207.
Plaques, polychrome, 198.
Plate, gold and silver, 202, 203 289, 290.
Plato, 259.
Portraits, 273, 275.
Posno, Sale, 278.

INDEX

Pottery, 91, 284.
Priest and Monkey, 188*, 193.
Priest, Statuette of a, 201*.
Private Person, Statue of a, 119, 120.
Pronaos, the, 221.
Proto-Doric or primitive Order, 103, 129, 144, 237; at Karnak, 129*.
Psammetichus I., 223, 239*, 243*, 243, 250.
Psammetichus II., 289.
Psammetichus III., 240*.
Psammetiknufisashmu, 263, 266; Bas-relief of, 271, 272.
Pselchis, 243.
Ptah, 113, 194, 201, 239, 283, 301; Memphite, 189*; Theban, 129; Propylæa and Façade of Oratory of Theban, 227*; Temple of, 133, 237.
Ptah-enekh, 65*, 66.
Ptah-hetep, 66, 71; and his Wife, 67*.
Ptahmes, 198.
Ptolemais, 273.
Ptolemaic Doorway, 226*.
Ptolemies, 215, 223, 230, 231, 232, 237, 239, 240, 242, 254, 259, 261, 265 272, 278, 287.
Ptolemy, 258. Euergetes, 240, 257; Euergetes charging, 260*; Philadelphus, 240; Philopator, 242; Philopator IV., 240; Physcon, 242, 259; Soter, 239.
Punt, 180.
Pylon, the, 48, 97, 126, 127; of Heru-em-Heb at Karnak, 126*.
Pyramid, of Cheops, 42; of Chephren, 41, 299; False, 40, 44*; Great Pyramid and Sphinx, 45*; with Obelisk, 44; origin of the, 40; of Pepi II., 35; of Rā-enuser, 45*; of Unas, Door in, 47*; of Unas, plan, 46*.
Pyramidion, the, 146, 147; of Dahshur, 100*.
Pyramid-mastaba, the, 100, 101, 146, 147; of an Apis, 140*; of Drah-Abu'l-Nekkah, 98*; section of a, 98*.
Pyramids, 26, 40, 42, 48, 62, 81, 83, 98, 113; of Gizeh, 45; of Meroë, 245.

Q.
Qa-au Stele, 20*, 21.
Queen, Statuette of a, 240*.
Quibell, 9, 92.

R.
Rameses I., 140, 154.
Rameses II., 139, 140, 143, 150, 154, 155, 165-167, 185, 188-191, 194, 214, 219, 220, 239, 260, 237; Alabaster Statue of, 184*, 185*; Bust on Coffin of, 194*; Coffin of, 199; Colossal Figure of, 189*; Colossal Head of, 186*; pushing a Boat, 158.
Rameses III., 133, 145, 151, 155, 159, 189, 192, 198, 208, 224, 247.
Rameses IV., 162, 199, 202; and a Libyan Prisoner, 186*, 193; Sandstone Bust of, 194.
Rameses XII., 206.
Rameses of the Twentieth Dynasty, the, 140, 151.
Rameses, Prince, afterwards Rameses II., 181*.
Ramesesnakht, 193.
Ramesseum, 127, 144, 154, 156, 165, 166, 221, 225; General View of, 144*.
Ramessids, the, 194, 213, 218, 219, 233, 262, 293.
Ramosis, 181.
Rā (the sun-god), 44, 46, 283.
Rā-hetep, 80, 84, 87, 167.
Rā-en-user, 44, 45, 49; Chape of, 49*, 56; Statuette of, 82.
Rā-nefer, 71, 82.
Reindeer Period, 2.
Reisner's Mycerinus, 80*.
Rekaknah, 7.
Relief en creux, 12, 260.
Renascence of Egyptian Art, 262.
Rhind, 287.
Ritual of the Pyramids. 216.
Rome, 161, 174, 275, 301.

S.
Sabni, Chapel of, 38.
es-Sabua, 189.

Sadunimet, 87*.
Saft-el-Henneh, Naos of, 6.
Sahu-Rā, 56; adopted by the goddess, 57*; Chapel of, 44, 49*; Temple of, 49.
Saïd, the, 20, 83, 215, 218, 223, 240.
Saïs, 213, 278; School of, 24.
Saite period, 15, 48, 242, 265.
Sakkarah, 32-34, 38, 44, 62, 63, 77, 80, 91, 114, 216, 217, 258, 282, 291
Sanhur, 230.
Sapui, 80.
Sarcophagus of Khefu-enekh, 27*; of Mycerinus, 27*; of Princess Kauit, 111*, 113.
Sa-Renput, Portico of, 100*; Tomb of, 101.
Sargonids, 289.
Scribes, Statues of, 86-88, 119; crouching, 86*; kneeling, 87*; seated, 87, 299.
Sebek-emsef, 118*, 119.
Sebek-hetep, 118*, 119, 124, 240.
Secret chambers, 234, 235.
Sekhet, 173, 278, 279, 281; Bronze, 284*; at Karnak, 163*.
Seneferu, 20, 40, 41, 44, 51, 62, 80.
Senmut, 171, 247.
Sennefer, 177; with his Wife and Daughter, 168*.
Septah Meneptah, 189; Scene in Tomb of, 183*; in his Tomb, 182*.
Septimius Severus, 244.
Serdab, 34, 37, 42.
Serpent-Isis, 290*.
Serpent, King, 21, 23; Stele of, 21*.
Servant carrying his Master's Baggage, 88*.
Servant tarring a Jar, 10*.
Service of Antiquities, 96.
Sesostris I., 97, 100, 111-113, 116, 119; Head of, 113*; Statues of, 108*, 109*.
Sesostris II., 118, 120.
Sesostris III., 114, 120; Head of, 114*.
Sesostris IV., 116; Head of, 114*.
Sesostris fighting, 183*, 190, 206, 299.
Set (god), 168, 228.

311

INDEX

Seti I, 21, 140, 151, 153, 154, 162, 185, 187-191, 258; at Abydos, 180'; and the three Goddesses, 181*, 188, 299.
Seti II., 189, 206; in his Tomb, 182*.
Severus, 275.
Sheikh-Abd-el-Kurnah, 148, 149, 153*, 163-165, 177, 180, 287.
Sheikh-el-beled, 83*, 84, 85, 112, 195, 299; supposed Wife of the, 83*.
Shepherd Kings, see Hyksos.
Shepsestah, 49.
Shoulder Movement, Tomb of Khnemu-hetep, 105*.
Shu (god), 243.
Shunet-ez-Zebib, 1*.
Siege of a Fortress, 104*; at Deshâsheh, 107*.
Siesis, 111; Portrait of, 108*.
Silsileh, 143; Speos at; Plan and Façade, 136*.
Silver Plate of Thmuis, 292*.
Simon, James, 201.
Sinai, 21, 26, 96; bas-reliefs at, 21, 22*, 59.
Siût, 108, 110.
Sketch Figure of a King, 263*.
Sketch in a Tomb, 153*.
Slave bearing a Jar, 159*.
Sloping Passage in Tomb of Ti, 29*.
Smendes, 196.
Sobek, 228, 229.
Sokaris, 292.
Soldiers at Siût, 105*.
Solar Temple of Rā-en-user, 50*.
Soul Statues, 256*.
Spain, 2.
Speos, the, 141-146.
Sphinx, 80, 81, 117, 118, 173; of Amenemhaal III., 116*, 124, 196; of Apries, 276, 279*; of Gizeh, 78*; of the Ptolemaic Period, 257*; of the Roman Period, 253*; Temple of the, 47, 48, 51*; Interior of Temple, 51*, 52*.
Squatting Figure, 236*.
Statue, with body in Sheath, 18*; finished but for the Head, 245*; full face, 15*; full face, walking, 16*; of the Hyksos Period, 125*;
"ready-made," 252; roughly blocked out, 245; seated, 74*; standing, bearing ensigns, 17*.
Statuette of petrified Wood, 176*.
Statues, 17.
Stelæ, 20, 21, 23, 33, 52, 54, 62, 148, 261, 266, 268, 270.
Stele Door of Nibera, 39*; of Usiru, 33*; of the Fayum, 268*; in form of False Door, 31*; of Horus and Crocodiles, 260*; of King Serpent, 21*; of Nikhafitka, 40; of Prince Antef, 113; of Ta-au, 20*; of Sesostris III., 112; of Seti, 28*.
Step Pyramid, 39, 40, 43*, 91; Section of, 44*.
Storehouses with Brick vaults in Ramesseum, 145*.
Stroganoff, 276.
Surveyor with Line, 157*.
Syene, 110, 242, 285.
Syria, 77, 159, 206, 300.

T.

Table of offerings, 32, 38, 46.
Tafeh, Temple of, 231*, 242.
Takushit, 277, 280*.
Tanagra, 285.
Tanis, 117, 217, 258; School of, 24, 195.
Tanite Statue, 248*.
Tantkalashiri, 271.
Tataharsias, 273; Coffin of, 275*.
Tchaho, 266.
Tefnut, 243.
Tefyeh, 105.
Tell-es-Sab, 278.
Temenos, the, 41.
Temples, 130; decoration of the, 18; small, 229, 230.
Teye, see Thi.
Thebaid, 220, 247, 273, 275, 300.
Theban Citizens, 152*.
Theban School, 24, 113, 213.
Thebes, 48, 101, 104, 114, 116, 117, 125, 127, 135, 147, 162, 179, 183, 189, 190, 193, 196, 206, 213, 218, 254, 259, 261, 263, 265, 274, 280, 289.

Thi, Queen, 171, 176, 181, 185, 186, 200; so-called Head of, 177*; Head of Statuette of, 171*.
Thinite Tablet, 25*; Period, 6, 7; Pharaohs, 7; School, 26, 61, 79, 81.
This, 80.
Thmuis, 278, 289.
Thoth, 60, 168, 193, 267, 285, 292.
Thoth Paotnuphis, 242.
Thothmes I., 148, 149, 170.
Thothmes II., 130.
Thothmes III., 113, 129, 130, 132, 133, 140, 150, 151, 171, 172, 173, 179, 199, 202, 214, 237, 239, 242, 247, 259, 288, 299; Head of a Statue of, 162*.
Thothmes IV., 140, 150, 151, 172, 198; and his Mother, 162*.
Thoueris, 242, 249.
Thuâa, 199; Coffin of, 194*.
Thuti, 202.
Ti, see under Tomb.
Ti, Statue of, 84.
Tiberius, 236.
Tirhakah, 219, 220, 222, 245, 248, 276; Head of, 239*; Statuette of, 279*.
Toilet utensils, 200, 204.
Tomb of Adu, Denderah, 42*.
Tomb of Ankhmara, Dancers in, 69*.
Tomb of Heru-hetep, Painted Interior in, 102*.
Tomb of Kha-em-het, Sketch in, 149.
Tomb of Mekhu, 38, 43*.
Tomb of Menthu-hetep, Plan, 99*.
Tomb of Nakht, wall in, 154*.
Tomb of Ptah-hetep, Brawl between Boatmen, 69*; Herdsman driving Bulls, 67*; Perspective of Registers, 66*; Sacrifice, 63*.
Tomb of Ra-hetep, wall, 63*.
Tomb of Sabui, 43*.
Tomb of Sa-Renput II., 101.
Tomb of Ti, 34, 65, 72, 73; Bringing Corn, 13*; Cramming Geese, 70*; Harvest Scenes, 12*; Hippopotamus Hunt, 55*; Plan of, 41*; Servants of Ti bringing of-

312

INDEX

ferings, 12*; Slaughter of Cattle, 13*; Sloping Passage in, 29*.
Tomb with pyramidal summit, Theban, 140*.
Tombs, 27, 23, 29, 97, 98; decoration of, 18.
Torso and Head of a Woman, 169*.
Trajan, 261; Kiosk of, 241, 243.
Triad of Heracleopolis, 190*.
Triumphal bas-relief of Seti I., 175.
Tuitishere, Queen, 160*, 169.
Tukh-el-Karamus, 289, 292.
Tuosret, 203, 206.
Turah limestone, 47, 67, 75, 84.
Turin Museum, 80, 169, 170, 171, 186, 191, 201.
Tut-ankhamen, 177*, 184-186.
Twin Statues at Cairo, 118*.
Two Prisoners tied Back to Back, 159*.
Types of archaic Chapels and Temples, 5*.

U.

Unas, 41, 56; Pyramid of, 43; Temple of, 49.
Ushabtiu, 198, 282, 284.

Utilitarian element in Egyptian art, 300.
Uzueri, 58.

Valley of the Kings, 164; of the Queens, 230.
Vase in the form of a Head in a Helmet, 285*.
Vassalli, 51.
Venice, 288.
Vespasian, 231.
Vienna Museum, 119.

W.

Wadi-es-Sabua, 144, 219; Avenue of Sphinxes at, 137*.
War-Dance, 104*.
Wood, use of, 77.
Wood-carving, 198.
Wooden Head from Lisht, 109*.
Wooden Naos, 5*.
Wooden Spoon for Cosmetics, 197*.
Wooden Statue, Bust of, 75*.
Wooden Statue, 84*, 85.
Wooden Statuettes, 168.

Woman grinding Corn, 9*, 72*.
Woman, Head and Bust of a, 252*; Torso and Head of a, 169*.
Woman in sculptured groups, 74.
Woman, Statuette of a, 200*, 249*.
Wrestling, Beni Hasan, 107*.

X.

Xois, 240.

Young Girl, 202*; Statuette of, 201*.

Z.

Zadamonefonukhu, 268.
Zaï, 187; and Nai, 178*.
Zakazik, 202.
Zanufi, 263, 266.
Zauti 37.
Zawyet-el-Aryan, 26, 43; Floor and Libation-trough, 48*; Inclined Way, 47*.
Zoser, 38, 39, 40, 91.

ERRATA.

P. 44, 1. 18. Substitute for lines 18-22 the following: "Sahu-Rā and Rā-en-user. They were approached by propylæa built at the foot of the plateau (Fig. 81), beyond which a long incline rose to the body of the building, the arrangements of which varied. In the chapel of Sahu-Rā (Fig. 82), for instance, there was a dark passage, then a colonnaded court, then a complicated series of cells and storehouses, and in the obscurity of the background, the stele, in the form of a closed door, where the office of the dead king was celebrated. It was a temple", etc.

P. 48, inscription of Fig. 79, for "Foor" read "Floor."

P. 49, inscription of Fig. 81, for "Plan of the Chapel" read "Plan of the Propylæa."

P. 268, inscription of Fig. 515, for "Diadumenian" read "Diadumenianus."

www.ingramcontent.com/pod-product-compliance
Lightning Source LLC
Chambersburg PA
CBHW042041240426
43667CB00047B/2937